The
Pergamon
Dictionary of
Perfect Spelling

CHRISTINE MAXWELL

ARNOLD-WHEATON

Arnold-Wheaton
A Division of E. J. Arnold & Son Limited
Parkside Lane, Leeds LS11 5TD

A subsidiary of Pergamon Press Ltd
Headington Hill Hall, Oxford, OX3 0BW

Pergamon Press Inc.
Maxwell House, Fairview Park, Elmsford, New York 10523

Pergamon Press Canada Ltd
Suite 104, 150 Consumers Road, Willowdale, Ontario M2J 1P9

Pergamon Press (Australia) Pty Ltd
P.O. Box 544, Potts Point, N.S.W. 2011

Pergamon Press GmbH
Hammerweg 6, D-6242 Kronberg, Federal Republic of Germany

First edition 1977
Second edition 1978
Reprinted 1979, 1983, 1984, 1985

ISBN 0-08-022863-1 non net
ISBN 0-08-022865-8 net

Printed in Great Britain by A. Wheaton & Co. Ltd., Exeter

Contents

Preface

This dictionary, the first of its kind in Great Britain (as far as the compiler knows), and its accompanying booklet, *Practise Your Spelling*, aim at being of service to children and adults of all ages who are weak at spelling and who therefore fail to locate quickly and easily the words they seek in standard dictionaries.

Compilers and publishers of English-language dictionaries overseas have long recognised this problem, and have successfully provided phonetically-arranged dictionaries to help pupils overcome these serious difficulties which so impede their progress.

Recent experience gained as a teacher in an Oxford middle school (age-group 9–13) and with students learning English as a foreign language has brought the compiler face to face with the problem. This has made her aware of the inordinate amount of time that has to be spent by teachers helping students with spelling difficulties which they could so easily have overcome for themselves had they had access to a phonetically-arranged dictionary.

The compiler gratefully acknowledges the co-operation of teachers and students in Oxfordshire schools for their help in testing the dictionary and its accompanying booklet, *Practise Your Spelling*, in a classroom environment. These successful tests, which were also carried out in several establishments that teach English as a foreign language, have revealed the following:

I. Students who assisted with the tests quickly understood that words printed in RED were incorrectly spelt and that only words printed in BLACK were correctly spelt. In tests which involved several hundred students, not one copied down incorrect spellings. Some teachers' initial concern over the possible negative effect of showing students incorrect spellings has proved unfounded.

II. Teachers (besides saving themselves time) found that regular use of the dictionary and the exercise booklet improved their pupils' ability to locate words easily and quickly and spell them correctly.

The mis-spellings (mainly phonetic) are printed in RED (RED is wrong), with the correct spellings given alongside in BLACK (BLACK is right). Even when users are unsure of the first two letters in a word, they may still find its correct spelling with the help of this dictionary. For instance, the word 'pheasant' will be found under the phonetic groups <u>fes</u> and <u>fez</u> as well as in its correct alphabetical place under <u>phe</u>:

fesant   pheasant

fezant   pheasant

pheasant

5

Some of the commonest spelling errors are made in adding suffixes and in forming derivatives from root words which in themselves may be quite easy to spell. In a conventional dictionary a student may be able to find the spellings of infinitives like 'picnic', 'abandon' and 'span', but may encounter difficulties spelling their present and past participles. How is one to know that the words 'spanning' and 'spanned' are not spelt 'spaning' and 'spaned'? There may be no indication that one must insert 'k' after 'picnic' in order to spell 'picnicking' and 'picnicked' correctly. This dictionary leaves no room for error in this respect, as difficult and irregular word derivatives are included.

It is hoped that this dictionary (and its accompanying booklet) will prove to be of practical, daily help, solving spelling problems and helping to increase the spelling skills of both children and adults—in the classroom, at home and at work.

Oxford, July 1977   CHRISTINE MAXWELL

On Choice of Words, Spelling and Arrangement of Entries

The words in this dictionary have been chosen because they are difficult to spell. Accordingly, many common words are omitted. Obsolete and highly technical words have also been left out, though special attention has been given to the selection of scientific and technical words. Very few proper names are given and foreign words are included only if they have passed into common use.

Where alternative spellings exist these have mostly been omitted. In the case of words ending in -ise, -isation, the -ize and -ization versions have not been given (nor have they been given as mis-spelt versions since they cannot be counted as such). In a very few instances two spellings have been given; where only one spelling is given the reader can assume that it is widely accepted as being correct. To help the user decide upon the correct spelling, brief word definitions are given in the case of words that are (1) pronounced alike but differ in meaning and spelling, (2) often mispronounced to give the same or almost the same sound but are entirely different in meaning and spelling, e.g.:

    (1) sail (of boat)   (2) poplar (tree)
        sale (of goods)   popular (well known)

The spellings and mis-spellings in the dictionary are arranged in alphabetical order.

Endings of words: It has not been possible to put in every derivation and many comparative endings have been excluded. In many cases there has been insufficient space for all the derivatives to be placed in one entry. They have therefore been split up in what the author considers to be the most obvious and practical way, e.g.:

             abnormal /ly
             abnormalit*y* /ies

Abbreviations Used in the Dictionary

adj(s).	adjective(s)
fem.	feminine
n.	noun
pl(s).	plural(s)
sing.	singular
v.	verb

How to Use the Dictionary

1. Think hard about the word you wish to spell and try to decide with which two letters it starts.
2. Find the two letters in the dictionary and look down the <u>left-hand column</u> under these two letters until you find the word you want. If you find the word printed in BLACK, then you have found the correct spelling. However, if the word is printed in RED, then you are not spelling the word correctly, but if you look across the same line you will find the correct spelling printed in BLACK, e.g.:

palis   palace

3. (a) It may be necessary to add the word endings which are individually separated by oblique strokes (/) in order to build up the complete word you want. In the example below you can see how this works:

neat /er/est/ly/ness

By adding er to neat you spell neater.
By adding est to neat you spell neatest.
By adding ly to neat you spell neatly.
By adding ness to neat you spell neatness.

(b) Where the last letter or letters of a word are in *italics* these <u>must</u> be left off before adding the endings, e.g.:

nast*y* /ier/iest/ily/iness

Here, the *y* must be left off before making:

nastier, nastiest, nastily, nastiness

(c) The plurals of most nouns may be formed by simply adding the letter **s**. Only where this does not apply, or where the spelling of a plural often gives trouble, is the plural spelling noted, e.g.:

dais*y* /ies	(daisies)	cello /s	(cellos)
cargo /es	(cargoes)	minutia /e	(minutiae)
circus /es	(circuses)		

4. NOTE
If the correct spelling given alongside a mis-spelling has a ⁺ sign after it, then this means that all other given derivations of the word may only be found by looking up the correct spelling again, but in its PROPER ALPHABETICAL PLACE, e.g.:

hapen	happen [1]
hapier	happier [+]
hapless	
happen [1]	
happi*er* /est/ly/ness	

Where the word <u>happier</u> occurs in its correct alphabetical place other forms of the word are given:

happiest, happily, happiness

If you thought that the word <u>elastic</u> began with an **i** you would find that you are spelling the word wrongly and, as the following example shows, the correct spelling of <u>elastic</u> has a ⁺ sign after it:

ilastic	elastic [+]

8

Now if you look up <u>elastic</u> under **e** instead of **i** you will find that other forms of the word are given:

elastic /ally/ity

5. All the words with the number ¹ or ² or ³ or ⁴ after them are verbs (doing words) or may be used as verbs. If you require the word to end in either <u>ed</u> or <u>ing</u>, then you must remember the following:

(a) If you see ¹ after a word you may add <u>ed</u> or <u>ing</u> to the word without changing it, thus:

add¹   add<u>ed</u>   add<u>ing</u>

(b) If you see ² after a word ending in **e**, the **e** must be dropped before adding <u>ed</u> or <u>ing</u>, thus:

name²   nam<u>ed</u>   nam<u>ing</u>

(c) If you see ³ after a word you must double the final consonant (the last letter) before adding <u>ed</u> or <u>ing</u>, thus:

pat³   patt<u>ed</u>   patt<u>ing</u>

(d) If you see ⁴ after a word (all words with a ⁴ after them end in **y**) you MUST change the **y** to an **i** before adding <u>ed</u>, but you may add <u>ing</u> to the word without changing it, thus:

carry⁴   carr<u>i</u><u>ed</u>   carry<u>ing</u>
cry⁴   cri<u>ed</u>   cry<u>ing</u>

BEWARE

A word having an asterisk (*) after it has the same sound, or almost the same sound, as another word, but it has a different meaning and spelling.

Explanations in brackets (not exact definitions) are only included where the words occur in their correct alphabetical place in the book, e.g.:

berry* (fruit) /ies
berry   bury⁴*
bury⁴* (cover)

If you want to check the meaning of the word <u>bury⁴*</u>, you must look it up in its correct alphabetical place under <u>bu</u> and not under <u>be</u>.

NOTES. (1) Where a dagger (†) appears after the *, the word definition is given on the next line, e.g.:

farth er *† /est
†(distant)

(2) The **hyphen** (-) is a sign used to join words and must not be left out, e.g.:

far /-fetched/-flung (far-fetched, far-flung)
fire-engine

KEY TO DICTIONARY SYMBOLS

A list of meanings of the various symbols used appears on the inside back cover of the dictionary.

Dictionary Exercises

Although the instructions on the use of the dictionary are set out clearly enough for a pupil to follow and understand, it would be helpful for the teacher to read through the rules with the pupils and make them do the exercises set out below. There is an exercise to help reinforce each rule, and the final exercise (V) gives the pupil practice in the use of all the rules.

Most pupils will quickly learn how to use the dictionary and the teacher can check whether they are using it accurately simply by giving a verbal test requiring written answers. For those who may need further practice, the teacher may use the exercises set out in *Practise Your Spelling* (O. B. Gregory/C. Maxwell, Wheaton, 1977), which exploit further the special features of the dictionary—and are designed to aid spelling, word study and development of vocabulary.

EXERCISE I
Look up the following words and write out in full all the other words that you can make up from the information you find. (The first question has been done for you.)

1. bite *(biting, bitten)*
2. abundant
3. bleak
4. bush

5. door
6. feeble
7. wealth

8. luck
9. sharp
10. tooth

EXERCISE II
Remember: When the last letter or letters of a word are in *italics*, these must be LEFT OFF before adding the other endings, e.g.:

nast*y* /ier/iest/ily/iness

The *y* in nasty must be left off before making the words

nastier, nastiest, nastily, nastiness

Look up the following words and write out in full all the other words that you can make up from the information you find. (The first question has been done for you.)

1. difficulty *(difficulties)*
2. rowdy
3. geography
4. giddy

5. mightier
6. lady
7. someone

8. greedier
9. busier
10. army

EXERCISE III **Using the numbers 1, 2, 3, and 4**
Use the following example as a guide,

Verb	*Past participle*	*Present participle*
peck	pecked	pecking

and write out the corresponding parts of the verbs listed in the following sections A–D. (The first items of sections A–D, respectively, have been done for you.)

A. Using the number 1
1. tick *(ticked, ticking)*
2. bang
3. dismay
4. help

5. thump
6. link
7. lisp

8. hurl
9. shatter
10. drill

10

B. Using the number **2**
1. cripple *(crippled, crippling)*
2. mime
3. rinse
4. blaze
5. slope
6. tremble
7. wrestle
8. fuse
9. chuckle
10. ache

C. Using the number **3**
1. dab *(dabbed, dabbing)*
2. skid
3. beg
4. whiz
5. jar
6. chip
7. hum
8. zigzag
9. prod
10. expel

D. Using the number **4**
1. dignify *(dignified, dignifying)*
2. satisfy
3. disqualify
4. pity
5. busy
6. marry
7. terrify
8. try
9. fry
10. crucify

EXERCISE IV
Combination of numbers and other word endings: e.g. dance² /r
In the above entry the ² tells us that we can write <u>dancing</u> and <u>danced</u>.
If we add the **r** to the main word <u>dance</u>, we get <u>dancer.</u>
See if you can do this exercise. Write out in full as many forms of the words
as you can from the information given. (The first question has been done for you.)
1. attract *(attracting, attracted, attraction)*
2. coach
3. narrow
4. dissatisfy
5. guide
6. hedge
7. learn
8. thin
9. mouth
10. travel

EXERCISE V
You are now ready to tackle an exercise containing a mixture of all the rules.
Look up the following words and write out as many words as you can from the
information given. (The first question has been done for you.)
1. close *(closed, closing, closure)*
2. further
3. playful
4. run
5. young
6. clever
7. police
8. wide
9. knife
10. water

Your teacher will now ask you to spell a number of words, and if you use the
dictionary correctly, you will get every word right.
You may also work with another member of your group or class, taking turns to
ask each other how to spell words that you are presently using, until you are quite
confident that you can use the dictionary successfully.

Remember, on the inside back cover there is a key to the symbols used in this
dictionary.

A

à la carte
aback
abac *us* /i (pl.)

abait   abate ²⁺
abanden   abandon ¹⁺
abandon ¹ /ment
abash /ed
abate ² /ment

abawd   aboard
abawshun   abortion ⁺
abawt   abort ¹⁺
abawtion   abortion ⁺
abayans   abeyance ⁺
abbey /s
abb *ot* /ess (fem.)
abbreviat *e* ² /ion
abdicat *e* ² /ion
abdomen
abdomin *al* /ally/ous
abduct ¹ /ion/or
abet ³ /tor

abetor   abettor
abeyan *ce* /t

abeyans   abeyance ⁺
abhaw   abhor ³⁺
abhor ³ /rence

abhorence   abhorrence
abhorens   abhorrence
abhorent   abhorrent ⁺
abhorrent /ly

abidans   abidance
abid *e* ² /ance
abilit *y* /ies

abismal   abysmal ⁺
abiss   abyss
abject /ion/ly/ness
ablative

ablbodid   able-bodied

able /-bodied/r/st
ablie   ably
ably

abnawmal   abnormal ⁺
abnawmalitey   abnormality ⁺
abnormal /ly
abnormalit *y* /ies
aboard
abode
aboli *sh* ¹ /tion

abolishun   abolition
A-bomb
abominabl *e* /y

abominabul   abominable ⁺
abominashun   abomination
abominat *e* ² /ion

abord   aboard
aborigin *al* /es
aborshun
abort ¹ /ive
abortion /ist
abound ¹
about
above /-board

abownd   abound ¹
abowt   about
abracadabra

abrashun   abrasion ⁺
abras *ion* /ive

abrawd   abroad
abreast

abrecadabra   abracadabra
abrest   abreast
abreviashun   abbreviation
abreviate   abbreviate ²⁺
abreviation   abbreviation
abridge ² /ment

abrige   abridge ²⁺

13

abroad		abyewse	abuse [2]+
abrord	abroad	abysmal /ly	
abrupt /ly/ness		abyss	
absaloot	absolute +	abyusiv	abusive
absawb	absorb [1]+	abzawb	absorb [1]+
absawbency	absorbency +	abzawbent	absorbent
absawbensey	absorbency +	abzolv	absolve [2]+
absawbent	absorbent	acacia	
absawpshun	absorption +	academic /al/ally	
abscess /es		academician	
abscond [1] /er		academishun	academician
absent [1] /ee/eeism		academ*y* /ies	
abserd	absurd +	acapuncture	acupuncture
abserditey	absurdity	accede [2] /nce	
absess	abscess +	accelerat*e* [2] /ion/or	
absolushun	absolution	accent [1] /ual	
absolut*e* /ely/ism		accentuat*e* [2] /ion	
absolution		accept [1] /ability	
absolv*e* [2] /able		acceptabl*e* /y	
absorb [1] /able		acceptabul	acceptable +
absorben*cy* /t		acceshun	accession +
absorbensey	absorbency +	access /ibility/ible	
absorpshun	absorption +	accessar*y* ★ (legal) /ies	
absorpt*ion* /ive		accession /al	
abstain [1] /er		accessor*y* ★† /ies	
abstayn	abstain [1]+	† (accompaniment)	
abstemious /ness		accident /al/ally	
abstemius	abstemious +	acclaim [1] /er	
abstenshun	abstention	acclamashun	acclamation +
abstention		acclamat*ion* /ory	
abstinen*ce* /t		acclaym	acclaim [1]+
abstinens	abstinence +	acclimatis*e* [2] /ation	
abstract [1] /ion/or		accolade	
abstroos	abstruse +	accommodat*e* [2] /ion	
abstruse /ness		accompani*st* /ment	
absurd /ity/ities		accompany [4]	
abul	able +	accomplice	
abundanc*e* /y		accomplish [1] /ment	
abundans	abundance +	accompliss	accomplice
abundant /ly		accord [1] /ance/ingly	
abundent	abundant +	accordion /ist	
abunduns	abundance +	accordyun	accordion+
abus*e* [2] /ive/iveness		accost [1]	
abut [3] /ment		account [1] /ancy/ant	
abuv	above +	accountab*le* /ility	

14

accountabul	accountable [+]	acootrements	accoutrements
accoutrements		acord	accord [1+]
accredit [1] /ation		acorn	
accru e [2] /al		acost	accost [1]
accumpany	accompany [4]	acount	account [1+]
accumulat e [2] /ion/or		acoustic /s	
accumulative		acownt	account [1+]
accuracy		acquaint [1] /ance	
accurasey	accuracy	acquiesce [2] /nce/nt	
accurate /ly/ness		acquire [2] /ment	
accursed /ly/ness		acquisit ion /ive	
accusative		acquit [3] /tal	
accus e [2] /ation/er		acre /age	
accustom [1]		acrid /ity/ness	
ace		acrimonious /ly	
acer	acre [+]	acrimonius	acrimonious [+]
acerige	acreage	acrimony	
acetate		acrobat /ic/ically	
acetic		acromatic	achromatic
acetone		acronim	acronym
acetylen e /ic		acronym	
ache [2]		acropolis	
achevabul	achievable	across	
acheve	achieve [2+]	acseed	accede [2+]
achievable		acselerate	accelerate [2+]
achieve [2] /ment/r		acselerater	accelerator
achromatic		acsent	accent [1+]
acid /ic/ity		acsentuate	accentuate [2+]
acidul ate [2] /ous		acsept	accept [1+]
acknoledge	acknowledge [2+]	acseptable	acceptable [+]
acknolidge	acknowledge [2+]	acsesary	accessary [*+]
acknowledge [2] /ment		acsesary	accessory [*+]
aclaim	acclaim [1+]	acseshun	accession [+]
aclamashun	acclamation [+]	acsess	access [+]
aclamation	acclamation [+]	acsessorey	accessory [*+]
aclaym	acclaim [1+]	acshun	action [+]
acme		acsident	accident [+]
acne		act [1] /able	
acolight	acolyte	actini c /um	
acolyte		action /able	
acommodate	accommodate [2+]	activat e [2] /ion/or	
acomodate	accommodate [2+]	active /ly/ness	
acompaniment	accompaniment	activis m /t	
acompany	accompany [4]	activit y /ies	
acompliss	accomplice	act or /ress (fem.)	

actual /ly	
actualit *y* /ies	
actuar *y* /ies	
actuat *e* [2] /ion/or	
acumen	
acumpany	accompany [4]
acumpliss	accomplice
acumulate	accumulate [2+]
acupuncture	
acupunkcher	acupuncture
acuracy	accuracy
acurate	accurate [+]
acustic	acoustic [+]
acustum	accustom [1]
acute /ly/ness	
ad	add [1]
ad hoc	
ad infinitum	
ad-lib [3]	
adage	
adagio /s	
adamant /ine	
adament	adamant [+]
adapt [1] /ation/ive	
adaptab *le* /ility	
adaptabul	adaptable [+]
adapter ⋆ (person)	
adaptor ⋆ (electric)	
add [1]	
addend *um* /a (pl.)	
addenoids	adenoids
adder	
addict [1] /ion/ive	
addition /al/ally	
addle [2]	
address [1] /ee/er	
ade	aid [1+]
adement	adamant [+]
adendum	addendum [+]
adenoids	
adept /ly/ness	
adequacy	
adequasey	adequacy
adequate /ly/ness	
adhear	adhere [2+]

adhearence	adherence
adhere [2] /nce/nt	
adheshun	adhesion [+]
adhes *ion* /ive	
adicshun	addiction
adiction	addiction
adidge	adage
adieu	
adige	adage
adikwacy	adequacy
adikwat	adequate [+]
adiquacy	adequacy
adiquate	adequate [+]
adishun	addition [+]
adition	addition [+]
adjacent /ly	
adjectiv *e* /al	
adjoin [1]	
adjourn [1] /ment	
adjudge [2]	
adjudicat *e* [2] /ion/or	
adjunct /ion/ive	
adjust [1] /able/ment	
adjutan *cy* /t	
adle	addle [2]
administ *er* [1] /rable	
administrat *e* [2] /ion/or	
administrater	administrator
administrative	
admirabl *e* /y	
admirabul	admirable [+]
admiral /ty	
admirashun	admiration
admir *e* [2] /ation/er	
admirul	admiral [+]
admishun	admission [+]
admisibul	admissible [+]
admissib *le* /ility	
admiss *ion* /ive	
admit [3] /tedly	
admitance	admittance
admitans	admittance
admittance	
admonish [1] /er/ment	
ado	

adobe	
adobi	adobe
adolescen *ce* /t	
adolesence	adolescence [+]
adolesens	adolescence [+]
adolesent	adolescent
adoor	adore [2+]
adopshun	adoption
adopt [1] /er/ion/ive	
adorabl *e* /y	
adorabul	adorable [+]
ador *e* [2] /ation	
adorn [1] /ment	
adrenal /in	
adrift	
adroit /ly/ness	
adsorpshun	adsorption [+]
adsorpt *ion* /ive	
adue	adieu
adul	addle [2]
adulashun	adulation
adulat *e* [2] /ion/or	
adult /hood	
adulterat *e* [2] /ion	
adulterus	adulterous
adulter *y* /er/ous	
advance [2] /ment	
advans	advance [2+]
advencher	adventure [2+]
advencherous	adventurous [+]
advencherus	adventurous [+]
advent	
adventishus	adventitious [+]
adventitious /ly/ness	
adventure [2] /some	
adventurous /ly/ness	
adverb /ial	
adversar *y* /ies	
adverse /ly/ness	
adversit *y* /ies	
advertise [2] /ment	
advice * (suggestion)	
advisabl *e* /y	
advisabul	advisable [+]
advise [2] * (suggest)	

advis *edly* /er/ory	
advocacy	
advocasey	advocacy
advocat *e* [2] /or	
advurse	adverse [+]
advurtisment	advertisement
aegis	
aerat *e* [2] /ion/or	
aerial /ly	
aerobatics	
aerodrome	
aerodynamics	
aerofoil	
aeronaut /ical/ics	
aeroplane	
aerosol	
aesthet *e* /ic/icism	
afable	affable [+]
afabul	affable [+]
afair	affair
afare	affair
afecshun	affection
afecshunate	affectionate [+]
afect	affect [1+]
afectation	affectation
afection	affection
afectionate	affectionate [+]
afective	affective
afeild	afield
afeld	afield
aferm	affirm [1+]
afermativ	affirmative [+]
affab *le* /ility/ly	
affair	
affect [1] /ion/ive	
affectation	
affectionate /ly/ness	
affidavit	
affiks	affix [1+]
affiliat *e* [2] /ion	
affinit *y* /ies	
affirm [1] /ation	
affirmative /ly	
affix [1] /er	
afflict [1] /ion	

P.D.P.S.—B

affluen *ce* /t	
affluens	affluence +
afford [1] /able	
afforest [1] /ation	
affray /s	
affront [1]	
afid	aphid +
afidavit	affidavit
afield	
afiks	affix [1]+
afiliashun	affiliation
afiliate	affiliate [2]+
afiliation	affiliation
afinitey	affinity +
afire	
afirm	affirm [1]+
afirmativ	affirmative +
afix	affix [1]+
aflaim	aflame
aflame	
aflicshun	affliction
aflict	afflict [1]+
afliction	affliction
afloat	
aflote	afloat
afluence	affluence +
afluens	affluence +
afluent	affluent
aford	afford [1]+
aforesaid	
aforest	afforest [1]+
aforestashun	afforestation
aforestation	afforestation
aforism	aphorism +
aforistic	aphoristic
aforsed	aforesaid
afrade	afraid
afraid	
afray	affray +
afrayd	afraid
African	
Afrikaans	
Afrikans	Afrikaans
afrodisiac	aphrodisiac
afront	affront [1]

after	
afterbirth	
afterburth	afterbirth
aftermath	
afternoon	
afterthort	afterthought
afterthought	
afterwards	
afterwerds	afterwards
afurm	affirm [1]+
afurmashun	affirmation
afurmation	affirmation
afurmativ	affirmative +
again	
against	
agast	aghast
agate	
agayn	again
age [2] /less	
agen	again
agenc *y* /ies	
agenda	
agensey	agency +
agenst	against
agent /ial	
agglomerat *e* [2] /ion	
aggrandise [2] /ment	
aggravat *e* [2] /ion	
aggregat *e* [2] /ely/ion	
aggreshun	aggression +
aggress *ion* /or	
aggressive /ly/ness	
aggrieved	
aghast	
agil *e* /ity	
agitat *e* [2] /ion/or	
aglomerashun	agglomeration
aglomerate	agglomerate [2]+
aglomeration	agglomeration
aglow	
agnostic /ism	
agonie	agony +
agonis *e* [2] /ingly	
agon *y* /ies	
agorafobia	agoraphobia

agoraphobia	
agrafobia	agoraphobia
agrandise	aggrandise [2+]
agrarian	
agravate	aggravate [2+]
agree /d/ing/ment	
agreeabl e /y	
agregate	aggregate [2+]
agrement	agreement
agreshun	aggression [+]
agresion	aggression [+]
agresiv	aggressive [+]
agression	aggression [+]
agreved	aggrieved
agriculcher	agriculture [+]
agricultur e /al/ally	
agrieved	aggrieved
aground	
agrownd	aground
agu e /ish	
ahead	
ahed	ahead
ahoi	ahoy
ahoy	
aid [1] /er	
ail [1]★ (trouble)	
ail	ale ★
ailment	
aim [1] /less/lessly	
air [1]★ (gases)	
air	ere ★
air	heir ★
airate	aerate [2+]
airborne	
air-brake	
aircondishner	air-conditioner
air-conditioner	
air-cooled	
aircraft	
aires	Aries
airey	airy [+]
airfeild	airfield
airfield	
air force	
air-gun	

air hostess /es	
airial	aerial [+]
airily	
airline /r	
air-lock	
airmail [1]	
airmale	airmail [1]
airobatics	aerobatics
airodinamics	aerodynamics
airodrome	aerodrome
airofoil	aerofoil
airofoyl	aerofoil
aironort	aeronaut [+]
aironortics	aeronautics
airoplane	aeroplane
airosol	aerosol
air-pocket	
airport	
air raid	
airworth y /iness	
airy /-fairy	
aisle ★ (passage)	
aisle	isle ★
ajar	
ajasent	adjacent [+]
ajectiv	adjective [+]
ajency	agency [+]
ajenda	agenda
ajensey	agency [+]
ajent	agent [+]
ajile	agile [+]
ajilitey	agility
ajitashun	agitation
ajitate	agitate [2+]
ajoyn	adjoin [1]
ajudicate	adjudicate [2+]
ajunct	adjunct [+]
ajurn	adjourn [1+]
ajusment	adjustment
ajust	adjust [1+]
ajustable	adjustable
ajutancy	adjutancy [+]
akimbo	
akin	
aksiomatic	axiomatic [+]

aksis	axis [+]	alegation	allegation
aksium	axiom	alege	allege [2+]
akwaintance	acquaintance	alegiance	allegiance
akwalung	aqualung	alegians	allegiance
akwamarine	aquamarine	alegorey	allegory [+]
akwaplane	aquaplane	alegorical	allegorical [+]
akwarium	aquarium [+]	alelooya	alleluia
akwarius	Aquarius	aleluia	alleluia
akwatic	aquatic	alergey	allergy [+]
akwatint	aquatint	alergic	allergic
akwiduct	aqueduct	alert [1] /ly/ness	
akwiesence	acquiescence	aleviate	alleviate [2+]
akwiesent	acquiescent	alfa	alpha
akwiline	aquiline	alfabet	alphabet [+]
akwire	acquire [2+]	alfabetical	alphabetical
akwisition	acquisition [+]	alfresco	
akwisitiv	acquisitive	alga /e (pl.)	
akwit	acquit [3+]	algebra	
akwital	acquittal	algibra	algebra
alabaster		ali	ally [4+]
alack		aliance	alliance
alacrit *y* /ous		alians	alliance
alagro	allegro	alias /es	
alah	Allah	alibi /s	
alarm [1] /ist		aliby	alibi [+]
alas		alien /able	
alay	allay [1+]	alienat *e* [2] /ion/or	
albatross		aligater	alligator
albeit		alight [1]	
albeno	albino [+]	align [1] /ment	
albino /s		alike /ness	
album		alimenta *ry* /tion	
albumen *[*][†]		alimentrey	alimentary [+]
†(white of egg)		alimony	
albumin *[*][†]		aline	align [1+]
†(soluble protein)		alite	alight [1]
alchem *y* /ist		aliterashun	alliteration
alcohol /ic/ism		aliterate	alliterate [2+]
alcove		aliteration	alliteration
alder		alive	
alderman /cy		alkali /s	
ale * (drink)		alkalin *e* /ity	
ale	ail [1]*	alkemey	alchemy [+]
alegashun	allegation	alkemist	alchemist
alegater	alligator	all * (everyone)	

20

all	awl ★
all right	
Allah	
allay[1] /er	
allegashun	allegation
allegation	
allege[2] /dly	
allegiance	
allegorical /ly	
allegor y /ies	
allegro	
alleluia	
allergic	
allerg y /ies	
alleviat e[2] /ion	
alley /s/way	
all-fours	
alli	ally[4+]
alliance	
alligator	
alliterat e[2] /ion/ive	
allmost	almost
allocat e[2] /ion	
allot[3] /ment	
allotropes	
allow[1] /able/ance	
alloy[1]	
all-round	
allrite	all right
allso	also
allude[2★] (refer to)	
allude	elude[2★]
allure[2] /ment	
allushun	allusion ★
allusion★ (reference to)	
allusion	illusion ★
allusive ★† /ly/ness † (suggestive)	
allusive	elusive ★+
allusive	illusive ★
alluvi al /um	
all y[4] /ies	
ally	alley +
almanac	
almighty	

almon er /ry	
almost	
alms ★ (charity)	
alms	arms ★
alms-house	
alocate	allocate[2+]
aloft	
aloi	alloy[1]
alone	
along /side	
alood	allude[2★]
aloof /ness	
alot	allot[3+]
alotment	allotment
aloud	
alow	allow[1+]
alowable	allowable
alowabul	allowable
alowance	allowance
alowans	allowance
alowd	aloud
aloy	alloy[1]
alp	
alpaca	
alpaka	alpaca
alpha	
alphabet /ical/ically	
alpine	
already	
alredy	already
alright	all right
alrite	all right
alsashun	Alsatian
Alsatian	
also	
altar ★ (church)	
altarpiece	
alter[1★] (change)	
altera ble /tion	
alterabul	alterable +
alterashun	alteration
altercat e[2] /ion	
alternashun	alternation
alternat e[2] /ion/or	

alternative /ly	
alterpeace	altarpiece
alterpiece	altarpiece
altho	although
although	
altimeter	
altitude	
alto /s	
altogether	
altrooism	altruism
altrooist	altruist [+]
altrooistic	altruistic
altruism	
altruist /ic/ically	
alude	allude [2][*]
alum	
aluminium	
aluminum	aluminium
alure	allure [2][+]
alurt	alert [1][+]
alushun	allusion [*]
alusion	allusion [*]
alusiv	allusive [*][+]
always	
amaise	amaze [2][+]
amalgam	
amalgamashun	amalgamation
amalgamat e [2] /ion	
amass [1] /able/ment	
amater	amateur [+]
amateur /ish/ism	
amaze [2] /ment	
Amazon /ian	
ambasader	ambassador [+]
ambassador /ial	
amber	
ambiant	ambient
ambidekstrus	ambidextrous
ambidextrous	
ambidextrus	ambidextrous
ambien ce /t	
ambiens	ambience [+]
ambiguit y /ies	
ambiguous /ly/ness	
ambiguus	ambiguous [+]

ambishun	ambition
ambishus	ambitious [+]
ambit	
ambition	
ambitious /ly/ness	
ambivalen ce /t	
amble [2] /r	
amboosh	ambush [1][+]
ambrosia /l	
ambul	amble [2][+]
ambulance	
ambulans	ambulance
ambulat e [2] /ory	
ambush [1] /er	
ame	aim [1][+]
ameba	amoeba
amelierashun	amelioration
amelierate	ameliorate [2][+]
ameliorat e [2] /ion	
amen	
amenabl e /y	
amenabul	amenable [+]
amend [1] /ment	
amenit y /ies	
American	
ameter	ammeter
amethyst /ine	
amfibian	amphibian
amfibious	amphibious [+]
amfibius	amphibious [+]
amfitheater	amphitheatre
amiab le /ility/ly	
amiabul	amiable [+]
amicab le /ility/ly	
amicabul	amicable [+]
amid /st	
amiss	
amiter	ammeter
amitey	amity
amithist	amethyst [+]
amity	
ammeter	
ammonia /c/cal	
ammonya	ammonia [+]
ammunishun	ammunition

ammunition		anakey	anarchy +
amnest y /ies		anakronism	anachronism
amoeba		anal	
amoner	almoner +	analgesi a /c	
among /st		analise	analyse 2+
amonia	ammonia +	analisis	analysis +
amonya	ammonia +	analist	analyst
amoral /ity/ly		analitic	analytic +
amorfus	amorphous +	analog	analogue
amorous /ly		analogey	analogy +
amorphous /ly/ness		analogous /ly	
amortise 2		analogue	
amorus	amorous +	analogus	analogous +
amount 1		analog y /ies	
amownt	amount 1	anals	annals
ampar	ampere +	analyse 2 /r	
amper e /age		analys is /es (pl.)	
amperige	amperage	analyst	
amphibian		analytic /al/ally	
amphibious /ly/ness		anarchi c /sm/st	
amphitheatre		anarch y /ical	
ampl e /y		anarkey	anarchy +
amplie	amply	anarkick	anarchic +
amplifi	amplify 4+	anarkism	anarchism
amplif y 4 /ier		anarkist	anarchist
amplitude		anathema	
ampool	ampoule	anatomic al /ally	
ampoule		anatomise 2	
ampul	ample +	anatom y /ist	
amputashun	amputation	ancest or /ress (fem.)	
amputat e 2 /ion		ancestr y /al	
amulet		anchor 1 /age	
amung	among +	anchov y /ies	
amunishun	ammunition	ancient /ly/ness	
amunition	ammunition	ancillar y /ies	
amuse 2 /ment/r		andante	
anachronism		androginus	androgynous +
anachronistic /ally		androgyn ous /y	
anaconda		anecdot e /al/ic	
anacronism	anachronism	aneks	annex 1*+
anacronistic	anachronistic +	aneks	annexe *
anaemi a /c		anelise	analyse 2+
anaesthe sia /tic/tist		aneksation	annexation
anaesthetis e 2 /ation		anemia	anaemia +
anagram /matic		anemic	anaemic

anemomet *er* /ry	
anemone	
anemya	anaemia [+]
aneroid	
anesthesia	anaesthesia [+]
anesthetic	anaesthetic
anesthetise	anaesthetise [2+]
anesthetist	anaesthetist
anew	
angel ★ (heavenly)	
angel	angle [2]★
angelic /al/ally	
angena	angina
anger	
angina	
angle [2]★ (fish, geometry)	
angler	
Anglican /ism	
anglicise [2]	
anglisise	anglicise [2]
anglosaksen	Anglo-Saxon
Anglo-Saxon	
angora	
angrie	angry [+]
angr *y* /ier/iest/ily	
angsietey	anxiety [+]
anguish [1]	
angular /ity	
anguler	angular [+]
angwish	anguish [1]
anhidrus	anhydrous
anhydrous	
anihilate	annihilate [2+]
aniilate	annihilate [2+]
anilen	aniline
aniline	
animal /ism/istic	
animashun	animation
animat *e* [2] /ion	
animatedly	
animosit *y* /ies	
animul	animal [+]
aniseed	
aniversarey	anniversary [+]
anjelic	angelic [+]

anjelical	angelical
anker	anchor [1+]
ankerage	anchorage
ankerige	anchorage
ankle /bone/t	
ankshous	anxious [+]
ankshus	anxious [+]
ankul	ankle [+]
annals	
anneal [1]	
annex [1]★† /ation	
†(take possession of)	
annexe ★ (of house)	
annihilat *e* [2] /ion	
anniversar *y* /ies	
Anno Domini	
annon	anon
annotat *e* [2] /ion/or	
announce [2] /ment/r	
announs	announce [2+]
annoy [1] /ance/ingly	
annoyans	annoyance
annual /ly	
annuit *y* /ies	
annul [3] /ment	
annular ./ity	
annunciat *e* [2] /ion	
Ano domini	Anno Domini
anod *e* /al	
anodine	anodyne
anodyne	
anoi	annoy [1+]
anoiance	annoyance
anoians	annoyance
anoint [1] /er/ment	
anomaley	anomaly [+]
anomalous /ly	
anomalus	anomalous [+]
anomal *y* /ies	
anon	
anonimitey	anonymity
anonimous	anonymous [+]
anonimus	anonymous [+]
anonymity	
anonymous /ly/ness	

anorak	
anotashun	annotation
anotate	annotate [2]+
anotation	annotation
another	
anounce	announce [2]+
anouns	announce [2]+
anounser	announcer
anownce	announce [2]+
anowns	announce [2]+
anoy	annoy [1]+
anoyance	annoyance
anoyans	annoyance
anoynt	anoint [1]+
anser	answer [1]+
anserable	answerable
anserabul	answerable
ansester	ancestor +
ansestrul	ancestral
ansestry	ancestry +
anshent	ancient +
ansilarey	ancillary +
answer [1] /able/er	
ant /-eater/-hill	
ant	aunt +
antacid	
antagonis e [2] /m	
antagonist /ic/ically	
Antarctic	
antasid	antacid
anteceden ce /t	
antecedens	antecedence +
antechamber	
antedate [2]	
antediluvian	
anteek	antique +
antelope	
antena	antenna +
antenatal	
antenna /e (pl.)	
anterier	anterior
anterior	
anteroom	
anthem	
anther	

antholog y /ies/ist	
anthracit e /ic	
anthraks	anthrax
anthrasite	anthracite +
anthrax	
anthropoid /al	
anthropologey	anthropology +
anthropologist	
anthropolog y /ical	
anthropoyd	anthropoid +
anti-aircraft	
antibiotic	
antibod y /ies	
antic	
antichamber	antechamber
antichrist	
anticiclone	anticyclone +
anticipat e [2] /ion/ory	
anticlimaks	anticlimax +
anticlima x /ctic	
anticyclon e /ic	
antidate	antedate [2]
antidiloovian	antediluvian
antidot e /al/ally	
anti-freeze	
antihistamine	
antikwarian	antiquarian
antikwate	antiquate [2]
antikwerey	antiquary +
antikwitey	antiquity +
antilope	antelope
antimon y /ial	
antinatul	antenatal
antipathey	antipathy +
antipath y /etic	
antipodes	
antiquar y /ies/ian	
antiquate [2]	
antique /ness	
antiquit y /ies	
antiroom	anteroom
antisedens	antecedence +
anti-semiti c /sm	
antiseptic /ally	
antisiclone	anticyclone +

25

antisipashun	anticipation	aparishun	apparition
antisipate	anticipate [2+]	aparition	apparition
antisipation	anticipation	apart	
antisocial /ly		apartat	apartheid
antisoshal	antisocial [+]	apartheid	
antithes *is* /es (pl.)		apartied	apartheid
antithisis	antithesis [+]	apartment	
antitoksic	antitoxic [+]	apase	apace
antitoksin	antitoxin	apathetic /al/ally	
antitoxi *c* /n		apathy	
antler /ed		ape [2]	
anu	anew	apeace	apiece
anual	annual [+]	apeal	appeal [1+]
anuitey	annuity [+]	apear	appear [1+]
anul	anal	apearance	appearance
anul	annul [3+]	apearans	appearance
anular	annular [+]	apease	apiece
anulment	annulment	apeel	appeal [1+]
anunciashun	annunciation	apeer	appear [1+]
anunciate	annunciate [2+]	apeice	apiece
anunciation	annunciation	apeks	apex [+]
anunsiashun	annunciation	apellant	appellant [+]
anunsiate	annunciate [2+]	apellashun	appellation
anunsiation	annunciation	apellation	appellation
anus		apend	append [1+]
anuther	another	apendage	appendage
anvil		apendicitis	appendicitis
anxiet *y* /ies		apendige	appendage
anxious /ly/ness		apendiks	appendix [+]
any		apendisitis	appendicitis
anybody		apendix	appendix [+]
anyhow		aperance	appearance
anyone		aperans	appearance
anything		apercher	aperture
anyual	annual [+]	apergey	apogee [+]
anyway		aperitif	
anywere	anywhere	apertain	appertain [1]
anywhere		aperture	
aorta		apetiser	appetiser
apace		apetising	appetising [+]
Apache		apetite	appetite
apal	appal [3+]	ap *ex* /e*x*es/ices (pls.)	
aparatus	apparatus [+]	aphid /ian	
aparel	apparel [+]	aphoris *m* /tic	
aparent	apparent [+]	aphrodisiac	

apiar *y* /ies		apparatus /es	
apiece		apparel /led	
apissul	epistle +	apparent /ly	
apitite	appetite	apparishun	apparition
aplaud	applaud [1]	appart	apart
aplause	applause	apparition	
aplawd	applaud [1]	appeal [1] /ingly	
aplawse	applause	appear [1] /ance	
aple	apple +	appease [2] /ment/r	
apli	apply [4]	appella *nt* /tion	
apliance	appliance	append [1] /age	
aplians	appliance	appendicitis	
aplicable	applicable +	appendiks	appendix +
aplicabul	applicable +	appendi *x* /xes/ces (pls.)	
aplicant	applicant	appertain [1]	
aplicashun	application	apperture	aperture
aplication	application	appetiser	
aplom	aplomb	appetising /ly	
aplomb		appetite	
apocalips	apocalypse +	applaud [1]	
apocalyp *se* /tic		applause	
apocrifal	apocryphal	applawd	applaud [1]
apocryphal		applaws	applause
apoge *e* /an		apple /-cart/-pie	
apoint	appoint [1]+	appli	apply [4]
apologetic /ally		appliance	
apologey	apology +	applians	appliance
apologise [2]		applicab *le* /ility	
apolog *y* /ies/ist		applicant	
apoplectic /ally		applicashun	application
apopleksey	apoplexy	application	
apoplexy		apply [4]	
aporshun	apportion [1]+	appoint [1] /ment	
aportion	apportion [1]+	apporshun	apportion [1]+
aposishun	apposition	apportion [1] /ment	
aposit	apposite	apposishun	apposition
aposition	apposition	apposite	
aposle	apostle +	apposition	
apost *le* /olate/olic		appreciabl *e* /y	
apostrofey	apostrophe	appreciabul	appreciable +
apostrophe		appreciat *e* [2] /ion/ive	
aposul	apostle +	apprehend [1]	
apothecar *y* /ies		apprehenshun	apprehension
apoynt	appoint [1]+	apprehension	
appal [3] /lingly		apprehensive /ly/ness	

27

apprentice² /ship	
apprentis	apprentice²⁺
apprise²	
approach¹ /able	
approbation	
approch	approach¹⁺
appropriate² /ly/ness	
appropriat*ion* /or	
approval	
approve²	
approximashun	approximation
approximate² /ly	
approximation	
aprehend	apprehend¹
aprehenshun	apprehension
aprehensiv	apprehensive⁺
apren	apron¹
aprentis	apprentice²⁺
apreshabul	appreciable⁺
apreshiable	appreciable⁺
apreshiativ	appreciative
apresiashun	appreciation
apricot	
April	
aprise	apprise²
aprize	apprise²
aproach	approach¹⁺
aprobashun	approbation
aprobation	approbation
aproch	approach¹⁺
aprochabul	approachable
aproksimashun	approximation
aproksimat	approximate²⁺
aproksimation	approximation
apron¹	
aproov	approve²
aprooval	approval
apropo	apropos
apropos	
apropriashun	appropriation⁺
apropriate	appropriate²⁺
apropriation	appropriation⁺
aproval	approval
aprove	approve²
aproximate	approximate²⁺

aproximation	approximation
apt /ly/ness	
aptitude	
aptley	aptly
apul	apple⁺
aqualung	
aquamarine	
aquaplane	
aquarelle	
aquari *um* /a/ums (pls.)	
Aquarius	
aquatic	
aquatint	
aqueduct	
aqueous	
aquiline	
aquius	aqueous
ar	are⁺
arabel	arable
arabesk	arabesque
arabesque	
Arabi *an* /c	
arable	
arabul	arable
araign	arraign¹⁺
arain	arraign¹⁺
Aramaic	
arange	arrange²⁺
arant	arrant⁺
aray	array¹⁺
arayn	arraign¹⁺
arber	arbour
arbiter	
arbitrar *y* /ily/iness	
arbitrashun	arbitration
arbitrat *e*² /ion/or	
arbour	
arc ★ (curved line)	
arc	ark ★
arcade	
arch /es/ly/ness	
archaeolog *y* /ical/ist	
archai *c* /sm	
archangel	
archaologey	archaeology⁺

archbishop		aright	
archdeacon		ariley	airily
archduke		arina	arena
archeologey	archaeology +	arise /n	
archer /y		aristocracy	
archetype		aristocrasey	aristocracy
archfeind	archfiend	aristocrat /ic	
archfiend		arite	aright
archipelago /s		arithmetic /ian	
architect /ure		arithmetical /ly	
architectural /ly		arival	arrival
archiv es /ist		arive	arrive 2+
archley	archly	arizen	arisen
archway		ark ★ (floating vessel)	
arcipeligo	archipelago +	ark	arc ★
arcitect	architect +	arkade	arcade
arcitectural	architectural +	arkaic	archaic +
arcives	archives +	arkangel	archangel
arc -lamp /-light		arkiologey	archaeology +
Arctic		arkiologist	archaeologist
ardent /ly		arkipeligo	archipelago +
arder	ardour	arkitect	architect +
ardewus	arduous +	arkitectural	architectural +
ardour		arkives	archives +
arduous /ly/ness		arktic	Arctic
arduus	arduous +	arktipe	archetype
are /n't		arm 1 /ful/let	
area ★ (surface)		armada	
area	aria ★	armadillo /es	
arears	arrears	armament	
arees	Aries	armchair	
arena		armer	armour +
arent	aren't	armey	army +
arest	arrest 1+	armistice	
argew	argue 2+	armistis	armistice
argu	argue 2+	armoner	almoner +
arguabul	arguable	armour /ed	
argu e 2 /able/ably		arms ★ (limbs)	
argument /ative		arms	alms ★
ari	awry	arm y /ies	
aria ★ (song)		arnt	aren't
aria	area ★	arogance	arrogance +
arial	aerial +	arogans	arrogance +
arid /ity		arogant	arrogant
Aries		arogate	arrogate 2+

29

aroma /s/tic		artiller *y* /ies	
arora	aurora	artisan	
aroroot	arrowroot	artist ★ (painter)	
arose		artiste ★ (performer)	
around		artistic /ally	
arouse [2]		artistry	
arow	arrow [+]	artizan	artisan
arownd	around	artless /ly/ness	
arowroot	arrowroot	asail	assail [1+]
arowse	arouse [2]	asailant	assailant
arpeggio /s		asalant	assailant
arpejo	arpeggio [+]	asale	assail [1+]
arraign [1] /ment		asalt	assault [1+]
arrange [2] /ment		asassin	assassin
arrant /ly		asassinashun	assassination
array [1] /s		asassinate	assassinate [2+]
arrears		asassination	assassination
arrest [1] /er		asault	assault [1+]
arrival		asay	assay [1+]
arrive [2] /r		asayl	assail [1+]
arrogan *ce* /t/tly		asbestos /is	
arrogans	arrogance [+]	ascend [1] /ancy/ant	
arrogat *e* [2] /ion		ascenshun	ascension
arrow /-head		ascension	
arrowroot		ascent ★ (rise)	
arsenal		ascent	assent [1★]
arsenic /al		ascertain [1] /able	
arsnic	arsenic [+]	ascetic /ally/ism	
arson /ist		ascrib *e* [2] /able	
artefact		ase	ace
arter *y* /ies		asemblage	assemblage
arteshun	artesian	asemble	assemble [2+]
artesian		asembley	assembly [+]
artful /ly/ness		asemblige	assemblage
arthriti *c* /s		asembul	assemble [2+]
arthropod		asend	ascend [1+]
artichoke		asendancy	ascendancy
article [2]		asendansey	ascendancy
articul	article [2]	asendant	ascendant
articular		asenshun	ascension
articulat *e* [2] /ion		asension	ascension
artifice /r		asent	ascent ★
artificial /ity/ly		asent	assent [1★]
artifis	artifice [+]	asep *sis* /tic	
artifishal	artificial [+]	asershun	assertion

asert	assert [1+]	asistance	assistance
asertain	ascertain [1+]	asistans	assistance
asertane	ascertain [1+]	asistant	assistant
asertayn	ascertain [1+]	asitic	acetic
asertion	assertion	ask [1]	
asertive	assertive	askance	
asess	assess [1+]	askans	askance
asesser	assessor	askew	
asessment	assessment	asku	askew
aset	asset	asleep	
asetic	ascetic [+]	asma	asthma [+]
aseticism	asceticism	asmatic	asthmatic
asfalt	asphalt	asociate	associate [2+]
asfixia	asphyxia	asociation	association
asfixiate	asphyxiate [2+]	asonance	assonance [+]
ash /es/en/-tray/y		asonans	assonance [+]
ashamed		asonant	assonant
ashfalt	asphalt	asort	assort [1+]
ashor	assure [2★]	asoshiashun	association
ashorance	assurance	asoshiate	associate [2+]
ashorans	assurance	aspadistra	aspidistra
ashore ★ (on beach)		asparagus	
ashore	assure [2★]	aspect	
aside		aspen	
asiditey	acidity	asperit y /ies	
asidulate	acidulate [2+]	aspershun	aspersion
asiduous	assiduous [+]	aspersion	
asiduus	assiduous [+]	asphalt	
asign	assign [1+]	asphyxia	
asignashun	assignation	asphyxiat e [2] /ion	
asignation	assignation	aspic	
asignment	assignment	aspidistra	
asilum	asylum	aspirashun	aspiration
asimetrical	asymmetrical	aspir e [2] /ation	
asimilashun	assimilation	aspirin	
asimilate	assimilate [2+]	asprin	aspirin
asimilater	assimilator	ass /es	
asimilation	assimilation	assail [1] /able/ant	
asimitrey	asymmetry [+]	assassin	
asinable	assignable	assassinat e [2] /ion	
asinabul	assignable	assault [1] /er	
asine	assign [1+]	assay [1] /er	
asinement	assignment	assembl e [2] /age	
asinin e /ity		assembl y /ies	
asist	assist [1+]	assembul	assemble [2+]

assend	ascend [1+]
assendancy	ascendancy
assendant	ascendant
assenshun	ascension
assension	ascension
assent [1]* (agree)	
assent	ascent *
assert [1] /ion/ive	
assess [1] /ment/or	
asset	
assiduous /ly	
assign [1] /able/ation/ment	
assignee	
assimilat *e* [2] /ion/or	
assine	assign [1+]
assist [1] /ance/ant	
associat *e* [2] /ion	
assonan *ce* /t	
assonans	assonance [+]
assort [1] /ment	
assoshiate	associate [2+]
assuage [2] /ment	
assum *e* [2] /able/ably	
assumption	
assumshun	assumption
assurance	
assurans	assurance
assure [2]* (make certain)	
aster * (flower)	
aster	astir *
asterisk	
astern	
asteroid	
asthma /tic	
astigmati *c* /sm	
astir * (motion)	
astonish [1] /ment	
astound [1] /ingly	
astownd	astound [1+]
astral /ly	
astray	
astrel	astral [+]
astride	
astringen *cy* /t	
astrolog *y* /er/ical	

astronaut /ic/ical	
astronomy	
astronort	astronaut [+]
astronortic	astronautic
astrul	astral [+]
astur	astir *
asturn	astern
astute /ly/ness	
asume	assume [2+]
asumpshun	assumption
asumption	assumption
asunder	
aswage	assuage [2+]
asylum	
asymetrey	asymmetry [+]
asymmetr *y* /ical	
atach	attach [1+]
atachable	attachable
atachabul	attachable
atachay case	attaché case
atack	attack [1+]
atain	attain [1+]
atane	attain [1+]
ate * (did eat)	
ate	eight *
ateen	eighteen [+]
atempt	attempt [1+]
atend	attend [1+]
atendance	attendance
atendans	attendance
atendant	attendant
atenshun	attention [+]
atention	attention [+]
atentiv	attentive
atenuashun	attenuation
atenuate	attenuate [2+]
atenuation	attenuation
aterney	attorney [+]
atest	attest [1+]
atestashun	attestation
atestation	attestation
atey	eighty [+]
atheis *m* /t/tic	
athiism	atheism [+]
athiist	atheist

athleet	athlete
athlete	
athletic /ism/s	
atic	attic
atipical	atypical +
atire	attire ²
atitude	attitude
Atlantic	
atlas /es	
atmosfere	atmosphere +
atmosferic	atmospheric
atmospher e /ic	
atom /ic/ically	
atomise ² /r	
atone ² /ment	
atract	attract ¹+
atraction	attraction
atractiv	attractive +
atribushun	attribution
atributable	attributable
atributabul	attributable
atribute	attribute ²+
atribution	attribution
atrishun	attrition
atrition	attrition
atrium	
atrocious /ly/ness	
atrocit y /ies	
atrofey	atrophy ⁴+
atroph y ⁴ /ic	
atroshus	atrocious +
atrositey	atrocity +
attach ¹ /able	
attachabul	attachable
attaché case	
attachment	
attack ¹ /er	
attain ¹ /able/ment	
attempt ¹ /able	
attend ¹ /ance	
attendant	
attenshun	attention +
attent ion /ive	
attenuat e ² /ion	
atterney	attorney +

attest ¹ /ation	
attic	
attire ²	
attitude	
attorney /s	
attract ¹ /ion	
attractive /ly/ness	
attributable	
attribut e ² /ion/ive	
attrishun	attrition
attrition	
attune ²	
atune	attune ²
aturney	attorney +
atypical /ly	
au pair	
aubergine	
auburn	
aucshun	auction ¹+
auction ¹ /eer	
audacious /ly	
audacity	
audashus	audacious +
audasitey	audacity
audib le /ility/ly	
audibul	audible +
audience	
audiens	audience
audiomet er /ric/ry	
audio-typist	
audio-visual	
audishun	audition ¹
audit ¹	
audition ¹	
auditor	
auditorium	
auditory	
auditrey	auditory
auger * (tool)	
aught * (anything)	
aught	ought *
augment ¹ /ation	
augur ¹* (predict)	
augur y /ies	
August	

aunt /ie/y		availab *le* /ility	
aura		avalable	available [+]
aural ★ (of the ear) /ly		avalabul	available [+]
auric *le* /ular		avalanche	
aurora		avale	avail [1]
auspic *es* /ious		avarey	aviary [+]
auspishus	auspicious	avaric *e* /ious	
austere /ly/ness		avenew	avenue
austerit *y* /ies		avenge [2] /r	
Australian		avenue	
authentic /ally/ity		aver [3] /ment	
authenticat *e* [2] /ion		average [2] /ly	
author /ess (fem.)		averige	average [2+]
authoris *e* [2] /ation		averishus	avaricious
authoritarian /ism		averiss	avarice [+]
authoritative /ly		averse /ly/ness	
authorit *y* /ies		avershun	aversion
autis *m* /tic		aversion	
autobiografey	autobiography [+]	avert [1] /edly	
autobiografical	autobiographi- cal [+]	aviar *y* /ies	
autobiographical /ly		aviashun	aviation [+]
autobiograph *y* /ies		aviater	aviator
autocrac *y* /ies		aviat *ion* /or	
autocrasey	autocracy [+]	avid /ity/ly	
autocrat		avlanch	avalanche
autocratic /ally		avocado	
autograf	autograph [1+]	avocashun	avocation
autograph [1] /ic		avocation	
automat *e* [2] /ion		avoid [1] /able/ably	
automatic /ally		avow [1] /al/edly	
automatism		avoyd	avoid [1+]
automaton		avoydable	avoidable
automobile		avoydabul	avoidable
autonomous /ly		avrige	average [2+]
autonomus	autonomous [+]	avur	aver [3+]
autonomy		avurs	averse [+]
autopilot		avurshun	aversion
autops *y* /ies		avursion	aversion
autum	autumn [+]	avurt	avert [1+]
autumn /al		await [1]	
auxiliar *y* /ies		awake [2]	
avaidable	available [+]	awaken [1]	
avaide	evade [2+]	award [1] /able/er	
avail [1]		aware /ness	
		awate	await [1]

away	
awb	orb [1]
awe [2]*(fear)/some/struck	
awear	aware +
awful /ly/ness	
awgsiliarey	auxiliary +
Awgust	August
awgy	orgy +
awhile	
awile	awhile
awiyul	awhile
awkward /ly/ness	
awl * (tool)	
awning	
awoard	award [1]+
awoke	
awry	
axe [2]	
axial	
axident	accident +
axiom	
axiomatic /ally	
ax is /es (pl.)	
axle	
axseed	accede [2]+
axsel	axle
axselerate	accelerate [2]+
axsent	accent [1]+
axsentuate	accentuate [2]+
axsept	accept [1]+
axseptable	acceptable +
axseptabul	acceptable +
axsesorey	accessory *+
axsess	access +
axsessible	accessible
axsessibul	accessible
ay * (yes) /es *	
ay	eye [2]*+
ay	I *+
aya	ayah
ayah	
aye * (always)	
azalea	
azalia	azalea
azure	

B

babble [2]	
babie	baby +
babmingten	badminton
babminten	badminton
baboon	
babul	babble [2]
bab y /ies	
baby-sitter	
baccarat	
bach	batch
bacheler	bachelor +
bachelor /hood	
bacill us /i (pl.)	
back [1] /ache/bone/er	
backara	baccarat
backbencher	
backbit e /er/ing	
backbone	
backcloth	
backfire [2]	
backgammon	
background	
backgrownd	background
backhand /ed/er	
backlash	
backlog	
backslid e /er/ing	
backspace [2]	
backstage	
backstitch [1]	
backstroke	
backward /ness/s	
backwater	
bacon	
bacteriological /ly	
bacteriolog y /ist	
bacteri um /a (pl.)	
bad * (no good) /ly	
bade * (asked)	
badge	
badger [1]	
badley	badly

badminton	
baffle² /r	
baful	baffle² +
bag³ /gy/gier/giest	
bagatelle	
baggage	
baggidge	baggage
baggi*ly* /ness	
bagier	baggier
bagiley	baggily +
bagpipe /r	
baige	beige
bail ★ (security, sport)	
bail	bale ²★
bailee ★ (person)	
bailey ★ (castle wall)	
bailful	baleful +
bailiff	
bain	bane +
bainful	baneful
bairn	
baist	baste²
bait ¹★ (fishing)	
bait	bate ²★
baize	
baje	beige
Balaclava	
balad	ballad +
balalaika	
balalika	balalaika
balance² /r	
balans	balance ²+
balast	ballast
balay	ballet
balcon*y* /ies	
bald ★ (no hair)	
bald	bawled ★
balderdash	
bald-headed	
bald*ing* /ness	
bale ²★ (bundle)	
bale	bail ★
baleful /ly	
balerina	ballerina
balihoo	ballyhoo

balistic	ballistic +
balk ¹	
balkoney	balcony +
ball ★ (dance) /room	
ball	bawl ★+
ballad /ry	
ballast	
ball-bearing	
ballerina	
ballet	
ballistic /s	
balloon ¹ /er/ist	
ballot ¹	
ball-point	
ballyhoo	
balm /y ★ (mild)	
balmoral	
baloney	
baloon	balloon ¹+
balot	ballot ¹
balsa	
balsam	
baluster	
balustrade	
bamboo	
bamboozle² /r	
bamboozul	bamboozle ²+
ban ³	
banal /ity/ities	
banalitey	banality
banana	
band ★(stripe, group)/s★	
band	banned ★
bandage ²	
bandanna	
bandey	bandy +
bandie	bandy +
bandige	bandage ²
bandit /ry	
bands	banns ★
bandstand	
bandwagon	
bandy /-legged	
bane /ful/fully	
baner	banner

bang [1]		barge [2] /-pole	
bangle		bargen	bargain [1]+
bangul	bangle	baricade	barricade [2]
banish [1] /ment		barier	barrier
banister		barige	barrage
banjo /s		baring * (exposing)	
bank [1] /er/note		baring	barring *
bankrupt [1] /cy		baring	bearing *
bankwet	banquet [1]	barister	barrister
banned * (barred)		baritone	
banner		barium	
banns * (marriage)		bark [1] /er	
banquet [1]		barley /-sugar	
bans	banns *	barly	barley +
bantam /-weight		barm	balm +
banter [1] /ingly		barmade	barmaid
Bantu		barmaid	
baonet	bayonet [3]	barmy * (crazy)	
baptis e [2] /m		barmy	balmy *
bar /red * (stop) /ring *		barn /yard	
barack	barrack [1]	barn	bairn
barb		barnacle /d	
barbarian		barnicul	barnacle +
barbar ic /ism/ous		barograf	barograph
barbarit y /ies		barograph	
barbarus	barbarous	barok	baroque
barbecue		baromet er /ric	
barbed wire		baron * (noble) /et/y	
barber		baroness (fem.)	
barbican		baroque	
barbique	barbecue	barow	barrow
barbiturate		barrack [1]	
bard * (poet)		barrage	
bard	barred *	barrel [3] /ful	
bare [2]* (naked) /foot		barren * (empty) /ness	
bare	bear *	barricade [2]	
bareback		barrier	
barefaced		barrister	
bareheaded		barrow	
barel	barrel [3]+	barter [1] /er	
barelegged		barul	barrel [3]+
baren	baron *+	basalt	
baren	barren *+	base * (station, foundation)	
bareskin	bearskin	base	bass *
bargain [1] /er			

baseball
base *less* /ly/ness
basement
baset   basset
bashful /ly/ness
basic /ally
basillus   bacillus [+]
basin /ful
bas *is* ⋆ (groundwork)/es
basit   basset
bask[1]
basket /ball/ful/ry
baskit   basket [+]
basoon   bassoon
bas-relief
bass ⋆ (deep tone)
bass clef
bass drum
basset
bassoon
bastard /ly
bastardis *e* [2] /ation
baste [2]
basterd   bastard [+]
bastion
bastyun   bastion
bat[3] /sman
batalion   battalion
batalyun   battalion
batch
bate [2]⋆ (lessen)
bate   bait[1]⋆
baten   baton ⋆
baten   batten[1]⋆
bater   batter[1]
baterey   battery [+]
batering ram   battering-ram
bathe [2] /r
bathroom
batie   batty [+]
batik
batle   battle [2+]
baton ⋆ (staff of office)
battalion
batten[1]⋆ (wood, grow fat)

batter[1]
battering-ram
batter *y* /ies
battle[2] /dress/ship
battle-axe
batt *y* /ier/iest
batul   battle[2+]
baty   batty [+]
bauble
baubul   bauble
bauxite
bawble   bauble
bawdie   bawdy [+]
bawdi *ly* /ness
bawd *y* /ier/iest
bawk   balk[1]
bawksite   bauxite
bawl ⋆ (cry)/ed ⋆ /ing
bawl   ball ⋆[+]
bawl-baring   ball-bearing
bawldedash   balderdash
bawldheded   bald-headed
bawldness   baldness
bawlpoint   ball-point
bawlroom   ballroom
baylif   bailiff
bayonet[3]
bayth   bathe [2+]
bazaar
bazar   bazaar
bazooka
be ⋆ (is-[verb]) /ing
be   bee ⋆[+]
beach[1]⋆ (shore) /es
beach   beech ⋆[+]
beachcomber
beachhead
beacon
bead /y
beadle
beadul   beadle
beaf   beef [+]
beafeter   beefeater
beafstake   beefsteak
beagl *e* /ing

beagul	beagle +	bed 3 /ridden/rock	
beak /er		bedaub 1	
beam 1		bedawb	bedaub 1
bean * (vegetable)		beday	bidet
bean	been *	bedevil 3	
beanstalk		bedlam	
bear * (carry, animal)		bedouin	
bear	bare 2*+	bedowin	bedouin
bearback	bareback	bedraggle 2	
beard 1		bedragul	bedraggle 2
bearfased	barefaced	bedriden	bedridden
bearfoot	barefoot	bedroom	
bearheded	bareheaded	bed-sitter	
bearing * (carrying)		bedspread	
bearing	baring *	bedstead	
bearleggid	barelegged	bedtime	
bearskin		bee * (insect) /hive	
beast /ly		beech * (tree) /es	
beastli er /est/ness		beech	beach 1*+
beat * (strike) /en		beechcomer	beachcomber
beat	beet *	beechhed	beachhead
beatif y 4 /ic/ication		beecon	beacon
beatitude		beed	bead +
beatle	beetle	beedle	beadle
beatroot	beetroot	beef /y	
beatul	beetle	beefeater	
beau * (dandy)		beefi er /est/ly/ness	
Beaufort scale		beefsteak	
beauteous		beegle	beagle +
beautician		beek	beak +
beautie	beauty +	beekun	beacon
beautiful /ly		beeline	
beautify 4		Beelzebub	
beautishun	beautician	beem	beam 1
beaut y /ies		been * (past of be)	
beaver		been	bean *
becalmed		beenstork	beanstalk
became		beer * (drink)	
becarmed	becalmed	beer	bier *
because		beerd	beard 1
beck		beest	beast +
beckon 1 /ingly		beestlier	beastlier +
becom e /ing		beeswaks	beeswax
becon	beacon	beeswax	
becos	because	beet * (vegetable)	

beet	beat *+	bel	bell *
beetle		bel	belle *
beetroot		belaber	belabour 1
beetul	beetle	belabour 1	
beever	beaver	belated /ly	
befall /en		belay 1	
befell		belch 1	
befier	beefier +	beleaf	belief
befit 3		beleager	beleaguer 1
before /hand		beleaguer 1	
befrend	befriend 1	beleavabul	believable +
befriend 1		beleave	believe 2+
befuddle 2		belfrey	belfry +
befudul	befuddle 2	belfr y /ies	
beg 3		Belgian	
began		beli	belie *+
beger	beggar 1+	belicose	bellicose +
beggar 1 /liness/ly		belie * (untruth) /d	
begile	beguile 2+	belief	
begin /ner/ning		believabl e /y	
begone		believe 2 /r	
begot /ten		beliful	bellyful
begrudge 2		beligerence	belligerence +
beguile 2 /ment/r		beligerency	belligerency
begun		beligerent	belligerent
behalf		beline	beeline
beharf	behalf	belittle 2 /r	
behave 2		belittul	belittle 2+
behavier	behaviour +	beliying	belying
behaviour /ism		bell * (rings)	
behead 1		belle * (beauty)	
behed	behead 1	bellicos e /ity	
beheld		belligerenc e /y	
behest		belligerent	
behind		bellow 1 /er	
behive	beehive	bellows	
behold /en/er/ing		bell y * (stomach) /ies/ied	
behove		bellyful	
beige		belong 1 /ings	
being		belose	bellows
bekoz	because	beloved	
bekweath	bequeath 1+	below * (beneath)	
bekwest	bequest	below	bellow 1+
bel *†		below	billow 1*+
†(unit = 10 decibels)		belows	bellows

bely	belly *+
belying	
bemoan 1	
bemuse 2	
bench /er/es	
bend /ing	
beneath	
benefaction	
benefact or /ress (fem.)	
beneficen ce /t	
beneficial	
beneficiar y /ies	
benefisens	beneficence +
benefisent	beneficent
benefisharey	beneficiary +
benefishul	beneficial
benefit 1	
benevolen ce /t/tly	
benevolens	benevolence +
benifacshun	benefaction
benifacter	benefactor +
benifactress	benefactress
benifit	benefit 1
benign /ant/ly	
benine	benign +
bent	
benum	benumb 1+
benumb 1 /ment	
benzene *†	
†(from coal-tar)	
benzine * (from mineral oils)	
bequeath 1 /ment	
bequest	
berate 2	
beray	beret
bereave 2 /ment	
bereft	
beret	
bereve	bereave 2+
bergler	burglar
berial	burial
beriberi	
berie	berry *+
berie	bury 4*

beril	beryl +
berilium	beryllium
berkelium	
berlap	burlap
berli	burly +
bern	burn 1+
bernish	burnish 1+
berr y * (fruit) /ies	
berry	bury 4*
berserk	
bersurk	berserk
berth 1* (moor, bunk)	
berth	birth *+
bery	berry *+
bery	bury 4*
beryl /line	
beryllium	
beseech /er	
beseige	besiege 2+
beset /ting	
beside /s	
besiege 2 /ment	
besort	besought
besot 3	
besought	
bespatter 1	
best /-seller	
bester	bestir 3
bestial /ism/ly	
bestiality /ies	
bestir 3	
bestow 1 /al/er	
bestrew 1 /n	
bet /ting	
beta particles	
betle	beetle
betoken 1	
betray 1 /al/er	
betroth 1 /al	
better 1 /ment	
betul	beetle
between	
betwixt	
beverage	
beveridge	beverage

beverige	beverage	bifell	befell
bevie	bevy +	bifocal	
bev y /ies		bifurcat e ² /ion	
bewail ¹ /er		big /ger/gest/gish	
beware		bigam ist /ous	
bewayl	bewail ¹⁺	bigamus	bigamous
bewich	bewitch ¹⁺	bigam y /ies	
bewilder ¹ /ment		bigan	began
bewitch ¹ /er		bighead	
beyond		bigile	beguile ²⁺
bezurk	berserk	bigin	begin +
bi election	by-election	biginer	beginner
biannual *† /ly		bigining	beginning
†(twice a year)		bigon	begone
biannual	biennial *+	bigone	bygone +
bias ¹ /es		bigot /ed/ry	
biatifi	beatify ⁴⁺	bigrudge	begrudge ²
biatitude	beatitude	bigun	begun
Bibl e /ical		biharf	behalf
bibliografey	bibliography +	bihave	behave ²
bibliografic	bibliographic +	bihavier	behaviour +
bibliographic /al		bihed	behead ¹
bibliograph y /ies/er		bihest	behest
bibul	Bible +	bihove	behove
bicame	became	bike	
bicarbonate		bikweath	bequeath ¹⁺
bicarmed	becalmed	bikwest	bequest
bicentenar y /ies		bil	bill ¹
bicentennial		bilaber	belabour ¹
bicentenyul	bicentennial	bilated	belated +
biceps		bilateral /ism/ly	
bich	bitch +	bilaw	by-law
bicicle	bicycle ²⁺	bilay	belay ¹
biciclist	bicyclist	bilberie	bilberry +
bicker ¹ /er		bilberr y /ies	
bicycl e ² /ist		bild	build +
bide ²		bilding	building
bidet		bile	
bidevil	bedevil ³	bileager	beleaguer ¹
biennial *† /ly		bileavable	believable +
†(every two years)		bileavabul	believable +
biennial	biannual *+	bileave	believe ²⁺
bier * (for coffin)		bileger	beleaguer ¹
bier	beer *	bileif	belief
bier	byre *	bilet	billet ¹

bilge		biografical	biographical +
bilief	belief	biographical /ly	
bilingual /ism/ly		biography /ies/er	
bilingwal	bilingual +	biokemist	biochemist +
bilious		biologey	biology +
bilittle	belittle ²+	biological /ly	
bilitul	belittle ²+	biology /ist	
bilius	bilious	biopsey	biopsy +
bilk ¹ /er		biopsy /ies	
bill ¹		biparti te /san	
billabong		bipartizan	bipartisan
billet ¹		bipass	by-pass ¹
billiards		biped	
billion /aire		biplane	
billit	billet ¹	biplay	byplay
billow ¹★ (wave) /y		bipolar /ity	
bilong	belong ¹+	biproduct	by-product
bilow	below ★	birate	berate ²
bilow	billow ¹★+	birch /es	
biluvd	beloved	bird	
bilyards	billiards	birdie	
bilyon	billion +	bird's-eye	
bilyus	bilious	bireft	bereft
bimetalli c /sm		bireve	bereave ²+
bimoan	bemoan¹	birode	byroad
bimonthly		birth ★ (born) /day	
bimuse	bemuse ²	birth	berth ¹★
bin ★ (box)		biscuit	
bin	been ★	bisecshun	bisection
binacle	binnacle	bisect ¹ /ion/or	
binacul	binnacle	biseech	beseech +
binary		biseege	besiege ²+
bind /er/ery/ing		biseksual	bisexual +
bineath	beneath	bisentenary	bicentenary +
bineeth	beneath	bisentenial	bicentennial
binge		bisentenyal	bicentennial
bingo		biseps	biceps
binine	benign +	biset	beset +
binnacle		bisexual /ly	
binocular /s		bishop /ric	
binomial		bisicle	bicycle ²+
binum	benumb ¹+	bisiclist	bicyclist
biochemist /ry		biside	beside +
biografer	biographer	bisier	busier +
biografey	biography +	bisiley	busily

biskit	biscuit
bismuth	
bisness	business +
bison	
bisort	besought
bisot	besot 3
bispatter	bespatter 1
bistander	bystander
bistow	bestow 1+
bistowal	bestowal
bistru	bestrew 1+
bistur	bestir 3
bisun	bison
bisy	busy 4
bitch /es	
bit *e* /ing/ten	
biter	bitter +
bitoken	betoken 1
bitray	betray 1+
bitrayal	betrayal
bitroth	betroth 1+
bitter /est/ly/ness	
bitum *en* /inous	
bitween	between
bitwixt	betwixt
bivalve	
bivouac /ked/king	
bivuac	bivouac +
biwail	bewail 1+
biware	beware
biwayul	bewail 1+
biwear	beware
biwhich	bewitch 1+
biwich	bewitch 1+
biwilder	bewilder 1+
biword	byword
biyond	beyond
bizar	bizarre +
bizarre /ly/ness	
bizier	busier +
biziley	busily
bizmuth	bismuth
bizness	business +
bizy	busy 4
blab 3 /ber	

blaber	blabber
black 1 /out	
black-beetle	
blackberie	blackberry +
blackberr *y* /ies	
blackbird	
blackboard	
blacken 1	
blackguard	
blackleg 3	
blacklist 1	
blackmail 1 /er	
blacksmith	
bladder	
blade	
blader	bladder
blagard	blackguard
blaid	blade
blaim	blame 2+
blaimless	blameless +
blair	blare 2
blaise	blaze 2
blaizer	blazer
blam *e* 2 /able	
blameless /ly	
blameworthy	
blamonge	blancmange
blanch 1	
blancmange	
bland /ly/ness	
blank /ly	
blanket 1	
blare 2	
blarney	
blasfeim	blaspheme 2+
blasfemey	blasphemy +
blasfemus	blasphemous
blasphem *e* 2 /ous	
blasphem *y* /ies	
blast 1 /-off	
blast-furnace	
blatancy	
blatansey	blatancy
blatant /ly	
blaze 2	

blazer		blo	blow [+]
blazon[1] /er		bloat[1] /edness	
bleach[1] /er		bloater	
blead	bleed [+]	blob[3]	
bleak /er/est/ly/ness		bloc ★ (group)	
blear[1] /y		blochie .	blotchy
bleari er /est/ly		block[1]★† /age	
bleat[1] /er		†(solid piece, stop)	
bled		block	bloc ★
bleech	bleach[1+]	blockade[2] /r	
bleed /er/ing		blockhead /ed	
bleek	bleak [+]	blond /ish/ness	
bleer	blear[1+]	blone	blown
bleerey	bleary	blood[1] /y	
bleerier	blearier [+]	blood pressure	
bleet	bleat[1+]	blood vessel	
blemish[1] /er		bloodhound	
blench[1] /er		blood ied /ier/iest	
blend[1] /er		bloodi ly /ness	
bless[1]		blood shed /shot	
blest		bloodthirst y /iness	
blew ★ (wind)		bloom[1] /ers	
blew	blue ★[+]	blossom[1] /y	
blewbell	bluebell	blosum	blossom[1+]
blewberie	blueberry [+]	blot[3] /ter	
blewbery	blueberry [+]	blot	bloat[1+]
blew-chip	blue-chip	blotch[1] /y	
blewish	bluish	bloter	bloater
blewprint	blue-print	bloter	blotter
blight[1] /er		blouse	
blind[1] /est/ly/ness		blow /er/ing/n/y	
blinder /s		blowse	blouse
blind-man's-buff		blowter	bloater
blink[1]		blowze	blouse
bliss /ful/fully		blowzey	blowzy [+]
blister[1]		blowz y /ier/iest	
blite	blight[1+]	blu	blue ★[+]
bliter	blighter	blubber[1] /y	
blith	blithe [+]	blubell	bluebell
blithe /ly/ness		bluberie	blueberry [+]
blithering		blubery	blueberry [+]
blits	blitz[1]	blud	blood[1+]
blitz[1]		blud presher	blood pressure
blizard	blizzard	blud vesel	blood vessel
blizzard		bludey .	bloody

bludgen	bludgeon [1]	bob-sled	
bludgeon [1]		bob-sleigh	
bludhound	bloodhound	boby	bobby [+]
bludhownd	bloodhound	boch	botch [1+]
bludid	bloodied [+]	bode [2]	
bludie	bloody	bodice	
bludily	bloodily [+]	bodie	body [+]
bludshed	bloodshed [+]	bodi *ed* /ly	
bludshot	bloodshot	bodigard	bodyguard
bludthurstey	bloodthirsty [+]	bodiley	bodily
blue * (colour) /bell		bodiss	bodice
blue	blew *	bodkin	
blueberr*y* /ies		bod*y* /ies	
bluebottle		bodyguard	
blue-chip		bogey * (golf)	
blue-print		bogey	bogy [*+]
bluf	bluff [1+]	boggle [2]	
bluff [1] /er		bogul	boggle [2]
bluish		bogus	
blummers	bloomers	bog*y* * (devil) /ies	
blunder [1] /er		bohemian	
blunderbuss		boi	boy *
blunt [1] /er/est/ly/ness		boi	buoy [1*]
blur [3] /riness/ry		boiansey	buoyancy [+]
blurb		boiant	buoyant
blurie	blurry	boicot	boycott [1+]
blurt [1]		boil [1] /er	
blush [1] /es/ingly		boisterous /ly	
bluster [1] /y		boisterus	boisterous [+]
boa-constrictor		boks	box [1+]
boar * (swine)		Boksing Day	Boxing Day
boar	boor *	bolard	bollard
boar	bore [2*+]	bolaro	bolero
board [1] /er * (lodger)		bold	
boarding /-house/-school		bolder * (braver)	
boast [1] /er		bolder	boulder *
boastful /ly/ness		bold *ly* /ness	
boat [1] /-house/-race		bole * (tree trunk)	
boater		bole	bowl [1*]
boatswain		bolero	
bobbin		bollard	
bobb*y* /ies		boloney	
bobie	bobby [+]	Bolshevi*k* /sm/st	
bobin	bobbin	bolster [1] /er	
bobslay	bob-sleigh	bolt [1]	

46

bom	bomb [1+]
bomb [1] /er	
bombard [1] /ment	
bombardier	
bombast /ic/ically	
bomberdeer	bombardier
bomer	bomber
bona fide	
bonanza	
bond [1] /age	
bondige	bondage
bon *e* [2] /y	
bonet	bonnet
bonfire	
bonie	bonny
bonier	bonnier [+]
bonit	bonnet
bonnet	
bonni *er* /est/ly/ness	
bonny	
bonus /es	
bony	bonny
boo [1] /er	
boobie	booby [+]
boob *y* /ies	
boodwar	boudoir
book /able/ish/let	
bookay	bouquet
bookie	
boolvar	boulevard
boomerang	
boor * (bad-mannered)	
boor	boar *
boorgwa	bourgeois
boost [1] /er	
boot /ee * (shoe) /less	
booteek	boutique
booth	
bootie	booty *
bootik	boutique
bootleg [3] /ger	
booty * (spoils)	
booty	bootee *
booze [2] /r	
boracic	

boraks	borax
borasic	boracic
borax	
bord	board [1+]
border [1]* (edge) /line	
border	boarder *
bording	boarding [+]
bordum	boredom
bordy	bawdy [+]
bore [2]*† /dom	
† (drill, dull)	
bore	boar *
bore	boor *
born * (birth)	
borne * (carried)	
boron	
borough * (town)	
borow	borrow [1+]
borrow [1] /er	
borstal	
bort	bought
bos	boss [1+]
bosie	bossy
bosier	bossier [+]
bosily	bossily
bosn	boatswain
bosn	bosun
bosom	
boss [1] /es/y	
bossi *er* /est/ly/ness	
bost	boast [1+]
bostful	boastful [+]
bosun	
bosy	bossy
bot	boat [1+]
botaney	botany [+]
botanical /ly	
botan *y* /ist	
botch [1] /y	
boter	boater
both	
bother [1] /ation/some	
botherashun	botheration
bothersum	bothersome
botom	bottom [+]

bottle [2]	
bottom /less/most	
botul	bottle [2]
boudoir	
bough * (tree)	
bough	bow [1]*
bought	
boukay	bouquet
boulder * (big rock)	
boulder	bolder *
boulevard	
bounc e [2] /y	
bound [1] /er	
boundar y /ies	
boundless	
bounteous	
bountius	bounteous
bount y /ies/iful	
bouquet	
bourgeois	
bourgwa	bourgeois
bout	
bouteek	boutique
boutique	
bovine	
bow [1]* (bend, arrow)	
bow	beau *
bow	bough *
bowel	
bower	
bowl [1]* (cricket, basin)	
bowl	bole *
bownce	bounce [2]+
bowncy	bouncy
bownd	bound [1]+
bowndarey	boundary +
bowndless	boundless
bowns	bounce [2]+
bowntey	bounty +
bowntiful	bountiful
bowntius	bounteous
bowt	bout
box [1] /er/es/-office	
Boxing Day	
boy * (lad)	

boy	buoy [1]*
boyancy	buoyancy+
boyansey	buoyancy+
boyant	buoyant
boycott [1] /er	
boykot	boycott [1]+
boyl	boil [1]+
boysterus	boisterous +
brace [2]* (strap up)	
bracelet	
bracken	
bracket [1]	
brackish	
brackit	bracket [1]
brade	braid [1]
brag [3] /gart	
braget	braggart
Brahm a /in	
brai	bray [1]
braid [1]	
brail	Braille
Braille	
brain /wave/y	
brain-drain	
braini er /est/ly	
brainwash [1]	
braise [2]* (cook)	
braise	braze [2]*+
braisen	brazen +
brakable	breakable
brakabul	breakable
brake [2]* (stop)	
brake	break *+
brakedown	breakdown
braken	bracken
brakeneck	breakneck
brakethrew	breakthrough
brakethrough	breakthrough
brakewater	breakwater
brakige	breakage +
braking	breaking
brakish	brackish
brale	Braille
brama	Brahma +
brambl e /y	

brambul	bramble +
bramin	Brahmin
branch¹ /es	
brand¹ /-new	
brandie	brandy +
brandnu	brand-new
brandy /-snap	
brane	brain +
branedrain	brain-drain
branewash	brainwash¹
branier	brainier +
bras	brass +
brase	brace²★
brase	braise²★
brase	braze²★+
brash /ly	
brasier	brassiere★
brasier	brazier★
braslet	bracelet
brass /iest/ily/y	
brassiere★†	
†(undergarment)	
brasy	brassy
brasyer	brazier★
brat	
bravado	
brave² /ly/ry	
bravo	
bravoora	bravura
bravrey	bravery
bravura	
brawd	broad +
brawl¹ /er	
brawn /ier/iest/y	
bray¹	
brayd	braid¹
braze²★ (solder) /r	
braze	braise²★
brazen /ly/ness	
brazier★ (fire basket)	
breach¹★†	
† (gap, violation)	
breach	breech★
bread★ (food)	
bread	bred★

breadth	
break★ (destroy) /able	
break	brake²★
break age /er/ing	
breakdown	
breakfast	
breakneck	
breakthrew	breakthrough
breakthrough	
breakwater	
bream	
breast¹ /bone/plate	
breast stroke	
breath /less/lessly	
breathalyse² /r	
breathe² /r	
breathtaking	
bred★ (reared)	
bred	bread★
bredth	breadth
breech★ (part of gun)	
breech	breach¹★
breed /er/ing	
breef	brief¹+
breef case	brief-case
breem	bream
breez e² /ily/iness	
breez y /ier/iest	
breif	brief¹+
breif case	brief-case
brekfast	breakfast
Bren-gun	
brest	breast¹+
brestbone	breastbone
brestplait	breastplate
breststroke	breast stroke
breth	breadth
breth	breath +
brethalise	breathalyse²+
brethless	breathless
brethren	
brethtaking	breathtaking
brevit y /ies	
brew¹ /er	
brewer y /ies

breze	breeze [2+]	brisket	
brezy	breezy [+]	brisle	bristle [2+]
briar		bristl *e* [2] /y	
bribabul	bribable	brisul	bristle [2+]
brib *e* [2] /able/er		brite	bright [+]
briber *y* /ies		briten	brighten [1]
bric-à-brac		brittle /ness/r/st	
brick /bat/yard		britul	brittle [+]
bricklay *er* /ing		broach [1] *†	
bridal * (of bride)		† (tool, discuss)	
bridal	bridle [2*+]	broach	brooch *+
bride /groom		broad /ly	
bridel	bridal *	broadcast	
bridel	bridle [2*+]	broadcloth	
bridelpath	bridle-path	broaden [1]	
bridesmaid		broadside	
bridge [2] /able		broad *ways* /wise	
bridle [2] *† /-path		brocade [2]	
†(for a horse)		broccoli	
bridle	bridal *	broch	broach [1]*
brief [1] /s/ly		broch	brooch *+
brief-case		brochure	
brigade		brock	
brigadear	brigadier	brocoli	broccoli
brigadier		brog	brogue
brigand /age		brogue	
brige	bridge [2+]	broil [1] /er	
bright /ly/ness		broke /r	
brighten [1]		broken /-hearted	
brillianc *e* /y		bromide	
brilliant /ly		bromine	
brilliantine		bronchial	
brilyance	brilliance [+]	bronchitis	
brilyancy	brilliancy	bronco	
brilyans	brilliance [+]	bronkitis	bronchitis
brilyansey	brilliancy	bronkiul	bronchial
brilyant	brilliant [+]	bronkyul	bronchial
brilyantine	brilliantine	bronze [2]	
brim [3] /ful		brooam	brougham
brimstone		brooch * (clasp) /es	
brindled		brood [1] /iness/y	
brin *e* /y		brook [1] /let	
bring /ing		broom /stick	
brink		broonet	brunette
brisk /ly/ness		broose	bruise [2+]

broot	brute +	buccaneer /ing	
brootal	brutal +	buck [1]	
brootalitey	brutality +	buckaneer	buccaneer +
brorn	brawn +	bucket /ful	
brornie	brawny	buckle [2] /r	
brorny	brawny	buckshot	
brort	brought	buckskin	
brosher	brochure	buckwheat	
broth		bucolic	
brothel		Buddhis m /t	
brother /hood		budge [2]	
brother(s)-in-law		budgerigar	
brotherl y /iness		budget [1] /ary	
brougham		budgigar	budgerigar
brought		Budism	Buddhism +
brow /s * (eyebrows)		budist	Buddhist
browbeat /en/ing		buf	buff
brown [1] /er/est		bufalo	buffalo +
browney	brownie	bufer	buffer [1]
Brownian motion		bufet	buffet [1]
brownie		buff	
browse [2] * (read) /r		buffalo /es	
broyl	broil [1]+	buffer [1]	
brud	brood [1]+	buffet [1]	
brudy	broody	buffoon [1]	
bruer	brewer	buffooner y /ies	
bruerey	brewery +	bufit	buffet [1]
bruise [2] /r		bufoonerey	buffoonery +
brunet	brunette	bufune	buffoon [1]
brunette		bufunerey	buffoonery +
brunt		bug [3] /bear	
bruse	bruise [2]+	bugbare	bugbear
brush [1] /wood		bugerigar	budgerigar
brusk	brusque +	buget	budget [1]+
brusque /ly/ness		bugg y /ies	
Brussels sprouts		bugie	buggy +
brutal /ly		bugl e [2] /er	
brutalis e [2] /ation		bugul	bugle [2]+
brutalit y /ies		bugy	buggy +
brut e /ish		build /er/ing	
bubbl e [2] /y		built	
bublie	bubbly	buksom	buxom +
bubly	bubbly	buksomness	buxomness
bubonic plague		bulb /ous	
bubul	bubble [2]+	bulbus	bulbous

51

buldoze	bulldoze [2+]	bungul	bungle [2+]
bulet	bullet [+]	bunie	bunny [+]
buletin	bulletin	bunion	
bulfinch	bullfinch [+]	bunk [1]	
bulfite	bullfight	bunker [1]	
bulg *e* [2] /y		bunkum	
bulie	bully [4+]	bunn *y* /ies	
bulit	bullet [+]	Bunsen burner	
bulit proof	bullet-proof	buny	bunny [+]
bulk /ier/iest/iness/y		bunyon	bunion
bulkey	bulky	buoy [1]★ (float)	
bulkhead		buoyan *cy* /t	
bull /fight		buoyansey	buoyancy [+]
bulldoze [2] /r		bur	
bullet /-proof		bura	borough ★
bulletin		burble [2] /r	
bullfinch /es		burbul	burble [2+]
bullion		burch	birch [+]
bullock		burd	bird
bullring		burden [1] /some	
bull's-eye		burdey	birdie
bull *y* [4] /ies		burdie	birdie
bulock	bullock	burds eye	bird's-eye
bulring	bullring	bureau /x (pl.)	
bulrush		bureaucrac *y* /ies	
bulseye	bull's-eye	bureaucrat /ic	
bulwark		burgandey	Burgundy
buly	bully [4+]	burger	burgher
bulyon	bullion	burgher	
bumbelbe	bumble-bee	burglar	
bumble-bee		burglar *y* /ies	
bump [1] /er/ily/iness		burgle [2]	
bumpey	bumpy [+]	burgler	burglar
bumpkin		burgul	burgle [2]
bumpshus	bumptious [+]	Burgundy	
bumptious /ly/ness		burial	
bump *y* /ier/iest		burlap	
bumshus	bumptious [+]	burlesk	burlesque [2+]
bunch [1] /es/y		burlesque [2] /r	
bundle [2]		burlie	burly [+]
bundul	bundle [2]	burl *y* /ier/iest/iness	
bung [1] /-hole		burn [1] /able/er/t	
bungalow		burnish [1] /er	
bungkum	bunkum	buro	bureau [+]
bungle [2] /r		burocracy	bureaucracy [+]

burocrasey	bureaucracy +	butress	buttress 1+
burocrat	bureaucrat +	butrey	buttery +
burow	burrow 1*+	butt 1* (end)	
burra	borough *	butter 1 /-fingered	
burro	bureau +	buttercup	
burrow 1* (hole, dig) /er		butterey	buttery +
burrow	borough *	butterfly	
bursar /y		buttermilk	
burser	bursar +	butterscotch	
burst /ing		butter y /ies	
burth	birth *+	buttock	
burthday	birthday	button 1 /hole	
bur y 4* (cover)		buttress 1 /es	
bus 3 /es		buxom /ness	
busbie	busby +	buy *† /ing/er * †(purchase)	
busb y /ies		buy	by *
bush /ily/iness		buy	bye *
bushel		buzz 1 /es	
bushie	bushy +	buzzard	
bush y /ier/iest		by * (near)	
busi er /est/ly		by	buy *+
business /-like		by	bye *
bust		by-and-by	
bustle 2 /r		bycicle	bicycle 2+
busul	bustle 2+	byciclist	bicyclist
busy 4		bye * (sport)	
but * (however)		by-election	
but	butt 1*	byer	buyer *
butcher 1 /y		byfocal	bifocal
buten	button 1+	bygone /s	
buter	butter 1+	bying	buying
buter fingerd	butter-fingered	byke	bike
butercup	buttercup	by-law	
buterfly	butterfly	byle	bile
butermilk	buttermilk	bylore	by-law
buterscotch	butterscotch	bymetalic	bimetallic +
butey	beauty +	bymonthly	bimonthly
butician	beautician	bynomial	binomial
butify	beautify 4	byopsey	biopsy +
butique	boutique	bypartisan	bipartisan
butishun	beautician	bypartite	bipartite +
butler		bypass 1	
butn	button 1+	byped	biped
butock	buttock	byplane	biplane
buton	button 1+		

byplay
bypolar   bipolar [+]
by-product
byre ★ (barn)
byroad
byrode   byroad
bysecshun   bisection
bysect   bisect [1+]
bysection   bisection
byseksual   bisexual [+]
bysexual   bisexual [+]
bystander
byvalv   bivalve
byword

C

cab /man
cabal [3]
cabaray   cabaret
cabaret
cabbage
cabbidge   cabbage
cabb y /ies
cabie   cabby [+]
cabin /-boy
cabinet
cable [2] /gram/way
cabul   cable [2+]
cacao
cach   catch [+]
cachay   cachet
cache [2]★ (hidden store)
cache   cash [1★]
cachet
cachou   cashew
cachwerd   catchword
cackle [2]
cacofony   cacophony [+]
cacophon y /ous
cact us /i (pl.)
cacul   cackle [2]
cad /dish
cadaver /ous

caddey   caddie ★
caddie ★ (golf)
caddis /-worm
cadd y [4★] (for tea) /ies
cadence
cadens   cadence
cadentsa   cadenza
cadenza
cadet corps
cadge [2]
cadis   caddis [+]
cadmium
Caesar
Caesarean
caesium
café /s
cafene   caffeine
cafeteria
caffeine
cafiene   caffeine
cafiteria   cafeteria
cage [2] /y
cagi er /est/ly/ness
cain   cane [2+]
cairn
cairngorm
caison   caisson
caisson
cajole [2] /ry
cake [2]
calabash
calamine
calamit y /ies/ous
calcareous
calcarius   calcareous
calcif y [4] /ication
calcin e /ation
calcium
calculable
calculabul   calculable
calculashun   calculation
calculat e [2] /ion/or
calculus
cale   kale
Caledonian

calendar * (time)		Calvary	
calender ¹* (machine)		calve ²* (produce a calf)	
cal f /ves (pl.)		calve	carve ²*
caliber	calibre	Calvinis m /t/tic	
calibrashun	calibration	calypso	
calibrat e ² /ion/or		calyx /es	
calibre		cam /shaft	
calicks	calyx +	camaflage	camouflage ²
calico /es		camaraderie	
calif	caliph +	camber ¹	
californium		Cambrian	
caligrafey	calligraphy +	cambric	
caligraphy	calligraphy +	came	
calipers	callipers	camellia	
caliph /ate		camelya	camellia
calipso	calypso	Camembert	
calix	calyx +	cameo /s	
calk ¹* (horseshoe)		camera /man	
calk	caulk ¹*	camerarderey	camaraderie
call ¹* (cry out)		camfor	camphor +
call	caul *	camforated	camphorated
calligraph y /er/ist		camio	cameo +
callipers		camisole	
callisthenics		camombare	Camembert
callosity		camomile	
callous * (unfeeling)		camouflage ²	
callous ly /ness		camp ¹ /-follower	
callow		campaign ¹	
callus * (hard skin)		campain	campaign ¹
calm ¹ /ly/ness		campanile	
calomel		campanology	
calorie /s		camphor /ated	
calorific		campus /es	
calorif y ⁴ /ier		can ³ /not/'t *	
calorimet er /ric/ry		canabis	cannabis
calory	calorie +	Canadian	
calositey	callosity	canal	
calow	callow	canalis e ² /ation	
calsify	calcify ⁴+	canar y /ies	
calsine	calcine +	cancan	
calsium	calcium	cancel ³ /lation	
calumniat e ² /ion/or		cancer /ous	
calumn y /ies/ious		cancerus	cancerous
calus	callous *	candela	
calus	callus *	candelabrum	

55

cander	candour	cantankerous /ly/ness	
candey	candy +	cantata /s	
candid * (frank)		canteen	
candid	candied *	canter [1]	
candidac y /ies		cantilever /ed	
candidat e /ure		cantle	
candie	candy +	canton [1] /al/ment	
candied * (sugared)		cantul	cantle
candle /light/stick		canvas * (cloth) /es	
candour		canvass [1]* (solicit)	
candul	candle +	cany	canny
cand y /ies		canyon	
cane [2] /-sugar		caolin	kaolin
canery	cannery +	caos	chaos +
cangaroo	kangaroo	caotic	chaotic
canibal	cannibal +	cap [3]	
canibalise	cannibalise [2]+	capabilit y /ies	
canie	canny	capabl e /y	
canine		capabul	capable +
canister		capacious /ly/ness	
canker [1]		capacit ance /ive/or	
cannabis		capacitans	capacitance +
canner y /ies		capacitate [2]	
cannibal /ism/istic		capacit y /ies	
cannibalis e [2] /ation		capashus	capacious +
cannon [1]* (gun)		capasitey	capacity +
cannonade		capasitor	capacitor
canny		cape	
canoe [2] /s		caper [1]	
canoeist		capilarey	capillary +
canon * (law) /ical		capillar y /ies	
canon	cannon [1]*	capital /ism/ly	
canonaid	cannonade	capitalis e [2] /ation	
canonis e [2] /ation		capitalist /ic	
canonry		capitashun	capitation
canooist	canoeist	capitation	
canop y [4] /ies		capitulat e [2] /ion	
cansel	cancel [3]+	capon	
canselashun	cancellation	capric e /ious	
canselation	cancellation	Capricorn	
canser	cancer +	caprishus	capricious
canserus	cancerous	capshun	caption [1]
cant * (hypocrisy)		capshus	captious
cant	can't *	capsiz e [2] /able	
cantaloup		capstan	

capsul *e* ² /ar	
captain ¹ /cy	
capter	captor
captin	captain ¹⁺
caption ¹	
captious	
captivashun	captivation
captivat *e* ² /ion	
captiv *e* /ity	
captor	
capture ² /r	
car /park	
caracter	character
caracteristic	characteristic ⁺
carafe	
caramel	
carat ★ (unit of gems)	
carat	caret ★
carate	karate
caravan ³	
caraway	
carbine	
carbohydrate	
carbolic	
carbon /aceous/ate	
carbon dioxide	
carbon monoxide	
carbonis *e* ² /ation	
carbuncle	
carbuncul	carbuncle
carbureter	carburettor
carburettor	
carcass	
carcino *ma* /genic	
card /board	
cardiac	
cardigan	
cardinal	
cardiograf	cardiograph ⁺
cardiogram	
cardiograph /y	
care ² /worn	
careen ¹	
career ¹ /ism/ist	
carefree	

careful /ly	
careless /ly/ness	
caress ¹	
caret ★ (mark)	
caret	carat ★
caretak *er* /ing	
cargo /es	
cariage	carriage ⁺
caribou	
caricacher	caricature ²⁺
caricatur *e* ² /ist	
caricter	character
caricteristic	characteristic ⁺
caridge	carriage ⁺
carie	carry ⁴⁺
carier	carrier
carion	carrion
carisma	charisma
carkey	khaki
carki	khaki
carm	calm ¹⁺
carmine	
carnage	
carnal /ity/ly	
carnashun	carnation
carnation	
carngorm	cairngorm
carnidge	carnage
carnival	
carnivor *e* /ous	
carol ³ /ler	
carot	carrot ⁺
carous *e* ² /al	
carowsal	carousal
carowse	carouse ²⁺
carp ¹ /er	
carpent *er* ¹ /ry	
carpet ¹	
carpus	
carriage /way	
carrier	
carrion	
carrot /y	
carr *y* ⁴ /ier	
carryon	carrion

carsinoma	carcinoma +
cart [1] /-horse	
cartel	
cartilage	
cartilidge	cartilage
cartografer	cartographer
cartografey	cartography +
cartograph y /er/ic	
carton	
cartoon [1] /ist	
cartridge	
cartrite	cart-wright
cart-wheel	
cart-wright	
carve [2]* (cut)	
carve	calve [2]*
cary	carry [4]+
cascade [2]	
cascara	
case [2]	
casein	
casement	
caserole	casserole [2]
casette	cassette
cash [1]* (money)	
cash	cache [2]*
cashay	cachet
casheer	cashier [1]
cashew	
cashier [1]	
cashmere	
cashoo	cashew
cashual	casual +
cashuist	casuist +
cashultey	casualty +
casing	
casino /s	
cask * (wine)	
cask	casque *
caskaid	cascade [2]
casket	
caskit	casket
casock	cassock
casque * (helmet)	
cassel	castle [2]

casserole [2]	
casset	cassette
cassette	
cassock	
cast * (throw) /ing	
cast iron	
castanet	
castaway	
caste *† /less	
† (social class)	
castigat e [2] /ion/or	
castle [2]	
cast-off	
castor	
castor-oil	
castrashun	castration
castrat e [2] /ion	
casual /ly/ness	
casualt y /ies	
casuist /ic/ry	
cat /tish/ty/walk	
catabolism	
cataclysm /ic	
catacomb	
catacoom	catacomb
catalep sy /tic	
catalise	catalyse [2]+
catalisis	catalysis +
catalist	catalyst
catalitic	catalytic
catalog	catalogue [2]+
catalogue [2] /r	
catalys e [2] /ation	
cataly sis /tic	
catalyst	
catamaran	
catapiler	caterpillar
catapult [1]	
catar	catarrh +
cataract	
catarrh /al	
catastrofey	catastrophe
catastrofic	catastrophic +
catastrophe	
catastrophic /ally	

catcall [1]		causeway	
catcawl	catcall [1]	caustic /ally	
catch /ing/ment		cauteris *e* [2] /ation	
catchword		caution [1] /ary	
catechis *e* [2] /m		cautious /ly/ness	
categoric /al/ally		cavalcade	
categorise [2]		cavalier	
categor *y* /ies		cavalr *y* /ies	
cater [1] /er		cave [2] /man	
caterpillar		cavern /ous	
caterwaul [1]		caveson	
catgut		caviare	
cathar *sis* /tic		cavil [3]	
cathedral		cavisun	caveson
Catherine-wheel		cavit *y* /ies	
cathod *e* /ic		cavort [1]	
catholic /ism		caw [1]★ (cry of a crow)	
caticise	catechise [2]+	caw	core ★
catigorey	category +	caw	corps ★
catigoric	categoric +	cawcashun	Caucasian
catigorise	categorise [2]	cawcasian	Caucasian
catikism	catechism	cayenne	
catish	cattish	cazm	chasm
catkin		cease [2] /-fire/less	
catle	cattle	cedar	
catnap [3]		cede [2]★ (give up)	
cat-o'-nine-tails		cede	seed [1]★
cat's-eye		ceder	cedar
cattle		cedilla	
catul	cattle	ceeling	ceiling ★
caucashun	Caucasian	ceese	cease [2]+
Caucasian		cefalic	cephalic +
caucus /es		ceiling ★ (roof)	
caught ★ (did catch)		ceiling	sealing ★
caught	court [1]★	celandine	
cauk	caulk [1]★	celebrant	
caul ★ (membrane)		celebrashun	celebration
caul	call [1]★	celebrat *e* [2] /ion	
cauldron		celebrit *y* /ies	
cauliflower		celerey	celery
caulk [1]★ (seal)		celerity	
caulk	calk [1]★	celery	
causal		celestial /ly	
causat *ion* /ive		celiba *cy* /te	
cause [2] /less		celibasey	celibacy +

celibrant	celebrant
celibrate	celebrate [2+]
cell * (prison, unit)	
cell	sell *[+]
cellar * (cave)	
celler	seller *
cellist	
cello /s	
cellophane	
cellular	
cellule	
celluler	cellular
celluloid	
cellulose	
celofane	cellophane
Celsius	
Celt /ic	
cement [1] /ation	
cemeter y /ies	
cemetrey	cemetery +
cemical	chemical +
cemist	chemist +
cemistrey	chemistry
cenotaf	cenotaph
cenotaph	
censer * (for incense)	
censer	censor [1]*[+]
censership	censorship
censher	censure [2+]
censor [1]*† /ious/ship †(moral overseer)	
censur e [2] /able	
census /es	
cent * (money)	
cent	scent [1]*
cent	sent *
centaur	
centeem	centime
centenarian	
centenar y /ies	
centennial /ly	
center	centre [2+]
center forwud	centre-forward
centigrade	
centigram	

centileter	centilitre
centilitre	
centime	
centimeter	centimetre
centimetre	
centipede	
centor	centaur
central /ity/ly	
centralis e [2] /ation	
centre [2] /board	
centre-forward	
centrifugal /ly	
centrifuge	
centripetal	
centuple	
centupul	centuple
centurion	
centur y /ies	
cephali c /tis	
ceramic /s	
cerculer	circular
cercumcise	circumcise [2+]
cercumference	circumference
cercumferens	circumference
cercumflex	circumflex
cercumnavigate	circumnavi-gate [2+]
cercumscribe	circumscribe [2]
cercumscripshun	circumscription
cercumscription	circumscription
cercumsise	circumcise [2+]
cercumspect	circumspect +
cercumstance	circumstance
cercumstans	circumstance
cercumstanshul	circumstantial +
cercumstantial	circumstantial +
cercumvent	circumvent [1+]
cercus	circus +
cereal * (grain)	
cereal	serial *[+]
cerebellum	
cerebra l /tion	
cerebrum	
ceremonial /ly	
ceremonious /ly	

ceremonius	ceremonious +	chalenge	challenge [2]+
ceremony /ies		chalet	
cerial	cereal ★	chalice	
cerial	serial ★+	chalinge	challenge [2]+
ceribelum	cerebellum	chalis	chalice
ceribrum	cerebrum	chalk [1] /y	
cerise		challenge [2] /r	
cerkit	circuit [1]+	chamber /-music	
cert		chamberlain	
certain /ly		chamberlin	chamberlain
certainty /ies		chambermade	chambermaid
certen	certain +	chambermaid	
certifiable /y		chameleon	
certifiabul	certifiable +	chamie	chamois
certificate [2] /ion		chamois	
certify [4] /ier		champ [1]	
certinty	certainty +	champagne	
certitude		champain	champagne
cervical		champion [1] /ship	
cervicul	cervical	champyun	champion [1]+
cerviks	cervix +	chamwa	chamois
cervix /es		chance [2] /y	
cesashun	cessation	chancel	
cesation	cessation	chancellery /ies	
ceshun	cession ★	chancellor	
ceshun	session ★	chancelor	chancellor
cespit	cesspit	chancelrey	chancellery +
cespool	cesspool	chancery /ies	
cessation		chandelier	
cession ★ (yielding)		chandler	
cession	session ★	chane	chain [1]+
cesspit		chane reacshun	chain-reaction
cesspool		chanel	channel [3]
chacoal	charcoal	change [2] /able/-over	
chafe [2]★ (rub)		changeling	
chaff ★ (grain husks)		channel [3]	
chaffer [1]		chans	chance [2]+
chaffinch /es		chansel	chancel
chagrin /ed		chanseler	chancellor
chain [1] /-gang		chanselrey	chancellery +
chain-armour		chanserey	chancery +
chain-mail		chansey	chancy
chain-reaction		chansie	chancy
chain-store		chant [1]	
chair [1] /man		chaos /tic	

chap [3]	
chapel	
chaperon [1] /age	
chaplain /cy	
chaplet	
chaplin	chaplain [+]
chapter /-house	
char [3] /woman/women	
character	
characteris *e* [2] /ation	
characteristic /ally	
charade	
charcoal	
chare	chair [1+]
charey	chary [+]
charge [2] /able	
chargé-d'affaires	
charger	
charie	chary [+]
chariot /eer	
charisma	
charitabl *e* /y	
charitabul	charitable [+]
charit *y* /ies	
charlatan	
charlot	charlotte
charlotte	
charm [1] /er	
charman	chairman
chart [1]	
charter [1] /er	
chartis *m* /t	
char *y* /ily/iness	
chas *ed* ★ (pursued) /ing	
chased	chaste ★
chasen	chasten [1]
chasis	chassis
chasm	
chassie	chassis
chassis	
chaste ★ (pure)	
chaste	chased ★[+]
chasten [1]	
chastise [2] /ment	
chastity	

chat [3] /ty	
chateau /x (pl.)	
chater	chatter [1+]
chaterbox	chatterbox
chattel	
chatter [1] /er	
chatterbox	
chaty	chatty
chauffeur	
chauvinis *m* /t/tic	
cheap ★ (inexpensive)	
cheap	cheep [1★]
cheap *ish* /ly/ness	
chear	cheer [1+]
chearful	cheerful [+]
chease	cheese [+]
cheat [1] /er	
check [1★] (stop) /er [1]	
check	cheque ★[+]
Check	Czech ★
checkmate [2]	
check-up	
Cheddar	
cheder	Cheddar
cheef	chief [+]
cheek *y* /ier/iest/ily/iness	
cheep [1★] (bird sound)	
cheep	cheap ★
cheer [1] /less	
cheerey	cheery [+]
cheerful /ly/ness	
cheerie	cheery [+]
cheerio	
cheer *y* /ier/iest/ily/iness	
chees *e* /y	
cheesecake	
cheese-cloth	
cheet	cheat [1+]
cheeta	cheetah [+]
cheetah /s	
cheeter	cheetah [+]
chef	
chef-d'oeuvre	
cheif	chief [+]
cheiften	chieftain [+]

chelist	cellist	chilli er /est/ly/ness	
chelo	cello +	chime 2	
chemical /ly		chimeric /al	
chemise		chimney /-piece	
chemist /ry		chimnie	chimney +
chemistrey	chemistry	chimpanzee	
cheque *† /-book		chin	
†(money)		china /-clay	
cherie	cherry +	Chinese	
cherio	cheerio	chink 1	
cherish 1		chintz /es	
cheroot		chip 3	
cherp	chirp 1+	chipendale	Chippendale
cherr y /ies		chipmunk	
cherub /ic		chipolata	
chery	cherry +	Chippendale	
ches	chess +	chiropod y /ist	
chesbord	chessboard	chirp 1 /y	
chess /board		chirrup 1	
chest		chisel 3 /ler	
Chesterfield		chit /-chat	
chestnut		chivalrus	chivalrous
chevalier		chivalr y /ous	
chevron		chive	
chew 1 /ing-gum		chlorate	
chic * (stylish)		chloride	
chicanery		chlorinat e 2 /ion	
chick *† /en/weed		chlorine	
†(baby bird)		chlorofill	chlorophyll
chicory		chloroform 1	
chide 2		chlorophyll	
chief /s		chloroplast	
chieftain /cy		chock /-a-block	
chiffon		chock-full	
chil	chill 1+	choclut	chocolate
chilblain		chocolate	
child /ren (pl.)		choice /st	
childbaring	childbearing	choir * (singers)	
childbearing		choir	quire *
child birth /hood		chois	choice +
child ish /less/like		choke 2 /r	
chili * (food) /es		choler * (rage) /ic	
chilie	chilly *	choler	collar 1*+
chilier	chillier +	cholera	
chill 1 /y * (cold)		cholester in /ol	

choo	chew [1+]	chub /by	
choos e /ing/y		chubbi er /est/ly/ness	
chop [3] /per		chubier	chubbier [+]
chopp y /ier/iest		chuck [1]	
chopsooey	chop-suey	chuckle [2]	
chopstick		chucul	chuckle [2]
chop-suey		chug [3]	
chopy	choppy [+]	chukker	
choral * (singing) /ly		chum [3] /my	
chorale * (metric hymn)		chump	
chord * (music)		chunk /y	
chord	cord *[+]	church /es/warden	
chore		churl /ish	
choreograph y /er		churn [1]	
chorister		churp	chirp [1+]
chork	chalk [1+]	chute * (drop)	
chortle [2]		chute	shoot *[+]
chortul	chortle [2]	chutney	
chorus [1] /es		chyle	
chose /n		chyme	
chow		cianide	cyanide
chrisalis	chrysalis [+]	cibernetics	cybernetics
chrisanthemum	chrysanthemum	cicada	
Christ		cicatrice	
christen [1]		cicatriss	cicatrice
Christendom		ciclamate	cyclamate
Christian /ity		ciclamen	cyclamen
Christmas /sy		cicle	cycle [2]
chromate		ciclic	cyclic [+]
chromatic /ally		ciclist	cyclist [+]
chromatin		ciclometer	cyclometer
chromatograf	chromatograph [+]	ciclone	cyclone [+]
chromatogram		ciclops	Cyclops
chromatograph /y		ciclostile	cyclostyle
chrom e /ic/ium		ciclotron	cyclotron
chromosome		cicul	cycle [2]
chronic /ally		cider	
chronicle [2] /r		cifer	cipher [1]
chronicul	chronicle [2+]	cigar /ette	
chronograph /ic		cigaret	cigarette
chronological /ly		cignet	cygnet *
chronolog y /ies		cignet	signet *
chronometer		cilestial	celestial [+]
chrysalis /es		cilinder	cylinder
chrysanthemum		cilindrical	cylindrical [+]

cilium	
cimbal	cymbal ★+
cimbal	symbol ★+
ciment	cement [1]+
cinamon	cinnamon
cinch /es	
cinder	
Cinderella	
cine camera	
cinema /tic	
cinematograph /er/y	
cinerama	
cinic	cynic +
cinical	cynical +
cinicul	cynical +
cinima	cinema +
cinimatograf	cinematograph +
cinimatograph	cinematograph +
cinnamon	
cinosure	cynosure
cipher [1]	
cipress	cypress
circa	
circit	circuit [1]+
circle [2]	
circuit [1] /ous/ry	
circul	circle [2]
circular	
circularis e [2] /ation	
circulat e [2] /ion	
circulator /y	
circumcis e [2] /ion	
circumference	
circumferens	circumference
circumflex	
circumfrence	circumference
circumnavigat e [2] /or	
circumscribe [2]	
circumscription	
circumspect /ion	
circumstance	
circumstans	circumstance
circumstanshul	circumstantial +
circumstantial /ly	
circumvent [1] /ion	

circus /es	
cirosis	cirrhosis
cirrhosis	
cirro-cumulus	
cirro-stratus	
cist	cyst +
cistern	
cistitis	cystitis
citadel	
cit e [2]★ (quote) /ation	
cite	sight [1]★+
cite	site [2]★
citie	city +
citizen /ship	
citologey	cytology
citric acid	
citr on /ate	
citrus	
cit y /ies	
civet	
civic /ism/s	
civil /ian/ly	
civilis e [2] /ation	
civilit y /ies	
civit	civet
clad /ding	
claim [1] /able/ant	
clairvoyan ce /t	
clam	
clamant	
clamber [1]	
clame	claim [1]+
clamer	clamour +
clamerous	clamorous
clamerus	clamorous
clamm y /ily/iness	
clamo ur /rous	
clamp [1]	
clamy	clammy +
clan /nish	
clandestine /ly	
clang [1] /our	
clank [1]	
clansman	
clap [3] /per	

claptrap	
claret	
clarif*y*[4] /ication/ier	
clarinet /tist	
clarion	
clarity	
clark	clerk +
claryun	clarion
clash[1]	
clasify	classify[4]+
clasroom	classroom
class[1] /less/y	
classic /al/ally/s	
classicis*m* /t	
classif*y*[4] /ication/ier	
classroom	
clatter[1]	
clause	
claustrofobia	claustrophobia
claustrophobia	
clavichord	
clavic*le* /ular	
clavicord	clavichord
clavicul	clavicle +
claw[1]	
clay /more	
claym	claim[1]+
clean[1] /able/liness/ly	
cleanse[2]	
clear[1] /ance/ly/ness	
cleav*e*[2] /age	
cleavidge	cleavage
cleek	clique +
clef	
cleft	
clematis	
clemen*cy* /t	
clemensey	clemency +
clench[1]	
clenliness	cleanliness
clense	cleanse[2]
clergy /man	
cleric /al/alism	
clerk /ship	
clever /er/est/ly	

clew[1]★ (thread)	
clew	clue ★+
clichay	cliché
cliché	
click[1]	
client /ele	
cliff /s	
climactic /ally	
climaks	climax[1]+
climat*e* /ology	
climatic /ally	
climax[1] /es	
climb[1]★ (go up) /er	
clime ★ (climate)	
clinch[1]	
cling /ing	
clinic /al/ally	
clink[1]	
clinker /-built	
cliontell	clientele
clip[3] /per	
cliqu*e* /ish/y	
clitoris	
cloak /room	
clobber[1]	
cloche	
clock[1] /wise/work	
clod /-hopper	
clog[3]	
cloister[1]	
clorate	chlorate
clore	claw[1]
cloride	chloride
clorinate	chlorinate[2]+
clorine	chlorine
clorofill	chlorophyll
cloroform	chloroform[1]
clorophil	chlorophyll
cloroplast	chloroplast
clos*e*[2] /ure	
closet[1]	
closher	closure
clot[3]	
cloth	
cloth*e*[2] /ier	

cloud [1] /ier/less/y	
clout[1]	
clove /n	
clover /-leaf	
clowd	cloud [1+]
clown[1] /ish	
club[3] /bable	
cluch	clutch[1]
cluck[1]	
clue * (guide) /less	
clue	clew[1]*
clump[1]	
clumsi*ly* /ness	
clums*y* /ier/iest	
clung	
cluster[1]	
clutch[1]	
clutter[1]	
coach[1] /ful/man	
coagulant	
coagulat*e*[2] /ion/or	
coaks	coax[1]
coal /field/-mine	
coala	koala
coalesans	coalescence
coalesce[2] /nce/nt	
coalesent	coalescent
coaless	coalesce[2+]
coalishun	coalition[+]
coalition /ist	
coal-scuttle	
coarse * (rough) /ly/ness	
coarse	course *[+]
coarsen[1]	
coast[1] /al	
coast*guard* /line	
coat[1] /ee	
coax[1]	
cob	
cobalt	
cobble[2] /r	
cobra	
cobul	cobble[2+]
cobweb /bed	
coca	

cocaine	
cocane	cocaine
coccyx /es	
coch	coach[1+]
cochineal	
cock[1] /crow/erel	
cockato	cockatoo
cockatoo	
cockchafer	
cocker	
cocket	coquette[+]
cocketrey	coquetry
cock-eyed	
cockle	
cockney /ish/ism/s	
cockpit	
cockroach	
cockscomb	
cockshore	cocksure
cocksis	coccyx[+]
cocksure	
cocktail	
cockul	cockle
cock*y* /ier/iest/ily	
coco * (palm tree)	
coco	cocoa *
cocoa * (cacao powder)	
coconut	
cocoon	
cocotte	
cod[3] /ling	
codak	Kodak
coddle[2]	
code[2]	
codecks	codex[+]
codeine	
cod*ex* /ices (pl.)	
codger	
codicil	
codif*y*[4] /ication/ier	
codisil	codicil
codle	coddle[2]
co-educate[2]	
co-education /al	
coefficient	

67

coefishent	coefficient	coinidge	coinage
coegsist	coexist [1+]	coinside	coincide [2]
coequal /ity/ly		coinsidence	coincidence +
coerc e [2] /ible		coinsidens	coincidence +
coerc ion /ive		coinsident	coincident
coerse	coerce [2+]	coir * (coconut fibre)	
coershun	coercion +	coir	choir *
coersive	coercive	coit us /ion	
coexist [1] /ence/ent		coke [2]	
cofee	coffee	coket	coquette +
cofer	coffer	cokoon	cocoon
cofey	coffee	col	
coff	cough [1+]	cola	koala
coffee		colaborate	collaborate [2+]
coffer		colage	collage
coffin		colander	
cog [3] /-wheel		colaps	collapse [2+]
cogen cy /t		colate	collate [2+]
coger	codger	cold /er/est/ly/ness	
cogitat e [2] /ion		cold-blooded	
cognac		cold-shoulder [1]	
cognate		cole	coal +
cognisabl e /y		colean	colleen
cognisan ce /t		colecshun	collection
cognishun	cognition +	colect	collect [1+]
cognition /al		colectabul	collectable +
cognitive		colection	collection
cognomen		colectiv	collective +
cohabit [1] /ation		coleeg	colleague
cohear	cohere [2+]	colege	college +
cohearent	coherent +	colegian	collegian
cohere [2] /nce		colegiate	collegiate
coherent /ly		coler	choler *+
coheshun	cohesion +	coler	collar [1]*+
cohes ion /ive		colera	cholera
cohort		coleric	choleric
coifer	coiffeur *+	colesterin	cholesterin +
coiffeu r *† /se (fem.)		colesterol	cholesterol
†(hairdresser)		colic /ky	
coiffure * (hair style)		colide	collide [2]
coifur	coiffure *	colier	collier
coil [1]		colinder	colander
coin [1] /age/er		colinear	collinear
coincide [2]		colishun	collision
coinciden ce /t		colision	collision

colitis	
collaborat *e* ² /ion/or	
collage	
collaps *e* ² /ible	
collar ¹*† /-bone	
†(seize, neckband)	
collar	choler *+
collat *e* ² /ion/or	
collateral	
colleague	
collect ¹ /ion/or	
collect *able* /edly	
collectiv *e* /ism/ist	
colleen	
colleg *e* /ian/iate	
coller	choler *+
coller	collar ¹*+
collide ²	
collie	
collier	
collinear	
collision	
collocate ²	
colloid /al	
colloquial /ism/ly	
colloqu *y* /ies	
collude ²	
collus *ion* /ive	
colly	collie
colokwey	colloquy +
colokwial	colloquial +
colon	
colonade	colonnade
colonel * (officer)	
colonial /ism	
colonis *e* ² /ation/er	
colonnade	
colon *y* /ies/ist	
coloqual	colloquial +
coloquy	colloquy +
color	colour ¹+
coloration	
colorful	colourful +
colossal /ly	
colossus /es	

colour ¹ /less	
colourful /ly	
coloyd	colloid +
colt /ish	
colude	collude ²
colum	column +
columbine	
column /ar/ist	
colushun	collusion +
colusion	collusion +
coma * (deep sleep)	
coma	comma *
comand	command ¹+
comandment	commandment
comando	commando +
comb ¹	
combat ¹ /ant/ive	
combinashun	combination
combin *e* ² /ation	
combuschun	combustion
combustib *le* /ility	
combustibul	combustible +
combustion	
com *e* /ing	
come	comb ¹
comedi *an* /enne (fem.)	
comed *y* /ies	
comel *y* /ier/iest	
comemorashun	commemoration
comemorate	commemorate ²+
comence	commence ²+
comend	commend ¹+
comendabul	commendable +
comendashun	commendation
comendation	commendation
comens	commence ²+
comenshurate	commensurate
coment	comment ¹+
comentater	commentator
comentrey	commentary +
comerce	commerce
comercial	commercial +
comercialise	commercialise ²+
comercialism	commercialism
comerse	commerce

69

comershal	commercial +
comershalise	commercialise 2+
comershalism	commercialism
comestibles	
comet	
comfert	comfort 1+
comfort 1 /er/less	
comfortabl e /y	
comic /al/ally	
comicalit y /ies	
comiserate	commiserate 2+
comiserey	commissary +
comishun	commission 1+
comission	commission 1+
comit	comet
comit	commit 3+
comital	committal
comitey	comity *
comitment	commitment
comittal	committal
comittey	committee *
comity * (courtesy)	
comma *(punctuation)	
comma	coma *
command 1 /ant/er	
commandeer 1	
commandment	
commando /s	
commemorat e 2 /ion	
commence 2 /ment	
commend 1 /ation	
commendabl e /y	
commensurate	
comment 1 /ator	
commentar y /ies	
commentrey	commentary +
commerce	
commercial /ism/ly	
commercialis e 2/ation	
commershal	commercial +
commershalise	commercialise 2+
commiserat e 2 /ion	
commissar /iat	
commissar y /ies	
commission 1 /aire/er	

commit 3 /ment/tal	
committee * (body)	
commity	comity *
commod e /ious	
commodit y /ies	
commodore	
common /er/est/ly	
Common Market	
commonplace	
Commons	
Commonwealth	
commoshun	commotion
commotion	
communal /ly	
communalise 2	
commune 2	
communicable	
communicat e 2 /ion	
communicat ive /or	
communikay	communiqué
communi on /cant	
communiqué	
communis m /t/tic	
communit y /ies	
commute 2 /r	
comode	commode +
comodious	commodious
comodity	commodity +
comodius	commodious
comodoor	commodore
comon	common +
Comon Market	Common Market
Comonwelth	Commonwealth
comoshun	commotion
comotion	commotion
compact	
compair	compère 2*
companion /ship	
compan y /ies	
companyun	companion +
comparabl e /y	
comparabul	comparable +
comparative /ly	
compare 2* (liken to)	
compare	compère 2*

comparison
compartment
compashonate · compassionate
compashun · compassion +
compass [1] /es
compassion /ate/ately
compatib *le* /ility
compatibul · compatible +
compatriot
compel [3]
compendium
compensat *e* [2] /ion
compensator /y
compère [2]★ (presenter)
competant · competent
compet *e* [2] /ition
competen *ce* /t
competit *ive* /or
compil *e* [2] /ation
complacenc *e* /y
complacens · complacence +
complacent /ly
complain [1] /ant/t
complane · complain [1]+
complasense · complacence +
complasent · complacent +
complement [1]★† /ary
  †(complete)
complete [2] /ly
completion
complex
complexion /ed
complexit *y* /ies
complian *ce* /t
complicat *e* [2] /ion
complicity
compliment [1]★† /ary
  † (praise)
compl *y* [4] /iable
component
comport [1] /ment
compose [2]
composher · composure
composishun · composition
composite /ly

composition
compositor
compost
composure
compot · compote
compote
compound [1] /able
comprehen *d* [1] /sible
comprehens *ion* /ive
compress [1] /ion/or
compressib *le* /ility
compris *e* [2] /able
compromise [2]
compulshun · compulsion +
compuls *ion* /ive
compulsor *y* /ily
compulsrey · compulsory +
compuncshun · compunction
compunction
comput *e* [2] /ation/er
computeris *e* [2] /ation
comrad · comrade +
comrade /ly/ship
comunal · communal +
comunalise · communalise [2]
comune · commune [2]
comunicable · communicable
comunicant · communicant
comunicashun · communication
comunicate · communicate [2]+
comunication · communication
comunikay · communiqué
comunion · communion+
comunism · communism +
comunist · communist
comunitey · community +
comunyun · communion+
comute · commute [2]+
con [3]
concave
concavit *y* /ies
conceal [1] /ment
concede [2]
conceit /ed
conceivabul · conceivable

conceiv e^2 /able/ably	
concentrat e^2 /ion	
concentric /ity	
concept /ual/ually	
conception	
concern [1]	
concert /ina	
concerto /s	
concession /ary	
conch	
concherto	concerto [+]
conciet	conceit [+]
concievabul	conceivable
concieve	conceive [2+]
conciliat e^2 /ion	
conciliator /y	
concise /ly/ness	
conclave	
conclude [2]	
conclus ion /ive	
concoct [1] /ion	
concomitant	
concord /ance/ant	
concorse	concourse
concourse	
concrete /ly/ness	
concubine	
concur [3]	
concurren ce /t/tly	
concuss [1] /ion	
condemn [1] /ation	
condens e^2 /ation/er	
condescen d^1 /sion	
condiment	
condisend	condescend [1+]
condisenshun	condescension
condisension	condescension
condishun	condition [1+]
condit	conduit
condition [1] /al/ally	
condole [2] /nce	
condon e^2 /ation/er	
conduc e^2 /ive	
conduct [1] /ion	
conductiv e /ity	

conduct or /ress (fem.)	
conduit	
cone	
conect	connect [1+]
conerbashun	conurbation
conerbation	conurbation
confabulat e^2 /ion	
confection /er/ery	
confederac y /ies	
confederasey	confederacy [+]
confederat e^2 /ion	
confer [3] /ment	
conference	
confeser	confessor
confess [1] /or	
confession /al	
confetti	
confidant *† /e (fem.)	
†(trusted friend)	
confide [2] /nce	
confidenshal	confidential [+]
confident *† /ly	
†(self-assured)	
confidential /ity/ly	
configerashun	configuration
configuration	
confine [2] /ment	
confirm [1] /ation	
confirmat ive /ory	
confiscat e^2 /ion	
conflagration	
conflict [1]	
conform [1] /able/ation	
conform ist /ity	
confound [1]	
confownd	confound [1]
confurm	confirm [1+]
confus e^2 /ion	
confut e^2 /ation	
congeal [1] •	
congenial /ity/ly	
congenital /ly	
conger /-eel	
congest [1] /ion/ive	
conglomerat e^2 /ion	

congratulat *e*² /ion/ory

congregat *e*² /ion

congregational /ist

congress /ional

conic /al/ally

conifer /ous

conjectcher   conjecture²⁺

conjectur *e*² /al

conjoin¹ /t

conjucive   conducive

conjugal

conjugat *e*² /ion

conjuice   conduce²⁺

conjuncshun   conjunction

conjunction

conjunctiv *e* /itis

conjur *e*² /ation/er

conker*(horse chestnut)

conker   conquer¹*⁺

conkwest   conquest

connect¹ /ion/ive

conneser   connoisseur

conning-tower

conniv *e*² /ance/er

connoisseur

connot *e*² /ation

connubial /ly

conosseur   connoisseur

conote   connote²⁺

conquer¹*(defeat) /or

conquest

consanguin *eous* /ity

conscience

conscienshus   conscientious⁺

conscientious /ly

conscious /ly/ness

conscript¹ /ion

conseal   conceal¹⁺

conseat   conceit⁺

consecrat *e*² /ion

consecutive

consekwence   consequence⁺

consensus

consent¹

consequen *ce* /t

consequential /ly

conservancy

conservansey   conservancy

conservashun   conservation

conservation

conservat *ive* /ism

conservatoire

conservator *y* /ies

conservatrey   conservatory⁺

conserv *e*²

consider¹ /able/ably

considerat *e* /ion

considrabul   considerable

consign¹ /ment

consiliate   conciliate²⁺

consine   consign¹⁺

consise   concise⁺

consist¹ /ence

consistenc *y* /ies

consistensey   consistency⁺

consolabul   consolable

consolashun   consolation

consol *e*² /able/ation

consolidat *e*² /ion

consommé

consonan *ce* /t

consonans   consonance⁺

consort¹ /ium

conspicuous /ly/ness

conspirac *y* /ies

conspirasey   conspiracy⁺

conspirater   conspirator⁺

conspirator /y

conspire²

constable

constabul   constable

constabular *y* /ies

constan *cy* /t

constansey   constancy⁺

constelashun   constellation

constellation

consternat *e*² /ion

constipat *e*² /ion

constituenc *y* /ies

constituensey   constituency⁺

constituent
constitute[2]
constitution /al/ally
constrain[1] /t
constrict[1] /ion
construct[1] /ion
constructive /ly
constru e[2] /able
consul /ar/ate
consult[1] /ant
consultat ion /ive
consumashun   consummation
consum e[2] /able/er
consummate[2] /ly
consummation
consumpt ion /ive
consumshun   consumption +
consumtion   consumption +
contact[1] /or
contag ion /ious
contagus   contagious
contain[1] /er/ment
contaminat e[2] /ion
contemplat e[2] /ion
contemplative /ly
contemporaneous
contemporar y /ies
contempt /ible/uous
contend[1]
content[1] /ment
content ion /ious
contest[1] /able/ant
context
contigu ous /ity
continence
continens   continence
continent /al
contingenc y /ies
contingensey   contingency +
contingent
continual /ly
continua nce /tion
continu e[2] /ity
continuous /ly
contorshun   contortion +

contort[1]
contortion /ist
contour
contraband
contracept ion /ive
contract[1] /ion/or
contractual /ly
contradict[1] /ion/ory
contralto /s
contrapshun   contraption
contraption
contrar y /ily/iness
contrast[1]
contraven e[2] /er/tion
contribut e[2] /ion
contributor /y
contrit e /ion
contriv e[2] /ance
control[3] /lable/ler
controvershal   controversial +
controversial /ly
controvers y /ies
contus e[2] /ion
conurbation
convalesce[2] /nce/nt
convaless   convalesce[2+]
convalessence   convalescence
convect ion /ive/or
convene[2] /r
convenien ce /t
conveniens   convenience +
convenshun   convention
convenshunal   conventional +
convent
convention
conventional /ism/ly
converge[2] /nce/nt
conversant
conversation /al/alist
converse[2] /ly
conversion
convert[1] /er/ible
convex /ity
convey[1]
conveyanc e /ing

conveyor belt
convict[1] /ion
convinc e[2] /ingly
conviscate   confiscate[2+]
convivial /ity/ly
convocashun   convocation
convocation
convoke[2]
convolut e[2] /ion
convoy[1]
convuls e[2] /ion
convulsive /ly
con y /ies
conyac   cognac
coo[1]
cooger   cougar
cook[1] /able
cooker /y
cool[1] /ant/est/ness
coolie * (labourer)
coolly * (calmly)
coop[1]
co-op
cooper /age
co-operat e[2] /ion/or
co-operative /ly/ness
co-opt[1] /ion
co-ordinat e[2] /ion
co-partner /ship
cope[2]
copeck
Copernican system
co-pilot
copious /ly
copiss   coppice
copper /plate
coppice
copra
copse
copulat e[2] /ion
cop y[4] /ies/ier
copyright
copyrite   copyright
coquetry
coquett e /ish

coral * (sea life)
coral   choral *+
coral   corral[3]*
corcus   caucus +
cord * (rope) /age
cord   chord *
cordial /ity/ly
cordite
cordon[1]
cordon bleu
corduroy
core * (centre)
core   caw[1]*
core   corps *
corecshun   correction
corect   correct[1+]
corection   correction
corectiv   corrective
corespond   correspond[1+]
corespondence   correspondence
corespondens   correspondence
co-respondent
coridoor   corridor
coriografey   choreography +
corispondence   correspondence
corispondens   correspondence
corister   chorister
cork /age/screw
corm
cormorant
corn /flour
cornea /l
corner[1] /-stone
cornet
cornia   cornea +
cornice
cornucopia
corny
coroborate   corroborate[2+]
coroborativ   corroborative +
corode   corrode[2+]
corollary
corona
coronary
coronashun   coronation

coronation	
coroner	
coronet	
coroshun	corrosion [+]
corosion	corrosion [+]
corosiv	corrosive
corporal	
corporat e /ion	
corporeal	
corps * (army)	
corpse * (body)	
corpulen ce /t	
corpus	
corpusc le /ular	
corpussel	corpuscle [+]
corral [3] * (animal pen)	
corral	coral *
correct [1] /ion/ive/or	
correlat e [2] /ion	
correlative /ly	
correspond [1] /ence/ent	
corridor	
corrigend um /a (pl.)	
corrigible	
corroborat e [2] /ion	
corroborative /ly	
corrod e [2] /ible	
corros ion /ive	
corrugat e [2] /ion	
corrupt [1] /ive/ness	
corruptib le /ility	
corsashun	causation [+]
corsation	causation [+]
corse	coarse *[+]
corse	course *[+]
corsen	coarsen [1]
corset /ed	
corshun	caution [1+]
corshus	cautious [+]
corslet	
corstic	caustic [+]
cort	caught *
cort	court [1]*
cort marshal	court-martial [3+]
cortège	

corterise	cauterise [2+]
cort ex /ices (pl.)	
cortion	caution [1+]
cortious	cautious [+]
cortisan	courtesan
cortisone	
cortship	courtship
cortyard	courtyard
corugate	corrugate [2+]
corupt	corrupt [1+]
coruptible	corruptible [+]
coruptibul	corruptible [+]
corus	chorus [1+]
corvet	corvette
corvette	
cosecant	
coset	cosset [1]
cosh [1]	
cosi er /est/ly/ness	
co-signator y /ies	
cosine	
cosmetic /ian	
cosmic /ally	
cosmografey	cosmography [+]
cosmograph y /ic	
cosmolog y /ical	
cosmonaut	
cosmonort	cosmonaut
cosmopolitan /ism	
cosmos	
cosmotron	
co-sponsor	
Cossack	
cosset [1]	
cost /ly	
cost	coast [1+]
costgard	coastguard [+]
costive	
costli er /est/ness	
costum e /ier	
cosy	
cot	
cotage	cottage [+]
cotangent	
cote	coat [1+]

coterie	
cotidge	cottage +
coton	cotton +
cottage /r	
cotton /wool	
cou dayta	coup d'état
couch [1] /es	
cougar	
cough [1] /er	
could /n't	
coulomb	
council * (assembly)	
councillor * (member of assembly)	
counsel [3]* (advice)	
counsellor * (adviser)	
count [1] /ess (fem.) /less	
countenance	
counter [1] /foil	
counteract [1] /ion	
counter-attack [1]	
counterbalance [2]	
counter-charge [2]	
counter-claim [1]	
counter-clockwise	
counterfeit [1] /er	
countermand [1]	
countermine [2]	
counterpane	
counterpart	
counterpoint	
counterpoise [2]	
countersign [1]	
countersine	countersign [1]
counterway	counter-weigh [1]
counter-weigh [1]	
countie	county +
countr y /ies	
countryside	
count y /ies	
coup d'état	
couple [2] /t	
coupon	
courage /ous/ously	
courier	

cours e *† /ing †(conduct, passage)	
course	coarse *+
coursen	coarsen [1]
court [1]* (law)	
court	caught*
courtesan	
courtes y /ies	
courtier	
courtley	courtly +
courtl y /iness	
court-martial [3] /s	
courtship	
courtyard	
cousin	
covalent bond	
cove	
coven	
covenant	
Coventry	
cover [1] /age/let	
covert	
covet [1] /er/ous	
covey /s	
cow	
coward *(runaway)/ice	
cowardl y /iness	
cowboy	
cowch	couch [1]+
cower /ed * (cringed)	
cowerd	coward *+
cowl /ing	
cownt	count [1]+
cowntenance	countenance
cowntenans	countenance
cownter	counter [1]+
cownteract	counteract [1]+
cowpox	
cowslip	
cox [1] /swain	
coxcomb	
coy /ly/ness	
coyn	coin [1]+
coyote	
crab [3] /-apple	

crack¹ /er		credence	
crackle²		credens	credence
cracknel		credential	
crackul	crackle²	credib le /ility/ly	
cradel	cradle²	credibul	credible +
cradle²		credit¹ /or	
cradul	cradle²	creditabl e /y	
craft /y		creditabul	creditable +
crafti er /est/ly/ness		crediter	creditor
craftsman /ship		credul ity /ous	
crag /gy		creed	
crain	crane²+	creek ★ (stream)	
cram³ /mer		creek	creak ¹★+
cramp¹ /on		creem	cream ¹+
cranberie	cranberry +	creep /er/ing/s/y	
cranberr y /ies		creepi er /est/ly/ness	
crane² /-fly		cremat e² /ion	
crani um /al		crematorium	
crank¹ /case/shaft/y		Cremlin	Kremlin
crann y /ies		crenellated	
crape²		creole	
crash¹		crep	crêpe
crash-land¹		crêpe	
crass		crept	
crate²		crepuscular	
crater		crescendo /s	
cravat		crescent	
crave² /n		cresent	crescent
crawl¹ /er		cresh	crèche
crayfish		creshendo	crescendo +
crayon		cresit	cresset
craz e² /y		cresset	
crazi er /est/ly/ness		crest /fallen	
creacher	creature	cretin /ism/ous	
creak ¹★ (noise) /y		cretonne	
creak	creek ★	creture	creature
cream¹ /y		crevasse	
creamer y /ies		crevice	
creami er /est/ness		crevis	crevice
crease²		crew¹ /s ★ (sailors)	
creat e² /ion/or		crews	cruise ²★+
creativ e /ity		crewsifix	crucifix +
creature		crib³ /ber	
crèche		cribbage	
crecher	creature	cribidge	cribbage

crick [1]
cricket /er
crime
criminal /ity/ly
criminolog *ist* /y
crimson
crincul   crinkle [2+]
cringe [2]
crinkl *e* [2] /y
crinoline
cripple [2]
cript   crypt [+]
criptograf   cryptograph [+]
criptogram   cryptogram
criptograph   cryptograph [+]
cripul   cripple [2]
crisalis   chrysalis [+]
crisanthemum   chrysanthemum
crisen   christen [1]
Crisendum   Christendom
Crishna   Krishna
cris *is* /es
Crismas   Christmas [+]
crisp /iness/ly/y
criss-cross [1]
Crist   Christ
cristal   crystal [+]
cristaline   crystalline
cristalise   crystallise [2+]
cristalografer   crystallographer [+]
Cristian   Christian [+]
Cristianity   Christianity
criteri *on* /a (pl.)
critic /al/ally
criticis *e* [2] /able
criticism
critisize   criticise [2+]
criy   cry [4+]
croak [1]
croch   crotch
crochet [1]
crock /ery
crocodile
crocus /es
croft /er

croissant
crokay   croquet
cromatic   chromatic [+]
cromatin   chromatin
cromatograf   chromatograph [+]
cromatogram   chromatogram
crome   chrome [+]
cromic   chromic
cromium   chromium
crone ★ (hag)
crone   krone ★[+]
cronic   chronic [+]
cronicul   chronicle [2+]
cronie   crony [+]
cronograf   chronograph [+]
cronograph   chronograph [+]
cronologey   chronology [+]
cronological   chronological [+]
cronometer   chronometer
cron *y* /ies
crood   crude [+]
crook
crooked /ly/ness
croon [1]
croop   croup
croopier   croupier
crop [3] /per
croquet
cross [1] /ly/ness
cross -*breed* /-bred
cross-country
cross-cut /ting
cross-examin *e* [2] /ation
cross-fertilis *e* [2] /ation
cross-fire
cross-legged
crosspatch
cross-purpose
cross-question [1]
cross-reference [2]
cross-road
crosswise
crossword
crotch
crotchet /y

79

crouch [1]		crysalis	chrysalis [+]
croup		crystal /line	
croupier		crystallis *e* [2] /ation	
crow [1]		crystallograph *er* /y	
crowbar		cub	
crowd [1]		cubby-hole	
crown [1]		cub *e* /age	
crucial /ly		cubical ★ (cube-shaped)	
crucible		cubicle ★ (small room)	
crucibul	crucible	cubihole	cubby-hole
crucifix /ion		cubis *m* /t	
crucify [4]		cuboard	cupboard
crude /ly/ness/st		cuckold [1]	
cruditey	crudity [+]	cuckoo	
crudit *y* /ies		cucumber	
cruel /ler/lest/ly		cuddle [2]	
cruelt *y* /ies		cudgel [3]	
cruet		cudul	cuddle [2]
cruise [2]★ (voyage) /r		cue [2]★ (billiards)	
crum	crumb [+]	cue	queue [2]★
crumb /iness/y		cuff [1]	
crumbl *e* [2]★ (break up)/y		cuisine	
crumbul	crumble [2]★[+]	culcher	culture [2+]
crumpet		cul-de-sac	
crumple [2]★ (crease)		culer	colour [1+]
crumpul	crumple [2]★	culerashun	coloration
crumy	crumby	culinary	
crunch [1] /iness/y		culinder	colander
cruper	crupper	culinrey	culinary
crupper		cull [1]	
crusade [2] /r		culminat *e* [2] /ion	
crush [1]		culpab *le* /ility	
crushal	crucial [+]	culpabul	culpable [+]
crusible	crucible	culprit	
crusibul	crucible	cult	
crust /y		cultivat *e* [2] /ion/or	
crustace *a* /an/ous		cultur *e* [2] /al/ist	
crustasha	crustacea [+]	culvert	
crutch		cumbersome /ly/ness	
crux /es		cumbersum	cumbersome [+]
cruze	cruise [2]★[+]	Cumbrian	
cr *y* [4] /ies/ier		cumfert	comfort [1+]
crypt /ic/ically		cumpas	compass [1+]
cryptogram		cumulative	
cryptograph /ic		cumulus	

cuneiform
cuniform   cuneiform
cunning
cuntreyside   countryside
cup ^{3} /ful
cupboard
cupidity
cupola
cupro-nickel
cur /rish
curab le /ility
curabul   curable $^+$
curac y /ies
curant   currant ★
curasey   curacy $^+$
curate
curater   curator $^+$
curator /ship
curb ^{1}★ (chain in bit)
curb   kerb ^{1}★
curd
curdle ^{2}
curdul   curdle ^{2}
cur e ^{2} /ative
curent   current ★$^+$
curfew
curiculum   curriculum $^+$
curie
curio /s
curiosit y /ies
curious /ly/ness
curium
curius   curious $^+$
curl ^{1} /er/iness/y
curlew
curnel   colonel ★
currage   courage $^+$
curragus   courageous
currant ★ (fruit)
currenc y /ies
currensey   currency $^+$
current ★ (flow) /ly
curricul um /a (pl.)
curry ^{4} /comb
curse ^{2}

cursive /ly
cursory
curt /ly/ness
curtail ^{1} /ment
curtain ^{1}
curtale   curtail $^1+$
curts y ^{4} /ies
curv e ^{2} /ature
curvilinear
cushion ^{1}
cushon   cushion ^{1}
cusp
cuss ^{1} /edness
custard
custod y /ial/ian
custom /er
customar y /ily
cut /ter/ting
cute /ly/ness/r/st
cuticle
cuticul   cuticle
cutlass /es
cutlery
cutlet
cuttle-fish
cuvenant   covenant
cuver   cover $^1+$
cuvet   covet $^1+$
cuvey   covey $^+$
cyanide
cybernetics
cyclamate
cyclamen
cycle ^{2}
cyclic /al/ally
cycl ist /ometer
cyclon e /ic
Cyclops
cyclostyle
cyclotron
cygnet ★ (swan)
cygnet   signet ★
cyle   chyle
cylinder
cylindrical /ly

81

cymbal *† /ist	
†(musical instrument)	
cymbal	symbol *+
cynic /ism	
cynical /ly	
cynosure	
cypress	
cyst /itis	
cytology	
czar	tsar
Czech * (nationality)	
Czechoslovakian	

D

dab ³ /ber	
dabble ² /r	
dable	dabble ²+
dabul	dabble ²+
dabutant	débutant +
dace	
dachshund	
dactill	dactyl
dactyl	
daddy /-long-legs	
daffodil	
daft /er/est	
dagger	
dahlia	
dail	dale
dailie	daily +
dail y /ies	
daintie	dainty +
daint y /ier/iest/ily/iness	
dairie	dairy +
dairimade	dairymaid
dair y /ies	
dairymaid	
daisie	daisy +
dais y /ies	
daitee	deity +
dakshound	dachshund
dale	
dalia	dahlia

dalie	dally ⁴+
dall y ⁴ /ier	
dam ³* (water)	
dam	damn ¹*+
damage ² /able	
damask	
dame	
damidge	damage ²+
damn ¹* (curse) /ation	
damnabl e /y	
damnabul	damnable +
damp /er/est/ness	
dampen ¹	
damsel	
damson	
dance ² /r	
dandelion	
dandie	dandy +
dandifi	dandify ⁴
dandify ⁴	
dandilion	dandelion
dandruff	
dand y /ies	
Dane * (from Denmark)	
dane	deign ¹*
danger /ous/ously	
dangerus	dangerous
dangle ² /r	
dangul	dangle ²+
danjer	danger+
danjerus	dangerous
dank /ness	
danse	dance ²+
daper	dapper +
daple	dapple ²
dapper /ness	
dapple ²	
dapul	dapple ²
dare ² /-devil	
dark /er/est/ly/ness	
darken ¹	
darling	
darn ¹ /er	
darnel	
dart ¹	

dase	dace
dash [1] /board	
dastard /ly	
data	
dat e [2] /able	
dater	data
dative	
daub [1] /er/y	
daufin	dauphin
daughter /(s)-in-law	
daunt [1] /less	
dauphin	
dauter	daughter [+]
davenport	
Davielamp	Davy lamp
davit	
Davy lamp	
dawb	daub [1+]
dawdle [2] /r	
dawdul	dawdle [2+]
dawn [1]	
dawnt	daunt [1+]
dawter	daughter [+]
day /-break/s * (dates)	
daybu	début
day-dream /t/ing	
dayify	deify [4+]
dayism	deism [+]
dayist	deist
dayity	deity [+]
daylight	
daylite	daylight
day-nurser y /ies	
daytant	détente
daze [2]* (stun)	
dazle	dazzle [2+]
dazul	dazzle [2+]
dazzl e [2] /er/ingly	
de luxe	
deacon /ess (fem.)	
deactivat e [2] /ion	
dead /-beat/-line	
deaden [1] /er	
dead-heat [1]	
deadlock	

deadl y /ier/iest/iness	
dead-nettle	
deaf /-mute/ness	
deafen [1] /ingly	
deal /er/ing/t	
deam	deem [1]
dean /ery	
deap	deep [+]
dear * (loved)	
dear	deer *
dear er /est/ly	
dearth	
death /-mask/-rate	
death ly /less/like	
death -trap /-watch	
débâcle	
debacul	débâcle
debar [3] /ment	
debark [1] /ation	
debase [2] /ment	
debat e [2] /able/ably	
debauch [1] /ery	
debilitat e [2] /ion	
debility	
debit [1] /able	
debonair /ness	
deborch	debauch [1+]
debree	debris
debrief [1]	
debris	
debt /or * (owe money)	
debunk [1] /er	
début	
débutant /e (fem.)	
decade	
decaden ce /t	
decagon /al	
deca gram /litre/metre	
decamp [1] /ment	
decant [1] /er	
decapitat e [2] /ion	
decapod	
decarbonis e [2] /ation	
decathlon	
decay [1]	

decease²	
deceit /ful/fully/fulness	
deceive² /r	
decelerat *e*² /ion	
December	
decenc *y* /ies	
decensey	decency +
decent * (good) /ly	
decent	descent *
decentralise²	
decepshun	deception
deception	
deceptive /ly/ness	
decerus	decorous +
decibel	
decide² /dly	
deciduous	
decifer	decipher ¹+
deci *gram* /litre/metre	
decimal /ism	
decimalis *e*² /ation	
decimat *e*² /ion	
decipher ¹ /able	
decision	
decisive /ly/ness	
deck ¹ /-chair/-hand	
declaim ¹ /er	
declamashun	declamation +
declamat *ion* /ory	
declarat *ion* /ory	
declare²	
declassif *y*⁴ /ication	
declension	
declin *e*² /able/ation	
declivit *y* /ies	
declutch ¹	
decockshun	decoction
decoction	
decode² /r	
decoi	decoy ¹
décollet *é* /age	
decompos *e*² /able/ition	
decompress ¹ /ion	
decompress *ive* /or	
decon	deacon +

decongestant	
decontaminat *e*² /ion	
decontrol ³	
décor	
decorashun	decoration
decorat *e*² /ion/ive/or	
decorous /ly/ness	
decorum	
decorus	decorous +
decoy ¹	
decreas *e*² /ingly	
decree /d/ing	
decrepit /ude	
decrese	decrease ²+
decri	decry ⁴+
decr *y*⁴ /ier	
ded	dead +
deden	deaden ¹+
dedheat	dead-heat ¹
dedicat *e*² /ion	
dedlie	deadly +
dedlier	deadlier
dedlock	deadlock
dedly	deadly +
dednetle	dead-nettle
dednetul	dead-nettle
deduc *e*² /ible	
deduct ¹ /ible/ion	
deed /-poll	
deel	deal +
deem ¹	
deen	dean +
deep /er	
deepen ¹	
deep-freez *e* /er/ing	
deep-frozen	
deep-fry ⁴	
deer * (animal)	
deer	dear *
de-escalat *e*² /ion	
def	deaf +
deface² /ment	
defamatory	
defamatrey	defamatory
defam *e*² /ation	

default [1] /er		
defeat [1] /ism/ist		
defecat e [2] /ion		
defect [1] /ion/ive/or		
defeet	defeat [1+]	
defen	deafen [1+]	
defence /less		
defend [1] /able/ant		
defens	defence [+]	
defensib le /ility		
defensibul	defensible [+]	
defensive /ly/ness		
defensless	defenceless	
defer [3]* (postpone)		
deferen ce /tial		
deferens	deference [+]	
deferenshal	deferential	
defesit	deficit	
defi	defy [4]	
defian ce /t/tly		
defians	defiance [+]	
deficienc y /ies		
deficient /ly		
deficit		
defile [2] /ment/r		
defin e [2] /able/ition		
definishun	definition	
definit	definite [+]	
definite /ly		
definitive /ly		
defishency	deficiency [+]	
defishent	deficient [+]	
defisit	deficit	
deflashun	deflation	
deflat e [2] /ion/ionary		
deflecshun	deflection	
deflect [1] /ion/ive/or		
deflour	deflower [1]	
deflower [1]		
defmute	deaf-mute	
deforest [1] /ation		
deform [1] /ation		
deformashun	deformation	
deformit y /ies		
defraud [1] /er		

defray [1] /able/al		
defreez e /ing		
defrord		defraud [1+]
defrost [1] /er		
defrozen		
deft /ly/ness		
defunct /ive/ness		
defy [4]		
degeneracy		
degenerat e [2] /ion		
degrad e [2] /ation		
degree		
dehidrate		dehydrate [2+]
dehydrat e [2] /ion		
de-ice [2] /r		
deifi		deify [4+]
deif y [4] /ier		
deign [1]* (condescend)		
de-ise		de-ice [2+]
deis m /t		
deitee		deity [+]
deit y /ies		
deject [1] /ion		
dejeneracy		degeneracy
dejenerate		degenerate [2+]
dejeneration		degeneration
dekstrose		dextrose
dekstrus		dextrous
delay [1] /er		
delectabl e /y		
delectabul		delectable [+]
delegac y /ies		
delegasey		delegacy [+]
delegat e [2] /ion		
delet e [2] /ion		
deleterious /ly		
deliberat e [2] /ely/ion		
delibratley		deliberately
delicac y /ies		
delicate /ly/ness		
delicatessen		
delicious /ly/ness		
deligacy		delegacy [+]
deligashun		delegation
deligate		delegate [2+]

delight [1] /ful/fully
delineat *e* [2] /ion
deliniashun   delineation
deliniate   delineate [2+]
delinkwasey   delinquency [+]
delinkwens   delinquence [+]
delinquen *ce* /t
delinquenc *y* /ies
delirious /ly/ness
delirium
delirius   delirious [+]
delishus   delicious [+]
delite   delight [1+]
deliteful   delightful
deliterius   deleterious [+]
deliver [1] /ance/er
deliver *y* /ies
delivrey   delivery [+]
dell
delouse [2]
delt   dealt
delta
delude [2]
deluge [2]
deluks   de luxe
delushun   delusion [+]
delusion /al
delus *ive* /ory
delve [2] /r
demagog   demagogue [+]
demagog *ue* /y
demand [1] /able/er
demarcat *e* [2] /ion
demarch   démarche
démarche
demean [1] /our
demeaner   demeanour
demented
demerara
demerit
demesne
demigod
demilitarise [2]
demis *e* [2] /able
demist [1] /er

demobilis *e* [2] /ation
democrac *y* /ies
democrasey   democracy [+]
democratic /ally
democratis *e* [2] /ation
demolish [1] /able
demolishun   demolition [+]
demolition /ist
demon /ic
demonstra *ble* /tive
demonstrashun   demonstration
demonstrat *e* [2] /ion/or
demoralise [2]
demot *e* [2] /ion
demur [3]★ (object)
demure ★(quiet, coy)/ly
denationalise [2]
dencher   denture
dendrology
deni   deny [4]
denial
denier
denigrat *e* [2] /ion/or
denim
denizen
denominat *e* [2] /or
denomination /al
denot *e* [2] /able/ation/ive
denounce [2] /ment
denownse   denounce [2+]
dense /ly/r
densitey   density [+]
densitie   density [+]
densit *y* /ies
dent [1]
dental
dentifrice
dentifriss   dentifrice
denti *ne* /tion
dentishun   dentition
dentist /ry
denture
denud *e* [2] /ation
denunciat *e* [2] /ion
deny [4]

deoderant	deodorant
deoderise	deodorise ²+
deodorant	
deodorise ² /r	
deparcher	departure
depart ¹ /ure	
department /al/ally	
departmentalise ²	
depen	deepen ¹
depend ¹ /able/ence	
dependant ★ (n.)	
dependenc y /ies	
dependensey	dependency +
dependent ★ (adj.)	
depict ¹ /ion	
depilat e ² /ion/or	
depilatory	
deplet e ² /ion	
deploi	deploy ¹+
deplor e ² /able/ably	
deploy ¹ /ment	
depo	depot
depopulat e ² /ion	
deport ¹ /ment	
deportashun	deportation
deportation	
depos e ² /able	
deposishun	deposition
deposit ¹ /ion/or	
depositor y /ies	
depositrey	depository +
depot	
deprav e ² /ity	
deprecat e ² /ion/ory	
depreciat e ² /ion	
depredat e ² /ion	
depresherise	depressurise ²
depreshurise	depressurise ²
depresiv	depressive
depress ¹ /ion/ive	
depressant	
depressurise ²	
depricate	deprecate ²+
depriv e ² /ation	
depth	

deput e ² /ation	
deputey	deputy +
deputise ²	
deput y /ies	
derail ¹ /ment	
derale	derail ¹+
derange ² /ment	
derelicshun	dereliction
derelict /ion	
derick	derrick
deride ² /r	
derishun	derision
derision	
deris ive /ory	
derivashun	derivation +
derivat ion /ive	
derivativ	derivative
deriv e ² /able/er	
dermatitis	
dermatolog y /ist	
derogat e ² /ive/ory	
derrick	
dert	dirt +
derth	dearth
derty	dirty ⁴+
dervish	
desalinat e ² /ion	
descant ¹ /er	
descend ¹ /er	
descendant ★ (n.)	
descendent ★ (adj.)	
descent ★ (go down)	
describ e ² /able	
descript ion /ive	
descry ⁴	
deseat	deceit +
deseave	deceive ²+
desecrat e ² /ion	
desegregat e ² /ion	
desel	diesel
deselerashun	deceleration
deselerate	decelerate ²+
Desember	December
desency	decency +
desend	descend ¹+

desensitise [2]	
desent	decent ★+
desent	descent ★
desentralise	decentralise [2]
desershun	desertion
desert [1]★ (abandon, dry land)	
desert	dessert ★
desert *er* /ion	
deserve [2] /dly	
desese	disease +
desibel	decibel
desiccat *e* [2] /ion	
desiduous	deciduous
design [1] /er	
designat *e* [2] /ion/or	
desimal	decimal +
desimalise	decimalise [2]+
desimate	decimate [2]+
desimation	decimation
desine	design [1]+
desirab *le* /ility	
desirabul	desirable +
desir *e* [2] /ous	
desist [1]	
desk	
deskant	descant [1]+
desolat *e* [2] /ion	
despair [1]	
desperado /es	
desperashun	desperation
desperate /ly/ness	
desperation	
despicabl *e* /y	
despise [2] /r	
despite	
despoil [1] /ment	
despoliation	
despond [1] /ent	
despondenc *e* /y	
despondens	despondence +
despot /ism	
despotic /ally	
dessert ★ (food)	
dessert	desert [1]★

destinashun	destination
destination	
destine [2]	
destin *y* /ies	
destitut *e* /ion	
destroy [1] /er	
destructib *le* /ility	
destructibul	destructible +
destruct *ion* /ive	
desultor *y* /ily	
det	debt +
detach [1] /ment	
detail [1]	
detain [1] /ment	
detale	detail [1]
detane	detain [1]+
detecshun	detection
detect [1] /ion/or	
detective	
détente	
detention	
deter [3]★ (hinder)	
deter	debtor ★
deterent	deterrent
detergent	
deteriorat *e* [2] /ion	
determinant	
determinashun	determination
determination	
determin *e* [2] /able	
deterrent	
detest [1] /able/ation	
deth	death +
dethrone [2] /ment	
detiriarate	deteriorate [2]+
detonat *e* [2] /ion/or	
detoor	detour
detour	
detract [1] /ion/or	
detriment /al	
detrishun	detrition
detrition	
deuce	
deuterium	
deuteron	

devalu *e*² /ation
devastat *e*² /ion/or
develop¹ /er/ment
devian *ce* /t
deviat *e*² /ion
device ★ (scheme, means)
devil /ry
devilish /ly
devious /ly
devis *e*²★ (invent) /able
devitalis *e*² /ation
devius   devious +
devoid
devolushun   devolution
devolution
devolve²
devot *e*² /ee/ion
devour¹
devout /ly/ness
dew ★ (moisture)
dew   due ★
dew *y* /-drop
dext *erity* /rous
dextrose
dextrus   dextrous
dhoti
dhow
diabetes
diabetic
diabolic /al/ally
diadem
diafanous   diaphanous +
diafanus   diaphanous +
diafram   diaphragm +
diagnose²
diagnos *is* /es (pl.)
diagnostic /ian
diagnostishun   diagnostician
diagonal /ly
diagram
diagrammatic /ally
dial³ /er
dialect /al/ally
dialectic /al/ally
dialisis   dialysis +

dialog   dialogue
dialogue
dialy *sis* /tic
diamet *er* /ral
diametric /al/ally
diamond
diapason
diaper
diaphanous /ly
diaphragm /atic
diarea   diarrhoea
diarey   diary +
diarrhoea
diar *y* /ies/ist
diatonic
diatribe

> If you cannot find your word
> under **di** look under **de**

dibase   debase ²+
dibate   debate ²+
dibble² /r
dice² (pl. of die)
dichotom *y* /ies
diciple   disciple
dicipul   disciple
dicotomey   dichotomy +
dicotyledon
dicshun   diction
dicshunrey   dictionary +
dictafone   dictaphone
dictaphone
dictat *e*² /ion
dictator /ial
diction
dictionar *y* /ies
dictum
didactic /ally/ism
diddle² /r
didget   digit +
didgitalis   digitalis
didn't (did not)
didnt   didn't
die ★ (sing. of dice)
die ★ (death) /d ★

die-hard
dieing   dyeing ⋆
dieing   dying ⋆
diernal   diurnal +
diesel
diet[1] /ary
dietetic /s
dietician
dietishun   dietician
difer   differ[1]⋆
diference   difference +
diferens   difference +
diferenshal   differential +
diferenshiate   differentiate[2]+
diferent   different
diferential   differential +
diferentiate   differentiate[2]+
differ[1]⋆ (disagree)
differ   defer[3]⋆
differen ce /t
differential /ly
differentiat e[2] /ion
difficult
difficult y /ies
diffiden ce /t
diffract /ion
diffus e[2] /ion/ive
dificult   difficult
dificultey   difficulty +
difidence   diffidence +
difident   diffident
difract   diffract +
diftheria   diphtheria
difthong   diphthong
difuse   diffuse[2]+
difushun   diffusion
difusion   diffusion
dig[3] /ger
digest[1] /ion/ive
digestib le /ility
digit /al/ally
digitalis
dignify[4]
dignitar y /ies
dignitrey   dignitary +

dignity
digress[1] /ion/ive
dike[2]
dil   dill
dilapidat e[2] /ion
dilatashun   dilatation
dilat e[2] /ation/or/ory
dilemma
diletant   dilettante +
dilettant e /i (pl.)
dilidalie   dilly-dally[4]
diligen ce /t
diligens   diligence +
dill
dilly-dally[4]
dilut e[2] /ion/or
diluvial
dim[3] /ly/ness
dime
dimenshun   dimension +
dimension /al
dimer   dimmer +
diminish[1] /able
diminuendo
diminut ive /ion
dimm er /est
dimpl e[2] /y
dimpul   dimple[2]+
dinamic   dynamic +
dinamite   dynamite[2]
dinamo   dynamo +
dinastey   dynasty +
dinastic   dynastic +
dine[2]⋆ (eat) /r
dine   dyne ⋆
diner   dinner
dingh y /ies
dingie   dinghy +
ding y /ily/iness
dinner
dinosaur
dinosore   dinosaur
dioces e /an
diode
diokside   dioxide

diosees	diocese +	disarange	disarrange ²⁺
dioxide		disaray	disarray
dip ³ /per		disarm ¹ /ament	
diper	diaper	disarrange ² /ment	
diphtheria		disarray	
diphthong		disasoshiate	disassociate ²⁺
diploma /s		disassociat e ² /ion	
diplomac y /ies		disast er /rous/rously	
diplomasey	diplomacy +	disastrus	disastrous
diplomat /ist		disatisfi	dissatisfy ⁴⁺
diplomatic /ally		disavow ¹ /al	
dipsomania /c		disband ¹ /ment	
dire /ful/ly/r/st		disbar ³ /ment	
direcshun	direction	disbeleif	disbelief
direct ¹ /ion/ive		disbeleive	disbelieve ²⁺
director /ate		disbelief	
director y /ies		disbelieve ² /r	
directrey	directory +	disberden	disburden ¹⁺
dirge /ful		disberse	disburse ²⁺
dirigib le /ility		disbileaf	disbelief
dirigibul	dirigible +	disbileve	disbelieve ²⁺
dirt /iness		disburden ¹ /ment	
dirt y ⁴ /ier/iest/ily		disburse ² /ment	
disabilit y /ies		disc /-brake/-jockey	
disable ² /ment		discard ¹	
disabul	disable ²⁺	discern ¹ /ible/ment	
disabuse ²		discernibul	discernible
disadvantage /ous		discharge ²	
disadvantidge	disadvantage +	disciple	
disafecshun	disaffection	disciplinar y /ian	
disaffected		discipline ²	
disaffection		discipul	disciple
disagreabul	disagreeable +	disclaim ¹	
disagree /d/ing/ment		disclaym	disclaim ¹
disagreeabl e /y		disclos e ² /ure	
disagrement	disagreement	discolor	discolour ¹⁺
disallow ¹		discolo ur ¹ /ration	
disapear	disappear ¹⁺	discomfert	discomfort ¹
disapearance	disappearance	discomfort ¹	
disapoint	disappoint ¹⁺	discompos e ² /ure	
disapoynt	disappoint ¹⁺	disconcert ¹	
disappear ¹ /ance		disconect	disconnect ¹⁺
disappoint ¹ /ment		disconnect ¹ /ion	
disapprov e ² /al		disconsert	disconcert ¹
disaproval	disapproval	disconsolate /ly	

91

discontent [1]
discontinu *e* [2] /ance
discontinu *ity* /ous
discord /ance/ant
discorse — discourse [2]
discotek — discotheque
discotheque
discount [1] /able/er
discountenance [2]
discourage [2] /ment
discourse [2]
discourteous /ly/ness
discourtes *y* /ies
discourtius — discourteous +
discover [1] /er
discover *y* /ies
discownt — discount [1]+
discowntenans — discountenance [2]
discredit [1] /able
discreet /ly/ness
discrepanc *y* /ies
discrepant
discrepensey — discrepancy +
discreshun — discretion +
discretion /ary
discribable — describable
discribe — describe [2]+
discriminat *e* [2] /ion
discripshun — description +
discriptiv — descriptive
disculer — discolour [1]+
discuridge — discourage [2]+
discurs *ion* /ive
discurtesey — discourtesy +
discurtius — discourteous +
discus *† /es
   †(heavy disc)
discushun — discussion
discuss [1]* (debate)
discussion
disdain [1] /ful/fully
dise — dice [2]
disease /d
diseave — deceive [2]+
disecshun — dissection

disect — dissect [1]+
disembark [1] /ation
disembarrass [1] /ment
disemble — dissemble [2]+
disembodie — disembody [4]+
disembod *y* [4] /iment
disembowel [3] /ment
disembroil [1]
disembul — dissemble [2]+
diseminashun — dissemination
diseminate — disseminate [2]+
disenchant [1] /ment
disengage [2] /ment
disenshent — dissentient
disenshun — dissension
disentangle [2] /ment
disentient — dissentient
disentrey — dysentery
disern — discern [1]+
disernible — discernible
disernibul — discernible
disertashun — dissertation
disertation — dissertation
diserviss — disservice
disfaver — disfavour [1]
disfavour [1]
disfiger — disfigure [2]+
disfigure [2] /ment
disfranchise [2] /ment
disgise — disguise [2]+
disgorge [2] /ment
disgrace [2] /ful/fully
disgruntled
disguise [2] /r
disgust [1]
dish /-cloth/ful
dishabille
disharmoney — disharmony +
disharmon *y* /ious
disharten — dishearten [1]
dishearten [1]
dishevel [3]
dishonest /ly/y
dishonour [1] /able/ably
dishonrabul — dishonourable

disidence	dissidence +
disidens	dissidence +
disident	dissident
disillusion [1] /ment	
disilushun	disillusion [1]+
disimilar	dissimilar +
disimulashun	dissimulation
disincentive	
disinclinashun	disinclination
disinclin *e* [2] /ation	
disinfect [1] /ant/ion	
disinherit [1] /ance	
disinsentiv	disincentive
disintegrat *e* [2] /ion	
disinter [3] /ment	
disinterest [1]	
disintigrate	disintegrate [2]+
disipate	dissipate [2]+
disiple	disciple
disiplin	discipline [2]
disiplinarey	disciplinary +
disipul	disciple
disjoint [1]	
diskwiet	disquiet [1]+
diskwolification	disqualification
diskwolify	disqualify [4]+
dislik *e* [2] /able	
dislocat *e* [2] /ion	
dislodge [2] /ment	
disloge	dislodge [2]+
disloial	disloyal +
disloialtey	disloyalty
disloyal /ly/ty	
dismal /ly	
dismantle [2]	
dismantul	dismantle [2]
dismast [1]	
dismay [1]	
dismember [1] /ment	
dismisal	dismissal
dismiss [1] /al	
dismount [1]	
dismownt	dismount [1]
disobay	disobey [1]
disobedien *ce* /t	

disobey [1]	
disoblige [2]	
disoloot	dissolute +
disoluble	dissoluble
disolute	dissolute +
disolution	dissolution
disolve	dissolve [2]+
disonance	dissonance +
disonans	dissonance +
disonant	dissonant
disone	disown [1]
disoner	dishonour [1]+
disonerabul	dishonourable
disonest	dishonest +
disonist	dishonest +
disonrabul	dishonourable
disorder [1] /ly	
disorganis *e* [2] /ation	
disorientate [2]	
disoshiate	dissociate [2]+
disown [1]	
disparage [2] /ment	
disparate /ly/ness	
disparidge	disparage [2]+
disparige	disparage [2]+
disparitey	disparity +
disparit *y* /ies	
dispashonate	dispassionate +
dispassionate /ly	
dispatch [1] /er	
dispel [3] /ler	
dispensar *y* /ies	
dispens *e* [2] /ation/er	
dispepsia	dyspepsia +
dispeptic	dyspeptic
dispers *e* [2] /al	
dispershun	dispersion
dispersion	
dispirit [1]	
displace [2] /ment	
displase	displace [2]+
display [1]	
displeas *e* [2] /ure	
displese	displease [2]+
displesher	displeasure

disport [1]
dispos *e* [2] /able/al
disposeshun   disposession
disposess   dispossess [1+]
disposishun   disposition
disposition
dispossess [1] /ion
disproof
disproov   disprove [2]
disproporshun   disproportion [+]
disproportion /ate
disprosium   dysprosium
disprove [2]
dispursal   dispersal
dispurse   disperse [2+]
dispurshun   dispersion
disputashun   disputation [+]
disputat *ion* /ious
disput *e* [2] /able
disqualif *y* [4] /ication
disquiet [1] /ude
disregard [1] /ful
disrepair
disreputabl *e* /y
disrepute
disrespect /ful/fully
disrigard   disregard [1+]
disripair   disrepair
disrispect   disrespect [+]
disrobe [2] /ment
disrupt [1] /ion/ive
dissapear   disappear [1+]
dissapoint   disappoint [1+]
dissaproov   disapprove [2+]
dissatisf *y* [4] /action
dissect [1] /ion/or
dissemble [2] /r
disseminat *e* [2] /ion/or
dissension
dissent [1]* (disagreement)
dissentient
dissentious
dissertation
disservice
dissiden *ce* /t

dissidens   dissidence [+]
dissimilar /ity/ities
dissimulat *e* [2] /ion
dissipat *e* [2] /ion
dissociat *e* [2] /ion
dissoluble
dissolute /ly/ness
dissolution
dissolve [2] /nt
dissonan *ce* /t
dissuade [2]
dissuas *ion* /ive
distaff
distance
distans   distance
distant /ly
distaste /ful/fully
distemper [1]
distend [1]
distenshun   distension
distens *ible* /ion
distensibul   distensible [+]
disterb   disturb [1+]
disterbance   disturbance
distil [3] /lation/ler
distiller *y* /ies
distinct /ive/ly
distinction
distinguish [1] /able
distingwish   distinguish [1+]
distorshun   distortion
distort [1] /ion
distracshun   distraction
distract [1] /ion
distrain [1] /t
distrane   distrain [1+]
distraught
distrawt   distraught
distress [1] /ful
distribut *e* [2] /ion
distribut *ive* /or
district /nurse
distrort   distraught
distrust [1] /ful
disturb [1] /ance

disunion	
disunit *e* [2] /y	
disurn	discern [1+]
disurnible	discernible
disuse [2]	
diswade	dissuade [2]
diswashun	dissuasion [+]
diswasion	dissuasion [+]
diswasiv	dissuasive
ditch [1] /er	
dither [1] /y	
ditie	ditty [+]
dito	ditto
ditto	
ditt *y* /ies	
dity	ditty [+]
diurnal /ly	
divan	
dive [2] /r	
diverge [2] /nce/nt	
divergens	divergence
divers	diverse [+]
diverse /ly	
divershun	diversion
diversifi	diversify [4+]
diversif *y* [4] /ication	
diversion	
diversitey	diversity [+]
diversity /ies	
divert [1] /er	
divest [1]	
divide [2] /r	
dividend	
divin *e* [2] /ation/ely/er	
divinitey	divinity [+]
divinit *y* /ies	
diviser	divisor
divishun	division [+]
divis *ible* /ive/ively	
divisibul	divisible [+]
division /al	
divisiv	divisive
divisor	
divorce [2] /é/ée (fem.)	
divorse	divorce [2+]

divulge [2] /nce/r	
dizier	dizzier [+]
dizmal	dismal [+]
dizolve	dissolve [2+]
dizy	dizzy
dizzi *er* /est/ly/ness	
dizzy	
do ★ (perform) /er/ing	
do ★ (music) /s ★ (pl.)	
do	doe ★[+]
docile /ly	
docility	
dock [1] /er/yard	
docket [1]	
dockit	docket [1]
docter	doctor [1+]
doctor [1] /ate/ial	
doctrin	doctrine [+]
doctrinair	doctrinaire
doctrin *e* /aire/al	
document [1] /ation	
documentar *y* /ies	
documentrey	documentary [+]
dodder [1] /er/y	
dodecagon	
doder	dodder [1+]
dodg *e* [2] /er/y	
dodgi *er* /est/ness	
doe ★ (deer) /s ★ (pl.)	
doe	do ★[+]
doe	dough ★[+]
does ★ (do-[verb])	
doesn't (does not)	
doff [1]	
dofin	dauphin
dog [3] /fight/fish	
dog-eared	
dogeared	dog-eared
dogeral	doggerel
dogfite	dogfight
doggerel	
dogma /tic/tically	
dogmatis *e* [2] /m	
doilie	doily [+]
doil *y* /ies	

doldrum		doom[1]	
dole[2]		doomsday book	Domesday Book
doleful /ly		door /step/way	
doler	dollar	door	dour
dolerus	dolorous[+]	doordle	dawdle[2+]
dolfin	dolphin	doormouse	dormouse
doll[1] /y		doosh	douche[2]
dollar		dope[2] /y	
doller	dollar	dophin	dauphin
dollop		dore	door[+]
dolman		dorman *cy* /t	
dolomite		dormansey	dormancy[+]
dolorous /ly/ness		dormice	
dolorus	dolorous[+]	dormise	dormice
dolphin		dormitor *y* /ies	
domain		dormitrey	dormitory[+]
domane	domain	dormouse	
dome		dorn	dawn[1]
Domesday Book		dorsal /ly	
domestic /ally		dorter	daughter[+]
domesticate[2]		dos *e*[2] /age	
domesticity		dosidge	dosage
domestisitey	domesticity	dosile	docile[+]
domicil *e* /iary		dositey	docility
dominan *ce* /t		dossier	
dominans	dominance[+]	dot[3]	
dominat *e*[2] /ion/or		dot *age* /ard	
dominear	domineer[1]	dote[2] /r	
domineer[1]		doti	dhoti
dominion		dotidge	dotage[+]
domino /es		dotti *er* /est/ly/ness	
dominyon	dominion	dotty	
domisile	domicile[+]	double[2] /-barrelled	
don[3]*† /nish		double-bass	
†(put on, tutor)		double-cross[1]	
donat *e*[2] /ion/or		doublet	
done * (finished)		doubloon	
doner	donor	doubly	
donkey /s		doubt[1] /er/less	
donky	donkey[+]	doubtful /ly/ness	
donor		douche[2]	
donut	doughnut	dough * (bread) /nut/y	
dooch	douche[2]	dought *y* /ily	
doodle[2] /r		dour	
doodul	doodle[2+]	douse[2]* (shower) /r	

douse	dowse ²★	draftiness	draughtiness
dout	doubt ¹⁺	drafts	draughts ★
doutey	doughty ⁺	draftsman ★ (drafter	
doutful	doubtful ⁺	of documents)	
doutless	doubtless	draftsman	draughtsman ★
dove /-cot		drafty	draughty ⁺
dovetail ¹		drag ³ /ger	
dow	dhow	dragon	
dow	doe ★⁺	dragonfl y /ies	
dow	dough ★⁺	dragoon ¹	
dowager		drain ¹ /age/er	
dowdie	dowdy ⁺	drainidge	drainage
dowd y /ily/iness		drake	
dowey	doughy	dram	
down ¹ /cast/hill		drama /s/tist	
downey	downy	dramatic /ally	
downfall /en		dramatis e ² /ation	
downgrade ²		drank	
downharted	downhearted	drape ² /r	
downhearted		draper y /ies	
downie	downy	drastic /ally	
downpoor	downpour	draught ★† /s ★	
downpour		†(air current, game)	
downright		draughtiness	
downrite	downright	draughtsman ★†	
downstairs		†(drawer of plans)	
downtrodden		draught y /ier/iest	
downward		draw /ing/n	
downwerd	downward	drawback	
downy		drawbridge	
dowrie	dowry ⁺	drawer	
dowr y /ies		drawing-room	
dowse ²★ (divine with rod)		drawl ¹ /er	
dowse	douse ²★⁺	dray ★ (low cart)	
dowt	doubt ¹⁺	dray	drey ★
dowtey	doughty ⁺	dread ¹ /ful/fully	
dowtful	doubtful ⁺	dreadnort	dreadnought
doz e ²★ (sleep) /y		dreadnought	
doze	does ★	dream ¹ /ily/less/t/y	
dozen		drearey	dreary
dozi ly /ness		drearie	dreary
drab		dreari er /est/ly/ness	
draft ¹★ (bank, military)		dreary	
draft	draught ★⁺	dred	dread ¹⁺
draftey	draughty ⁺	dredful	dreadful

dredge² /r	
drednort	dreadnought
dreem	dream¹⁺
drege	dredge²⁺
dregs	
dremt	dreamt
drench¹ /er	
drerey	dreary
drerie	dreary
drerier	drearier⁺
dresage	dressage
dresie	dressy
dresmaker	dressmaker⁺
dress¹ /er/es/iness/y	
dressage	
dressmaker /ing	
dresy	dressy
drew	
Drewid	Druid
drey ★ (squirrel's nest)	
dri	dry⁴⁺
dribble² /r	
driblet	
dribul	dribble²⁺
driclean	dry-clean¹
drift¹ /er/wood	
dril	drill¹
drill¹	
drily	
drink /able/er	
drip³ /-dry	
drive /en/er/ing	
drivel³ /ler	
drizul	drizzle²⁺
drizzle² /y	
droll /ness	
drollery /ies	
dromedary /ies	
drone²	
Drooid	Druid
drool¹	
droop¹ /y	
drop³ /let	
droper	dropper
drop-out	

dropper	
dropsey	dropsy⁺
dropsie	dropsy⁺
dropsy /ical/ied	
dross /iness	
drought	
drout	drought
drove /r	
drown¹	
drowse² /y	
drowsey	drowsy
drowsie	drowsy
drowsier /ly/ness	
drowt	drought
dru	drew
drub³ /ber	
drudge² /ry	
drug³	
druge	drudge²⁺
drugery	drudgery
drugget	
druggist	
Druid	
drum³ /mer/stick	
drumedarey	dromedary⁺
drum-major	
drunk /ard/en/enness	
dry⁴ /ier/iest	
dry-clean¹	
dryer	drier
dual ★ (two) /ism/ity	
dual	duel³★
dub³	
dubbin	
dubious /ly	
dubius	dubious⁺
duble	double²⁺
dublebareld	double-barrelled
dublet	doublet
dublie	doubly
dubloon	doubloon
dubly	doubly
ducal	
ducat	
duce	deuce

duchess /es		dun ★ (colour)	
duchey	duchy +	dun	done ★
duchie	duchy +	dunce	
duch y /ies		dune	
duck¹ /ling		dung /hill	
ducket	ducat	dungaree /s	
ducktile	ductile +	dungen	dungeon
duct /ing/less		dungeon	
ductil e /ity		dunjon	dungeon
du e ★ (owing, expected)		duns	dunce
due	dew ★	dunse	dunce
duedrop	dew-drop	duolog	duologue
duel ³★ (fight)		duologue	
duel	joule ★	dup e² /able	
dueler	dueller +	dupleks	duplex +
duelist	duellist	duplex /ity	
duell er /ist		duplicat e² /ion/or	
duet /tist		duplicity	
duey	dewy +	duplisitey	duplicity
dufel	duffel	durab le /ility/ly	
duffel		durabul	durable +
duffer		durashun	duration
dug /-out		duration	
dul	dull +	duress	
dulcet		durge	dirge +
dulcimer		during	
duler	duller +	durt	dirt +
dulie	duly	durtie	dirty ⁴+
dull /ard/y		durtier	dirtier
dull er /est/ish		durty	dirty ⁴+
dulset	dulcet	dusbin	dustbin +
dulsimer	dulcimer	duse	deuce
duly		dusk /y	
dum	dumb +	dust¹ /er/y	
dumb /ly/ness		dust bin /man/pan	
dumb-bell		dusti er /est/ness	
dumbell	dumb-bell	Dutch /man/woman	
dumbfound¹		dutie	duty +
dumfound	dumbfound¹	dutifree	duty-free
dumfownd	dumbfound¹	dutiful /ly	
dumm y /ies		dut y /ies	
dumness	dumbness	duty-free	
dump¹ /er/y		duv	dove +
dumpling		duvtail	dovetail¹
dumy	dummy +	duvtale	dovetail¹

duz	does ★
duzn	dozen
duznt	doesn't
dwarf[1] /ish	
dwell /er/ing	
dwelt	
dwindle[2]	
dwindul	dwindle[2]
dworf	dwarf[1+]
dye ★† /d ★† /ing ★†	
†(change colour)	
dye	die ★+
dyed	died ★
dyehard	die-hard
dying ★ (death)	
dying	dyeing ★
dynamic /ally	
dynamics	
dynamite[2]	
dynamo /s	
dynast	
dynastey	dynasty +
dynastic /ally	
dynast y /ies	
dyne ★ (unit of force)	
dysentery	
dysentrey	dysentery
dyspep sia /tic	
dysprosium	

E

each	
eager /ly/ness	
eagle /-eyed/t	
eal	eel
ear /-ache/-drum	
earie	eerie ★
earie	eyrie ★
earl /dom	
earli er /est	
early /ish	
earmark[1]	
earn[1]★ (gain) /ings	

earnest /ly/ness	
ear-ring	
earshot	
earth[1] /iness	
earthen /ware	
earthl y /iness	
earthquake	
earth work /worm	
earwig	
ease[2]	
easel	
east /erly/ward/wards	
easten	eastern +
Easter	
eastern /er	
eas y /ier/ily/iness	
easy-going	
eat /able/en/er/ing	
eau-de-Cologne	
eaves	
eavesdrop[3] /per	
ebb[1]	
ebonie	ebony +
ebon y /ite	
ebulience	ebullience +
ebuliens	ebullience +
ebulient	ebullient
ebullien ce /t	
eccentric /ally/ity	
ecclesiastic /al/ally	
ecentric	eccentric +
ech	each
echelon	
echo[1] /es	
eclair	
eclare	eclair
eclectic	
eclesiastic	ecclesiastic +
eclipse[2]	
ecliptic	
ecolog	ecologue
ecologey	ecology +
ecological /ly	
ecologue	
ecolog y /ist	

economic /al/ally/s	
economise [2]	
economist	
econom y /ies	
ecsema	eczema
ecsentric	eccentric [+]
ecstas y /ies	
ecstatic /ally	
ectoplasm	
ecumenical	
eczema	
edd y [4] /ies	
edge [2] /ways/wise	
edgey	edgy [+]
edgie	edgy [+]
edg y /ily/iness	
edib le /ility	
edibul	edible [+]
edict	
edie	eddy [4+]
edifice	
edifiss	edifice
edif y [4] /ication	
edishun	edition
edit [1] /ion	
editer	editor [+]
editor /ial/ially	
educab le /ility	
educashun	education [+]
educat e [2] /ive/or	
education /al/ally/ist	
edy	eddy [4+]
eeger	eager [+]
eegle	eagle [+]
eel	
eer	ear [+]
eerie ★ (strange)	
eerie	eyrie ★
eeri er /est/ly/ness	
eermark	earmark [1]
eface	efface [2+]
efect	effect [1]
efectiv	effective [+]
efectual	effectual
efeet	effete

efemeral	ephemeral [+]
efeminacy	effeminacy
efeminasey	effeminacy
efeminate	effeminate [+]
efert	effort [+]
efervesence	effervescence
efervesent	effervescent
efervess	effervesce [2+]
efface [2] /ment	
effect [1]	
effective /ly	
effectual	
effeminacy	
effeminate /ly	
effervesce [2] /nce/nt	
effervess	effervesce [2+]
effete	
efficacious /ly/ness	
efficacy	
efficashus	efficacious [+]
efficienc y /ies	
efficient /ly	
effigey	effigy [+]
effig y /ies	
efflorescen ce /t	
effluen ce /t	
effluvium	
effort /less/lessly	
effronter y /ies	
effulgen ce /t	
effulgens	effulgence [+]
effus e [2] /ion/ive	
eficacious	efficacious [+]
eficacy	efficacy
eficasey	efficacy
eficashus	efficacious [+]
eficiency	efficiency [+]
eficient	efficient [+]
efigey	effigy [+]
efishency	efficiency [+]
efishensey	efficiency [+]
efishent	efficient [+]
efloresence	efflorescence [+]
efluence	effluence [+]
efluens	effluence [+]

efluent	effluent
efluvium	effluvium
efort	effort +
efronterey	effrontery +
efulgence	effulgence +
efuse	effuse 2+
efusiv	effusive
eg	egg 1+
egalitarian /ism	
ege	edge 2+
egg 1 /-cup/-shell	
Egipshun	Egyptian
Egiptian	Egyptian
egis	aegis
ego /ism/tism	
egocentric /ity	
egoist /ic/ically	
egosentric	egocentric +
egotist /ical/ically	
egress 1	

If you cannot find your word
under **egs** look under **ex**

egsact	exact 1+
egsamine	examine 2+
egsample	example
egsaust	exhaust 1+
egsecutive	executive
egsempt	exempt 1+
egsert	exert 1+
Egyptian	
eiderdown	
Eiffel (Tower)	
eight * (number)	
eighteen /th	
eighth /ly	
eight y /ies	
einsteinium	
either	
ejaculat e 2 /ion/ory	
eject 1 /ion/or	
ejis	aegis
eke 2	
eko	echo 1+

If you cannot find your word
under **eks** look under **ex**

ekscavate	excavate 2+
ekschange	exchange 2+
eksclaim	exclaim 1
eksite	excite 2+
ekumenical	ecumenical
ekwable	equable +
ekwabul	equable +
ekwal	equal 3+
ekwalise	equalise 2+
ekwalitey	equality +
ekwanimitey	equanimity
ekwashun	equation
ekwate	equate 2
ekwater	equator +
ekwation	equation
ekwerey	equerry +
ekwestrian	equestrian
ekwianguler	equiangular
ekwidistant	equidistant
ekwilateral	equilateral
ekwilibrium	equilibrium
ekwine	equine
ekwinox	equinox
ekwip	equip 3+
ekwitable	equitable +
ekwitabul	equitable +
ekwity	equity +
ekwivalence	equivalence +
ekwivocate	equivocate 2+
elaborat e 2 /ely/ion	
elapse 2	
elastic /ally/ity	
elat e 2 /ion	
elbow 1 /-room	
elder /ly	
elderberie	elderberry +
elderberr y /ies	
eldest	
elect 1 /ive/or/orate	
election /eering	
electoral /ly	
electric /al/ally	
electrician	

electricity
electrif *y* ⁴ /ication
electrocut *e* ² /ion
electrode
electrolight   electrolyte ⁺
electrolite   electrolyte ⁺
electrolysis
electrolyt *e* /ic
electromagnet /ic/ism
electromotive
electron /s
electronic /ally/s
electroplate ²
electroscope
electrovalency
elefant   elephant ⁺
elegan *ce* /t
elegans   elegance ⁺
elegey   elegy ⁺
eleg *y* /ies/iac
element /al/ary
elephant /ine
elevat *e* ² /ion/or
eleven /th
elf /in/ish
elfs   elves
elicit ¹★ (draw out)
elicit   illicit ★⁺
elide ²
elifant   elephant ⁺
eligans   elegance ⁺
eligant   elegant
eligib *le* /ility
eligibul   eligible ⁺
elikser   elixir
eliment   element ⁺
elimental   elemental
elimentarey   elementary
elimentrey   elementary
eliminat *e* ² /ion/or
elips   ellipse
elipsis   ellipsis
eliptic   elliptic ⁺
elision
élit *e* /ism/ist

elivashun   elevation
elivate   elevate ²⁺
elivater   elevator
elivation   elevation
elixir
Elizabethan
elk
ellipse
ellipsis
elliptic /al/ally
elocution /ary/ist
elokwence   eloquence ⁺
elokwens   eloquence ⁺
elokwent   eloquent
elongat *e* ² /ion
elope ² /ment/r
eloquen *ce* /t
eloquens   eloquence ⁺
else /where
elswere   elsewhere
elucidat *e* ² /ion/or
elude ²★ (avoid)
elude   allude ²★
elushun   elusion ★
elusidate   elucidate ²⁺
elusion ★ (escape)
elusive ★ (evasive) /ness
elusive   illusive ★
elver
elves (pl. of elf)
emaciat *e* ² /ion
emanat *e* ² /ion/ive
emancipat *e* ² /ion/or
emansipate   emancipate ²⁺
emasculat *e* ² /ion
emasiate   emaciate ²⁺
embalm ¹ /er/ment
embankment
embarass   embarrass ¹⁺
embargo ¹ /es
embark ¹ /ation
embarm   embalm ¹⁺
embarrass ¹ /ment
embass *y* /ies
embattle ²

embatul	embattle [2]	eminens	eminence [+]
embed [3]		eminent	imminent [*+]
embellish [1] /ment		emisarey	emissary [+]
ember		emishun	emission
embezul	embezzle [2+]	emissar*y* /ies	
embezzle [2] /ment/r		emission	
embitter [1] /ment		emit [3] /ter	
emblazon [1]		emollient	
emblem		emolument	
emblematic /ally		emoshun	emotion [+]
embodie	embody [4+]	emotion /al/ally	
embod*y* [4] /iment		emotive	
embolism		empanel [3]	
emboss [1]		emperer	emperor [+]
embrace [2]		emp*eror* /ress (fem.)	
embrase	embrace [2]	emphas*is* /es (pl.)	
embrio	embryo [+]	emphasise [2]	
embriologist	embryologist [+]	emphatic /ally	
embrocashun	embrocation	empire [*] (dominion)	
embrocation		empire	umpire [2*]
embroider [1] /y/ies		empiric /ism/ist	
embroil [1] /ment		empirical /ly	
embryo /s/nic		empirisist	empiricist
embryolog*ist* /y		emplacement	
emend	amend [1+]	emploi	employ [1+]
emerald		employ [1] /able/ee/er	
emerey	emery	emporium /s	
emerge [2] /nce		empower [1]	
emergenc*y* /ies		empress	impress [1+]
emergensey	emergency [+]	emptie	empty [4]
emergent		empti*er* /est/ness	
emerie	emery	empty [4]	
emershun	emersion	emulashun	emulation
emersion		emulat*e* [2] /ion/ive/or	
emery		emulshun	emulsion
emetic		emulsif*y* [4] /ication	
emfasis	emphasis [+]	emulsion	
emfasise	emphasise [2]	en route	
emfatic	emphatic [+]	enable [2] /ment	
emigrant		enabul	enable [2+]
emigrat*e* [2] /ion		enact [1] /able/ment	
emigray	émigré [+]	enamel [3] /ler	
émigré /e (fem.)		enamer	enamour [1]
eminen*ce* /t [*†]		enamour [1]	
†(distinguished)		encamp [1] /ment	

Word	Correction
encapsulat *e*[2] /ion	
encase[2] /ment	
encefalic	encephalic
encephalic	
enchant[1] /ment	
enchant *er* /ress (fem.)	
enciclical	encyclical
enciclopedia	encyclopedia[+]
encircle[2] /ment	
enclave	
enclos *e*[2] /ure	
encompass[1]	
encore[2]	
encounter[1]	
encourage[2] /ment	
encownter	encounter[1]
encroach[1] /er/ment	
encrust[1]	
encumb *er*[1] /rance	
encuridge	encourage[2+]
encurige	encourage[2+]
encyclical	
encyclopedi *a* /c	
end[1] /less/lessly	
endanger[1]	
endear[1] /ment	
endeavour[1]	
endeer	endear[1+]
endever	endeavour[1]
endive	
endocrine	
endorse[2] /ment/r	
endow[1] /ment	
end-product	
endur *e*[2] /able/ance	
enema /s	
enem *y* /ies	
energetic /ally	
energey	energy[+]
energise[2] /r	
energ *y* /ies	
enervat *e*[2] /ion	
enfebul	enfeeble[2+]
enfeeble[2] /ment	
enfold[1]	
enforce[2] /ment	
enforceab *le* /ility	
enfors	enforce[2+]
enforsible	enforceable[+]
enforsibul	enforceable[+]
enfranchise[2] /ment	
engage[2] /ment	
engender[1]	
engine /-driver	
enginear	engineer[1]
engineer[1]	
English /man/woman	
engraft[1] /ment	
engrain[1]	
engrave[2] /r	
engrayn	engrain[1]
engross[1]	
engulf[1]	
enhance[2] /ment	
enhans	enhance[2+]
eni	any
enibodie	anybody
enigma /tic/tically	
enihow	anyhow
enima	enema[+]
enithing	anything
eniware	anywhere
eniway	anyway
eniwhere	anywhere
eniwun	anyone
enjender	engender[1]
enjin	engine[+]
enjineer	engineer[1]
enjoi	enjoy[1+]
enjoiable	enjoyable[+]
enjoiabul	enjoyable[+]
enjoiment	enjoyment
enjoin[1]	
enjoy[1] /ment	
enjoyabl *e* /y	
enlace[2]	
enlarge[2] /able/ment/r	
enlase	enlace[2]
enlighten[1] /ment	
enlist[1]	

enliten	enlighten [1+]
enliven [1]	
enmit y /ies	
ennoble [2] /ment	
ennui	
enobul	ennoble [2+]
enormit y /ies	
enormous /ly/ness	
enormus	enormous [+]
enough	
enquire [2] /r	
enquir y /ies	
enrage [2]	
enrap	enwrap [3]
enrapcher	enrapture [2]
enrapture [2]	
enrich [1] /ment	
enrol [3] /ment	
enroot	en route
ensconce [2]	
enscons	ensconce [2]
ensefalic	encephalic
ensemble	
ensembul	ensemble
ensercal	encircle [2+]
enshore	ensure [2★]
enshore	insure [2★+]
enshrine [2]	
enshure	ensure [2★]
ensiclical	encyclical
ensiclopedia	encyclopedia [+]
ensign	
ensine	ensign
enslave [2] /ment	
ensnare [2]	
ensue [2]	
ensure [2★] (make certain)	
ensure	insure [2★+]
entail [1]	
entale	entail [1]
entangle [2] /ment	
entangul	entangle [2+]
enteprise	enterprise [+]
enter [1]	
enteritis	

enterpris e /ing	
entertain [1] /er/ment	
entertane	entertain [1+]
enthral [3] /ment	
enthrone [2] /ment	
enthuse [2]	
enthusias m /t	
enthusiastic /ally	
entice [2] /ment/r	
entire /ly/ty	
entise	entice [2+]
entitey	entity [+]
entitle [2] /ment	
entitul	entitle [2+]
entit y /ies	
entomb [1] /ment	
entomolog y /ical/ist	
entoom	entomb [1+]
entrails	
entrain [1]	
entrales	entrails
entrance [2] /ment	
entrans	entrance [2+]
entrant	
entrap [3]	
entreat [1] /ingly	
entreat y /ies	
entrée	
entreet	entreat [1+]
entrench [1] /ment	
entreprener	entrepreneur [+]
entrepreneur /ial	
entrey	entry [+]
entrust [1]	
entr y /ies	
entwine [2]	
enuf	enough
enumerat e [2] /ion/or	
enunciat e [2] /ion/or	
enunsiate	enunciate [2+]
envelop [1★†] /ment	
†(to surround)	
envelope ★ (stationery)	
envenom [1]	
envie	envy [4+]

envious /ly/ness		epok	epoch +
environ¹ /s		eporlet	epaulet
environment /al/ally		equab *le* /ility/ly	
envisage²		equal³ /ly	
envisidge	envisage²	equalis *e*² /ation/er	
envisige	envisage²	equalitey	equality +
envius	envious +	equalit *y* /ies	
envoi	envoy	equanimity	
envoy		equashun	equation
env *y*⁴ /iable/ier		equate²	
enwrap³		equater	equator +
enzime	enzyme	equation	
enzyme		equator /ial	
epaulet		equerr *y* /ies	
epawlet	epaulet	equestrian	
ephemeral /ly		equiangular	
epic /ally		equidistant	
epicenter	epicentre	equilateral	
epicentre		equilibrium	
epicure /an/anism		equine	
epidemic		equinoks	equinox
epiderm *is* /al		equinox	
epidiascope		equip³ /ment	
Epifaney	Epiphany	equitabl *e* /y	
epiglottis		equitabul	equitable +
epigraf	epigraph +	equit *y* /ies	
epigram		equivalen *ce* /t	
epigrammatic /ally		equivalens	equivalence +
epigraph /ic		equivocal /ly	
epilep *sy* /tic		equivocat *e*² /ion/or	
epilog	epilogue	equmenical	ecumenical
epilogue		er	err¹
Epiphany		era /s	
episcopacy		eradicat *e*² /ion/or	
episcopal /ian		erand	errand
episcopasey	episcopacy	erant	errant
episod *e* /ic/ical		eras *e*² /er/ure	
epist *le* /olary		erasher	erasure
episul	epistle+	erata	errata
epitaf	epitaph	eratic	erratic +
epitaph		eratum	erratum +
epithet		erban	urban
epitome		erbane	urbane +
epitomise²		erbanise	urbanise²+
epoch /al		erbanitey	urbanity

107

erchin	urchin	erudit *e* /ely/ion	
ere ★ (before)		erupt [1] /ion/ive	
erecshun	erection	erwig	earwig
erect [1] /ile/or		esay	essay [1+]
erection		escalat *e* [2] /ion/or	
erer	error	escallop [1]	
erge	urge [2+]	escapade	
ergency	urgency	escape [2] /ment	
ergensey	urgency	escapis *m* /t	
ergent	urgent	escarpment	
erie	eerie ★	eschew [1]	
erie	eyrie ★	eschu	eschew [1]
ering	ear-ring	escort [1]	
erk	irk [1+]	esel	easel
erksome	irksome	esence	essence
erksum	irksome	esens	essence
erl	earl [+]	esenshal	essential [+]
erlier	earlier [+]	esential	essential [+]
erly	early [+]	eshelon	echelon
ermine		eshoo	eschew [1]
ern	earn [1★+]	Eskimo /s (pl.)	
ern	urn ★	eskwire	esquire
ernest	earnest [+]	esofagus	esophagus
erode [2]		esophagus	
eroneous	erroneous [+]	esoteric /ally/ism	
eronius	erroneous [+]	especial /ly	
eror	error	espeshal	especial [+]
eroshun	erosion	espi	espy [4]
erosion		espionage	
erotic /a/ally/ism		esplanade	
err [1]		esplanaid	esplanade
errand		espous *e* [2] /al	
errant		espowse	espouse [2+]
erratic /ally		espresso	
errat *um* /a (pl.)		espy [4]	
erroneous /ly		esquire	
erronius	erroneous [+]	essay [1] /s/ist	
error		essence	
erstwhile		essens	essence
erstwile	erstwhile	essenshal	essential [+]
erth	earth [1+]	essential /ly	
erthen	earthen [+]	est	east [+]
erthley	earthly [+]	establish [1] /able/ment	
erthquake	earthquake	estate	
erudishun	erudition	esteam	esteem [1]

esteem [1]		eunuch	
Ester	Easter	euphemism	
estern	eastern [+]	euphemistic /ally	
esthet	aesthete [+]	euphon *y* /ious	
esthetic	aesthetic	euphori *a* /c	
estimable		Eurashun	Eurasian
estimabul	estimable	Eurasian	
estimat *e* [2] /ion/or		eurhythmics	
estrange [2] /ment		eurithmics	eurhythmics
estuar *y* /ies		European	
et cetera		euthanasia	
etch [1] /er		evacuashun	evacuation
ete	eat [+]	evacuat *e* [2] /ion	
eternal /ly		evacuee	
eternit *y* /ies		evad *e* [2] /able	
ether /eal		evaluat *e* [2] /ion	
ether	either	evangelic /al/ally	
ethic /al/ally/s		evangelis *e* [2] /m/t	
ethnic /ally		evanjelic	evangelic [+]
ethnolog *y* /ical		evaperate	evaporate [2+]
etholog *y* /ical		evaporat *e* [2] /ion/or	
ethos		evaquee	evacuee
etiket	etiquette	evashun	evasion
etimology	etymology [+]	evasion	
etiquet	etiquette	evasive /ly/ness	
etiquette		eve	
etsetera	et cetera	even [1] /ly/ness	
etymolog *y* /ical/ist		even *song* /tide	
eucalyptus /es		event /ful	
Eucharist		eventual /ly	
Euclid		eventualit *y* /ies	
eufemism	euphemism	ever /green/lasting	
eufoney	euphony [+]	evermore	
eufonious	euphonious	every /body/day/one	
eufonius	euphonious	every *thing* /where	
eufony	euphony [+]	eves	eaves
euforia	euphoria [+]	evesdrop	eavesdrop [3+]
euforic	euphoric	evict [1] /ion	
eugenic /ally/s		eviden *ce* [2] /tial	
Eukarist	Eucharist	evidens	evidence [2+]
Euklid	Euclid	evident /ly	
eulogey	eulogy [+]	evil /ly	
eulogis *e* [2] /m		evince [2]	
eulogistic /ally		evins	evince [2]
eulog *y* /ies		evocat *ion* /ive	

evoke [2]	
evolushun	evolution [+]
evolushunist	evolutionist
evolution /ary/ist	
evolve [2]	
evrie	every [+]
evry	every [+]
ewe ★ (sheep)	
ewe	yew ★
ewe	you ★
exacerbat *e* [2] /ion	
exacrabul	execrable
exact [1] /itude/ly/ness	
exaggerat *e* [2] /ion/or	
exalt [1] /ation	
examination	
examine [2] /r	
example	
exampul	example
exaserbate	exacerbate [2+]
exasperat *e* [2] /ion	
excavat *e* [2] /ion/or	
exceed [1] /ingly	
excel [3]	
excellen *ce* /t	
excellenc *y* /ies	
excellens	excellence [+]
excellensey	excellency [+]
excepshun	exception [+]
except [1]	
exception /able/al/ally	
excerpt [1]	
excess /ive/ively	
exchange [2] /able/r	
exchequer	
excis *e* [2] /able/ion	
excitab *le* /ility	
excitabul	excitable [+]
excite [2] /dly/ment	
exclaim [1]	
exclamashun	exclamation [+]
exclamat *ion* /ory	
exclu *de* [2] /sion	
exclusiv *e* /ely/ity	
excommunicat *e* [2] /ion	

excoriat *e* [2] /ion	
excrement	
excrescence	
excresens	excrescence
excreta	
excret *e* [2] /ion	
excruciating /ly	
excrushiating	excruciating [+]
excursion /ist	
excus *e* [2] /able/ably	
exebition	exhibition [+]
execrable	
execrabul	execrable
execrat *e* [2] /ion	
execut *e* [2] /ant/or/rix (fem.)	
execution /er	
executive	
exemplary	
exemplif *y* [4] /ication	
exempt [1] /ion	
exentric	eccentric [+]
exentricitey	eccentricity
exercise [2]	
exert [1] /ion	
exhal *e* [2] /ation	
exhaust [1] /ion	
exhaust *ible* /ive	
exhibit [1] /or	
exhibition /er	
exhibitionis *m* /t	
exhilara *te* [2] /nt/tion	
exhort [1] /ation	
exhum *e* [2] /ation	
exibition	exhibition [+]
exigence	
exigenc *y* /ies	
exigens	exigence
exigensey	exigency [+]
exigu *ous* /ity	
exile [2]	
exist [1] /ence/ent	
existens	existence
exit [1]	
exkwisit	exquisite [+]
exonerat *e* [2] /ion	

exorbitan ce /t	
exorcise² /r	
exorcis m /t	
exorsism	exorcism +
exorst	exhaust ¹+
exorstibul	exhaustible +
exort	exhort ¹+
exortashun	exhortation
exoteric	
exotic /ness	
expand¹	
expans e /ion	
expanshun	expansion
expansive /ly/ness	
expatriat e² /ion	
expect¹ /ation	
expectanc e /y	
expectans	expectance +
expectant /ly	
expedien ce /t	
expedienc y /ies	
expediens	expedience +
expedishun	expedition
expedishus	expeditious +
expedite² /r	
expedition	
expeditious /ly/ness	
expel³	
expend¹ /iture	
expendab le /ility	
expendabul	expendable +
expendicher	expenditure
expens e /ive	
experience²	
experiens	experience²
experiment¹ /ation	
experimental /ly	
expert /ise/ly	
expiat e² /ion	
expir e² /ation/y	
explain¹ /able	
explanashun	explanation +
explanat ion /ory	
explane	explain ¹+
explanetrey	explanatory

expletive	
explicabl e /y	
explicabul	explicable +
explicit /ly	
explisit	explicit +
explode²	
exploit¹ /ation/er	
explorashun	exploration +
explorat ion /ory	
explore² /r	
exploshun	explosion +
explos ion /ive	
exponent	
export¹ /ation/er	
expos e² /ure	
exposher	exposure
expostulat e² /ion	
expound¹	
expreshun	expression +
expresibul	expressible +
expresive	expressive +
express¹	
expressibl e /y	
expression /less	
expressive /ly	
expresso	espresso
expropriat e² /ion/or	
expulsion	
expunge²	
expurgate²	
expurgat ion /ory	
expurt	expert +
exquisite /ly/ness	
exseed	exceed ¹+
exsel	excel³
exselence	excellence +
exselens	excellence +
ex-service	
exstravagans	extravagance +
exsurpt	excerpt¹
extant	
extasey	ecstasy +
extatic	ecstatic +
extempor e /aneous	
extemporis e² /ation	

extend [1] /ible		eye [2]*† /ball/brow/s *†	
extenshun	extension	†(sight)	
extension		eyeglass /es	
extensive /ly		eyelash /es	
extent		eyelet * (hole for lace)	
extenuat e [2] /ion		eyelet	islet *
exterier	exterior	eye lid /sight	
exterior		eye-opener	
exterminat e [2] /ion/or		eye-witness	
external /ly		eyrie * (bird's nest)	
exterpate	extirpate [2]+	eyrie	eerie *
extinct /ion		eze	ease [2]
extinguish [1] /er		ezel	easel
extingwish	extinguish [1]+	ezier	easier
extirpat e [2] /ion		ezy	easy +
extol [3]			
extorshun	extortion +		
extort [1]		**F**	
extortion /ate/er/ist			
extra		fable /d	
extract [1] /able/ion/or		fabric	
extradishun	extradition	fabricat e [2] /ion/or	
extradit e [2] /able/ion		fabul	fable +
extramural		fabulous /ly	
extraneous /ly/ness		fabulus	fabulous +
extranius	extraneous +	façade	
extraordinar y /ily		face [2] /less	
extra-sensory		faceshus	facetious +
extravagan ce /t/tly		facet /ed	
extravaganza		facetious /ly	
extrawdinrey	extraordinary +	facia * (shop-front)	
extream	extreme +	facia	fascia *
extreme /ly		facial /ly	
extremist		facile	
extremit y /ies		facilitat e [2] /ion	
extricable		facilit y /ies	
extricabul	extricable	facshun	faction +
extricat e [2] /ion		facshus	factious
extrordinary	extraordinary +	facsimile /s	
extrover t /sion		fact /ual/ually	
exuberan ce /t		factio n /us	
exuberans	exuberance +	factishus	factitious
exud e [2] /ation		factitious	
exult [1] /ant/ation		factor	
exume	exhume [2]+	factor y /ies	

facultative	
facult y /ies	
fad /dish/dy	
fade ²	
faec es /al	
faeton	phaeton
fag ³ /-end	
faggot /-stitch	
fagot	faggot +
Fahrenheit	
fail ¹ /ure	
failier	failure
faim	fame ²
faimus	famous +
fain * (glad)	
fain	feign ¹*
faint ¹* (unconscious)	
faint	feint ¹*
faint-hearted	
fair ¹* (beauty, just)	
fair	fare ²*
fair er /est/way	
fairie	fairy +
fairwell	farewell
fairy /ies	
fairy land /-tale	
fait	fate ²*
faitful	fateful +
faith /ful/fully	
faithless /ly	
fake ² /r * (deceiver)	
fakir * (holy man)	
fal	fall +
falacious	fallacious
falacy	fallacy +
falanks	phalanx +
falanx	phalanx +
falasey	fallacy +
falashus	fallacious
falcon /er/ry	
fale	fail ¹+
falibility	fallibility
falible	fallible +
falibul	fallible +
falic	phallic +

fall /en/er/ing/-out	
fallacious	
fallac y /ies	
fallasey	fallacy +
fallib le /ility	
fallibul	fallible +
fallow ¹	
fallus	phallus
falout	fall-out
falow	fallow ¹
fals	false +
false /hood/ly/r/st	
falsetto /s	
falsif y ⁴ /ication/ier	
falsit y /ies	
falt	fault ¹+
falter ¹	
falure	failure
falus	phallus
fame ²	
familey	family +
familiar /ity	
familiaris e ² /ation	
familiaritey	familiarity
familier	familiar +
famil y /ies	
famine	
famish ¹	
famous /ly/ness	
famus	famous +
fan ³ /-belt	
fanatic /al/ally/ism	
fanatisism	fanaticism
fanci er /est/ly/ness	
fanciful /ly	
fanc y ⁴ /ies	
fane	feign ¹*
fanfair	fanfare
fanfare	
fansie	fancy ⁴+
fansier	fancier +
fansiful	fanciful +
fansy	fancy ⁴+
fant	faint ¹*
fantasey	fantasy +

fantasia	
fantasm	phantasm
fantasmagoria	phantasmagoria +
fantastic /ally	
fantas y /ies	
fantharted	faint-hearted
fantom	phantom
far /-fetched/-flung	
farad /ay	
farc e ² /ical/ically	
fare ²★ (get along)	
fare	fair ¹★
Farenheight	Fahrenheit
Farenhite	Fahrenheit
farer	fairer +
farewell	
fariland	fairyland +
faringeal	pharyngeal +
faringitis	pharyngitis
farinks	pharynx
farinx	pharynx
farisee	Pharisee +
faritale	fairy-tale
farm ¹ /er/house	
farmacist	pharmacist
farmacologey	pharmacology +
farmacopea	pharmacopoeia
farmacy	pharmacy +
farmasey	pharmacy +
farmasist	pharmacist
farmasutic	pharmaceutic +
farm stead /yard	
faro	Pharaoh
farse	farce ²+
farshal	farcical
far-sighted	
farth er ★† /est †(distant)	
farther	father ¹★
farthing /gale	
faryngeal	pharyngeal +
faryngitis	pharyngitis
farynx	pharynx
fasade	façade
fasces	

fascia ★ (architecture)	
fascia	facia ★
fascinat e ² /ion	
fascis m /t	
fase	face ²+
fase	phase ²
fasees	fasces
fasen	fasten ¹+
fasener	fastener
faseshus	facetious +
faset	facet +
fasetious	facetious +
fasha	facia ★
fasha	fascia ★
fashal	facial +
fashion ¹ /able/ably	
fashism	fascism +
fashist	fascist
fashon	fashion ¹+
fashonable	fashionable
fashonabul	fashionable
fasile	facile
fasilitate	facilitate ²+
fasilitey	facility +
fasinashun	fascination
fasinate	fascinate ²+
fasination	fascination
fast ¹	
fasten ¹ /er	
fastidious /ly/ness	
fastidius	fastidious +
fat ³ /ness/ter/test/ty	
fatal /ism/ly	
fatalist /ic/ically	
fatalit y /ies	
fate ²★ (destiny)	
fate	fête ²★
fateeg	fatigue ²
fateful /ly	
faten	fatten ¹
fath	faith +
father ¹★ (parent)	
father	farther ★+
father hood /land	
father(s)-in-law	

father *less* /ly		febus	Phoebus
fathom [1] /able		feces	faeces +
fatig	fatigue [2]	fech	fetch [1]
fatigue [2]		feckless	
faton	phaeton	fecund /ity	
fatten [1]		fed /-up	
fatuous /ly		federal /ism/ist/ly	
fatuus	fatuous +	federalis *e* [2] /ation	
faty	fatty	federat *e* [2] /ion	
faucet		fee	
fault [1] /ily/less/y		feeble /r/st	
faun ★ (Roman god)		feebul	feeble +
faun	fawn [1]★	feed /back/er/ing	
fauna		feef	fief
faux pas		feel /er/ing	
faver	favour [1]+	feeld	field [1]+
faverable	favourable	feend	fiend +
faverabul ·	favourable	feest	feast [1]
faverit	favourite +	feet ★ (pl. of foot)	
faveritism	favouritism	feet	feat ★
favour [1] /able/ably		feetle	foetal
favourit *e* /ism		feetus	foetus +
favrable	favourable	feif	fief
fawn [1]★ (young deer)		feign [1]★ (invent)	
fawn	faun ★	feign	fain ★
fawna	fauna	feild	field [1]+
fay ★ (fairy)		feildmarshal	field-marshal
fay	fey ★	feind	fiend +
fayton	phaeton	feint [1]★ (pretend)	
fea	fee	feint	faint [1]★
feacher	feature [2]+	fekless	feckless
fealty		fekund	fecund +
fear [1] /less/some		fekunditey	fecundity
fearful /ly		fel	fell
feasable	feasible +	fela	fellah
feasib *le* /ility/ly		felial	filial +
feasibul	feasible +	felicitat *e* [2] /ion	
feast [1]		felicit *y* /ous	
feat ★ (act)		feline	
feat	feet ★	felisitate	felicitate [2]+
feather [1] /weight/y		felisitey	felicity +
featherbed /ding		felisitus	felicitous
feature [2] /less		fell	
February		fellah	
Febuary	February	fellow /ship	

felon /ious		fertil e /ity	
felon y /ies		fertilis e ² /ation/er	
felow	fellow +	fertiv	furtive +
felt		ferule	ferrule
femail	female	ferus	ferrous
female		ferven cy /t	
femer	femur	ferver	fervour
feminin e /ity		fervour	
feminis m /t		fery	ferry ⁴+
femur		fes	fez
fence ² /r		fesant	pheasant
fenel	fennel	fesees	faeces +
feniks	phoenix	fesible	feasible+
fenix	phoenix	fesibul	feasible +
fennel		fester ¹	
fenobarbitone	phenobarbitone	festiv e /al	
fenol	phenol	festivit y /ies	
fenomenon	phenomenon +	festoon ¹	
fenomina	phenomena	fetch ¹	
fenominal	phenomenal +	fête ²★ (festival)	
fense	fence ²+	fête	fate ²★
fer	fir ★	feter	fetter ¹
fer	fur ★	fether	feather ¹+
feret	ferret ¹	fetherbed	featherbed +
feric	ferric +	fetherwait	featherweight
ferie	ferry ⁴+	fetid	
feris wheel	Ferris-wheel	fetish /ism/ist	
ferite	ferrite	fetlock	
ferl	furl ¹	fetter ¹	
ferlong	furlong	fettle ²	
ferment ¹ /ation		fetul	fettle ²
fermium		feud ¹	
fern /ery		feudal /ism	
fernis	furnace	fever /ed/ish	
feroci ous /ty		few	
feroshus	ferocious +	fewdal	feudal +
ferositey	ferocity	fewdalism	feudalism
ferous	ferrous	fey ★ (fated to die)	
ferret ¹		fey	fay ★
ferr ic /ous		fez	
Ferris-wheel		fezant	pheasant
ferrite		fial	file ²★+
ferrule		fial	phial ★
ferr y ⁴ /ies		fiancé /e (fem.)	
ferthest	furthest	fiansay	fiancé +

fiasco /s		fiksativ	fixative
fib [3] /ber		fikscher	fixture
fiber	fibre +	filament	
fibr e /ous		filander	philander [1]+
fibreglass		filanthropey	philanthropy +
fibrus	fibrous	filanthropic	philanthropic
fibula		filanthropist	philanthropist
fickle /ness		filantropy	philanthropy +
ficshun	fiction +	filarmonic	philharmonic
fiction /al		filateley	philately +
fictishus	fictitious +	filatelist	philatelist
fictitious /ly/ness		filch [1]	
ficul	fickle +	file [2]★ (tool, folder) /r	
fiddl e [2] /er/y		file	phial ★
fiddlesticks		filet	fillet [1]
fidelity		filharmonic	philharmonic
fidget [1] /iness/y		filial /ly	
fidle	fiddle [2]+	filibuster [1]	
fidul	fiddle [2]+	filie	filly +
fie		filigree	
fief		filip	fillip [1]
field [1] /-day/er		filistine	Philistine
field-marshal		fill [1] /er	
fiend /ish		fillet [1]	
fierce /ly/ness/r/st		fillip [1]	
fierey	fiery +	fill y /ies	
fierse	fierce +	film [1] /y	
fier y /ier/iest/ily		film-star	
fife		film-strip	
fifteen /th		filologey	philology +
fiftey	fifty +	filosofer	philosopher +
fifth		filosofey	philosophy
fift y /ies/ieth		filosofical	philosophical +
figer	figure [2]+	filosofise	philosophise [2]
figerativ	figurative +	filosopher	philosopher +
figerhead	figurehead	filosophical	philosophical +
figerhed	figurehead	filosophise	philosophise [2]
figet	fidget [1]+	filosophy	philosophy
fight /er/ing		filter [1]★ (pass, strainer)	
figment		filter	philtre ★
figurative /ly		filth /ier/iest/ily/iness/y	
figure [2] /head		filtrat e [2] /ion	
fiks	fix [1]+	filum	phylum
fiksashun	fixation +	fily	filly +
fiksation	fixation +	fin /ned/ny	

117

final * (at last)
finale * (the end)
finalis *e²* /t
finalit*y* /ies
finally
financ *e²* /ier
financial /ly
finans   finance ²⁺
finanshul   financial ⁺
finansier   financier
finch /es
find /er/ing
fine ² /r/ry/st
finerey   finery
finess   finesse
finesse
finger ¹ /print/tips
finicky
finikey   finicky
finish ¹ /er
finite
fiord
fir * (tree)
fir   fur *
fire ² /arm
fire-brigade
fire-engine
fire-escape
fire-extinguisher
firefl*y* /ies
fire *place* /work
firm ¹ /er/est/ness
firmament
first /-aid/-class/-rate
firth
firy   fiery ⁺
fiscal /ism/ly
fiseek   physique *
fish ¹ /ier/iest/iness/y
fisher   fissure
fisherm *an* /en (pl.)
fisher*y* /ies
fish- *hook* /monger
fishmunger   fishmonger
fishun   fission ⁺

fisic   physic *
fisic   physique *
fisical   physical ⁺
fisician   physician
fisicist   physicist
fisics   physics
fisile   fissile
fisiologey   physiology ⁺
fision   fission ⁺
fisionomey   physiognomy
fisiotherapey   physiotherapy
fisiotherapist   physiotherapist ⁺
fisique   physique *
fisishun   physician
fisisist   physicist
fissile
fission /able
fissure
fit ³ /ment/ness/ter/test
fite   fight ⁺
fitful /ly
five /pence/r
fix ¹ /edly
fixat *ion* /ive
fixcher   fixture
fixture
fiy   fie
fizle   fizzle ²
fizul   fizzle ²
fizz ¹ /y
fizzle ²
fjord
flabbergast ¹
flabb*y* /ier/iest/iness
flabergast   flabbergast ¹
flabie   flabby ⁺
flaby   flabby⁺
flaccid /ity/ness
flag ³ /ship/staff
flagellate ²
flagon
flagrancy
flagransey   flagrancy
flagrant /ly
flail ¹

flair ★ (instinct)	
flair	flare ²★
flak *e* ² /iness/y	
flaks	flax +
flaksen	flaxen
flaksid	flaccid +
flamable	flammable
flamabul	flammable
flamboiant	flamboyant
flamboyan *ce* /cy/t	
flamboyans	flamboyance +
flame ²	
flamingo /es	
flammable	
flammabul	flammable
flanel	flannel ³+
flange ²	
flank ¹	
flanle	flannel ³+
flannel ³ /ette/graph	
flanul	flannel ³+
flap ³ /per	
flare ²★ (light)	
flare	flair ★
flash ¹ /ier/iest/ily/y	
flash *back* /light	
flask	
flat /let/ly/test	
flaten	flatten ¹
flater	flatter ¹+
flatten ¹	
flatter ¹ /er	
flatulen *ce* /t	
flatulens	flatulence +
flaunt ¹	
flautist	
flaver	flavour ¹
flavour ¹	
flaw ¹★ (blemish) /less	
flaw	floor ¹★
flax /en	
flay ¹	
flea ★ (insect)	
flea	flee ★+
flea-bite	

fleat	fleet ¹
flebitis	phlebitis
fled	
fledgling	
flee ★ (run) /ing	
flee	flea ★
fleec *e* ² /y	
flees	fleece ²+
fleet ¹	
flegling	fledgling
flegm	phlegm+
flegmatic	phlegmatic
fleks	flex ¹
fleksible	flexible +
fleksibul	flexible +
flem	phlegm +
Flemish	
fler de lis	fleur-de-lis
flert	flirt ¹+
flesh /iness/y	
fleur-de-lis	
flew ★ (flight)	
flew	flu ★
flew	flue ★
flex ¹	
flexib *le* /ility/ly	
flexibul	flexible +
fli	fly +
flick ¹	
flicker ¹	
flier	flyer
flight /iness/y	
flimsie	flimsy +
flims *y* /ier/iest/ily/iness	
flinch ¹	
fling	
flint /y	
flipancy	flippancy +
flipansey	flippancy +
flipant	flippant
fliper	flipper
flippan *cy* /t	
flipper	
flirt ¹ /ation/atious	
flit ³	

flite	flight [+]	flower [1]* (plant) /y	
flo	floe *	flower	flour [1]*
flo	flow [1]*[+]	flownder	flounder [1]
float [1]		flownse	flounce [2]
flock [1] /s * (groups)		flowt	flout [1]
flocks	phlox *	flox	phlox *
floe * (ice)		flu * (cold)	
floem	phloem	flu	flew *
flog [3]		flu	flue *
flood [1] /-gate/lit		fluctuashun	fluctuation
floodlight /ing		fluctuat e [2] /ion	
flooid	fluid [+]	flud	flood [1+]
floor [1]* (in room)		fludlight	floodlight [+]
floor	flaw [1]*[+]	fludlite	floodlight [+]
flooride	fluoride [+]	flue * (pipe)	
floorine	fluorine	flue	flew *
floot	flute [2]	flue	flu *
flop [3] /pily/py		fluen cy /t	
flora /l/lly		fluff /iness/y	
Florentine		fluid /ity	
florescen ce *† /t *†		fluke [2]	
†(flowering)		fluks	flux
florescence	fluorescence *[+]	flummox [1]	
floresent	florescent *	flumuks	flummox [1]
florid		flumux	flummox [1]
floridate	fluoridate [2+]	flung	
florin		fluorescen ce*(light)/t *	
florist		fluoridat e [2] /ion	
floss /y		fluori de /ne	
flotashun	flotation	flurie	flurry [4+]
flotation		flurish	flourish [1]
flote	float [1]	flurr y [4] /ies	
flotilla		flurt	flirt [1+]
flotsam		flurtashun	flirtation
flotsum	flotsam	flurtation	flirtation
flounce [2]		flury	flurry [4+]
flounder [1]		flush [1]	
flouns	flounce [2]	fluster [1]	
flour [1]* (powder)		flute [2]	
flour	flower [1]*[+]	flutter [1]	
flourey	flowery	fluvial	
flourish [1]		flux	
flout [1]		fl$y$ /ies/yer/ying	
flow [1]* (to move) /n		flycatcher	
flow	floe *	flylea f /ves (pl.)	

fly *weight* /wheel	
fo	foe +
foal [1]	
foam [1]	
fob [3]	
fobia	phobia
focal	
focus [1] /er	
fodder [1]	
foder	fodder [1]
foe /s	
foet *us* /al	
fog [3] /horn	
fogg *y* /ier/iest/ily/iness	
foible	
foibul	foible
foier	foyer
foil [1]	
foist [1]	
foks	fox +
fold [1] /er	
fole	foal [1]
foliage	
foliat *e* [2] /ion	
folie	folly +
foliidge	foliage
folio [1] /s	
folk /-dance/-song	
folklor *e* /ist	
follow [1] /er	
foll *y* /ies	
folow	follow [1+]
foly	folly +
fome	foam [1]
foment [1] /ation/er	
fon	phon *
fond /er/est/ly/ness	
fondant	
fondle [2]	
fondul	fondle [2]
fone	phone [2]*
fonetic	phonetic +
fonie	phony
fonograf	phonograph +
fonografic	phonographic
fonograph	phonograph +
fonographic	phonographic
fonologey	phonology +
font	
fony	phony
food /s	
fool [1] /proof	
foolhard *y* /iness	
foolscap	
foot [1] /fall/hold/note	
football /er	
foot *path* /print	
foot *sore* /step/stool	
fop /pish	
for * (on behalf of)	
for	fore *
for	four *+
for ever	
forage [2] /r	
foram *en* /ina (pl.)	
forarm	forearm [1]
forbade	
forbarance	forbearance
forbare	forbear +
forbear /ance/ing	
forbid /den/ding	
forbode	forebode [2+]
forbore	
forcasel	forecastle
forcast	forecast +
forcastle	forecastle
forc *e* [2] /ible/ibly	
forceful /ly/ness	
forceps	
forclose	foreclose [2+]
ford [1] /able	
fore * (golf)	
fore	four *+
forearm [1]	
forebode [2] /r	
forecast /er	
forecastle	
foreclos *e* [2] /ure	
fored	forehead
forefathers	

forefinger		
forefoot		
forefront		
forego *(precede)/ing */ne *		
forego	forgo *+	
foreground		
forehand		
forehead		
foreign /er/ness		
foreknowledge		
foreland		
foreleg		
forelock		
forem *an* /en (pl.)		
foremast		
foremost		
foren	foreign +	
forener	foreigner	
forenoledge	foreknowledge	
forensic		
forerunner		
foresail		
foresaw		
foresee /able/ing/n		
foreshadow [1]		
foreshorten [1]		
foresight		
foresite	foresight	
foreskin		
forest [1] /ation/er/ry		
forestall [1]		
foretaste [2]		
foretell		
forethought		
foretold		
forewarn [1]		
foreword * (preface)		
foreword	forward [1]*	
forfathers	forefathers	
forfeit [1] /ure		
forficher	forfeiture	
forfinger	forefinger	
forfit	forfeit [1]+	
forfiture	forfeiture	
forfoot	forefoot	

forfront	forefront	
forfrunt	forefront	
forgather [1]		
forgave		
forge [2] /r		
forger *y* /ies		
forget /table/ting		
forgetful /ness		
forget-me-not		
forgiv *e* /able/eness/ing		
forgo *(waive)/ing*/ne*		
forgo	forego *+	
forgot /ten		
forground		foreground
forhand		forehand
forhead		forehead
forhed		forehead
forige		forage [2]+
forin		foreign +
fork [1]		
forland		foreland
forleg		foreleg
forlock		forelock
forlorn		
form [1] /al/ation		
formalis *e* [2] /ation		
formalit *y* /ies		
formally *†		
†(conventionally)		
formally		formerly *
forman		foreman +
format		
formative		
former /ly *†		
†(before now)		
formerly		formally *
formic		
formidabl *e* /y		
formidabul		formidable +
formost		foremost
formula /e/s (pls.)		
formulat *e* [2] /ion		
forn		faun *
forn		fawn [1]*
fornicat *e* [2] /ion		

fornolidge	foreknowledge
forruner	forerunner
forsable	forcible
forsail	foresail
forsak e /en/ing	
forsaw	foresaw
forse	force [2+]
forsee	foresee [+]
forseps	forceps
forsful	forceful [+]
forshadow	foreshadow [1]
forshorten	foreshorten [1]
forsible	forcible
forsite	foresight
forsithia	forsythia
forskin	foreskin
forsook	
forstall	forestall [1]
forsythia	
fort ★ (military)	
fort	fought ★
fortaste	foretaste [2]
forte ★ (strong point)	
forteen	fourteen [+]
fortel	foretell
forth ★ (forward)	
forth	fourth ★
forthcoming	
forthort	forethought
forth right /with	
fortie	forty [+]
fortif y [4] /ication/ier	
Fortin barometer	
fortissimo	
fortitude	
fortnight /ly	
fortnite	fortnight [+]
fortold	foretold
fortress	
fortuitous /ly	
fortuitus	fortuitous [+]
fortun e [2] /ate/ately	
fort y /ies/ieth	
forum	
forward [1]★ (advance)	

forward	foreword ★
forwarn	forewarn [1]
forwent	
forword	foreword ★
fosfate	phosphate
fosforesce	phosphoresce [2+]
fosforescent	phosphorescent
fosforess	phosphoresce [2+]
fosforus	phosphorous ★[+]
fosforus	phosphorus ★
fosil	fossil
fosilise	fossilise [2+]
fosphate	phosphate
fossil	
fossilis e [2] /ation	
foster [1] /-father/-mother	
foto	photo [+]
fotocopy	photocopy [+]
fotoelectric	photo-electric
fotofinish	photo-finish
fotogenic	photogenic
fotograf	photograph [1+]
fotografey	photography
fotograph	photograph [1+]
fotometer	photometer [+]
fotometrey	photometry
foton	photon
fotosinthesis	photosynthesis
fotostat	photostat
fototropism	phototropism
fought ★ (did fight)	
foul [1]★ (dirty) /ly/ness	
foul	fowl [1]★[+]
found [1] /ation/er/ling	
foundr y /ies	
fount	
fountain	
four ★ (number) /th ★	
four fold /some	
fourt	fort ★
fourt	fought ★
fourteen /th	
fourth	forth ★
fourty	forty [+]
fow	foe [+]

fowl [1]★ (bird) /er	
fowl	foul [1]★+
fownd	found [1]+
fowndashun	foundation
fowndation	foundation
fowndrey	foundry +
fownt	fount
fowntain	fountain
fox-hunt /ing	
fox-terrier	
foyble	foible
foyer	
fracshun	fraction +
fracshus	fractious
fraction /al/ally	
fractious	
fracture [2]	
fraeltey	frailty
fragile /ly	
fragility	
fragment [1] /ary/ation	
fragran ce /t	
fragrans	fragrance +
frail /ty/ties	
frait	freight +
frame [2] /work	
franc ★ (money)	
franchise [2]	
francium	
frank [1]★ (blunt) /ly/ness	
frankfurter	
frankincense	
frankium	francium
frantic /ally	
frase	phrase [2]★+
frasologey	phraseology
frate	freight +
fraternal /ly	
fraternis e [2] /ation	
fraternit y /ies	
fraud	
fraudulen ce /t	
fraudulens	fraudulence +
fraught	
fraut	fraught

frawd	fraud
frawdulence	fraudulence +
frawdulens	fraudulence +
frawdulent	fraudulent
frawt	fraught
fray [1] /s ★ (fights)	
frayl	frail +
frays	phrase [2]★+
freak [1] /ish	
freckle [2]	
frecul	freckle [2]
free /d/ing/ly/r/st	
freedom	
free-hand	
freehold /er	
freek	freak [1]+
freelance [2]	
freelans	freelance [2]
freemason /ry	
free-wheel [1]	
freez e ★ (cold) /er/ing	
freeze	frieze ★
freight /age/er	
freind	friend +
frekwency	frequency +
frekwensey	frequency +
frekwent	frequent [1]+
French /man/woman	
frend	friend +
frendly	friendly +
frendship	friendship
frenetic	phrenetic
frenologey	phrenology +
frenologist	phrenologist
frenzie	frenzy +
frenz y /ies/ied	
frequenc y /ies	
frequensey	frequency +
frequent [1] /er/ly	
fresco /es	
fresh /er/ly/ness	
freshen [1]	
fresko	fresco +
fret [3] /ful/fully	
fret -saw /work	

Freudian		frostbit *e* /ten	
fri	fry⁴	froth¹ /iness/y	
friable		frown¹	
friabul	friable	frowzie	frowzy⁺
friar		frowz *y* /ier/iest	
fricshun	friction⁺	froze /n	
friction /al		frugal /ity/ly	
friend /ship		fruishun	fruition
friendl *y* /ier/iest/iness		fruit¹ /ion	
frier	friar	fruiterer	
frieze * (ornament)		fruitful /ly/ness	
frigate		fruitless /ly/ness	
fright		fruit *y* /ier/iest/iness	
frighten¹		frump /ish	
frightful /ly/ness		frunt	front¹⁺
frigid /ity		fruntal	frontal
frill¹		fruntier	frontier
fringe²		fruntispiece	frontispiece
fripper *y* /ies		frustrat *e* ² /ion	
frisk¹ /ily/iness/y		frut	fruit¹⁺
frite	fright	fruterer	fruiterer
friteful	frightful⁺	frutful	fruitful⁺
friten	frighten¹	frutie	fruity⁺
friter	fritter¹⁺	frutier	fruiterer
fritter¹ /er		fry⁴	
frivol³ /ous		fu	few
frivolit *y* /ies		fucher	future⁺
frivolus	frivolous	fucherist	futurist⁺
frizul	frizzle²⁺	fucheristic	futuristic
frizz¹ /y		fuchsia	
frizzl *e* ² /y		fudal	feudal⁺
frock¹		fudalism	feudalism
frog /man/men (pl.)		fuddle²	
froidian	Freudian	fude	feud¹
frolic /some		fudge²	
frolick *ed* /ing		fudul	fuddle²
front¹ /age/al/ally		fuel³	
frontier		fug /gy	
frontispiece		fugitive	
froogal	frugal⁺	ful	full⁺
frooishun	fruition	fulblooded	full-blooded
frooition	fruition	fulbluded	full-blooded
froot	fruit¹⁺	fulcrum	
frootful	fruitful⁺	fulfil³ /ment	
frost¹ /ily/y		full /-blooded/er/-time	

125

fulscap	foolscap	furst	first [+]
fulsome /ly/ness		furstaid	first-aid
fulsum	fulsome [+]	furstrate	first-rate
fumble [2] /r		furth	firth
fumbul	fumble [2+]	further [1] /more/most	
fume [2]		furtherance	
fumigat *e* [2] /ion/or		furthest	
fun /nily/ny		furtive /ly	
funcshun	function [1+]	fur *y* /ies	
funcshunrey	functionary	furze	
function [1] /ary		fus	fuss [1+]
functional /ly		fus *e* [2] /ion	
fund [1]		fuselage	
fundamental /ly		fusha	fuchsia
funel	funnel [3]	fusib *le* /ility	
funer *al* /eal		fusibul	fusible [+]
fung *us* /i (pl.)		fusie	fussy
funicular		fusier	fussier [+]
funiculer	funicular	fusilade	fusillade
funily	funnily	fusilage	fuselage
funk [1]		fusilier	
funnel [3]		fusilige	fuselage
funn *y* /ier/iest/ily		fusillade	
fur ★ (coat)		fuss [1] /y	
fur	fir ★	fussie	fussy
furie	furry [+]	fussi *er* /est/ly/ness	
furie	fury [+]	fustie	fusty [+]
furier	furrier	fust *y* /ier/iest/ily/iness	
furious /ly		fusy	fussy
furius	furious [+]	futil *e* /ity	
furl [1]		futur *e* /ism/ity	
furlong		futurist /ic	
furm	firm [1+]	fuzz /ily/iness	
furmament	firmament	fwayay	foyer
furment	ferment [1+]	fyord	fiord
furmentashun	fermentation	fyord	fjord
furmentation	fermentation	fysical	physical [+]
furn	fern [+]	fysically	physically
furnace		fysician	physician
furnicher	furniture	fysicist	physicist
furnis	furnace	fysick	physic ★
furnish [1] /er		fysick	physique ★
furniture		fysicks	physics
furrow [1]		fysicley	physically
furr *y* /ier/iest/iness		fysiologey	physiology [+]

fysionomey	physiognomy	galery	gallery [+]
fysiotherapey	physiotherapy	Galic	Gaelic ★
fysiotherapist	physiotherapist [+]	Galic	Gallic ★
fysique	physique ★	galie	galley
fysishun	physician	galium	gallium
fysisist	physicist	galivant	gallivant [1]
		gall [1]	

G

gabardine		gallant /ry	
gabble [2]★ (talk) /r		galler*y* /ies	
gable ★ (on roof)		galley	
gabul	gabble [2]★[+]	Gallic ★†	
gabul	gable ★	†(of Gaul, French)	
gad [3] /about		gallic	Gaelic ★
gadget /ry		gallium	
gadolinium		gallivant [1]	
gael	gale	gallon	
Gaelic ★ (language)		gallop [1] /er	
gaf	gaffe	gallows	
gaffe		galon	gallon
gag [3]		galop	gallop [1][+]
gaga		galore	
gage	gauge [2][+]	galoshes	
gagercounter	Geiger counter	galows	gallows
gaget	gadget [+]	galvanic	
gaggle [2]		galvanis*e* [2] /ation/m	
gagit	gadget [+]	galvanometer	
gagul	gaggle [2]	galy	galley
gai*ety* /ly		gambit	
gain [1] /er/ful/fully		gamble [2]★ (games) /r	
gait ★ (walk)		gambol [3]★ (frolic)	
gait	gate [2]★[+]	game /-bird/-cock	
gaiter /ed		gamekeeper	
gaitey	gaiety [+]	gamesmanship	
gal	gall [1]	gamie	game [+]
gala		gaming	
galactic		gammon	
galaksey	galaxy [+]	gamon	gammon
galant	gallant [+]	gamut	
galantrey	gallantry	gamy	game [+]
galaw	galore	gander [1]	
galax*y* /ies		ganet	gannet
gale		gang [1] /er	
		gangling	
		gang-plank	
		gangreen	gangrene [+]

gangren *e* /ous		gash [1]	
gangrenus	gangrenous	gasha	geisha
gangster /ism		gasket	
gangway		gaslight	
gannet		gaslite	gaslight
gaol [1]★ (prison) /bird/er		gasoline	
gape [2]		gasometer	
garage [2]		gasp [1]	
garantee	guarantee ★+	gastley	ghastly +
garantor	guarantor +	gastri *c* /tis	
garb [1]		gastronom *y* /ic/ical	
garbage		gate [2]★ (entrance) /way	
garbige	garbage	gate	gait ★
garble [2]		gate-crash [1]	
garbul	garble [2]	gater	gaiter +
gard	guard [1]+	gather [1] /er	
garden [1] /er		gauche	
gardenia		gaudie	gaudy +
gardian	guardian +	gaud *y* /ily/iness	
gardroom	guard-room	gauge [2] /r	
gardsman	guardsman	gaunt /let	
garet	garret	gauze	
gargantuan		gave	
gargle [2]		gawdie	gaudy +
gargoil	gargoyle	gawk [1] /iness	
gargoyle		gawl	gall [1]
gargul	gargle [2]	gawnt	gaunt +
garish		gawntlet	gauntlet
garison	garrison [1]	gawse	gorse
garland [1]		gay /er/est	
garlic /ky		gayety	gaiety +
garment [1]		Gaylic	Gaelic ★
garner [1]		gayn	gain [1]+
garnet		gaysha	geisha
garnish [1]		gaze [2] /r	
garnit	garnet	gazel	gazelle
garot	garrotte [2]	gazelle	
garret		gazer	geyser
garrison [1]		gazet	gazette [2]
garrot	garrotte [2]	gazette [2]	
garrotte [2]		ge gaw	gew-gaw
garrulous /ly		gear [1] /box	
garter /ed		gees	geese
garulus	garrulous +	geese (pl. of goose)	
gas [3] /eous/es/-mask		Geiger counter	

geisha		genus	
gel [3]		geny	genie
gelatin	gelatine [+]	geocentric	
gelatin e /ous		geofisical	geophysical
gelatinus	gelatinous	geofisics	geophysics [+]
geld [1]		geofysical	geophysical
gelignite		geofysics	geophysics [+]
gem [3] /my		geografey	geography [+]
Gemini		geografic	geographic
gendarme		geografical	geographical [+]
gender [1]		geographical /ly	
gene		geograph y /er/ic	
genealog y /ist		geological /ly	
genee	genie	geolog y /ist	
general /ly		geometrey	geometry
generalis e [2] /ation		geometric /al/ally	
generalit y /ies		geometry	
generat e [2] /ion/or		geophysic s /al/ist	
generative		geosentric	geocentric
generic /ally		geranium /s	
generosity		gerd	gird [1+]
generous /ly/ness		gerder	girder
generus	generous [+]	gerdle	girdle [2]
genetic /ally/s		gerdul	girdle [2]
geney	genie	geriatric /ian/s	
genial /ity/ly		gerilla	gorilla ★
genie		gerilla	guerrilla ★
geniologey	genealogy [+]	gerkin	gherkin
genital /s		gerl	girl [+]
genitive		gerlish	girlish
geni us /i/uses (pls.)		germ	
genocide		German	
genoside	genocide	germane	
genre		Germanic	
genteel /ism/ly		germanium	
gentile		germicid e /al	
gentility		germinat e [2] /ion	
gentle [2] /ness/r/st		germiside	germicide [+]
gentlem an /en (pl.)		gerontology	
gentrey	gentry	gerth	girth
gentry		gerund /ive	
gentul	gentle [2+]	gescher	gesture [2]
gentulman	gentleman [+]	gess	guess [+]
genuin	genuine [+]	gesswerk	guesswork
genuine /ly/ness		gesswork	guesswork

P.D.P.S.—I

gest	guest ★
gesticulat *e* [2] /ion	
gesture [2]	
get /ting	
getto	ghetto +
gew-gaw	
geyser	
ghastl *y* /ier/iest/iness	
gherkin	
ghetto /s	
ghost [1] /ly	
ghoul /ish	
giant /ess (fem.)	
gibber [1] /ish	
gibbet [1]	
gibbon	
gibe [2]★ (taunt)	
gibe	gybe [2]★
giber	gibber [1]+
giberish	gibberish
gibet	gibbet [1]
giblets	
gibon	gibbon
gidance	guidance
gidans	guidance
gidd *y*/ier/iest/ily/iness	
gide	guide [2]+
gidie	giddy +
gidily	giddily
gidy	giddy +
gift /ed	
gig	
gigantic /ally	
giggle [2] /r	
gigolo	
gigul	giggle [2]+
gil	gill [1]
gild [1]★ (gold cover)	
gild	guild ★
gilder	guilder
Gildhall	Guildhall
gile	guile +
gileless	guileless
gill [1]	
giloteen	guillotine [2]

gilotine	guillotine [2]
gilt ★ (gold leaf)	
gilt	guilt ★
gilt-edged	
giltey	guilty +
gilty	guilty +
gim	gym +
gimick	gimmick +
gimkana	gymkhana
gimlet	
gimmick /ry/y	
gimnasium	gymnasium +
gimnastics	gymnastics
gin [3]	
ginecologey	gynaecology +
ginecologist	gynaecologist
gingam	gingham
ginger [1] /bread/ly	
gingham	
ginie	guinea +
ginifowl	guinea-fowl
ginipig	guinea-pig
ginjer	ginger [1]+
ginjerbred	gingerbread
gipsey	gipsy +
gipsie	gipsy +
gipsum	gypsum
gips *y* /ies	
giraf	giraffe
giraffe	
girashun	gyration
girate	gyrate [2]+
giration	gyration
gird [1] /er	
girdle [2]	
girdul	girdle [2]
girl /hood/ish	
giro ★ (banking)	
giro	gyro ★+
girth	
gise	guise
gist	
gitar	guitar +
gitarist	guitarist
give /n/r	

giving
Giy Forks   Guy Fawkes
gizerd   gizzard
gizzard
glacia *l* /tion
glacier
glad /der/dest/ly
gladden [1]
glade
gladen   gladden [1]
gladiater   gladiator
gladiator
gladiol *us* /i (pl.)
glamer   glamour
glamerus   glamorous +
glamoris *e* [2] /ation
glamorous /ly/ness
glamour
glance [2]
gland /ular
glanduler   glandular
glans   glance [2]
glare [2]
glas   glass +
glashal   glacial +
glasiashun   glaciation
glasiation   glaciation
glasier   glacier
glass /es/ily
glassware
glaswear   glassware
glaz *e* [2] /ier
glea   glee +
gleam [1]
glean [1] /er
glee /ful/fully
gleem   gleam [1]
gleen   glean [1+]
glib /ber/best/ly
glicerine   glycerine
glide [2] /r
glimmer [1]
glimpse [2]
glint [1]
glisen   glisten [1]

gliserin   glycerine
glisten [1]
glitter [1]
glo   glow [1]
gloaming
gloat [1]
glob *e* /al/ally
globe-trott *er* /ing
globul *e* /ar
globuler   globular
gloming   gloaming
gloo   glue [2+]
gloocose   glucose
glooie   gluey
gloom /y
gloomi *er* /est/ly/ness
glooten   gluten *+
glorie   glory [4+]
glorif *y* [4] /ication
glorius   glorious
glor *y* [4] /ies/ious
glos   gloss [1+]
glosarey   glossary +
gloss [1] /ier/iest/iness/y
glossar *y* /ies
glote   gloat [1]
glotis   glottis +
glott *is* /al
glove [2] /r
glow [1]
glower [1]
glucose
glue [2] /y
glum /ly/mer/mest
glut [3]
glut *en* *† /inous*†
    †(sticky substance)
gluten   glutton *+
glutinus   glutinous *
gluton   glutton *+
glutonus   gluttonous *
glutony   gluttony
glutton *† /ous *† /y
    †(greedy)
glutton   gluten *+

gluv	glove [2+]
glycerine	
gnarl [1]	
gnash [1]	
gnat	
gnaw [1]	
gnom e /ish	
gnu ★ (animal)	
go /er/es/ing	
goad [1]	
go -ahead /-kart	
goal ★† /ie/keeper/less	
†(aim, sport)	
goal	gaol [1★+]
goat /ee	
goatherd	
gobble [2] /r	
go-between	
goblet	
goblin	
gobul	gobble [2+]
gocart	go-kart
god /child/like	
god -daughter /son	
goddess (fem.)	
gode	goad [1]
god father /mother	
god forsaken /head	
goggle [2]	
gogul	goggle [2]
goiter	goitre
goitre	
gold /en/finch/fish	
goldsmith	
gole	goal ★+
golf [1] /er	
golie	goalie
golliwog	
gon	gone +
gondol a /ier	
gone /r	
gong [1]	
gonoria	gonorrhoea
gonorrhoea	
good /ly/ness/will	

good-bye	
good-humered	good-humoured
good-humoured	
goodie	goody +
good-looking	
good y /ies	
gool	ghoul +
goolash	goulash
goolish	ghoulish
goord	gourd
goormand	gourmand +
goormay	gourmet
goose /flesh	
gooseberie	gooseberry +
gooseberr y /ies	
Gordian	
Gordyan	Gordian
gor e [2] /y	
gorge [2] /r	
gorgeous /ly/ness	
Gorgonzola	
gorgus	gorgeous +
gorilla ★ (ape)	
gorilla	guerrilla ★
gorse	
gosamer	gossamer
gosip	gossip [1+]
gosling	
gospel /ler	
gossamer	
gossip [1] /er/y	
gost	ghost [1+]
gostly	ghostly
got /ten	
gote	goat +
goteherd	goatherd
Gothic	
gouge [2] /r	
goulash	
gourd	
gourmand /ism	
gourmet	
gout /y	
govern [1] /able/ance	
governer	governor +

government /al	
govern*or* /ess (fem.)	
govner	governor [+]
gowge	gouge [2+]
gown	
gowt	gout [+]
grab [3] /ber	
grace [2] /less	
graceful /ly	
gracious /ly/ness	
gradashun	gradation
grad*e* [2] /ation/er	
gradient	
gradual /ly	
graduat*e* [2] /ion/or	
graf	graph [1]
graffiti	
grafic	graphic [+]
graficley	graphically
grafite	graphite
grafiti	graffiti
grafologey	graphology [+]
grafologist	graphologist
graft [1] /er	
grail	
grain [1]	
graling	grayling
gramar	grammar [+]
gramatical	grammatical [+]
gramefone	gramophone
gramer	grammar [+]
grammar /ian	
grammatical /ly	
gramophone	
granar*y* /ies	
grand /ee/eur/stand	
grandchild /ren (pl.)	
grand -*daughter* /son	
grand*father* /mother	
grandiloquen*ce* /t	
grandios*e* /ity	
grane	grain [1]
grange	
granie	granny [+]
granit	granite

granite	
grann*y* /ies	
grant [1]	
granulat*e* [2] /ion	
granul*e* /ar/arity	
grany	granny [+]
grape /fruit/-shot	
graph [1]	
graphic /al/ally	
graphite	
grapholog*y* /ist	
graple	grapple [2]
grapnel	
grapple [2]	
grapul	grapple [2]
gras	grass [1+]
grase	grace [2+]
grashus	gracious [+]
grasp [1]	
grass [1] /es/hopper	
grasshoper	grasshopper
grate [2★] (fire) /r	
grate	great [★+]
grateful /ly/ness	
gratif*y* [4] /ication	
gratis	
gratitude	
gratuitey	gratuity [+]
gratuitous /ly/ness	
gratuitus	gratuitous [+]
gratuit*y* /ies	
grave /ly/yard	
gravel [3] /ly	
gravie	gravy
gravitashun	gravitation [+]
gravitate [2]	
gravitation /al	
gravity	
gravy	
gray	grey [+]
grayhound	greyhound
grayhownd	greyhound
grayl	grail
grayling	
grayn	grain [1]

graz *e* ² /ier		griffin	
greas *e* ² /y		gril	grill ¹⁺
greasie	greasy	grill ¹ /-room	
greasi *er* /est/ly/ness		grim /ly/mer/mest/ness	
great ★ (big) /er/est		grimace ²	
great	grate ²★⁺	grimas	grimace ²
greatful	grateful ⁺	grim *e* ² /ier/iest/iness/y	
grede	greed ⁺	grin ³	
greed /y		grind /er/ing	
greedi *er* /est/ly/ness		grip ³★ (hold)	
green /er/ery/ness		grip	gripe ²★
green*gage* /grocer		gripe ²★ (colic pain)	
green *horn* /house		grisel	gristle
Greenwich mean time		grisly ★ (ghastly)	
greese	grease ²⁺	grisly	gristly ★
greesie	greasy	grist	
greet ¹		gristle	
gref	grief	gristly ★ (full of gristle)	
gregarious /ly/ness		grisul	gristle
gregarius	gregarious ⁺	grit ³ /tily/ty	
greif	grief	grizul	grizzle ²
greive	grieve ²⁺	grizzle ²	
greivus	grievous	gro	grow ⁺
gremlin		groan ¹★ (moan)	
grenad *e* /ier		groän	grown ★⁺
grene	green ⁺	grocer ★ (shop) /y/ies	
grenegage	greengage ⁺	grocer	grosser ★
grengroser	greengrocer	grogg *ily* /iness/y	
grenich	Greenwich ⁺	groin	
gresier	greasier ⁺	grone	groan¹★
grete	greet ¹	grone	grown ★⁺
grevance	grievance	groo	grew
grevans	grievance	grooel	gruel ³
greve	grieve ²⁺	groom ¹	
grevus	grievous	groop	group ¹
grew		groosum	gruesome ⁺
grey /er/est/hound		groov *e* ² /y	
grid		grope ²	
griddle ²		gros	gross ¹⁺
gridiron		groser	grocer ★⁺
gridul	griddle ²	groser	grosser ★
grief		groserey	grocery
grievance		gross ¹ /er ★ (fatter) /ly	
grievans	grievance	grotesk	grotesque ⁺
griev *e* ² /ous/ously		grotesque /ly	

groto	grotto [+]	gufaw	guffaw [1]
grotto /es		guffaw [1]	
ground [1] /less		guid *e* [2] /ance	
ground -*swell* /work		guild ★ (association)	
group [1]		guild	gild [1]★
grouse [2] /r		guilder	
grove		Guildhall	
grovel [3] /ler		guile /ful/less	
grow /er/ing		guillotine [2]	
growl [1] /er		guilt ★ (law-breaking)	
grown ★† /-up		guilt *y* /ier/iest/ily	
†(matured)		guinea /-fowl/-pig	
grownd	ground [1+]	guise ★ (pretence)	
growndswell	ground-swell [+]	guitar /ist	
growse	grouse [2+]	gul	gull [1]
growth		gulash	goulash
grub [3] /by		gulet	gullet
grubbi *er* /est/ly/ness		gulf [1]	
grudge [2]		Gulf-stream	
gruel [3]		gulible	gullible [+]
gruesome /ly/ness		gulibul	gullible [+]
gruf	gruff [+]	gulie	gully [4+]
gruff /er/est		gull [1]	
gruge	grudge [2]	gullet	
grumble [2] /r		gullib *le* /ility	
grumbul	grumble [2+]	gull *y* [4] /ies	
grumpie	grumpy [+]	gulp [1]	
grump *y* /ily/iness		guly	gully [4+]
grunt [1] /er		gum [3] /boil/my/-tree	
grusome	gruesome [+]	gumption	
grusum	gruesome [+]	gumshun	gumption
gruyare	gruyère	gun [3] /powder	
gruyère		gunl	gunwale
guano		gunner /y	
guarantee ★ (pledge) /d/ing		gunwale	
guarant *or* /y ★ (undertaking)		gurgle [2]	
guard [1] /sman		gurgul	gurgle [2]
guardian /ship		gush [1]	
guard-room		gust [1]	
guava		gusto	
guerrilla ★ (war)		gut [3]	
guerrilla	gorilla ★	guter	gutter [+]
guess /ing/work		guteral	guttural [+]
guessed ★ (estimated)		gutersnipe	guttersnipe
guest ★ (visitor)		gutter /snipe	

guttural /ly	
guvern	govern [1+]
guvernable	governable
guvernabul	governable
guvernance	governance
guvernans	governance
guverness	governess
guvernment	government [+]
guvnable	governable
guvner	governor [+]
guy [1] /s * (effigies)	
Guy Fawkes	
guzul	guzzle [2+]
guzzle [2] /r	
gwano	guano
gwave	guava
gybe [2]* (sailing)	
gybe	gibe [2]*
gym /nast/nastics	
gymkana	gymkhana
gymkhana	
gymnasium /s	
gynaecolog y /ist	
gypsum	
gyrat e [2] /ion/ory	
gyro * /compass	
gyro	giro *
gyroscop e /ic	

H

habeas corpus	
haberdasher /y	
habias corpus	habeas corpus
habichual	habitual [+]
habichuate	habituate [2+]
habitab le /ility	
habitabul	habitable [+]
habitashun	habitation
habitat	
habitation	
habitual /ly	
habituat e [2] /ion	
hach	hatch [1+]

hacherey	hatchery [+]
hachet	hatchet
hack [1] /-saw	
hackle [2]	
hackney [1]	
hackul	hackle [2]
had /n't	
haddock	
Hades	
hadock	haddock
haemofilia	haemophilia [+]
haemoglobin	
haemophilia /c	
haemoroids	haemorrhoids
haemorrhage	
haemorrhoids	
haf	half [+]
hafnium	
hafpenie	halfpenny [+]
hafpeny	halfpenny [+]
hagard	haggard
hagerd	haggard
haggard	
haggis	
haggle [2] /r	
hagis	haggis
hagul	haggle [2+]
hai	hay *[+]
haifever	hay fever
hail [1]* (salute, icy rain)	
hail	hale *
hailo	halo *[+]
hailstone	
hair * (on head) /line/y	
hair	hare *[+]
hair	heir *
hairbreadth	
hairi er /est/ness	
hair-raising	
hake	
halcion	halcyon
halcyon	
hale * (hearty)	
hale	hail [1]*
haleluya	hallelujah

halestone	hailstone
hal *f* /ves (pl.)	
half-*cast*/-hearted/-way	
halfpenn *y* /ies	
half-wit /ted	
halibut	
halilooya	hallelujah
hall ★ (room)	
hall	haul [1]★+
hallelujah	
hall-mark [1]	
hallo ★ (cry)	
hallow [1]★ (make holy)	
Hallowe'en	
hallucinat *e* [2] /ion/ory	
hallucinogen	
halmark	hall-mark [1]
halo ★(disc of light) /es	
halo	hallow [1]★
halogens	
halow	hallow [1]★
Haloween	Hallowe'en
halsiun	halcyon
halt [1] /er/ingly	
halusinate	hallucinate [2]+
halusinogen	hallucinogen
halve [2]	
halyard	
halyerd	halyard
ham /burger	
hamer	hammer [1]+
ham-fisted	
hamlet	
hammer [1] /er	
hammock	
hamper [1]	
hamster	
hamstring	
hand [1] /ful/fuls	
handbag	
handcuff [1]	
handicap [3]	
handicraft	
handie	handy +
handiwork	

handkerchief /s	
handle [2] /bar/r	
hand-made	
handriten	handwritten
handriting	handwriting +
handshake	
handsome ★ (looks) /ly	
handul	handle [2]+
handwrit *ing* /ten	
hand *y* /ier/iest/ily	
hang [1] /over	
hangar ★ (shelter)	
hanger ★ (for clothes)	
hangkerchif	handkerchief +
hangman	
hank	
hanker [1]	
hankerchief	handkerchief +
hankuf	handcuff [1]
hansom ★ (cab)	
hansom	handsome ★+
hansum	handsome ★+
hapen	happen [1]
haphazard /ly/ness	
hapie	happy +
hapier	happier +
hapless	
happen [1]	
happi *er* /est/ly/ness	
happy /-go-lucky	
hapy	happy +
hara-kiri	
harang	harangue [2]
harangue [2]	
haras	harass [1]+
harass [1] /ment	
harber	harbour [1]+
harbour [1] /age	
hard /er/est/ly/ship	
harden [1]	
hard-hearted	
hardie	hardy +
hardware	
hardwear	hardware
hard *y* /ier/iest/ily	

hare ★ (animal) /bell		hash ¹	
hare	hair ★+	hashish	
hare-brained		hasock	hassock
harem		hassock	
harico	haricot	hast *e* /ily/iness/y	
haricot		hasten ¹	
harier	hairier +	hat ³ /ter	
hark ¹		hatch ¹ /es/way	
harlekwin	harlequin +	hatcherey	hatchery +
harlequin /ade		hatcher *y* /ies	
harlot /ry		hatchet	
harm ¹ /ful/fully		hate ² /ful/r	
harmless /ness		hatred	
harmonic /a/ally		hatrid	hatred
harmonious /ly/ness		haught *y* /ier/iest/ily	
harmonis *e* ² /ation		haul ¹★ (pull in) /age	
harmonium		haul	hall ★
harmonius	harmonious +	haulm	
harmon *y* /ies		haunch /es	
harness ¹ /er		haunt ¹	
harow	harrow ¹	hav	have +
harp ¹ /ist		Havana	
harpoon ¹ /er		have /n't	
harpsichord		haven	
harpsicord	harpsichord	havent	haven't
harrier		haversack	
harrow ¹		having	
harsh /ly/ness		havoc	
hart ★ (deer)		hawk ¹ /er/ish	
hart	heart ★+	hawl	haul ¹★+
hartbrake	heartbreak +	hawlidge	haulage
hartbroken	heartbroken +	hawlige	haulage
hartburn	heartburn +	hawm	haulm
harten	hearten ¹	hawnch	haunch +
harth	hearth	hawnet	hornet
hartie	hearty +	hawnpipe	hornpipe
hartless	heartless +	hawnt	haunt ¹
harty	hearty +	hawser	
harum-scarum		hawthorn	
harve	halve ²	hawticulcher	horticulture +
harvest ¹ /er		hawticulture	horticulture +
harvist	harvest ¹+	hawtie	haughty +
hary	hairy	hawtier	haughtier
has /-been/n't		hawty	haughty +
hasen	hasten ¹	hay ★ (grass) /cock	

hay	hey ★	heavyweight	
hay fever		Hebrew	
hayday	heyday	hebroo	Hebrew
hazard ¹ /ous		heckle ² /r	
haz e /ier/iest/y		heckul	heckle ²⁺
hazel		hectic /ally	
hazerd	hazard ¹⁺	hecto gram /litre/metre	
hazerdus	hazardous	hed	head ¹⁺
hazi ly /ness		hedake	headache
he /'ll ★ (he will)		heddress	head-dress ⁺
head ¹ /ache/board		heder	header ⁺
head -dress /way		hedge ² /hog/row	
head er /less/line/y		hedland	headland ⁺
head land /long/strong		hedmaster	headmaster ⁺
head master /mistress		hedmistriss	headmistress
headquarters		hedonis m /t	
heal ¹★ (to cure) /er		hedquarters	headquarters
heal	heel ¹★	heed ¹ /ful/less	
health /y		heel ¹★ (of foot)	
healthi er /est/ly/ness		heel	heal ¹★⁺
heap ¹		heep	heap ¹
hear ★ (sound) /er/ing		heet	heat ¹⁺
hear	here ★	heeth	heath
hearabouts	hereabouts	hefer	heifer
hearafter	hereafter	heftie	hefty ⁺
heard ★ (sound)		heft y /ier/iest/ily/iness	
heard	herd ¹★⁺	hege	hedge ²⁺
hearken ¹		heifer	
hearsay		height	
hearse		heighten ¹	
heart ★ (body) /broken		heinous /ly/ness	
heartbreak /ing		heinus	heinous ⁺
heartburn /ing		heir ★ (inheritance)	
hearten ¹		heir ess /loom	
hearth		hel	hell ⁺
heartless /ly/ness		held	
heart y /ier/iest/ily		helicks	helix ⁺
heat ¹ /edly/er/-wave		helicopter	
heath		heliocentric	
heathen /ish		heliograf	heliograph
heather		heliograph	
heave ²		heliotrope	
heaven /ly		heliport	
heaviwait	heavyweight	helium	
heav y /ier/iest/ily		heli x /ces (pl.)	

hell /ish	
hello /s	
helm /sman	
helmet	
helo	hello⁺
help ¹ /er	
helpful /ly/ness	
helpless /ness	
helpmate	
helter-skelter	
helth	health ⁺
helthier	healthier ⁺
hem ³ /stitch	
hemerige	haemorrhage
hemeroids	haemorrhoids
hemisfere	hemisphere ⁺
hemispher *e* /ical	
hemlock	
hemofilia	haemophilia ⁺
hemoglobin	haemoglobin
hemorige	haemorrhage
hemp /en	
hen /pecked	
hena	henna
hence /forth	
henceforward	
hench *man* /men (pl.)	
henna	
henrey	henry ⁺
henry /s	
hens	hence ⁺
hensforth	henceforth
hensforwerd	henceforward
henus	heinous ⁺
hepatitis	
heptagon /al	
her /s/self	
herald ¹ /ic/ry	
heraldrey	heraldry
herb /age	
herbaceous	
herbal /ist	
herbashus	herbaceous
herbicide	
herbiside	herbicide

herbivor *e* /ous	
herbivorus	herbivorous
herd ¹★ (animals) /sman	
herd	heard ★
here ★ (this place)	
here	hear ★⁺
hereabouts	
hereafter	
here *by* /in/of	
heredit *ary* /y	
hereditey	heredity
hereditrey	hereditary ⁺
heresay	hearsay
heresie	heresy ⁺
heres *y* /ies	
heretic /al	
here *to* /upon/with	
hering	herring
heritage	
herita *nce* /ble	
heritans	heritance ⁺
heritige	heritage
herl	hurl ¹
hermafrodite	hermaphrodite
hermaphrodite	
hermetic /ally	
hermit /age	
hernia	
hero /es/ic/ically/ism	
heroin ★ (drug)	
heroine ★ (fem. hero)	
heron /ry	
herring	
herse	hearse
hert	hurt ⁺
hertle	hurtle ²
hertul	hurtle ²
hertz	
hesian	hessian
hesitan *cy* /t	
hesitansey	hesitancy ⁺
hesitat *e* ² /ion	
hessian	
heterodoks	heterodox ⁺
hetero *dox* /sexual	

heterogeneous	
heterogenus	heterogeneous
heteroseksual	heterosexual
hethen	heathen +
hether	heather
heve	heave [2]
heven	heaven +
hevenly	heavenly
hevie	heavy +
heviwait	heavyweight
heviweight	heavyweight
hevy	heavy +
hew [1]* (cut) /er/n	
hew	hue *
hexagon /al	
hexahedr on /al	
hey * (call out)	
hey	hay *+
heyday	

> *If you cannot find your word under* **hi** *look under* **hy**

hi * (call attention)	
hi	high *+
hiasinth	hyacinth
hiatus /es	
hibernat e [2] /ion/or	
hibrid	hybrid
hiccup [1]	
hich	hitch [1]+
hichhike	hitch-hike [2]+
hicup	hiccup [1]
hid /den/ing	
hide /bound/-out	
hideous /ly/ness	
hidius	hideous +
hier	higher *
hier	hire [2]*+
hierarch /ical	
hierarch y /ies	
hierark	hierarch +
hierarkey	hierarchy +
hieroglif	hieroglyph +
hieroglyph /ic	
hi-fi	

higgledy-piggledy	
high * (tall) /est/ly	
higher * (taller)	
higher	hire [2]*+
highfaluting	
highland	
highlight [1]	
highness	
highway /man/men (pl.)	
hijack [1] /er	
hike [2] /r	
hil	hill +
hiland	highland
hilari ous /ty	
hilaritey	hilarity
hilarius	hilarious +
hilight	highlight [1]
hilite	highlight [1]
hill /ock	
hill y /ier/iest/iness	
him * (he) /self	
him	hymn *+
hind /sight	
hinder [1]	
hindoo	Hindu +
hindrance	
hindrans	hindrance
hindsite	hindsight
Hindu /ism	
hiness	highness
hinge [2]	
hint [1]	
hinterland	
hipie	hippy +
hipodrome	hippodrome
hipopotamus	hippopotamus
hippodrome	
hippopotamus	
hipp y /ies	
hipy	hippy +
hire [2]* (employ) /ling	
hire	higher *
hiroglif	hieroglyph +
hiss [1]	
histerey	history +

141

histeria	hysteria +	holie	holly ★+
histerical	hysterical +	holie	holy ★
historian		holi *er* /est/ness	
historic /al/ally		holihock	hollyhock
histor *y* /ies		hollow ¹	
histrey	history +	holly ★ (tree) /hock	
histrionic /s		holly	holy ★
hit /ter/ting		holly	wholly ★
hitch ¹ /es		holm ★ (river islet)	
hitch-hike ² /r		holmium	
hite	height	holocaust	
hither /to		holocorst	holocaust
hive ²		holow	hollow ¹
hiway	highway +	holster ¹	
ho ★ (surprise)		holy ★ (sacred)	
ho	hoe ²★+	holy	holey ★
hoaks	hoax ¹+	holy	holly ★+
hoard ¹ ★ (collect) /er		holy	wholly ★
hoard	horde ²★	homage	
hoarse ★ (voice)		home ² ★ /ward/work	
hoarse	horse ²★	home	holm ★
hoarse *ly* /ness/st		home *ly* /less	
hoax ¹ /es/er		homesick /ness	
hobble ²		homicid *e* /al	
hobb *y* /ies		homige	homage
hobie	hobby +	homiley	homily
hobnob ³		homily	
hobul	hobble ²	homiopath	homoeopath +
hoby	hobby +	homisidal	homicidal
hochpoch	hotchpotch	homiside	homicide +
hock		homoeopath /ic	
hockey		homogene *ity* /ous	
hockie	hockey	homogenius	homogeneous
hocus-pocus		homonim	homonym +
hoe ²★ (dig) /s ★		homonym /ic	
hoes	hose ²★	homoseksual	homosexual +
hog ³ /gish		homosexual /ity	
hogshead		hone ²	
hogshed	hogshead	honest /ly/y	
hoist ¹		honey /dew	
hold /-all/er/ing		honeycomb ¹	
hole ²★ (cavity) /y ★		honeymoon ¹ /er	
hole	whole ★	honeysuckle	
holey	wholly ★	honie	honey +
holiday /er/ing		honorari *um* /a/ums (pls.)	

honorary	
honorific	
honour [1] /able/ably	
hony	honey [+]
hood [1]	
hoodwink [1]	
hoo f [1] /fs/ves (pls.)	
hook [1] /-up	
hooligan /ism	
hoop [1]★ (circle)	
hoop	whoop [1]★
hooping coff	whooping cough
hoot [1] /er	
hoover [1]	
hop [3] /per/scotch	
hope [2] /ful/fully	
hopeless /ness	
horde [2]★ (swarm)	
horde	hoard [1]★[+]
hore	whore [2][+]
horer	horror
horible	horrible [+]
horibul	horrible [+]
horid	horrid [+]
horific	horrific [+]
horify	horrify [4]
horizon	
horizontal /ly	
hormone	
horn [1] /beam/y	
hornet	
hornpipe	
horology	
horor	horror
horoscope	
horribl e /y	
horribul	horrible [+]
horrid /ness	
horrific /ally	
horrify [4]	
horror	
hors-d'oeuvre	
horse [2]★ (animal)	
horse	hoarse ★
horse back /-chestnut	

horsely	hoarsely [+]
horse power /radish	
horseshoe /s	
horsewhip [3]	
horswip	horsewhip [3]
horthorn	hawthorn
horticulcher	horticulture [+]
horticultur e /al/ist	
hortie	haughty [+]
horty	haughty [+]
hose [2]★ (stockings, water down)	
hose	hoes ★
hosier /y	
hospitabl e /y	
hospitabul	hospitable [+]
hospital	
hospitalis e [2] /ation	
hospitality	
host [1] /ess (fem.)	
hostage	
hostel	
hostelr y /ies	
hostige	hostage
hostile /ly	
hostilit y /ies	
hot /ly/-plate/ter/test	
hotchpotch	
hotel /ier	
hoter	hotter
hotest	hottest
hotheaded	
hotheded	hotheaded
hound [1]	
hour ★ (time) /ly	
hour	our ★
house [2] /boat/ful	
household /er	
house keeper /master	
housewi fe /ves (pl.)	
hovel	
hover [1] /craft	
how /ever	
howl [1] /er	
hownd	hound [1]

143

howse	house ²⁺	humock	hummock
howsekeeper	housekeeper ⁺	humorist /ic	
howsewife	housewife ⁺	humorous ★ (funny)	
howshold	household ⁺	humorous	humerus ★
hu	hew ¹★⁺	humour ¹	
hu	hue ★	hump ¹ /back	
hubbub		humus	
huch	hutch ⁺	hunch ¹ /back/es	
huddle ²		hundred /fold/th	
hudul	huddle ²	hundredwait	hundredweight
hudwink	hoodwink ¹	hundredweight	
hue ★ (tint, pursuit)		huney	honey ⁺
hue	hew ¹★⁺	hung	
huf	huff ¹⁺	hunger ¹	
huff ¹ /ily/iness/y		hungrie	hungry
hug ³		hungri er /est/ly/ness	
huge /ly/r/st		hungry	
Hugeno	Huguenot	huni	honey ⁺
Huguenot		hunk	
hul	hull ¹	hunt ¹ /er/ress (fem.)	
hulabaloo	hullabaloo	huntsman	
hulk /ing		hura	hurrah
hull ¹		huray	hurray
hullabaloo		hurd	heard ★
hum ³		hurd	herd ¹★⁺
human ★ (person) /ly		hurdigurdie	hurdy-gurdy
humane ★ (kindly) /ly		hurdle ²	
humanis e ² /ation		hurdul	hurdle ²
humanis m /t/tic		hurdy-gurdy	
humanitarian /ism		huricane	hurricane
humanit y /ies		hurie	hurry ⁴
humble ² /ness		hurl ¹	
humbly		hurmit	hermit ⁺
humbug ³		hurnia	hernia
humbul	humble ²⁺	hurrah	
humdrum		hurray	
humer	humour ¹	hurricane	
humerist	humorist ⁺	hurry ⁴	
humerus ★ (bone)		hurse	hearse
humerus	humorous ★	hurt /ful/ing	
humid /ity		hurtle ²	
humidif y ⁴ /ier		hurtul	hurtle ²
humiliat e ² /ion		hurtz	hertz
humility		hury	hurry ⁴
hummock		husband ¹ /ry	

husel	hustle ²⁺	hyperbola ★ (curve)	
hush ¹ /-hush		hyperbole ★ (exaggeration)	
husie	hussy ⁺	hyperbolical /ly	
husk ¹ /ily/iness		hypermarket	
huskie	husky ⁺	hyphenate ²	
husk y /ies		hypnosis	
huss y /ies		hypnoti c /sm/st	
hustle ² /r		hypnotise ²	
husul	hustle ²⁺	hypochondria /c	
husy	hussy ⁺	hypocris y /ies	
hutch /es		hypocrit e /ical	
hyacinth		hypodermic	
hybrid		hypotenuse	
hydra		hypothermia	
hydrangea		hypothes is /es (pl.)	
hydranja	hydrangea	hypothetical	
hydrant		hysteri a /cs	
hydraulic /ally/s		hysterical /ly	
hydrocarbon			
hydrochloric			
hydro-electric			

I

hydrofobia	hydrophobia		
hydrofoil		I ★ /'ll ★ (I will)	
hydrogen		I	eye ²★⁺
hydrografey	hydrography	iambic	
hydrography		ice ² /-apron/berg	
hydrokside	hydroxide	ice -bucket /-rink	
hydrolysis		ich	itch ¹⁺
hydromet er /ry		icicle	
hydropath /ic/y		iclesiastic	ecclesiastic ⁺
hydrophobia		iclips	eclipse ²
hydroplane		icliptic	ecliptic
hydrostat /ic		icon	
hydrotherapy		iconomey	economy ⁺
hydrous		iconomist	economist
hydroxide		icy	
hydrus	hydrous	idea /s	
hyena		ideal /ism	
hygene	hygiene ⁺	idealise ²	
hygien e /ic/ically		identical	
hygromet er /ric		identif y ⁴ /ication	
hygroscopic		identit y /ies	
hym	hymn ★⁺	ideological /ly	
hymen		ideolog y /ies	
hymn ★ (song) /al		iderdown	eiderdown

idilic	idyllic	igwana	iguana
idill	idyll +	ijaculashun	ejaculation
idioc y /ies		ijaculate	ejaculate 2+
idiologey	ideology +	ijaculation	ejaculation
idiological	ideological +	ijecshun	ejection
idiom /atic		iject	eject 1+
idiosincrasy	idiosyncrasy +	ijection	ejection
idiosincratic	idiosyncratic	ikon	icon
idiosyncra sy /tic		ikwip	equip 3+
idiot /ic		ikwivocal	equivocal +
idium	idiom +	ikwivocate	equivocate 2+
idle 2★ (lazy) /ness/r		il	I'll ★
idol ★ (worship)		ilaberate	elaborate 2+
idol	idle 2★+	ilaborashun	elaboration
idolatr y /ous		ilaborate	elaborate 2+
idolise 2		iland	island +
idyl	idyll +	ilapse	elapse 2
idyll /ic		ilash	eyelash +
iface	efface 2+	ilashun	elation
ifect	effect 1	ilastic	elastic +
ifectiv	effective +	ilasticity	elasticity
ifectual	effectual	ilastisitey	elasticity
Ifel	Eiffel	ilate	elate 2+
ifeminate	effeminate +	ilation	elation
ificiency	efficiency +	ile	aisle ★
ificient	efficient +	Ile	I'll ★
ifishensey	efficiency +	ile	isle ★
ifishent	efficient +	ilect	elect 1+
ifrunterey	effrontery +	ilection	election +
igalitarian	egalitarian +	ilectoral	electoral +
igloo		ilectorate	electorate
igneous		ilectrocute	electrocute 2+
ignishun	ignition	ilectron	electron +
ignit e 2 /ion		ilectronic	electronic +
ignius	igneous	ilectroplate	electroplate 2
ignoble		ilegal	illegal +
ignominious /ly		ilegalitey	illegality
ignominius	ignominious +	ilegible	illegible +
ignominy		ilegibul	illegible +
ignor	ignore 2	ilegitimacy	illegitimacy +
ignoramus		ilegitimasey	illegitimacy +
ignoran ce /t		ilegitimate	illegitimate
ignorans	ignorance +	ilet	islet ★
ignore 2		ileven	eleven +
iguana		ilicit	elicit 1★

ilikser	elixir	imaciate	emaciate [2+]
iliminashun	elimination	imaculate	immaculate
iliminate	eliminate [2+]	image [2]	
ilimination	elimination	imagin	imagine [2+]
ilips	ellipse	imaginashun	imagination
iliptic	elliptic [+]	imagin *e* [2] /ation	
iliptical	elliptical	imancipate	emancipate [2+]
ilisit	elicit [1]★	imansipashun	emancipation
iliteracy	illiteracy [+]	imansipate	emancipate [2+]
iliterasey	illiteracy [+]	imansipation	emancipation
iliterat	illiterate	imasculate	emasculate [2+]
ilixir	elixir	imashiate	emaciate [2+]
ill		imaterial	immaterial
illegal /ity		imature	immature [+]
illegib *le* /ility		imaturitey	immaturity
illegibul	illegible [+]	imbalance	
illegitima *cy* /te		imbalans	imbalance
illicit ★ (illegal) /ly		imbecil *e* /ity	
illicit	elicit [1]★	imbesile	imbecile [+]
illitera *cy* /te		imbibe [2]	
illogical /ity		imbue [2]	
illuminat *e* [2] /ion		imediacy	immediacy
illusion ★ (false idea)		imediasey	immediacy
illusion	allusion ★	imediate	immediate [+]
illusion	elusion ★	imense	immense [+]
illusive ★ (deceptive)		imensitey	immensity
illusive	allusive ★[+]	imerge	emerge [2+]
illusive	elusive ★[+]	imergence	emergence
illustrat *e* [2] /ion		imergency	emergency [+]
illustrious		imergens	emergence
ilogical	illogical [+]	imergent	emergent
ilope	elope [2+]	imerse	immerse [2+]
ilucidate	elucidate [2+]	imershun	immersion
ilude	elude [2]★	imersion	immersion
iluminashun	illumination	imesurable	immeasurable [+]
iluminate	illuminate [2+]	imesurabul	immeasurable [+]
ilumination	illumination	imetic	emetic
ilusidate	elucidate [2+]	imige	image [2]
ilusion	illusion ★	imigrant	immigrant
ilusive	elusive ★[+]	imigrashun	immigration
ilusive	illusive ★	imigrate	immigrate [2+]
ilustrate	illustrate [2+]	imigration	immigration
ilustration	illustration	iminent	imminent ★[+]
ilustrius	illustrious	imishun	emission
I'm (I am)		imission	emission

imit	emit [3+]	imp /ish/ishness	
imitat e^2 /ion		impact [1] /ion	
immaculate		impair [1] /ment	
immaterial		impalpabl e /y	
immatur e /ity		imparshal	impartial [+]
immeasurabl e /y		imparshialitey	impartiality
immediacy		impart [1]	
immediasey	immediacy	impartial /ity/ly	
immediate /ly		impas	impasse
immens e /ely/ity		impasabul	impassable
immers e^2 /ion		impashence	impatience
immigrant		impashens	impatience
immigrat e^2 /ion		impashent	impatient [+]
imminent *† /ly		impashund	impassioned
†(about to happen)		impasioned	impassioned
imminent	eminent *	impasiv	impassive [+]
immobil e /ity		impassable	
immobilis e^2 /ation		impasse	
immoderate /ly		impassioned	
immodest /ly/y		impassive /ness	
immoral /ity/ly		impassivity	
immortal /ity/ly		impatience	
immortalis e^2 /ation		impatient /ly	
immovabl e /y		impeach [1] /able/ment	
immun e /ity		impecabul	impeccable [+]
immunis e^2 /ation		impeccabl e /y	
immunology		impecunio us /sity	
imobile	immobile [+]	impecunius	impecunious [+]
imoderate	immoderate [+]	impede [2]	
imodest	immodest [+]	impediment /a	
imodestey	immodesty	impeech	impeach [1+]
imolient	emollient	impel [3] /ler	
imolument	emolument	impend [1]	
imoral	immoral [+]	impenetrab le /ility	
imoralitey	immorality	impeniten ce /t	
imortal	immortal [+]	impenitens	impenitence [+]
imortalise	immortalise [2+]	imperative /ly/ness	
imortalitey	immortality	imperceptibl e /y	
imoshun	emotion [+]	imperfect /ion	
imoshunal	emotional	imperial /ism/ly	
imotion	emotion [+]	imperialist /ic	
imotional	emotional	imperil [3] /ment	
imotiv	emotive	imperious /ly/ness	
imovable	immovable [+]	imperishable	
imovabul	immovable [+]	imperius	imperious [+]

impermeable		imposter	impostor ★
impermiabul	impermeable	impostor ★ (swindler)	
imperseptible	imperceptible +	imposture ★ (deception)	
imperseptibul	imperceptible +	impoten *ce* /t	
impersonal /ly		impotens	impotence +
impersonat *e* ² /ion/or		impound ¹	
imperterbable	imperturbable +	impoverish ¹ /ment	
impertinen *ce* /t		impownd	impound ¹
impertinens	impertinence +	impracticab *le* /ility	
imperturbab *le* /ility		impracticabul	impracticable +
impervious /ly/ness		imprecat *e* ² /ion	
impervius	impervious +	imprecise /ly	
impetuosity		impregnab *le* /ility	
impetuous /ly/ness		impregnat *e* ² /ion	
impetus /es		impres	impress ¹+
impetuus	impetuous +	impresario /s	
impiety		impreshun	impression +
impinge ² /ment		impreshunism	impressionism +
impious /ly		impresible	impressible
impius	impious +	impresibul	impressible
implacabl *e* /y		impresionism	impressionism +
implacabul	implacable +	impresionist	impressionist
implant ¹ /ation		impresise	imprecise +
implement ¹ /ation		impresiv	impressive +
impli	imply ⁴+	impress ¹ /ible	
implicat *e* ² /ion		impression /able	
implicit /ly/ness		impressionis *m* /t/tic	
implisit	implicit +	impressive /ly/ness	
implore ²		imprint ¹	
impl *y* ⁴ /ication		imprison ¹ /ment	
impolite /ly/ness		improbab *le* /ility/ly	
impolitic		improbabul	improbable +
imponderable /s		impromptu	
impondrabul	imponderable +	impromtoo	impromptu
import ¹ /able/ation		improper /ly	
importan *ce* /t/tly		impropriet *y* /ies	
importans	importance +	improve ² /ment	
importunate /ly		improviden *ce* /t/tly	
importun *e* ² /ity		improvidens	improvidence +
imposcher	imposture ★	improvis *e* ² /ation	
impos *e* ² /able/ition		impruden *ce* /t/tly	
imposible	impossible +	imprudens	imprudence +
imposibul	impossible +	impruve	improve ²+
imposishun	imposition	impuden *ce* /t/tly	
impossib *le* /ility/ly		impudens	impudence +

impugn [1]	
impuls e /ion/ive/ively	
impune	impugn [1]
impunity	
impure /ly	
impurit y /ies	
imput e [2] /able/ation	
imulshun	emulsion
imulsion	emulsion
imune	immune +
imunise	immunise [2]+
imunitey	immunity
imunologey	immunology
imurge	emerge [2]+
in * (on inside)	
in	inn *+
inability	
inaccessib le /ility	
inaccurac y /ies	
inaccurate /ly	
inacsesible	inaccessible +
inacsesibul	inaccessible +
inacshun	inaction
inaction	
inactive /ly	
inactivit y /ies	
inacuracy	inaccuracy +
inacurasey	inaccuracy +
inacurate	inaccurate +
inadekwacy	inadequacy +
inadekwasey	inadequacy +
inadekwat	inadequate +
inadequac y /ies	
inadequate /ly	
inadmisibul	inadmissible +
inadmissib le /ility	
inadverten ce /t	
inadvertens	inadvertence +
inalienab le /ility	
inalienabul	inalienable +
inane /ly	
inanimate	
inanit y /ies	
inaplicable	inapplicable +
inapplicabl e /y	

inapplicabul	inapplicable +
inappropriate /ly	
inapropriat	inappropriate +
inaptitude	
inarticulate /ly	
inasmuch	
inate	innate +
inatenshun	inattention +
inatention	inattention +
inatentiv	inattentive
inattent ion /ive	
inaudib le /ility	
inaugural	
inaugurat e [2] /ion/ive	
inauspicious /ly	
inawmus	enormous +
inawspicious	inauspicious +
inawspishus	inauspicious +
inborn	
inbred	
inbreeding	
incalculab le /ility	
incandescen ce /t	
incandesence	incandescence +
incant [1] /ation	
incapab le /ility/ly	
incapabul	incapable +
incapacitat e [2] /ion	
incapacity	
incapasitate	incapacitate [2]+
incapasitey	incapacity
incarcerat e [2] /ion	
incarnat e [2] /ion	
incarserate	incarcerate [2]+
incendiar y /ies	
incense [2]	
incentive	
incept ion /ive	
incertitude	
incessant /ly	
incest /uous	
inch [1] /es	
incidence * (bearing)	
incident /al/ally	
incidents * (events)	

incinerat *e* ² /ion/or

incipient

incis *e* ² /ion

incisive /ly/ness

incisor

incite ²★ (stir up)

incite   insight ★

incivilit *y* /ies

inclemen *cy* /t

inclemensey   inclemency ⁺

inclin *e* ² /ation

inclose   enclose ²⁺

inclu *de* ² /sion

inclusive /ly

incognito

incoheren *ce* /t

incoherens   incoherence ⁺

incombustible

income tax

incomensurat   incommensurate

incoming

incommensurate

incommod *e* ² /ious

incommunicado

incomparabl *e* /y

incompatib *le* /ility

incompatibul   incompatible ⁺

incompeten *ce* /t/tly

incompetens   incompetence ⁺

incomplete

incomprehensible

incomunicado   incommunicado

inconceivabl *e* /y

inconclusive /ly

incongru *ent* /ous

incongruit *y* /ies

incongruus   incongruous

inconseavable   inconceivable ⁺

inconsiderable

inconsiderate /ly

inconsistenc *y* /ies

inconsistensey   inconsistency ⁺

inconsistent /ly

inconsolable

inconsolabul   inconsolable

inconspicuous /ly

inconstan *cy* /t

incontestabl *e* /y

incontestabul   incontestable ⁺

incontinen *ce* /t

incontinens   incontinence ⁺

incontrovertibl *e* /y

inconvenien *ce* ² /t

inconveniens   inconvenience ²⁺

incorect   incorrect ⁺

incorigible   incorrigible ⁺

incorigibul   incorrigible ⁺

incorporat *e* ² /ion/or

incorrect /ly

incorrigib *le* /ility

incorruptib *le* /ility

increase ²

incredibl *e* /y

incredibul   incredible ⁺

incredul *ity* /ous

incredulus   incredulous

increment /al

increse   increase ²

incriminat *e* ² /ion

incrust   encrust ¹

incubat *e* ² /ion/or

inculcat *e* ² /ion

inculpat *e* ² /ion

incum   income ⁺

incumbenc *y* /ies

incumbensey   incumbency ⁺

incumbent

incur ³

incurab *le* /ility/ly

incurabul   incurable ⁺

incurshun   incursion ⁺

incurs *ion* /ive

indebted /ness

indecenc *y* /ies

indecensey   indecency ⁺

indecent /ly

indecipherable

indecishun   indecision

indecision

indecisive /ly

151

indecorous /ness		indigenus	indigenous
indecorum		indigeschun	indigestion +
indecorus	indecorous +	indigestibl e /y	
indeed		indigestibul	indigestible +
indefatigabl e /y		indigest ion /ive	
indefatigabul	indefatigable +	indignant /ly	
indefensibl e /y		indignashun	indignation
indefensibul	indefensible +	indignation	
indefinable		indignit y /ies	
indefinabul	indefinable	indigo	
indefinite /ly		indipendence	independence +
indeks	index 1+	indipendens	independence +
indelibl e /y		indipendent	independent
indelibul	indelible +	indirect /ly	
indelicac y /ies		indiscre et /tion	
indelicasey	indelicacy +	indiscreshun	indiscretion
indelicate /ly		indiscriminate	
indemnifi	indemnify 4+	indisishun	indecision
indemnif y 4 /ication		indisision	indecision
indemnit y /ies		indisisiv	indecisive +
indencher	indenture	indispensabl e /y	
indent 1 /ation/ure		indispensabul	indispensable +
independen ce /t		indispos e 2 /ition	
independens	independence +	indisputabl e /y	
indescribabl e /y		indisputabul	indisputable +
indescribabul	indescribable +	indistinct	
indesency	indecency +	indistinguishable	
indesensey	indecency +	indite 2★ (compose)	
indesent	indecent +	indite	indict 1★+
indesiferable	indecipherable	indium	
indestructib le /ility		individual /ity/ly	
indestructibul	indestructible +	individualis m /t	
indeted	indebted +	indivisibl e /y	
indeterminate /ly		indivisibul	indivisible +
ind ex 1 /exes/ices (pls.)		indoctrinat e 2 /ion	
Indian		indolen ce /t/tly	
indicat e 2 /ion/ive/or		indolens	indolence +
indict 1★(accuse)/ment		indomitabl e /y	
indiference	indifference +	indomitabul	indomitable +
indiferens	indifference +	indoor /s	
indiferent	indifferent	indubitabl e /y	
indifferen ce /t		indubitabul	indubitable +
indigen ce /t		induce 2 /ment	
indigenous		inducshun	induction +
indigens	indigence +	inductance	

inductans	inductance	inequity * (injustice)	
induct *ion* /ive/ively		inequity	iniquity *
indulge ² /nce/nt		iner	inner +
indulgens	indulgence	ineradicabl *e* /y	
induse	induce ²+	ineradicabul	ineradicable +
industrey	industry +	inersha	inertia
industrial /ism/ist/ly		inert /ia/ly/ness	
industialis *e* ² /ation		inescapabl *e* /y	
industrious /ly		inescapabul	inescapable +
industrius	industrious +	inesenshal	inessential
industr *y* /ies		inesential	inessential
inebriat *e* ² /ion		inessential	
inedib *le* /ility		inestimabl *e* /y	
inedibul	inedible +	inestimabul	inestimable +
inefectiv	ineffective +	inestinium	einsteinium
inefectual	ineffectual +	inevitability	
ineffective /ly/ness		inevitabl *e* /y	
ineffectual /ly		inevitabul	inevitable +
inefficienc *y* /ies		inexact /itude	
inefficient /ly		inexcusabl *e* /y	
ineficiency	inefficiency +	inexhaustibl *e* /y	
ineficient	inefficient +	inexorabl *e* /y	
inefishensey	inefficiency +	inexpedient /ly	
inefishent	inefficient +	inexpensive /ly	
inegsact	inexact +	inexperience /d	
inegsactitude	inexactitude	inexperiens	inexperience +
inegsawstible	inexhaustible +	inexplicabl *e* /y	
inekscusable	inexcusable +	inexpressibl *e* /y	
inekserable	inexorable +	inextinguishable	
inekspedient	inexpedient +	inextingwishabul	inextinguishable
inekspensive	inexpensive +	inextricabl *e* /y	
ineksperience	inexperience +	infalible	infallible +
ineksplicable	inexplicable +	infalibul	infallible +
inekspresible	inexpressible +	infallib *le* /ility/ly	
inekstricable	inextricable +	infamey	infamy
inekwitable	inequitable +	infamous /ly	
inekwity	inequity *	infamus	infamous +
inelegan *ce* /cy/t		infamy	
inelegens	inelegance +	infancy	
ineligib *le* /ility		infansey	infancy
ineligibul	ineligible +	infant /icide/ile	
inept /itude/ly		infantrey	infantry +
inequalit *y* /ies		infantr *y* /ies	
inequitabl *e* /y		infatuat *e* ² /ion	
inequitabul	inequitable +	infecshun	infection

153

infecshus	infectious +
infect [1] /ion	
infectious /ness	
infer [3] /ence	
inferens	inference
inferier	inferior +
inferior /ity	
inferm	infirm
infermarey	infirmary +
infermitey	infirmity +
infernal /ly	
inferno /s	
infertil e /ity	
infest [1] /ant/ation	
infidel	
infidelit y /ies	
infiltrat e [2] /ion/or	
infinite /ly	
infinitesimal /ly	
infinitey	infinity +
infinitive	
infinit y /ies	
infirm	
infirmar y /ies	
infirmit y /ies	
inflamable	inflammable +
inflamabul	inflammable +
inflamashun	inflammation
inflamatrey	inflammatory
inflame [2]	
inflamma ble /tion	
inflammatory	
inflashun	inflation +
inflat e [2] /able	
inflation /ary	
inflect [1] /ion	
inflexib le /ility	
inflict [1] /ion	
inflooenza	influenza
influence [2]	
influens	influence [2]
influenshal	influential +
influential /ly	
influenza	
influks	influx

influx	
inform [1] /ative/er	
informal /ity/ly	
informant	
informashun	information
information	
infracshun	infraction
infraction	
infra-red	
infrastructure	
infrekwency	infrequency +
infrekwent	infrequent
infrequen cy /t/tly	
infringe [2] /ment	
infuriate [2]	
infus e [2] /er/ion	
ingenious /ly	
ingenius	ingenious +
ingenuity	
ingenuous /ly/ness	
ingenuus	ingenuous +
ingle-nook	
Inglish	English +
inglorious /ly	
inglorius	inglorious +
ingot	
ingrained	
ingrashiate	ingratiate [2]
ingratiate [2]	
ingratitude	
ingredient	
ingrowing	
ingulnook	ingle-nook
inhabit [1] /able/ant	
inhal e [2] /ant/ation	
inherent /ly	
inherit [1] /ance/or	
inheritans	inheritance
inhibishun	inhibition
inhibit [1] /ion/or/ory	
inhospitabl e /y	
inhospitabul	inhospitable +
inhuman /ity/ly	
inikwalitey	inequality +
inikwitey	iniquity *

154

inikwitous	iniquitous
inikwitus	iniquitous
inimical	
inimitabl e /y	
inimitabul	inimitable +
inings	innings
iniquitey	iniquity ★
iniquitous	
iniquitus	iniquitous
iniquity ★ (badness)	
iniquity	inequity ★
inishal	initial 3+
inishativ	initiative
inishiashun	initiation
inishiate	initiate 2+
inishiation	initiation
initial 3 /ly	
initiat e 2 /ion/ive	
inject 1 /ion/or	
injer	injure 2+
injunction	
injunkshun	injunction
injur e 2 /ious	
injurey	injury +
injurius	injurious
injur y /ies	
injustice	
injustis	injustice

> **If you cannot find your word under ink look under inc**

ink 1 /-pot/-well	
inkalculable	incalculable +
inkeeper	innkeeper
inkling	
inkrement	increment +
inkwest	inquest
inkwire	enquire 2+
inkwisitiv	inquisitive +
inkwisitor	inquisitor
inlade	inlaid
inland	
in-law	
inla y /id	
inlet	

inmate	
inmost	
inn ★ (tavern) /keeper	
innate /ly	
inner /most	
innings	
innocen ce /t/tly	
innocuous /ly	
innovat e 2 /ion/ive	
innuendo /es	
innumerabl e /y	
inocence	innocence +
inocens	innocence +
inocent	innocent
inoculat e 2 /ion	
inocuous	innocuous +
inocuus	innocuous +
inofensiv	inoffensive +
inoffensive /ly/ness	
inoperative /ness	
inoportune	inopportune +
inopportune /ly	
inordible	inaudible +
inordinate /ly	
inorganic	
inorgural	inaugural
inorgurate	inaugurate 2+
inormitey	enormity +
inormous	enormous +
inormus	enormous +
inorspicious	inauspicious +
inorspishus	inauspicious +
inosent	innocent
inough	enough
inovashun	innovation
inovate	innovate 2+
inovation	innovation
inovativ	innovative
input	
inquest	
inquisitive /ly/ness	
inquisitor	
inroad	
inrode	inroad
insan e /ely/ity	

155

insanitar *y* /iness	
insanitey	insanity
insanitrey	insanitary +
insashable	insatiable +
insashabul	insatiable +
insatiabl *e* /y	
inscribe²	
inscripshun	inscription
inscription	
inscrutab *le* /ility	
insect /icide	
insectiside	insecticide
insecure /ly	
insecurity	
inseminat *e*² /ion	
insendiarey	incendiary +
insense	incense²
insensib *le* /ility/ly	
insensibul	insensible +
insensitive /ly	
insensitivity	
insentiv	incentive
inseparabl *e* /y	
inseprabul	inseparable +
insepshun	inception +
inseption	inception +
insermountable	insurmountable +
insert¹ /ion	
insertitude	incertitude
insesant	incessant +
insest	incest +
insestuous	incestuous
insestuus	incestuous
inset³	
inshorance	insurance
inshorans	insurance
inshore	ensure²★
inshore	insure²★+
inside /r	
insidence	incidence ★
insidens	incidence ★
insidens	incidents ★
insident	incident +
insidental	incidental
insidious /ly/ness	

insidius	insidious +
insight ★ (keen understanding)	
insight	incite²★
insignia	
insignifican *ce* /t/tly	
insincere /ly	
insincerity	
insinerate	incinerate²+
insinerater	incinerator
insinsere	insincere +
insinseritey	insincerity
insinuat *e*² /ion/or	
insipid /ly/ness	
insipient	incipient
insiser	incisor
insishun	incision
insision	incision
insisiv	incisive +
insist¹ /ence/ent/ently	
insite	incite²★
insite	insight ★
insivilitey	incivility +
insolen *ce* /t/tly	
insolens	insolence +
insolub *le* /ility/ly	
insolubul	insoluble +
insolven *ce* /cy/t	
insolvens	insolvence +
insomnia /c	
insomuch	
inspecshun	inspection
inspect¹ /ion	
inspecter	inspector +
inspector /ate	
inspir *e*² /ation	
instability	
instal	install¹+
install¹ /ation	
instalment	
instance²	
instans	instance²
instant /ly	
instantaneous /ly	
instantanius	instantaneous +

instead		intangibl *e* /y	
insted	instead	intangibul	intangible [+]
instep		integer	
instigat *e* [2] /ion/or		integral /ly	
instigater	instigator	integrashun	integration
instill [1]		integrat *e* [2] /ion/or	
instinct /ive/ively		integrity	
institushun	institution [+]	intelect	intellect
institut *e* [2] /or		intelectual	intellectual [+]
institution /al		inteligence	intelligence [+]
institutionalis *e* [2] /m		inteligens	intelligence [+]
instrement	instrument [+]	inteligensia	intelligentsia
instruct [1] /ion/ive/or		inteligent	intelligent [+]
instrument /ation		inteligible	intelligible [+]
instrumental /ist		intellect	
insubordinashun	insubordination	intellectual / ly	
insubordinat *e*/ely/ion		intelligen *ce* /tsia	
insufferabl *e* /y		intelligent /ly	
insufficien *cy* /t/tly		intelligibl *e* /y	
insuficiency	insufficiency [+]	intelligibul	intelligible [+]
insuficient	insufficient	intemperance	
insufishensey	insufficiency [+]	intemperans	intemperance
insufishent	insufficient	intemperate /ly	
insufrable	insufferable [+]	intend [1]	
insular /ity		intense /ly	
insulat *e* [2] /ion/or		intenshun	intention [+]
insulin		intensif *y* [4] /ication	
insult [1]		intensit *y* /ies	
insuperabl *e* /y		intensive /ly/ness	
insuprabul	insuperable [+]	intent	
insurance		intention /al/ally	
insurans	insurance	inter [3] /ment	
insure [2]★(insurance)/r		interbred	
insure	ensure [2]★	interbreeding	
insurecshun	insurrection	intercede [2]	
insurection	insurrection	intercept [1] /ion/or	
insurgen *ce* /t		interceshun	intercession [+]
insurgens	insurgence [+]	intercess *ion* /or	
insurmountabl *e* /y		interchange [2] /able	
insurrection		interconnect [1] /ion	
insurshun	insertion	intercorse	intercourse
insurt	insert [1+]	intercourse	
insurtion	insertion	interelate	interrelate [2]
intact		interest [1]	
intake		interfere [2] /nce	

157

interier	interior	intervenshun	intervention
interim		interview [1]	
interior		intervue	interview [1]
interject [1] /ion		interweav e /ing	
interlock [1]		interwoven	
interloper		intestin e /al	
interlude		intiger	integer
intermarie	intermarry [4]	intigral	integral +
intermarry [4]		intigrashun	integration
intermediar y /ies		intigrate	integrate [2]+
intermediate		intigration	integration
interment ★ (burial)		intijer	integer
interment	internment ★	intimacy	
interminable		intimasey	intimacy
interminabul	interminable	intimate /ly	
intermingle [2]		intimidashun	intimidation
intermingul	intermingle [2]	intimidat e [2] /ion	
intermishun	intermission	intoksicant	intoxicant
intermission		intoksicate	intoxicate [2]+
intermittent		intolerabl e /y	
intern [1] /ment ★ (detention)		intoleran ce /t	
internal		intolerans	intolerance +
internashunal	international +	intolrabul	intolerable +
international /ly		intonashun	intonation
internecine		intonation	
internisine	internecine	intoxicant	
interogashun	interrogation	intoxicat e [2] /ion	
interogate	interrogate [2]+	intractable	
interplanetary		intractabul	intractable
Interpol		intramuscular	
interpolat e [2] /ion		intransigen ce /t	
interpret [1] /ation		intransigens	intransigence +
interrelate [2]		intransitive	
interrogat e [2] /ion/or		intreeg	intrigue [2]+
interrupt [1] /ion		intrepid /ly	
intersect [1] /ion		intricac y /ies	
interseed	intercede [2]	intricasey	intricacy +
intersepshun	interception	intricate /ly	
intersept	intercept [1]+	intrigue [2] /r	
intersepter	interceptor	intrinsic /ally	
interseshun	intercession +	introduce [2]	
interupshun	interruption	introducshun	introduction +
interuption	interruption	introduct ion /ory	
interval		introduse	introduce [2]
interven e [2] /tion		introod	intrude [2]+

introoshun		invenshun	invention
introosion		invent [1] /ion/or	
introosiv		inventer	inventor
introspect [1] /ion /ive		inventive /ness	
introver t [1] /sion		inventor y /ies	
intrude [2] /r		inventrey	inventory [+]
intrushun	intrusion [+]	invers e /ion	
intrus ion /ive		invershun	inversion
intuishun	intuition	invert [1] /er	
intuition		invertebrate	
intuitive /ly		invest [1] /ment	
inturn	intern [1+]	investicher	investiture
inturnal	internal	investigashun	investigation
inuendo	innuendo [+]	investigat e [2] /ion	
inuf	enough	investiture	
inumerable	innumerable [+]	inveterate	
inumerashun	enumeration	invidious /ly	
inumerate	enumerate [2+]	invidius	invidious [+]
inumerater	enumerator	invigilat e [2] /ion/or	
inumeration	enumeration	invigilater	invigilator
inumrabul	innumerable [+]	invigorat e [2] /ion	
inunciashun	enunciation	invincibl e /y	
inunciate	enunciate [2+]	invinsible	invincible [+]
inunciation	enunciation	inviolate	
inundat e [2] /ion		invisib le /ility/ly	
inunsiate	enunciate [2+]	invisibul	invisible [+]
inure [2]		invitashun	invitation
inursha	inertia	invit e [2] /ation	
inurt	inert [+]	invoice [2]	
invade [2] /r		invois	invoice [2]
invalid /ity		invoke [2]	
invalidate [2]		involuntar y /ily	
invaluable		involuntrey	involuntary [+]
invaluble	invaluable	involve [2] /ment	
invalubul	invaluable	invulnerab le /ility	
invariabl e /y		invulnerabul	invulnerable [+]
invariabul	invariable [+]	invurs	inverse [+]
invashun	invasion	invurt	invert [1+]
invasion		invurtebrate	invertebrate
invay	inveigh [1]	inward /ly/ness/s	
invaygul	inveigle [2]	inwud	inward [+]
invective		iodene	iodine
inveigh [1]		iodine	
inveigle [2]		iodise [2]	
inveigul	inveigle [2]	ion /ic	

159

ionis *e* ² /ation	
ionosfere	ionosphere
ionosphere	
iota	
ira	era +
iradiate	irradiate ²+
iradicate	eradicate ²+
irascib *le* /ility	
irascibul	irascible +
irase	erase ²+
irasher	erasure
irashonal	irrational +
irasible	irascible +
irate	
irational	irrational +
ire	
ireclaimable	irreclaimable
ireconcilable	irreconcilable +
ireconcilabul	irreconcilable +
irecoverable	irrecoverable +
irect	erect ¹+
irecuvrable	irrecoverable +
irefutable	irrefutable +
iregular	irregular +
iregularitey	irregularity +
ireguler	irregular +
irelegious	irreligious
irelevance	irrelevance +
irelevans	irrelevance +
irelevansey	irrelevancy +
irelevant	irrelevant
ireligus	irreligious
iremediable	irremediable +
iremediabul	irremediable +
iremovable	irremovable +
iremovabul	irremovable +
ireplacable	irreplaceable
ireplasable	irreplaceable
ireprable	irreparable
ireprabul	irreparable
irepressible	irrepressible
iresolute	irresolute +
irespectiv	irrespective +
iresponsible	irresponsible +
iresponsibul	irresponsible +

ireverence	irreverence +
ireverens	irreverence +
ireverent	irreverent
ireversible	irreversible +
irevocable	irrevocable +
irevocabul	irrevocable +
irideemable	irredeemable +
irideemabul	irredeemable +
iridium	
irigashun	irrigation
irigate	irrigate ²+
irigation	irrigation
iris	
Irish	
irisistible	irresistible +
irisistibul	irresistible +
iritable	irritable +
iritant	irritant
iritashun	irritation
iritate	irritate ²+
iritation	irritation
iriversible	irreversible +
irk ¹ /some	
irode	erode ²
iron ¹ /monger	
ironeous	erroneous +
ironey	irony +
ironic /al/ally	
ironie	irony +
ironius	erroneous +
iron *y* /ies	
iroshun	erosion
irosion	erosion
irotic	erotic +
irradiat *e* ² /ion	
irrational /ly	
irreclaimable	
irreclaimabul	irreclaimable
irreconcilabl *e* /y	
irreconcilabul	irreconcilable +
irrecoverabl *e* /y	
irrecoverabul	irrecoverable +
irredeemabl *e* /y	
irredeemabul	irredeemable +
irrefutabl *e* /y	

irrefutabul	irrefutable +
irregular /ly	
irregularit y /ies	
irrelevan ce /t	
irrelevanc y /ies	
irrelevansey	irrelevancy +
irreligious	
irreligus	irreligious
irremediabl e /y	
irremediabul	irremediable +
irremovabl e /y	
irremovabul	irremovable +
irreparable	
irreplacabul	irreplaceable
irreplaceable	
irreprabul	irreparable
irrepresibul	irrepressible
irrepressible	
irresistibl e /y	
irresolute /ly/ness	
irrespective /ly	
irresponsibility	
irresponsibl e /y	
irresponsibul	irresponsible +
irretrievabl e /y	
irretrievabul	irretrievable +
irreveren ce /t/tly	
irreverens	irreverence +
irreversibl e /y	
irreversibul	irreversible +
irrevocabl e /y	
irrevocabul	irrevocable +
irrigat e 2 /ion/or	
irrisistable	irresistible +
irritab le /ility/ly	
irritabul	irritable +
irritant	
irritashun	irritation
irritat e 2 /ion	
irrupt 1 /ion/ive	
irupshun	irruption
irupt	irrupt 1+
iruption	irruption
ise	ice 2+
ishuance	issuance

ishuans	issuance
ishue	issue 2+
isicle	icicle
isight	eyesight
isinglass	
isite	eyesight
island /er	
isle * (island)	
isle	aisle *
islet * (small island)	
islet	eyelet *
isn't (is not)	
isnt	isn't
isobar	
isolashun	isolation +
isolate 2	
isolation /ist	
isometric /ally	
isosceles	
isosilese	isosceles
isotherm	
isotope	
Israeli	
Isralie	Israeli
issuans	issuance
issu e 2 /ance	
isthmus	
Italian	
italic /s	
italicise 2	
italisize	italicise 2
Italyun	Italian
itch 1 /y	
item	
itemise 2	
iternal	eternal +
iternally	eternally
iternitey	eternity +
ither	either
itinerant	
itinerar y /ies	
itinerey	itinerary +
it's * (it is)	
its * (possessive)	
iun	iron 1+

iunmunger	ironmonger	jackdaw	
ivacuashun	evacuation	jackdoor	jackdaw
ivacuate	evacuate ²⁺	jacket ¹	
ivacuation	evacuation	jack-kni *fe* ² /ves (pl.)	
ivacuee	evacuee	Jacobean	
ivade	evade ²⁺	Jacobi *n* /te	
ivaluashun	evaluation	jade ²	
ivaluate	evaluate ²⁺	Jaffa	
ivaluation	evaluation	jaffer	Jaffa
ivangelise	evangelise ²⁺	jag ³	
ivangelist	evangelist	jaguar	
ivaperator	evaporator	jail ¹ /bird/er	
ivaporashun	evaporation	jam ³★ (preserve) /my	
ivaporate	evaporate ²⁺	jamb ★ (side post)	
ivaporation	evaporation	jamboree	
ivashun	evasion	jambori	jamboree
ivasion	evasion	jangle ²	
ivasiv	evasive ⁺	jangul	jangle ²
I've (I have)		janiter	janitor
Ive	I've	janitor	
ivent	event ⁺	January	
iventful	eventful	Janurey	January
iventual	eventual ⁺	Japanese	
iventualitey	eventuality ⁺	jar ³	
ivicshun	eviction	jargon	
ivict	evict ¹⁺	jasmin	jasmine
iviction	eviction	jasmine	
ivie	ivy	jasper	
ivocashun	evocation ⁺	jaundice ²	
ivocation	evocation ⁺	jaundis	jaundice ²
ivocativ	evocative	jaunt ¹ /ily/iness/y	
ivoke	evoke ²	jauntie	jaunty
ivolve	evolve ²	javelin	
ivory		jaw /bone	
ivry	ivory	jawndice	jaundice ²
ivy		jawndis	jaundice ²
		jawnt	jaunt ¹⁺
		jawntey	jaunty
J		jay /-walker	
		jaz	jazz ¹⁺
jab ³		jazz ¹ /y	
jabber ¹ /er		jealous /ly/y	
jabot		jeans	
jack ¹ /boot/pot		jeep	
jackal		jeer ¹	
jackass /es			

Jehovah		jingo /es/ism	
jelie	jelly +	jingul	jingle [2]
jell *y* /ies		jirashun	gyration
jelous	jealous +	jirate	gyrate [2]+
jelus	jealous +	jiration	gyration
jely	jelly +	jiro	giro ★
jemie	jemmy +	jiro	gyro ★+
jemm *y* /ies		jiroscope	gyroscope +
jemy	jemmy +	jist	gist
jenes	jeans	jiter	jitter [1]+
jeopard *ise* [2] /y		jitter [1] /y	
jepadise	jeopardise [2]+	jive [2]	
jepardy	jeopardy	job [3] /less	
jeribilt	jerry-built	jockey [1] /s	
jerie	jerry +	jockie	jockey [1]+
jerk [1] /ily/iness/y		jocky	jockey [1]+
jerkin		jocose /ly	
jerry /-building/-built		jocular /ity/ly	
jersey /s		jocund /ity	
jersie	jersey +	jodhpurs	
jersy	jersey +	jodpers	jodhpurs
jery	jerry +	jodpurs	jodhpurs
jest [1] /er		jog [3]	
jet [3] /-propelled		joggle [2]	
jetie	jetty +	jogul	joggle [2]
jetison	jettison [1]	joi	joy +
jetsam		joiful	joyful
jettison [1]		join [1] /er/ery	
jett *y* /ies		joint [1] /er/ly	
jety	jetty +	joiride	joy-ride +
Jew /ish/ry ★ (Jews)		joist [1]	
jewel [3]★ (gem)		joius	joyous +
jewel	duel [3]★	jok *e* [2] /er/ingly	
jewel	joule ★	joll *y* [4] /ier/iest/ily/ity	
jeweler	jeweller +	jolt [1] /y	
jeweller /y		joly	jolly [4]+
jewelrey	jewellery	jonkwil	jonquil
jib [3]		jonquil	
jiffy		Joo	Jew +
jifie	jiffy	Jooish	Jewish
jify	jiffy	jool	joule ★
jig [3] /saw		joon	June
jilt [1]		joopiter	Jupiter
jim	gym +	joos	juice +
jingle [2]		joosey	juicy

joot	jute	jugle	juggle [2+]
jostle [2]		jugular ★ (vein)	
josul	jostle [2]	juic e /ier/iest/ily/y	
jot [3]		Juish	Jewish
joule ★ (unit of energy)		jujoob	jujube
joule	duel [3★]	jujube	
joule	jewel [3★]	juke-box	
journal /ism/ist		jukstapose	juxtapose [2+]
journey [1] /s		jukstaposition	juxtaposition
jovial /ity/ly		Juli	July
jowl		July	
joy /ful/fully		jumble [2]	
joyous /ly		jumbo	
joy-rid e /ing		jumbul	jumble [2]
joyus	joyous [+]	jump [1] /er/iness/y	
ju	Jew [+]	junkcher	juncture
jubilant /ly		junction	
jubilashun	jubilation	juncture	
jubilation		June	
jubilee		jungle	
jubili	jubilee	jungul	jungle
juce	juice [+]	junier	junior
jucy	juicy	junior	
Judas		juniper	
judder [1]		junk	
judge [2] /ment		junket [1]	
judicacher	judicature	junta	
judicature		Jupiter	
judicial /ly		jurer	juror
judiciar y /ies		juri	jury ★ [+]
judicious /ly		juridical /ly	
judishal	judicial [+]	juriman	juryman [+]
judisharey	judiciary [+]	jurisdicshun	jurisdiction [+]
judishus	judicious [+]	jurisdiction /al	
judo		jurispruden ce /t	
juel	duel [3★]	jurisprudens	jurisprudence [+]
juel	jewel [3★]	jur ist /or	
juel	joule ★	jurnal	journal [+]
jueller	jeweller [+]	jurnalism	journalism
juelrey	jewellery	jurnalist	journalist
jug [3]		jurnie	journey [1+]
juge	judge [2+]	jurny	journey [1+]
jugernawt	juggernaut	jur y ★(legal)/ies	
juggernaut		jury man /men (pl.)	
juggle [2] /r ★ (conjurer)		juse	juice [+]

jusie	juicy
just	
justice	
justifiabl *e* /y	
justifiabul	justifiable +
justificashun	justification
justif *y* [4] /ication	
justis	justice
jut [3]	
jute	
juvenil *e* /ity	
juwel	jewel [3]★
juweller	jeweller +
juwellrey	jewellery
juxtapos *e* [2] /ition	
jym	gym +
jymkana	gymkhana
jymnasium	gymnasium +
jymnast	gymnast
jymnastics	gymnastics
jyroscope	gyroscope +

K

If you cannot find your word under **k** *look under* **c**

---

kacao	cacao
kaen	cayenne
Kaiser	
kaison	caisson
kakey	khaki
kakie	khaki
kale	
kaleidoscop *e* /ic	
kalidascope	kaleidoscope +
kameliun	chameleon
kangaroo	
kaolin	
kaos	chaos +
kaotick	chaotic
karate	
karicter	character
karicterisashun	characterisation
karicterise	characterise [2]+

karicteristic	characteristic +
karizma	charisma
kayak	
kedgeree	
keel [1] /age	
keelige	keelage
keen [1] /ly/ness	
keep /er/ing/sake	
keg	
kegeree	kedgeree
kejery	kedgeree
kelp	
kelsius	Celsius
kelt	Celt +
keltic	Celtic
kemical	chemical +
kemist	chemist +
kemistrey	chemistry
ken [3]	
kenl	kennel
kennel	
kept	
kerb [1]★ (stone edging)	
kerb	curb [1]★
kerchief	
kernel ★ (seed)	
kernel	colonel ★
keropodie	chiropody +
keropody	chiropody +
keroseen	kerosene
kerosene	
kestrel	
ketch /es	
ketchup	
ketle	kettle +
kettle /drum	
ketul	kettle +
kew	cue [2]★
kew	queue [2]★
key [1]★† /hole/stone †(with lock)	
key	quay ★
khaki	
khan	
khrist	Christ

khristianity	Christianity	kiropodey	chiropody +
kiak	kayak	kiropodist	chiropodist
kibbutz		kiropody	chiropody +
kick [1] /er		kiser	Kaiser
kick-off		kiss [1] /er/es	
kid [3]		kit [3]	
kidd*y* /ies		kitchen	
kidie	kiddy +	kite	
kidnap [3] /per		kiten	kitten
kidney		kith	
kidy	kiddy +	kitie	kitty
kile	chyle	kitn	kitten
kill [1] /er		kitten	
kiln		kitty	
kilo		kity	kitty
kilocycle		kiyak	kayak
kilogram		klorate	chlorate
kilohertz		kloride	chloride
kiloliter	kilolitre	klorinashun	chlorination
kilolitre		klorinate	chlorinate [2+]
kilometer	kilometre	klorination	chlorination
kilometre		klorine	chlorine
kilosicle	kilocycle	klorofil	chlorophyll
kilotonne		kloroform	chloroform [1]
kilotun	kilotonne	klorophill	chlorophyll
kilowatt		knack /er	
kilowhat	kilowatt	knapsack	
kilt		knave ★ (rascal) /ry	
kime	chyme	knead [1]★ (press)	
kimono		knee /-cap/d ★†/ing	
kin /dred/ship		† (touch with knee)	
kinaesthesis		kneel [1]	
kind /ly/ness		knell [1]	
kindergarten		knelt	
kindle [2]		knew ★ (did know)	
kindrid	kindred	knew	gnu ★
kindul	kindle [2]	knew	new ★+
kinesthesis	kinaesthesis	knickerbockers	
kinetic		knickers	
king /ly/-pin/-size		knick-knack	
kink /ier/iest/y		kni*fe* [2] /ves (pl.)	
kins *man* /woman/folk		knight ★ (rank)	
kiosk		knit [3]★ (with needles)	
kipper [1]		knob [3]★ (handle) /by	
kirk		knob	nob ★

knock [1] /er/-kneed
knoll [1]
knot [3]★ (what you tie) /ty
know ★† /ing/ingly/s ★†
　†(understand)
knowledge /able
knuckle [2] /duster
koala
Kodak
kola   koala
koolom   coulomb
kopeck   copeck
koral   choral ★+
koral   coral ★
koral   corral [3]★
kord   chord ★
kord   cord ★+
Kremlin
kresh   crèche
krisalis   chrysalis +
krisanthimum   chrysanthemum
Krishna
kroisant   croissant
kromate   chromate
kromatic   chromatic +
kromatin   chromatin
kromatograf   chromatograph +
kromatogram   chromatogram
krome   chrome +
kromic   chromic
kromium   chromium
kromosome   chromosome
krone★(money)/r(pl.)
krone   crone ★
kronicul   chronicle [2]+
kronie   crony +
kronik   chronic +
kronologey   chronology +
kuisine   cuisine
Ku-Klux-Klan
kul de sac   cul-de-sac
kurb   curb [1]★
kurb   kerb [1]★
kurchif   kerchief
kurd   curd

kurdle   curdle [2]
kurdul   curdle [2]
kurk   kirk
kurl   curl [1]+
kurlew   curlew
kurlu   curlew
kurly   curly
kurnel   colonel ★
kurnel   kernel ★

> *If you cannot find your word
> under* **kw** *look under* **qu**

kwack   quack [1]
kwaff   quaff [1]
kwafur   coiffeur ★+
kwafur   coiffure ★
kwagmire   quagmire
kwail   quail [1]
kwaint   quaint +

L

label [3]
laber   labour [1]+
labernum   laburnum
labirinth   labyrinth +
labium
labor   labour [1]+
laborator *y* /ies
laboratrey   laboratory +
laborious /ly
laborius   laborious +
labour [1] /er
Labrador
labrum
laburnum
labyrinth /ine
lac *e* [2] /y
lacerat *e* [2] /ion
lach   latch [1]+
lachrym *al* /ose
lack [1] /-lustre
lackadaisical
lackadaysical   lackadaisical
lacker   lacquer [1]

lackey /s		lakrimal	lachrymal +
lacky	lackey +	lakross	lacrosse
laconic /ally		laks	lax +
lacquer ¹		laksativ	laxative
lacrimal	lachrymal +	lama ★ (Tibetan monk)	
lacros	lacrosse	lama	llama ★
lacrosse		lamb /'s-wool	
lactashun	lactation	lame ² /ly/ness	
lactation		lament ¹ /ation	
lactic		lamentabl e /y	
lad /die		lamentabul	lamentable +
ladder ¹		lamentashun	lamentation
lad e ★† /en/ing		laminate ²	
†(load cargo)		lamp /light/shade	
lade	laid ★	lampoon ¹ /er/ist	
lader	ladder ¹	lampray	lamprey
ladie	lady +	lamprey	
ladilike	ladylike +	lance ² /r/t	
ladiship	ladyship	land ¹ /lord	
ladle ²		landau	
ladul	ladle ²	landaw	landau
lad y /ies		landing /-place	
lady like /ship		landlad y /ies	
laer	lair ★	landlocked	
laer	layer ¹★	landlubber /ly	
laerd	laird	landmark	
laf	laugh ¹+	landoner	landowner
laffing stock	laughing-stock	landowner	
lafter	laughter	landscape ²	
lag ³		landsli de /p	
lagard	laggard	lane ★ (path)	
lager		lane	lain ★
laggard		langger	languor +
lagoon		language	
laid ★ (lay)		languid /ly/ness	
laid	lade ★+	languish ¹	
lain ★ (did lie on)		languor /ous	
lain	lane ★	langwid	languid +
lair ★ (den)		langwidge	language
lair	layer ¹★	langwige	language
laird		langwish	languish ¹
laitie	laity	lanjerie	lingerie
laity		lank /iness/y	
lake		lanladie	landlady +
laker	lacquer ¹	lanlord	landlord

lanolin		lateral	
lans	lance ² +	lath * (wooden strip)	
lanset	lancet	lathe * (machine)	
lantern		lather ¹	
lanthanum		Latin	
lanyard		latis	lattice +
lap ³		latitude	
lapel /led		latrine	
lapidary		latter * (last) /ly	
lapis lazuli		lattice /d	
lapse ²		lattis	lattice +
larcen y /ies/ous		laud ¹* (praise)	
larch /es		laud	lord ¹*+
larconic	laconic +	lauda ble /bly/tory	
lard ¹ /er		laugh ¹ /ter	
large /ly/r/sse/st		laughing-stock	
lariat		launch ¹ /er/es	
laringitis	laryngitis	laund er ¹ /erette/ress	
larinks	larynx +	laundrey	laundry +
larinx	larynx +	laundr y /ies	
lark ¹ /er		laureate	
larseny	larceny +	laurel ³	
larva *† /e (pl.)/l		lava * (of volcano)	
†(of insects)		lava	larva *+
larva	lava *	lavator y /ies	
laryn x /gitis		lavatrey	lavatory +
lascivious /ly/ness		lavender	
lase	lace ² +	lavish ¹ /ly/ness	
laser		law * (rule) /-abiding	
laserashun	laceration	law	lore *
laserate	lacerate ² +	law court /suit/yer	
laseration	laceration	lawd	laud ¹*
lasitude	lassitude	lawd	lord ¹*+
lasivious	lascivious +	Lawd Maer	Lord Mayor
lasivius	lascivious +	lawdable	laudable +
lasoo	lasso ¹ +	lawdabul	laudable +
lassitude ✎		lawdatorey	laudatory
lasso ¹ /es		lawditrey	laudatory
last ¹ /ly		lawful /ly	
latch ¹ /key		lawless /ness	
late /ly/st		lawn	
laten cy /t		lawnch	launch ¹+
latensey	latency +	lawnder	launder ¹+
later * (afterwards)		lawnderet	launderette
later	latter *+	lawndress	laundress

169

lawndrey	laundry [+]
lax /ity/ly/ness	
laxative	
lay /by/ing/-out	
laybie	layby
layer [1]★ (thickness)	
layer	lair ★
layman	
laz e [2] /y	
lazi er /est/ly/ness	
lea ★ (open ground)	
lea	lee ★+
leach [1]★ (purge)	
leach	leech ★+
lead ★ (guide) /er/ing	
lead ★ (element) /en	
lea f /flet/ves (pl.)	
leaf y /iness	
league	
leak [1]★ (hole) /age/y	
leak	leek ★
lean [1]	
leant ★ (inclined)	
leant	Lent ★
leant	lent ★
leap /ing/t	
leap -frog /-year	
learn [1] /er/t	
lease [2]	
leash [1]	
least /ways/wise	
leather /iness/n/y	
leav e /er ★ (school-)/ing	
leaven [1]	
leaver	lever ★
lebra	libra
lecher /ous/y	
lecherus	lecherous
lectern	
lecture [2] /r/ship	
led ★ (did guide)	
led	lead ★+
ledge	
ledger	
ledo	lido

lee ★† /ward/way †(shelter)	
lee	lea ★
leech ★ (worm) /es	
leech	leach [1]★
leed	lead ★+
leef	leaf +
leeflet	leaflet
leeg	league
leege	liege
leek ★ (vegetable)	
leek	leak [1]★+
leen	lean [1]
leep	leap +
leep yeer	leap-year
leer [1] /y	
leesh	leash [1]
left /ist/ward	
leftenancy	lieutenancy +
leftenansey	lieutenancy +
leftenant	lieutenant
left-hand /ed	
leg [3] /gy	
legac y /ies	
legal /ly	
legalis e [2] /ation	
legalit y /ies	
legasey	legacy +
legashun	legation
legation	
legend /ary	
legendrey	legendary
leger	ledger
legib le /ility/ly	
legibul	legible +
legion /ary/aries	
legislacher	legislature
legislashun	legislation
legislat e [2] /ion/or	
legislature	
legitima cy /te/tely	
legitimasey	legitimacy +
legitimis e [2] /ation	
legonrey	legionary
leisure /ly	

lejun	legion [+]	lest	least [+]
lejunrey	legionary	lesure	leisure [+]
leksicografer	lexicographer [+]	let /table/ting	
leksicographer	lexicographer [+]	leter	letter [1]
leksicon	lexicon	lethal /ly	
lemon /ade		lethargey	lethargy [+]
lemur		letharg *y* /ic	
lend /er/ing		lether	leather [+]
length /wise/y		letice	lettuce
lengthen [1]		letis	lettuce
lenienc *e* /y		letre	litre
leniens	lenience [+]	letter [1]	
lenient /ly		lettuce	
lens /es		letus	lettuce
Lent ★ (40 days)		leucocytes	
lent ★ (did lend)		leukaemia	
lent	leant ★	Levant	
lenth	length [+]	leve	leave [+]
lenthen	lengthen [1]	level [3] /ler/ly	
lenticel		level-headed	
lentil		levelheded	level-headed
Leo		leven	leaven [1]
leopard		lever [1] ★ (bar) /age	
leotard		lever	leaver★
lep *er* /rous		leviathan	
leperd	leopard	levie	levy [4+]
lepidopterous		levitashun	levitation
leprosy		levitat *e* [2] /ion	
lept	leapt	levity	
lerch	lurch [1+]	levy [4] /ies	
lerk	lurk [1]	lewd /ly/ness	
lern	learn [1+]	lexicografer	lexicographer [+]
les	less [+]	lexicograph *er* /y	
Lesbian		lexicon	
lese	lease [2]	lezbian	Lesbian
lesen	lessen [1★]	li	lie ★
lesher	leisure [+]	li	lye ★
leshon	lesion	lia	liar ★
lesion		liabilit *y* /ies	
leson	lessen [1★]	liable	
leson	lesson ★	liabul	liable
less /ee/er ★ (minor)		liaise [2]	
lessen [1★] (to belittle)		liaison [1]	
lesson ★ (learnt)		liar ★ (tells lies)	
lessor ★ (grants lease)		liar	lyre ★+

libel [3] /ler/lous		lignin	
libelus	libellous	lignite	
liberal /ity/ly		likeable	
liberalis *e* [2] /ation		likabul	likeable
liberashun	liberation	like [2] /ly/ness	
liberat *e* [2] /ion/or		likelihood	
libertey	liberty [+]	liken [1]	
libertine		liker	liqueur [1]★
libert *y* /ies		liker	liquor [1]★
libid *o* /inal/inous		likewise	
libra		likoris	liquorice
libralise	liberalise [2+]	likwefi	liquefy [4+]
librar *y* /ies/ian		likwid	liquid [+]
lice		likwidashun	liquidation
licee	lycée	likwidate	liquidate [2+]
licence ★ (n.)		likwidation	liquidation
license [2]★ (v.) /e/r		likwiditey	liquidity
licenshiate	licentiate	lilac	
licenshus	licentious [+]	lilak	lilac
licentiate		lile	lisle
licentious /ness		lilie	lily [+]
lichen /ed		Lilipushun	Lilliputian
lick [1]		Lilliputian	
licoriss	liquorice	lilt [1]	
lid /ded		lil *y* /ies	
lido		limb [1] /less	
lie ★ (untruth)		limber [1]	
lie	lye ★	limbo /s	
liege		lime /-kiln/light	
lieu ★ (place)		limelite	limelight
lieutenan *cy* /t		limerick	
li *fe* /ves (pl.)		limestone	
life *belt* /-blood/less/long		limf	lymph [+]
life-size		limfatic	lymphatic
lift [1] /-off		limit [1] /ation	
ligacher	ligature	limoosene	limousine
ligament		limousine	
ligature		limp [1] /er/ness	
light /er/est/ing		limpet	
lighten [1]		limph	lymph [+]
lighthouse		limphatic	lymphatic
light *ly* /ness		limpid	
lightning		linage ★†	
light-weight		†(number of lines)	
light-year		linch	lynch [1]

line[2] /r		lire	lyre ★[+]
lineage ★ (ancestry)		lirical	lyrical
lineament ★ (features)		lisay	lycée
lineament	liniment ★	lise	lice
linear /ity/ly		lisen	listen[1][+]
linet	linnet	lisence	licence ★
linger[1]		lisence	license[2]★[+]
lingerie		lisener	listener
lingo /es		lisensee	licensee
lingual		lisenshiat	licentiate
linguist /ic/ics		lisenshus	licentious[+]
lingwal	lingual	lisentiate	licentiate
lingwist	linguist[+]	lisentious	licentious[+]
liniament	lineament ★	lisle	
linier	linear[+]	lisp[1]	
liniige	lineage ★	lissom	
liniment ★ (salve)		list[1]	
liniment	lineament ★	listen[1] /er	
link[1] /age		listless /ly/ness	
links ★ (joins)		lisum	lissom
links	lynx ★[+]	lit	
linnet		litan*y* /ies	
lino /cut/leum		lite	light[+]
linolium	linoleum	litehowse	lighthouse
linseed		litely	lightly[+]
lint		liten	lighten[1]
lintel /led		liter	litre
lintul	lintel[+]	liter	litter[1]
linx	lynx ★[+]	literacher	literature
lio	Leo	litera *cy* /te	
lion /ess (fem.)		literal /ly	
lion-hearted		literar*y* /ily	
liotard	leotard	literasey	literacy[+]
lip[3] /stick		literat	literate
lip-read /er/ing		literature	
liquef*y*[4] /action		litergic	liturgic[+]
liquer	liquor[1]★	litergy	liturgy[+]
liqueur[1]★†		litewait	light-weight
†(sweet liquor)		lithe /ly/some	
liquid /ity		lithium	
liquidat *e*[2] /ion/or		lithograf	lithograph[+]
liquor[1]★ (drink)		lithografey	lithography
liquor	liqueur[1]★	lithograph /ic/y	
liquorice		litig *ant* /ious	
liquoris	liquorice	litigashun	litigation

litigat *e* ² /ion		loby	lobby ⁴⁺
litijus	litigious	local ★ (of place)	
litle	little	locale ★ (locality)	
litmus paper		localis *e* ² /ation	
litning	lightning	localit *y* /ies	
litracher	literature	locashun	location
litre		locat *e* ² /ion/or	
litter ¹		loch ★ (lake)	
little		lock ¹★ (door) /er/jaw	
litul	little	locket	
liturgey	liturgy ⁺	locksmith	
liturgic /al		lockwacious	loquacious ⁺
liturg *y* /ies		lockwacity	loquacity
liv	live ²⁺	lockwashus	loquacious ⁺
livable		locomoshun	locomotion ⁺
livabul	livable	locomot *ion* /ive	
live ² /lihood/ly		locum	
liveli *er* /est/ness		locust	
liven ¹		lode ★ (mineral) /stone	
liver /ish		lode	load ¹★⁺
liver *y* /ies		lodge ² /ment/r	
livid		lof	loaf ¹⁺
living-room		loft ¹ /ier/iest/ily/iness	
livlie	lively	log ³ /ger	
livlier	livelier ⁺	loganberie	loganberry ⁺
livrey	livery ⁺	loganberr *y* /ies	
liying	lying	logarithm /ic	
lizard		log-book	
lizerd	lizard	loge	lodge ²⁺
llama ★ (animal)		logerhed	loggerhead
lo	low ¹⁺	loggerhead	
load ¹★† /er		logic /al/ally/ian	
†(heavy weight)		logishun	logician
load	lode ★⁺	logistics	
loa *f* ¹ /ves (pl.)		loial	loyal ⁺
loam /y		loialist	loyalist
loan ¹★ (lending)		loialtey	loyalty ⁺
loan	lone ★⁺	loier	lawyer
loath ★ (reluctant)		loin	
loath *e* ²★ (hate) /some		loiter ¹ /er	
lob ³		lokust	locust
lobby ⁴ /ist		lol	loll ¹
lobe		lolipop	lollipop
lobie	lobby ⁴⁺	loll ¹	
lobster		lollipop	

174

lom	loam[+]
lone ★ (lonely) /r	
lone	loan[1]★
loneliness	
lonesome	
lonesum	lonesome
long[1] /er/est/wise	
longevity	
longitud e /inal/inally	
loo[1]★ (card game)	
loo	lieu ★
loobricant	lubricant
loobricashun	lubrication
loobricate	lubricate[2+]
loocrativ	lucrative
loodicrous	ludicrous[+]
loodicrus	ludicrous[+]
look[1]	
lookemia	leukaemia
looker	lucre[+]
looking-glass	
lookwarm	lukewarm
loom[1]	
loominus	luminous[+]
loona	luna
loop[1]	
loose[2]★† /ly/ness/r/st †(not tight)	
loose	lose ★[+]
loosen[1]	
loosing	losing
loot[1]★ (booty) /er	
loot	lute ★
lop[3]	
lope[2]	
loquacious /ly/ness	
loquacity	
loquashus	loquacious[+]
lord[1]★ (noble) /ly/ship	
lord	laud[1]★
lord(s) justice(s)	
Lord Mayor	
lore ★ (teaching)	
lore	law ★[+]
lorel	laurel[3]

lorgnette	
loriat	laureate
lorie	lorry[+]
lornch	launch[1+]
lornderet	launderette
lornyet	lorgnette
lorr y /ies	
lory	lorry[+]
los	loss
los e ★† /ing/er/t †(fail to win)	
lose	loose[2]★[+]
loshun	lotion
loss	
lotery	lottery[+]
lothe	loathe[2]★[+]
lothsum	loathsome
lotion	
lotter y /ies	
lotus	
loud /er/ly/ness	
loud-speaker	
lounge[2] /r	
lous e /y	
lout /ish	
lov e[2] /able/ely/er	
loveli er /est/ness	
loves	loaves
low[1] /est/liness/ly	
lowd	loud[+]
lower[1]	
lownge	lounge[2+]
lowse	louse[+]
lowt	lout[+]
loyal /ism/ist/ly	
loyalt y /ies	
lozenge	
lozinge	lozenge
lu	lieu ★
lu	loo[1]★
lubber /ly	
luber	lubber[+]
lubricant	
lubricat e[2] /ion	
lucer	lucre[+]

175

lucid /ity/ly/ness	
luck /ier/iest/ily/y	
lucr e /ative	
lude	lewd +
ludicrous /ly	
luff [1]	
lug [3] /ger	
luggage	
lugige	luggage
lugsuriant	luxuriant
lugubrious	
lukemia	leukaemia
lukewarm	
luksurey	luxury +
luksuriant	luxuriant
luksuriate	luxuriate [2]
luksurious	luxurious +
luksurius	luxurious +
lul	lull [1]
lulabie	lullaby +
lull [1]	
lullab y /ies	
lumbago	
lumbar ★ (back)	
lumber [1]★ (wood)	
lumberjack	
luminary	
lumino us /sity	
luminus	luminous +
lump [1] /iness/y	
luna	
luna cy /tic	
lunasey	lunacy +
lunch [1] /eon/es	
lung	
lunge [2]	
lurch [1] /er	
lure [2]	
lurid /ly	
lurk [1]	
lurn	learn [1]+
lurner	learner
lurnt	learnt
luscious	
lushus	luscious

lusid	lucid +
lust [1] /ful	
luster	lustre +
lustie	lusty +
lustr e /ous	
lust y /ily/iness	
lute ★ (instrument)	
lute	loot [1]★+
lutetium	
Lutheran	
luv	love [2]+
luver	lover
luvley	lovely
luvlier	lovelier +
luxurey	luxury +
luxurian ce /t/tly	
luxuriate [2]	
luxurious /ly	
luxur y /ies	
lycée	
lye ★ (chemical)	
lye	lie ★
lying	
lymph /atic	
lynch [1]	
lynx ★ (animal) /es	
lynx	links ★
lyre ★† /-bird †(instrument)	
lyre	liar ★
lyric /al/ism/ist	

M

ma'am	
mac ★ (macintosh)	
mac	mach ★
macabre	
macadam /ise [2]	
macaroni	
macaroon	
mace	
macerat e [2] /ion	
mach ★ (speed ratio)	

mach	match[1]+	magnificens	magnificence+
machate	machete	magnifisence	magnificence+
machete		magnifisent	magnificent
machiage	maquillage	magnif$y$[4] /ication	
Machiavellian		magnitude	
machination		magnolia	
machine[2] /ry		magnum	
machinist		magot	maggot+
mackerel		magpie	
mackintosh /es		Magyar	
macrocosm		maharaja /nee (fem.)	
macroscopic		mahem	mayhem
mad /der/dest/ly/ness		mahjong	
madam /e (French)		mahogany	
madden[1]		maid * (girl) /en/enly	
made * (built)		maid	made *
made	maid *+	mail[1]* (letters)	
Madeira		mail	male *
mademoiselle		maim[1]	
mademwoisel	mademoiselle	main *† /land/ly	
maden	madden[1]	†(most important)	
madera	Madeira	main	mane *
madonna		maintain[1]	
madrigal		maintenance	
maelstrom		maintenans	maintenance
maer	mayor+	maisonette	
magazine		maize * (corn)	
magenta		maize	maze[2]*
maggot /y		majenta	magenta
Magi		majer	major[1]+
magic /al/ally/ian		majestey	majesty+
magishun	magician	majestic /ally	
magisterial /ly		majest$y$ /ies	
magistrac$y$ /ies		majong	mahjong
magistrat$e$ /ure		major[1] /ette	
magnanimity /ous		majorit$y$ /ies	
magnanimus	magnanimous	mak	mac *
magnate *†		mak	mach *
†(prominent person)		makaber	macabre
magnesi$a$ /um		makadam	macadam+
magnet *† /ic/ism		makaroon	macaroon
†(attracts iron)		mak$e$ /ing/er/eshift	
magnetis$e$[2] /ation		Makiavelian	Machiavellian
magneto /s		makination	machination
magnificen ce /t/tly		maksila	maxilla+

177

maksim	maxim	malnutrishun	malnutrition
maksimise	maximise [2]	malnutrition	
maksimum	maximum [+]	malodorous	
malachite		Malpighian (layer)	
maladey	malady [+]	malstrom	maelstrom
maladjust *ed* /ment		malt [1] /ose	
maladministration		Maltese	
maladroit /ness		maltreat [1] /ment	
malad *y* /ies		maltreet	maltreat [1+]
malaise		mam	ma'am
malakite	malachite	mamal	mammal [+]
malaprop *ism* /os		mamarey	mammary
malard	mallard	mame	maim [1]
malaria		mammal /ian	
malase	malaise	mammary	
malcontent		mammon	
male * (man)		mammoth	
male	mail [1]*	mamon	mammon
maledicshun	malediction	mamoth	mammoth
malediction		man [3] /fully/ly/-of-war	
malefactor		mana	manna *
malet	mallet	manacle [2]	
maleus	malleus	manacul	manacle [2]
malevolen *ce* /t		manage [2] /able/ment	
malevolens	malevolence [+]	manager /ial	
malform [1] /ation		mandarin	
malformashun	malformation	mandat *e* [2] /ary * (law)	
malfuncshun	malfunction [1]	mandatory *(command)	
malfunction [1]		mandatrey	mandatory *
maliable	malleable [+]	mandible	
malice		mandibul	mandible
malicious /ly/ness		mandolin	
malign [1] /er/ity		mane * (hair)	
malignanc *y* /ies		mane	main *[+]
malignansey	malignancy [+]	maner	manner *[+]
malignant		maner	manor *[+]
maline	malign [1+]	manganese	
malinger [1] /er		mang *e* /y	
malis	malice	mangel-wurzel	
malishus	malicious [+]	manger	
mallard		mangle [2]	
malleab *le* /ility		mango /es	
malleabul	malleable [+]	mangrove	
mallet		mangul	mangle [2]
malleus		manhandle [2]	

178

manhandul	manhandle [2]	maple	
manhole		mapul	maple
manhood		maquillage	
mania /c/cal		mar [3]	
manicur *e* [2] /ist		marathon	
manidge	manage [2+]	maraud [1] /er	
manie	many	marawd	maraud [1+]
manifest [1] /ation		marble [2]	
manifesto /s		marbul	marble [2]
manifold [1]		march [1] /er/es	
manige	manage [2+]	marchioness (fem.)	
manikin	mannequin	Marconi	
manila	manilla	mare	
manilla		mareen	marine [+]
manipulashun	manipulation	margarine	
manipulat *e* [2] /ion		margerit	marguerite
manipulat *ive* /or		margin /al/ally	
manjer	manger	marguerite	
manliness		mariage	marriage [+]
manna * (food)		marie	marry [4]
mannequin		marige	marriage [+]
manner *† /ed/ism/ly		marigold	
†(method)		marijuana	
manoeuvr *e* [2] /able		marina	
manoover	manoeuvre [2+]	marinade	
manoovrable	manoeuvrable	marinate [2]	
manoovrabul	manoeuvrable	marine /r	
manor * (estate) /ial		marionet	marionette
manshun	mansion	marionette	
mansion		marital	
manslaughter		maritime	
manslorter	manslaughter	maritul	marital
mantel *† /piece		mariwana	marijuana
†(shelf at fireplace)		marjoram	
mantilla		mark [1] /edly/er	
mantle [2]* (cloak)		market [1] /ability	
mantul	mantle [2]*	markey	marquee *
manual /ly		markey	marquis *
manufaccher	manufacture [2+]	markoni	Marconi
manufacture [2] /r		marksism	Marxism [+]
manure [2]		marksman	
manuscript		markwis	marquis *
many		marline-spike	
maonaise	mayonnaise	marmalade	
map [3]		marmoreal	

marmorial	marmoreal	maserate	macerate [2+]
marmoset		mash [1]	
marmot		mashene	machine [2+]
maroon [1]		mashenerey	machinery
marow	marrow	mashenist	machinist
marquee * (tent)		mashine	machine [2+]
marquis * (noble)		mashinerey	machinery
marriage /able		mashinist	machinist
marrow		masiv	massive [+]
marry [4]		mask [1]* (cover)	
Mars		mask	masque *
Marseillaise		maskerade	masquerade [2]
Marselase	Marseillaise	masochis m /t/tic	
marsh /-mallow/y		masocism	masochism [+]
marshal [3]*†		masocist	masochist
†(arrange in order)		mason /ic/ry	
marshal	martial *[+]	masonet	maisonette
marshoness	marchioness	masque * (ball)	
marshun	Martian	masque	mask [1]*
marsupial		masquerade [2]	
marten * (animal)		mass [1] /es	
marten	martin *	massacer	massacre [2]
marter	martyr [1+]	massacre [2]	
marterdom	martyrdom	massage [2]	
marterise	martyrise [2]	masseu r /se (fem.)	
martial *† /ly		massive /ly/ness	
†(relating to war)		massur	masseur [+]
martial	marshal [3]*	master [1] /ly	
Martian		masterbate	masturbate [2+]
martin * (bird)		masterful /ly/ness	
martin	marten *	masterpeace	masterpiece
martinet		masterpiece	
martyr [1] /dom		masticat e [2] /ion	
martyrise [2]		mastiff /s	
marvel [3] /lous/lously		masturbat e [2] /ion	
Marxis m /t		mat [3]* (rug)	
mary	marry [4]	mat	matt *
marzipan		matador	
mas	mass [1+]	match [1] /es/less	
masacer	massacre [2]	mate [2]	
masacre	massacre [2]	mater	matter [1]
masage	massage [2]	material /ism/ist/ly	
mascot		materialis e [2] /ation	
masculin e /ity		maternal /ly	
mase	mace	maternit y /ies	

mathematic s /al/ian		
mathematishun	mathematician	
maths		
matinay	matinée	
matinée		
mating	matting	
matins		
matress	mattress +	
matriarch /al/y		
matriculat e ² /ion		
matriks	matrix +	
matrikulate	matriculate ²+	
matrimon y /ial		
matri x /ces/xes (pls.)		
matron /ly		
matt ★ (dull surface)		
matter ¹		
matting		
mattress /es		
mature ² /ly		
maturity		
maul ¹		
mausoleum		
mauve		
maverick		
mawgage	mortgage ²+	
mawkish /ness		
mawl	maul ¹	
mawsoleum	mausoleum	
maxilla /e (pl.)		
maxim		
maximise ²		
maxim um /a (pl.)		
may /be /-fly		
May Day		
mayhem		
mayonnaise		
mayor /al/alty		
maypole		
maze ²★†		
†(confusing paths)		
maze	maize ★	
mazurka		
mead		
meadow		

meager	meagre +	
meagre /ly		
meak	meek +	
meal /time/y		
mean ★ (nasty) /s		
mean	mien ★	
meander ¹		
mean er /est/ly/ness		
meaning /ful/fully/less		
meant		
meantime		
meanwhile		
measl es /y		
measuls	measles +	
measurable		
measure ² /less/ment		
meat ★ (flesh)		
meat	meet ★+	
meat	mete ²★	
mecanic	mechanic +	
mecanise	mechanise ²+	
mecanism	mechanism	
mechanic /al/ally		
mechanis e ² /ation/m		
medal ★ (award) /list		
medal	meddle ²★+	
medallion		
medalyon	medallion	
medcine	medicine +	
meddle ²★† /some/r ★		
†(interfere /r)		
meddler	medlar ★	
medeval	medieval	
medi an /al/ally		
medical /ly		
medicament		
medicat e ² /ion		
medicin e /al		
medieval		
mediocer	mediocre	
mediocre		
mediocrit y /ies		
medisinal	medicinal	
meditat e ² /ion/ive/or		
Mediterranean		

medi *um* /a/ums (pls.)
medlar * (fruit)

medle	meddle [2]*+
medler	meddler *
medler	medlar *
medley	
medly	medley
medow	meadow
medsin	medicine +
medul	meddle [2]*+
medulla	
meed	mead
meek /ly/ness	
meel	meal +
meeltime	mealtime
meen	mean *+
meener	meaner +
meening	meaning +
meeningful	meaningful
meens	means
meentime	meantime
meenwile	meanwhile
meerschaum	
meershum	meerschaum
meesels	measles +
meesley	measly
meet *(encounter)/ing	
meet	meat *
meet	mete [2]*
megacycle	
megafone	megaphone
megalith /ic	
megalomania /c	
megaphone	
meger	meagre +
megohm	
megom	megohm
mekanic	mechanic +
mekanical	mechanical
mekanise	mechanise [2]+
mekanism	mechanism
melanchol *y* /ia/ic	
melay	mêlée
mêlée	
melifluous	mellifluous

melifluus	mellifluous
mellifluous	
mellow [1]	
melodey	melody +
melodic /ally	
melodius	melodious
melodrama /tic	
melod *y* /ies/ious	
melon	
melow	mellow [1]
melt [1]	
member /ship	
membrain	membrane +
membran *e* /ous	
memento /es	
memo /s	
memoir	
memorabl *e* /y	
memorand *um*/a/ums(pls.)	
memorey	memory +
memorial	
memorise [2]	
memor *y* /ies	
memrable	memorable +
men (pl. of man)	
menace [2]	
menagerie	
menajerey	menagerie
menas	menace [2]
mend [1]	
mendacious /ly	
mendacity	
mendashus	mendacious +
mendasitey	mendacity
mendelevium	
mendicity	
menial /ly	
meningitis	
meninjitis	meningitis
menopause	
menopaws	menopause
menshun	mention [1]
menstrooal	menstrual
menstrooate	menstruate [2]+
menstrual	

menstruat *e* ² /ion	
ment	meant
mental /ity/ly	
mentalitey	mentality
menthol	
mention ¹	
mentor	
menu /s	
merang	meringue
mercantil *e* /ism	
mercenar *y* /ies	
mercenrey	mercenary +
merchandise	
merchant	
mercur *y* /ial	
merc *y* /iful/ifully/iless	
mere /ly/st	
meretricious	
meretrishus	meretricious
merge ² /r	
meridian	
meridional	
merie	merry +
meriment	merriment
meringue	
merit ¹	
meritorious	
meritorius	meritorious
mermade	mermaid
mermaid	
merr *y* /ier/ily/iment	
merry-go-round	
merry-making	
mersenrey	mercenary +
mersie	mercy +
mersiful	merciful
mersy	mercy +
mery	merry +
mesenger	messenger
mesh ¹	
Mesia	Messiah +
mesidge	message
mesie	messy
mesige	message
mesmeris *e* ² /m	

mesofill	mesophyll
mesophyll	
mess ¹ /ier/iest/ily/y	
message	
messenger	
Messia *h* /nic	
mesur	monsieur
mesurable	measurable
mesurabul	measurable
mesure	measure ²+
metabol *ic* /ism	
metacarpals	
metafisical	metaphysical +
metafisics	metaphysics
metafor	metaphor
metaforical	metaphorical +
metal ³★ (material)	
metal	mettle ★
metalic	metallic
metalise	metallise ²+
metallic	
metallis *e* ² /ation	
metallurg *y* /ical/ist	
metalurgey	metallurgy +
metamorfose	metamorphose ²+
metamorfosis	metamorphosis
metamorphos *e* ² /is/es (pl.)	
metaphor	
metaphorical /ly	
metaphysical /ly	
metaphysics	
metatarsals	
mete ²★ (measure)	
mete	meat ★
mete	meet ★+
meteor /ic/ite	
meteorolog *y* /ical	
meter ¹★ (machine)	
meter	metre ★+
methane	
methilate	methylate ²
method /ical/ically	
methylate ²	
meticulous /ly	
meticulus	meticulous +

183

metior	meteor [+]	midshipman	
metiorite	meteorite	midst	
metiorologey	meteorology [+]	midsummer	
metiorological	meteorological	midul	middle [+]
metr e * (measure) /ic		midwi fe /ves (pl.)/fery	
metre	meter [1]*	mien * (bearing)	
metricashun	metrication	mige	midge [+]
metricat e [2] /ion		might * (strength, may)	
metronome		might	mite *
metropoli s /tan		might ier /iest/ily/y	
mettle * (spirit)		migit	midget
mettle	metal [3]*	migraine	
metul	mettle *	migrane	migraine
mew [1] /s *†		migrant	
†(cat's cry, stable)		migrat e [2] /ion/or	
mezanin	mezzanine	mika	mica
mezzanine		miklmas	Michaelmas
mi	my [+]	miks	mix [1+]
miander	meander [1]	miksamatosis	myxomatosis
miaow		mikscher	mixture
mica		mikser	mixer
mice (pl. of mouse)		miksture	mixture
Michaelmas		mil	mill [1+]
microb e /ial		milch-cow	
microbiolog y /ist		mild /ly/ness	
microcosm		mildew /y	
microfilm		mildu	mildew [+]
microfone	microphone [+]	mile /age/stone	
micrometer		milenium	millennium [+]
micron		milet	millet
micro-organism		miligram	milligram [+]
microphon e /ic		milileter	millilitre
micropyle		milimeter	millimetre
microscop e /ic/ical/y		miliner	milliner [+]
microwave		milinerey	millinery
mid-brain		milinrey	millinery
midday		milion	million [+]
middle /-weight		milionair	millionaire
middling		milipede	millepede
midge /t		milisha	militia
Midlands		militan cy /t	
midling	middling	militansey	militancy [+]
midnight		militarey	military [+]
midnite	midnight	militar y /ily/ism/ist	
midriff		militate [2]	

militia	
milivolt	millivolt +
miliwot	milliwatt
milk ¹ /er/iness/y	
milkmade	milkmaid +
milk *maid* /sop	
mill ¹ /er	
millenni *um* /a (pl.)	
millepede	
millet	
milli *gram* /litre/metre	
milliner /y	
million /aire/th	
milli *volt* /watt	
milyun	million +
milyunair	millionaire
mime ²	
mimeograph ¹	
mimic /ry	
mimick *ed* /ing	
mimiograf	mimeograph ¹
mimosa	
minaret	
mince ² /meat/-pie/r	
mind ¹ /er/ful/less	
mine ² /sweeper	
miner *†	
†(works in a mine)	
miner	minor *
mineralog *y* /ical/ist	
minestrone	
minestrony	minestrone
mingle ²	
mingul	mingle ²
mini /skirt	
miniatur *e* /ist	
minicher	miniature +
minim /al/um/a (pl.)	
minimise ²	
minion	
miniscule	minuscule
minister ¹	
ministerial /ly	
ministra *tion* /nt	
ministrey	ministry +

ministr *y* /ies	
minit	minute ²+
mink	
minks	minx
minnow	
minor * (lesser)	
minor	miner *
minorit *y* /ies	
minow	minnow
minse	mince ²+
minsmeat	mincemeat
minspie	mince-pie
minster	
minstrel	
mint ¹	
minuet	
minus /sign	
minuscule	
minushia	minutia +
minute ² /ly	
minutia /e (pl.)	
minx	
minyouet	minuet
minyun	minion
miopia	myopia +
miow	miaow
mirac *le* /ulous	
miracul	miracle +
miraculus	miraculous
mirage	
mir *e* /y	
mirer	mirror ¹
miriad	myriad
mirror ¹	
mirth /ful/fully	
mis	miss ¹+
misadvencher	misadventure
misadventure	
misal	missal *
misal	missile *
misaliance	misalliance
misalians	misalliance
misalliance	
misanthrop *e* /ic/ist/y	
misapli	misapply ⁴+

185

misappl *y* [4] /ication
misapprehen *d* [1] /sion
misappropriat *e* [2] /ion
misaprehend — misapprehend [1+]
misaprehenshun — misapprehension
misaprehension — misapprehension
misapropriate — misappropriate [2+]
misbehav *e* [2] /iour
misbehavier — misbehaviour
misbihave — misbehave [2+]
miscalculat *e* [2] /ion
miscariage — miscarriage
miscarie — miscarry [4+]
miscarige — miscarriage
miscarr *y* [4] /iage
miscast
miscelanius — miscellaneous
miscellaneous
miscellan *y* /ies
mischance
mischans — mischance
mischie *f* /vous
mischif — mischief [+]
mischivus — mischievous
miscible
misconceive [2]
misconception
misconcieve — misconceive [2]
misconduct [1]
misconsepshun — misconception
misconstru *e* [2] /ction
miscount [1]
miscownt — miscount [1]
miscreant
misdeed
misdemeanour
misdemener — misdemeanour
mise — mice
miselaneous — miscellaneous
miselaney — miscellany [+]
miselanius — miscellaneous
miself — myself
miselium — mycelium
miser /liness/ly
miserabl *e* /y

miserabul — miserable [+]
miser *y* /ies
misfire [2]
misfit
misfortune
misgave
misgidance — misguidance
misgidans — misguidance
misgide — misguide [2+]
misgiv *e* /en/ing
misgovern [1] /ment
misguid *e* [2] /ance
misguven — misgovern [1+]
mishandle [2]
mishandul — mishandle [2]
mishap
mishun — mission [+]
mishunarey — missionary
mishunrey — missionary
misile — missile ★
misinform [1] /ation
misinterpret [1] /ation
misiv — missive
misjudge [2] /ment
misjuge — misjudge [2+]
miskwotashun — misquotation
miskwotation — misquotation
miskwote — misquote [2+]
mislade — mislaid
mislaid
mislay /ing
misle — missal ★
misle — missile ★
mislead /ing
misled
misleed — mislead [+]
misnomer
misogyn *y* /ism/ist
misojinist — misogynist
misojiny — misogyny [+]
mispell — misspell [+]
mispelt — misspelt
mispend — misspend [+]
mispent — misspent
misplace [2] /ment

misplase	misplace [2+]
misprint [1]	
mispronounce [2]	
mispronownce	mispronounce [2]
misquot *e* [2] /ation	
misrable	miserable +
misrabul	miserable +
misread /ing	
misred	misread +
misrepresent [1] /ation	
misrool	misrule [2]
misrule [2]	
miss [1] /es	
missal *(prayer book)	
missal	missile *
missellaneous	miscellaneous
missellany	miscellany +
missel-thrush	
misshapen	
missible	miscible
missile * (weapon)	
mission /ary/aries	
missive	
misspell /ing	
misspelt	
misspend /ing	
misspent	
misstate [2] /ment	
mist /ily/iness/y	
mistak *e* /able/en/ing	
misterey	mystery +
misterious	mysterious +
misterius	mysterious +
mistic	mystic *+
mistic	mystique *
mistifi	mystify [4+]
mistime [2]	
mistisism	mysticism
mistletoe	
mistook	
mistress /es	
mistrust [1] /ful	
misul	missal *
misul	missile *
misul thrush	missel-thrush

misultoe	mistletoe
misunderstand /ing	
misunderstood	
misuse [2]	
mite * (very small)	
mite	might *
miten	mitten
miter	mitre [2]
mith	myth +
mithical	mythical
mithologey	mythology
mitie	mighty
mitigat *e* [2] /ion	
mitre [2]	
mitten	
mix [1] /er/ture	
mixamatosis	myxomatosis
mixcher	mixture
mnemonic	
mo	mow +
moan *[1] (complain) /er	
moat [1]	
mob [3]	
mobil *e* /ity	
mobilis *e* [2] /ation	
mobilitey	mobility
moca	mocha
moccasin	
mocha	
mock [1] /ery	
mod *e* /ish	
model [3]	
moderashun	moderation
moderat *e* [2] /ion/or	
modern /ism/ity	
modernis *e* [2] /ation	
modest /y	
modicum /s	
modifi	modify [4+]
modificashun	modification
modif *y* [4] /ication	
modul	model [3]
modulat *e* [2] /ion/or	
modul *us* /i (pl.)	
mohair	

187

mohare	mohair	monkey /s	
moischer	moisture	monochord	
moisen	moisten [1]	monochrom *e* /atic/ic	
moist /ness/ure		monocle	
moisten [1]		monocotyledon	
moka	mocha	monocul	monocle
mokasin	moccasin	monogamus	monogamous
molar		monogam *y* /ist/ous	
molasses		monograf	monograph [1]
mold	mould [1+]	monogram	
molder	moulder [1]	monograph [1]	
moldey	mouldy	monokord	monochord
mole		monokrome	monochrome +
molecul *e* /ar		monokside	monoxide
molest [1] /ation		monolith /ic	
molicodle	mollycoddle [2]	monolog	monologue
molicodul	mollycoddle [2]	monologue	
mollify [4]		monomania /c	
mollusc		monophonic	
mollycoddle [2]		monoplane	
molt	moult [1]	monopoley	monopoly +
molten		monopolis *e* [2] /ation	
molusk	mollusc	monopolist /ic	
molybdenum		monopol *y* /ies	
moment /arily/ary		monorail	
momentous		monosilabic	monosyllabic
momentum		monosilable	monosyllable +
monak	monarch +	monosyllab *le* /ic	
monakey	monarchy +	monothaism	monotheism +
monarch /al/ical		monotheis *m* /t/tic	
monarch *y* /ies		monotipe	Monotype
monaster *y* /ial/ies		monoton *e* /ic	
monastic /ism		monoton *ous* /y	
monastrey	monastery +	monotonus	monotonous +
Monday		Monotype	
mone	moan [1+]	monoxide	
monetar *y* /ism/ist		monsieur	
money /s (pl.)/ed		monsoon	
Mongol /ian		monst *er* /rous	
Mongol *ism* /oid		monstrosit *y* /ies	
mongoose /s		monstrus	monstrous
mongrel		month /ly	
moniter	monitor [1]	monument /al/ally	
monitor [1]		moo [1]	
monk /ish		mooch [1]	

mood /ily/iness/y	
moon [1] /beam/lit/y	
moonlight	
moor [1]*† /age	
†(waste ground)	
moor	more *+
moose * (animal)	
moose	mousse *
moot [1]	
moov	move [2]+
moovable	movable
moovabul	movable
mop [3]	
mope [2]	
moped	
moraine	
moral /e/ity/ly	
moralise [2]	
moralitey	morality
morass	
moratorium /s	
morbid /ity	
mordant	
more *† /over	
†(greater quantity)	
more	moor [1]*+
morfia	morphia +
morfine	morphine
morg	morgue
morgage	mortgage [2]+
morganatic /ally	
morgige	mortgage [2]+
morgue	
moribund	
morn * (morning)	
morn	mourn [1]*+
mornful	mournful +
moron /ic	
morose /ly	
morover	moreover
morow	morrow
morphi a /ne/nism	
morrow	
Morse	
morsel	

mortal /ity/ly	
mortar [1] /-board	
mortary	mortuary +
mortgag e [2] /ee/or	
mortifi	mortify [4]+
mortif y [4] /ication	
mortise [2]	
mortuar y /ies	
mos	moss +
mosaic	
moshun	motion [1]+
mosk	mosque
moskito	mosquito +
Moslem	
mosque	
mosquito /es	
moss /es/y	
most	
mote	
moteef	motif *+
motel	
moter	motor [1]+
moterboat	motorboat
motercycle	motorcycle
moterise	motorise [2]+
moterist	motorist
moterway	motorway
moth /-eaten	
mother [1] /ly/(s)-in-law	
mother-tongue	
motif * (ornament) /s	
motion [1] /less	
motivat e [2] /ion	
motive * (movement)	
motled	mottled
motley	
motlie	motley
motly	motley
moto	motto +
motor [1]/boat/cycle/way	
motoris e [2] /t	
mottled	
motto /es	
mould [1] /iness/y	
moulder [1]	

moult [1]
mound [1]
mount [1]
mountain /eer/ous
mountebank
mountenus   mountainous
mourn [1]★ (grieve) /er
mournful /ly
mous e ★(rodent)/er/y
mouse   moose ★
mousse ★ (pudding)
moustache
mouth [1] /ful/piece
movable
movabul   movable
move [2] /ment
move   mauve
mow /er/n
mownd   mound [1]
mownt   mount [1]
mowntain   mountain +
mowntbank   mountebank
mownten   mountain +
mowntenear   mountaineer
mowntenus   mountainous
mowse   mouse ★+
mowth   mouth [1]+
mowthful   mouthful
mu   mew [1]+
much
muchooal   mutual +
mucilag e /inous
muck [1] /y
mucous ★ (adj.)
mucus ★ (n.)
mud /dy/guard
muddid   muddied +
muddi ed /er/est
muddle [2] /r
mudid   muddied +
mudie   muddy
mudul   muddle [2]+
muff [1]
muffin
muffle [2] /r

mufin   muffin
mufti
muful   muffle [2]+
mug [3] /gy
mukus   mucous ★
mukus   mucus ★
mulatto /s
mulberie   mulberry +
mulberr y /ies
mulch [1]
mulct [1]
mul e /eteer/ish
mulkt   mulct [1]
mullion
multifarious
multifarius   multifarious
multiform
multilateral /ly
multiple
multipleks   multiplex
multiplex
multipli   multiply [4]+
multiplicashun   multiplication
multiplicity
multipl y [4] /ication
multipul   multiple
multiracial
multirashul   multiracial
multitud e /inous
multitudinus   multitudinous
mulyun   mullion
mumble [2]
mumbo-jumbo
mumbul   mumble [2]
mumie   mummy +
mumifi   mummify [4]
mummify [4]
mumm y /ies
mumy   mummy +
munch [1]
mundane
Munday   Monday
munetarey   monetary +
munetrey   monetary +
mungrel   mongrel

municipal /ity/ities	
munie	money +
munificen ce /t	
munifisens	munificence +
munifisent	munificent
munishun	munition ¹
munisipal	municipal +
munisipalitey	municipality
munition ¹	
munk	monk +
munky	monkey +
munth	month +
muny	money +
mur	myrrh
mural /ly	
murder ¹ /er/ess/ous	
murk /ily/iness/y	
murmer	murmur ¹
murmur ¹	
murth	mirth +
murtle	myrtle
mus	mews *
mus	muse ²*
muscat /el	
muscle ²* (in body)	
muscle	mussel *
muscular /ity	
muse ²* (think)	
muse	mews *
musel	muscle ²*
musel	mussel *
museum /s	
mush /y	
mushroom ¹	
music /al/ally/ian	
musilage	mucilage +
musishun	musician
musk	
musket /eer/ry	
muskwash	musquash
musquash	
mussel * (shellfish)	
mussel	muscle ²*
must /n't	
mustach	moustache

mustang	
mustard	
muster ¹	
mustie	musty +
must y /iness	
mutashun	mutation
mutation	
mute ² /ly	
muter	mutter ¹
mutilat e ² /ion/or	
mutinear	mutineer +
mutin eer /ous	
mutinus	mutinous
mutin y ⁴ /ies	
muton	mutton
mutter ¹	
mutton	
mutual /ly	
muzie	muzzy +
muzul	muzzle ²
muzzle ²	
muzz y /ily/iness	
my /self	
mycelium	
myopi a /c	
myriad	
myrrh	
myrtle	
mysterious /ly/ness	
mysterius	mysterious +
myster y /ies	
mystic *† /al/ism †(spiritual)	
mystif y ⁴ /ication	
mystique * (mystery)	
myth /ical/ology	
myxomatosis	

N

nab ³	
naber	neighbour +
nabob	
nabour	neighbour +

nacher	nature	nascen *ce* /t	
nacheral	natural +	nasel	nasal +
nacheralise	naturalise ²+	nash	gnash ¹
nachural	natural +	nashanality	nationality +
nack	knack +	nashnalism	nationalism +
nacker	knacker	nashun	nation +
nader	nadir	nastie	nasty +
nadir		nast *y* /ier/iest/ily/iness	
naftha	naphtha	nat	gnat
nag ³ /ger		natal	
nail ¹		natie	natty
naive /té/ty		nation /al/ally	
naked /ness		nationalis *e* ² /ation	
nakid	naked +	nationalis *m* /t/tic	
nale	nail ¹	nationalit *y* /ies	
namby-pamby		native	
name ² /less/ly		Nativity	
nanie	nanny +	natle	natal
nann *y* /ies		natsi	Nazi
nany	nanny +	natty	
nap ³		natul	natal
napalm		natural /ism/ist/ly	
naparm	napalm	naturalis *e* ² /ation	
nape		nature	
naphtha		naty	natty
napie	nappy +	naught	
napkin		naughtie *r* /st	
napp *y* /ies		naught *y* /ily/iness	
napsack	knapsack	nause *a* /ous	
narate	narrate ²+	nauseate ²	
narativ	narrative	nautical	
narcissis *m* /t/tic		naval ★ (navy)	
narcissus		nave ★ (of church)	
narcosis		nave	knave ★+
narcotic		navel ★ (stomach)	
nar-do-well	ne'er-do-well	naverey	knavery
narl	gnarl ¹	navie	navvy ★+
narow	narrow ¹+	navie	navy ★+
narrat *e* ² /ion/or		navigab *le* /ility	
narrative		navigabul	navigable +
narrow ¹ /er/ly/ness		navigashun	navigation
narsissism	narcissism +	navigat *e* ² /ion/or	
narsissist	narcissist	navul	naval ★
narsisus	narcissus	navv *y* ★ (labourer) /ies	
nasal /ly		nav *y* ★ (warships) /ies	

naw	gnaw [1]
nay ★ (no)	
nay	neigh [1]★
naybour	neighbour [+]
nayl	nail [1]
Nazi	
nead	knead [1]★
nead	need [1]★[+]
neadle	needle [2]
neadless	needless [+]
Neapolitan	
near /-by/ly/ness	
neat /er/est/ly/ness	
nebul *a* /ous	
nebulus	nebulous
necesarey	necessary [+]
necesitate	necessitate [2]
necesitey	necessity [+]
necessar *y* /ily	
necessitate [2]	
necessit *y* /ies/ous	
neck /lace/tie	
necksus	nexus
necrofilia	necrophilia
necrophilia	
necropolis	
nectar /y	
nee	knee [+]
need [1]★ (lack) /ful/y	
need	knead [1]★
need	kneed ★
needle [2]	
needless /ly	
needul	needle [2]
neel	kneel [1]
neer	near [+]
ne'er-do-well	
neet	neat [+]
nefarious /ly	
nefarius	nefarious [+]
nefew	nephew
negashun	negation
negation	
negative /ly	
neglect [1] /ful	

négligé	
negligen *ce* /t	
negligens	negligence [+]
negligibl *e* /y	
negligibul	negligible [+]
neglijay	négligé
negoshable	negotiable
negoshabul	negotiable
negoshiate	negotiate [2+]
negotiable	
negotiat *e* [2] /ion/or	
negr *o* /oes/ess (fem.)	
negroid	
neice	niece
neigh [1]★ (horse's cry)	
neighber	neighbour [+]
neighberhood	neighbourhood
neighbour /ing/ly	
neighbourhood	
neither	
nek	neck [+]
neklace	necklace
necklis	necklace
nekrofilia	necrophilia
nekropolis	necropolis
nekst	next [+]
neksus	nexus
nell	knell [1]
nelt	knelt
Nemesis	
nemisis	Nemesis
nemonic	mnemonic
neodimium	neodymium
neodymium	
neolithic	
neon	
nephew	
nepotism	
Neptune	
neptunium	
nerv *e* [2] /y	
nervous /ly/ness	
nervus	nervous [+]
nesesarey	necessary [+]
nesesitate	necessitate [2]

193

nesesitey	necessity +	next /-of-kin	
neslin	nestling	nexus	
nest [1] /ling		ni	nigh
net [3] /ball		nibble [2]	
netha	neither	nibul	nibble [2]
nether		nice /ly/ness/r/st	
nettle [2] /rash		nicet y /ies	
netul	nettle [2+]	nich	niche
network		niche	
neumatick	pneumatic	nick [1]	
neural /gia		nickel	
neuritis		nickerbockers	knickerbockers
neurologist		nickers	knickers
neuron		nickle	nickel
neuro sis /tic		nicknack	knick-knack
neuter		nickname [2]	
neuton	newton	nicotine	
neutral /ity		niece	
neutralis e [2] /ation		niether	neither
neutron /s		nifarious	nefarious +
neva	never +	nifarius	nefarious +
never /more/theless		nife	knife [2+]
nevu	nephew	niftie	nifty +
new * (not old) /er/est		nift y /iness	
new	gnu *	nigerd	niggard +
new	knew *	niggard /ly	
newclear	nuclear	niggl e [2] /y	
newcleus	nucleus +	nigh	
new comer /fangled		night *† /dress/gown	
new ly /ness		†(the dark)	
newmatic	pneumatic	night	knight *
newmonia	pneumonia	night fall /jar	
newral	neural +	nightingale	
newritis	neuritis	nightmar e /ish	
newrologist	neurologist	night -shift /-time	
newron	neuron	night-watch /man	
newrosis	neurosis +	nigle	niggle [2+]
newrotic	neurotic	niglect	neglect [1+]
news /-agent/-flash		nigul	niggle [2+]
news paper /print/y		niks	nix
newt		nilon	nylon
newter	neuter	nimble /ness	
newton		nimblie	nimbly
newtralise	neutralise [2+]	nimbly	
newtron	neutron +	nimbul	nimble +

nimbus /es		nobie	knobby
nimf	nymph	nobility	
nimph	nymph	noble /man/men(pl.)/r/st	
nincompoop		noblie	nobly
nin e /th/thly		nobly	
nineteen /th		nobul	noble +
ninet y /ies/ieth		nock	knock [1]+
ningcumpoop	nincompoop	nocker	knocker
ninie	ninny +	nockneed	knock-kneed
ninn y /ies		nodes	
niobium		nodule	
nion	neon	noes * (negative)	
nip [3] /per/py		noes	knows *
nipie	nippy	noes	nose *+
nipple		nois e /y	
nipul	nipple	noledge	knowledge +
nipy	nippy	nolidge	knowledge +
nise	nice +	noll	knoll [1]
nisitey	nicety +	nome	gnome +
niss	niece	none * (not any)	
nit * (insect)		none	nun *+
nit	knit [3]*	nor	gnaw [1]
nite	knight *	norsia	nausea +
nite	night *+	norsiate	nauseate [2]
niter	nitre	nort	naught
nither	neither	nortey	naughty +
nitrate		nortickle	nautical
nitre		nortie	naughty +
nitric		Norwegian	
nitrifi	nitrify [4]	nose * (on face) /y	
nitrify [4]		nose	knows *
nitrite		nose	noes *
nitrogen /ous		nostril	
nitrogliserine	nitroglycerine	not * (no)	
nitroglycerine		not	knot [3]*+
nitrojen	nitrogen +	notie	knotty
nitrous /oxide		notty	knotty
nitrus	nitrous +	nova	
nitwit		nowing	knowing
nives	knives	nowledge	knowledge +
nix		nu	gnu *
no * (negative reply)		nu	knew *
no	know *+	nu	new *+
nob * (cribbage)		nuance	
nob	knob [3]*+	nuans	nuance

nuckle	knuckle [2+]	nuspaper	newspaper [+]
nuclear		nut /cracker/shell	
nucle us /i (pl.)		nuta	neuter
nud e /ist/ity		nuter	neuter
nudge [2]		nutie	nutty
nuge	nudge [2]	nutmeg	
nugget		nuton	newton
nulifi	nullify [4+]	nutralise	neutralise [2+]
nulitey	nullity	nutrishun	nutrition
null		nutrition	
nullif y [4] /ication		nutron	neutron [+]
nullity		nutty	
numatic	pneumatic	nuty	nutty
numb [1] /ness		nuzul	nuzzle [2]
number [1] /-plate		nuzzle [2]	
numer able /acy/al		nylon	
numerabul	numerable [+]	nymf	nymph
numerasey	numeracy	nymph	
numerat e [2] /ion			
numerical			
numerous /ly/ness			
numerus	numerous [+]		
numismatic /s			

O

numonia	pneumonia	O ★ (addressing)	
numrable	numerable [+]	o	oh ★
numrabul	numerable [+]	o	owe [2★]
numskull		oaf /ish	
nun ★ (religious) /nery		oak /en	
nun	none ★	oakum	
nupshal	nuptial	oar ★ (of a boat)	
nuptial		oar	ore ★
nural	neural [+]	oas is /es (pl.)	
nuralgia	neuralgia	oast	
nurcher	nurture [2]	oat /meal	
nuritis	neuritis	oath	
nurologist	neurologist	obay	obey [1]
nuron	neuron	obduracy	
nurosis	neurosis [+]	obdurasey	obduracy
nurotic	neurotic	obdurate /ly	
nurse [2]		obedien ce /t	
nurser y /ies		obediens	obedience [+]
nursrey	nursery [+]	obelisk	
nurture [2]		obes e /ity	
nurv	nerve [2+]	obey [1]	
nus	news [+]	obituar y /ies	
		objecshun	objection [+]

object [1] /or		obstacul	obstacle
objection /able		obstetric /ian/s	
objectiv e /ely/ity		obstetrishun	obstetrician
obligashun	obligation +	obstinacy	
obligat ion /ory		obstinasey	obstinacy
obligatrey	obligatory	obstinate /ly	
oblige [2]		obstreperous	
oblik	oblique +	obstreperus	obstreperous
oblique /ly/ness		obstrucshun	obstruction
obliterashun	obliteration	obstruct [1] /ion/ive	
obliterat e [2] /ion		obtain [1] /able	
obliv ion /ious		obtane	obtain [1]+
oblivius	oblivious	obtroode	obtrude [2]+
oblivyun	oblivion +	obtrooshun	obtrusion +
oblokwey	obloquy +	obtroosion	obtrusion +
oblong		obtroosiv	obtrusive
obloqu y /ies		obtrude [2] /r	
obnokshus	obnoxious +	obtrus ion /ive	
obnoxious /ly		obtuse /ly/ness	
obo	oboe +	obverse	
obo e /ist		obviate [2]	
obscene /ly		obvious /ly	
obscure [2] /ly		obvius	obvious +
obscurit y /ies		ocasion	occasion[1]+
obseen	obscene +	ocasional	occasional
obsekwies	obsequies	occashun	occasion [1]+
obsekwius	obsequious +	occasion [1] /al/ally	
obsequies		occident /al	
obsequious /ly		occlu de [2] /sion	
observable		occlushun	occlusion
observabul	observable	occult [1] /ation	
observan ce /t		occupan cy /t	
observashun	observation	occupation /al	
observator y /ies		occupi	occupy [4]+
observatrey	observatory +	occup y [4] /ier	
observ e [2] /ation/er		occur [3] /rence	
observence	observance +	occurens	occurrence
observens	observance +	ocean	
obseshun	obsession	ocell us /i (pl.)	
obsess [1] /ion/ive		ocelot	
obsolescen ce /t		ochre	
obsolesens	obsolescence +	o'clock	
obsolesent	obsolescent	oclude	occlude [2]+
obsolete		oclusion	occlusion
obstacle		ocsident	occident +

197

octagon /al	
octane	
octav *e* /o	
octet	
October	
octogenarian	
octopus /es	
ocul *ar* /ist	
ocult	occult [1]+
ocupancy	occupancy +
ocupant	occupant
ocupashun	occupation +
ocupation	occupation +
ocupi	occupy [4]+
ocur	occur [3]+
ocurence	occurrence
ocurens	occurrence
od	odd +
odd /er/est/ly/ment	
oddit *y* /ies	
ode	
odecolone	eau-de-Cologne
oder	odour +
oderiferus	odoriferous
oderous	odorous
oderus	odorous
odiferus	odoriferous
odious /ly	
oditey	oddity +
odium	
odius	odious +
odontology	
odoriferous	
odorous	
odour /less	
oesofagus	oesophagus
oesophagus	
of ★ (belonging to)	
of	oaf +
of	off ★+
ofal	offal
ofence	offence
ofend	offend [1]+
ofens	offence
ofensiv	offensive +

ofer	offer [1]
off ★ (away from) /ing	
offal	
offence	
offend [1] /er	
offens	offence
offensive /ly/ness	
offer [1]	
offhand /ed/edness	
office /r	
official /ly	
officiate [2]	
officious /ly/ness	
offis	office +
offishal	official +
offishus	officious +
offprint	
offset /ting	
offshoot	
offside	
ofhand	offhand +
oficial	official +
oficiate	officiate [2]
oficious	officious +
ofing	offing
ofis	office +
ofiser	officer
ofishal	official +
ofishiate	officiate [2]
ofishus	officious +
ofprint	offprint
ofset	offset +
ofshoot	offshoot
ofside	offside
oft /en	
ofthalmia	ophthalmia +
ofthalmologist	ophthalmologist +
oger	ogre +
ogle [2] /r	
ogre /ss (fem.)	
ogul	ogle [2]+
oh ★ (exclaim)	
oh	O ★
ohm /ic/meter	
oil [1] /y	

198

ointment		
oister	oyster	
oiyay	oyez	
ok	oak +	
oks	ox +	
oksalic	oxalic	
oksbridge	Oxbridge	
oksbrige	Oxbridge	
oksen	oxen	
oksiasetilene	oxy-acetylene	
oksidashun	oxidation	
oksidation	oxidation	
okside	oxide +	
oksident	occident +	
oksidise	oxidise 2+	
oksigen	oxygen	
oksigenate	oxygenate 2+	
oksigenise	oxygenise 2	
oksihemoglobin	oxyhaemoglobin	
oksonian	Oxonian	
okstail	oxtail	
okstale	oxtail	
okstung	ox-tongue	
okum	oakum	
old /en/er		
olfacshun	olfaction +	
olfact ion /ory		
olfactrey	olfactory	
oligarch y /ies		
oligarkey	oligarchy +	
olimpic	Olympic +	
oliv	olive	
olive		
Olympi c /an		
om	ohm +	
ombudsman		
omega		
omelet	omelette	
omelette		
omen 1		
ominous /ly		
ominus	ominous +	
omishun	omission	
omission		
omit 3		

omlet	omelette	
omnibus /es		
omnipoten ce /t		
omnipotens	omnipotence +	
omnipresent		
omniscien ce /t		
omnisiens	omniscience +	
omnisient	omniscient	
omnivorous /ly		
omnivorus	omnivorous +	
on	own 1	
once		
oncoming		
oncore	encore 2	
one * (single) /self		
oner	honour 1+	
oner	owner +	
onerable	honourable	
onerabul	honourable	
onerous		
onership	ownership	
onerus	onerous	
oniks	onyx	
onion		
onist	honest +	
onistey	honesty	
onley	only	
onlook er /ing		
only		
onomatipea	onomatopoeia +	
onomatopoei a /c		
onorarey	honorary	
onorarium	honorarium +	
onrable	honourable	
onrabul	honourable	
onrush		
onset		
onslaught		
onslawt	onslaught	
onslort	onslaught	
onto		
ontray	entrée	
ontreprener	entrepreneur +	
onus		
onward /s		

onyx	
oolit *e* /ic	
ooze [2] /y	
opacity	
opake	opaque [+]
opal /ine	
opalescen *ce* /t	
opalesens	opalescence [+]
opaque /ly	
opasitey	opacity
open [1] /er	
open sesame	
opera /tic/tically	
operab *le* /ility	
operabul	operable [+]
operashun	operation [+]
operat *e* [2] /ive/or	
operater	operator
operation /al	
operetta	
ophthalmi *a* /c	
ophthalmolog *ist* /y	
opiate	
opine [2]	
opinion /ated	
opinyun	opinion [+]
opium	
oponent	opponent
oportune	opportune [+]
oportunism	opportunism [+]
oportunist	opportunist
oportunitey	opportunity [+]
opose	oppose [2+]
oposishun	opposition
oposit	opposite [+]
oposition	opposition
opossum	
oposum	opossum
opponent	
opportune /ly/ness	
opportunis *m* /t	
opportunit *y* /ies	
oppose [2] /r	
opposishun	opposition
opposit *e* /ion	

oppress [1] /ion/ive	
oprable	operable [+]
oprabul	operable [+]
opreshun	oppression
opresiv	oppressive
opress	oppress [1+]
opshun	option [+]
opshunal	optional
opt [1] /ative	
opthalmia	ophthalmia [+]
opthalmic	ophthalmic
opthalmologist	ophthalmologist [+]
opthalmology	ophthalmology
optic /al/ally	
optician	
optimise [2]	
optimism	
optimistic /ally	
optimum	
option /al/ally	
optishun	optician
opulen *ce* /t	
opulens	opulence [+]
opus	
or * (alternative)	
or	awe [2]*[+]
or	oar *
or	ore *
ora	aura
orac *le* /ular	
oracul	oracle [+]
oral * /ly (verbal)	
oral	aural *[+]
orangatang	orang-outang
orange /ade	
orang-outang	
orashun	oration [+]
orater	orator
orat *ion* /or	
oratorio /s	
orator *y* /ies	
oratrey	oratory [+]
orb [1]	
orbit [1] /al	
orcestra	orchestra

orcestrate	orchestrate ² ⁺	original /ity/ly	
orchard		originat *e* ² /ion/or	
orchestra		oringe	orange ⁺
orchestrat *e* ² /ion/or		oriole	
orchid		orkestrate	orchestrate ² ⁺
ordain ¹		orkid	orchid
ordane	ordain ¹	orlder	alder
ordeal		ornament ¹ /al/ation	
ordenrey	ordinary ⁺	ornate /ly	
order ¹ /liness/ly		orning	awning
ordinal		ornitholog *y* /ist	
ordinance ★ (rule)		orphan ¹ /age	
ordinance	ordnance ★	orspishus	auspicious
ordinar *y* /ily		orstralian	Australian
ordinat *e* ² /ion		orstruck	awestruck
ordinrey	ordinary ⁺	orsum	awesome
orditer	auditor	ort	aught ★
orditorey	auditory	ort	ought ★
orditrey	auditory	orthedoks	orthodox
ordnance ★ (survey, guns)		orthodox	
ordure		orthografey	orthography ⁺
ore ★ (mineral)		orthograph *y* /ic/ical	
ore	awe ² ★ ⁺	orthopaedic	
ore	oar ★	orthopeadic	orthopaedic
orfan	orphan ¹ ⁺	orthoritarian	authoritarian ⁺
orfanage	orphanage	ortolan	
orfanige	orphanage	oscilashun	oscillation ⁺
orful	awful ⁺	oscilation	oscillation ⁺
organ /ist		oscillate ² ★ (swing)	
organic		oscillat *ion* /or/ory	
organis *e* ² /ation/er		oscillogra *m* /ph	
organism		oscilloscope	
orgasm		osculate ² ★ (contact)	
orger	auger ★	oselot	ocelot
orger	augur ¹ ★	oshun	ocean
orgey	orgy ⁺	osicul	ossicle
org *y* /iastic/ies		osier	
orical	auricle ⁺	osifi	ossify ⁴ ⁺
oriel		osius	osseous
orient /al/ally		osler	ostler
orientashun	orientation	osmium	
orientat *e* ² /ion		osmosis	
orifice		ospray	osprey ⁺
orifis	orifice	osprey /s	
origin		osseous	

osseus	osseous
ossicle	
ossifi	ossify [4+]
ossif y [4] /ication	
ossilate	oscillate [2*]
ossilation	oscillation [+]
ossilograf	oscillograph
ossilogram	oscillogram [+]
ossiloscope	oscilloscope
ost	oast
ostensibl e /y	
ostensibul	ostensible [+]
ostentashun	ostentation [+]
ostentashus	ostentatious
ostentat ion /ious	
osteo-arthritis	
osteology	
osteopath /y	
ostintashun	ostentation [+]
ostioarthritis	osteo-arthritis
ostiologey	osteology
ostler	
ostracis e [2] /m	
ostrasism	ostracism
ostrasize	ostracise [2+]
ostrich /es	
ote	oat [+]
oter	otter
oth	oath
other /wise	
otoman	ottoman
otter	
ottoman	
ought * (should)	
ought	aught *
ouija	
ounce	
ouns	ounce
our * (belonging to us)	
our	hour [*+]
ourly	hourly
ourselves	
oust [1]	
out [1]	
outback	

outbid /ding	
outbilding	outbuilding
outboard	
outbound	
outbownd	outbound
outbrake	outbreak
outbreak	
outbuilding	
outburst	
outcase	
outclass [1]	
outcome	
outcri	outcry [+]
outcrop	
outcr y /ies	
outdate [2]	
outdistance [2]	
outdo /ing/ne	
outdoor /s	
outer /most	
outface	
outfall	
outfit /ter	
outflank [1]	
outflow	
outgoing /s	
outgrow /n/th	
outhouse	
outhowse	outhouse
outlandish /ness	
outlast [1]	
outlaw [1] /ry	
outlay	
outlet	
outliing	outlying
outline [2]	
outlive [2]	
outlook	
outlying	
outmanoeuvre [2]	
outmanoover	outmanoeuvre [2]
outmatch [1]	
outmoded	
outnumber [1]	
outpace [2]	

outpashent	out-patient	overawe [2]	
out-patient		overawl	overall [+]
outpoor	outpour [1]	overbalance [2]	
outpost		overbalans	overbalance [2]
outpour [1]		overbaring	overbearing
output		overbearing	
outrage [2] /ous/ously		overberden	overburden [1]
outragus	outrageous	overblown	
outran		overboard	
outreach [1]		overbord	overboard
outrid *e* /den/ing/er		overburden [1]	
outright		overcame	
outrite	outright	overcast	
outrun /ning		overcharge [2]	
outset		overcoat	
outshin *e* /ing		overcom *e* /ing	
outshone		overcrowd [1]	
outside /r		overdew	overdue
outsize		overdo /ing/ne	
outskirts		overdose [2]	
outspoken /ness		overdraft	
outstanding /ly		overdraw /n	
outstare [2]		overdrive	
outstay [1]		overdu	overdue
outstretch [1]		overdue	
outstrip [3]		overdun	overdone
outvote [2]		overeach	overreach [1]
outward /ly/s		overeat /en/ing	
outwit [3]		overeet	overeat [+]
outworn		overestimate [2]	
ov	of ★	overflow [1]	
oval		overground	
ovarey	ovary [+]	overgrow /n/th	
ovarian		overgrownd	overground
ovar *y* /ies		overhand	
ovashun	ovation	overhang /ing	
ovation		overhaul [1]	
oven		overhawl	overhaul [1]
over		overhead /s	
overact [1]		overhear /ing	
overall /s		overheard	
overan	overran	overheat [1]	
overarm		overhed	overhead [+]
overate ★ (overeat)		overheet	overheat [1]
overate	overrate [2]★	overherd	overheard

overhere	overhear +
overhung	
overide	override +
overjoi	overjoy +
overjoy /ed	
overladen	
overland	
overlap [3]	
overla *y* /id	
overleaf	
overleef	overleaf
overload [1]	
overlode	overload [1]
overlook [1]	
overmuch	
overnight	
overnite	overnight
overore	overawe [2]
overought	overwrought
overpass	
overpower [1]	
overproduc *e* [2] /tion	
overproducshun	overproduction
overran	
overrate [2]★ (overvalue)	
overrate	overate ★
overrawt	overwrought
overreach [1]	
overreech	overreach [1]
overrid *e* /den/ing	
overrool	overrule [2]
overrule [2]	
overrun /ning	
oversaw	
oversea ★ (abroad) /s ★	
oversee ★† /ing/n/r/s ★†	
†(supervise)	
overshadow [1]	
overshoot	
overshot	
oversight	
oversite	oversight
oversle *ep* /pt	
oversore	oversaw
overspill [1]	

overstate [2] /ment	
overstep [3]	
overstock [1]	
overstrung	
overt /ly	
overtak *e* /en/ing	
overtaks	overtax [1]
overtax [1]	
overtern	overturn [1]
overthrow /n	
overtime	
overtire [2]	
overtone	
overtook	
overture	
overturn [1]	
overwate	overweight
overweight	
overwelm	overwhelm [1]+
overwerk	overwork [1]
overwhelm [1] /ingly	
overw *ind* /ound	
overwork [1]	
overwownd	overwound
overwrought	
oviduct	
ovine	
oviparous	
oviparus	oviparous
ovipositor	
ovoid	
ovoyd	ovoid
ovulashun	ovulation
ovulat *e* [2] /ion	
ovule	
ov *um* /a (pl.)	
owe [2]★ (in debt)	
ower	hour ★+
ower	our ★
owerselves	ourselves
owl /ish	
own [1]	
ownce	ounce
owner /less/ship	
owns	ounce

owst	oust [1]	packet	
owt	out [1]	packiderm	pachyderm [+]
owtbilding	outbuilding	packidge	package [2]
owtbord	outboard	packing-case	
owtbound	outbound	pact	
owtbownd	outbound	pad [3]	
owtbreak	outbreak	paddle [2] /r/-wheel	
owtlaw	outlaw [1+]	paddock	
ox /en (pl.)		paddy /-field	
oxalic		pade	paid [+]
Oxbridge		padie	paddy [+]
oxbrige	Oxbridge	padlock [1]	
oxidashun	oxidation	padock	paddock
oxid *e* /ation		padray	padre
oxidis *e* [2] /ation		padre	
oxigenate	oxygenate [2+]	padul	paddle [2+]
oxigenise	oxygenise [2]	pady	paddy [+]
oxihemoglobin	oxyhaemoglobin	pagan /ism	
Oxonian		pag *e* [2] /ination	
oxtail		pageant /ry	
oxtale	oxtail	pagentrey	pageantry
ox-tongue		paginashun	pagination
oxy-acetylene		pagoda	
oxygen		paid /-up	
oxygenat *e* [2] /ion		pail ★ (bucket)	
oxygenise [2]		pail	pale [2★]
oxyhaemoglobin		pain [1★] (suffering) /less	
oyez		pain	pane ★
oyster		painful /ly	
ozier	osier	pain-killer	
ozone layer		painstaking	
		paint [1] /er	
		pair [1★] (two)	
P		pair	pare [2★]
		pair	pear [★+]
pace [2] /-maker		pakiderm	pachyderm [+]
pach	patch [1+]	pakidurm	pachyderm [+]
pachwerk	patchwork	pal /ly	
pachwork	patchwork	pala *ce* /tial	
pachyderm /atous		paladium	palladium
pacific /ally		palankwin	palanquin
pacifis *m* /t		palanquin	
pacif *y* [4] /ication/ier		palas	palace [+]
pack [1] /-horse/-ice		palashul	palatial
package [2]		palatabl *e* /y	

palatabul	palatable +
palat *e* /al	
palatinate	
palaver	
pale ²* (whitish)	
pale	pail *
paleografey	paleography
paleography	
paleolithic	
paleontolog *y* /ist	
paleozoic	
pale *r* /ly/ness/st	
palet	palette *+
palet	pallet *
palette *† /-knife	
†(artist's board)	
palfrey	
paliass	palliasse
paliate	palliate ²+
palid	pallid +
palindrome	
palis	palace +
palisade	
pall ¹ /-bearer	
palladium	
pallet * (bed)	
pallet	palette *+
palliasse	
palliat *e* ² /ive	
pall *id* /or	
palm ¹ /ist/istry	
palmie	palmy
palmy	
palor	pallor
palpabl *e* /y	
palpabul	palpable +
palpitashun	palpitation
palpitat *e* ² /ion	
palsie	palsy +
pals *y* /ied	
paltrie	paltry +
paltr *y* /iness	
pamflet	pamphlet +
pampas	
pamper ¹ /er	

pamphlet /eer	
pan ³ /cake	
panacea	
panache	
pan-African	
Panama	
pan-American	
panasea	panacea
panash	panache
panchromatic	
pancrea *s* /tic	
pancromatic	panchromatic
panda * (animal)	
pandemonium	
pander ¹* (indulge)	
pane * (of glass)	
pane	pain ¹*+
paneful	painful +
panegyric	
panekiller	pain-killer
panel ³ /list	
panestaking	painstaking
pang	
panic /-stricken/-struck	
panick *ed* /ing/y	
panickt	panicked +
panier	pannier
panigiric	panegyric
panikey	panicky
panikstriken	panic-stricken
pannier	
panopl *y* /ied	
panorama /s	
panoramic /ally	
pansie	pansy +
pansnay	pince-nez
pans *y* /ies	
pant ¹	
pantaloon	
pantechnicon	
panteknicon	pantechnicon
pantheis *m* /t/tic	
pantheon	
panther	
panthiism	pantheism +

panthion	pantheon
pantile	
pantograf	pantograph +
pantograph /y	
pantomime	
pantrey	pantry +
pantr y /ies	
papa cy /l	
papasey	papacy +
paper ¹ /back/-chase	
paperwait	paperweight
paperweight	
papier-mâché	
papirus	papyrus +
papist /ical	
papoose	
paprika	
papyamashay	papier-mâché
papyr us /i (pl.)	
parable	
parabol a /ic	
parabul	parable
parachut e ² /ist	
parade ²	
paradigm	
paradim	paradigm
paradise	
paradoks	paradox +
paradox /ical/ically	
parafernalia	paraphernalia
paraffin	
parafrase	paraphrase ²
paragon	
paragraf	paragraph
paragraph	
parakeet	
paralaks	parallax
paralax	parallax
paralel	parallel ¹+
paralelogram	parallelogram
paralise	paralyse ²+
paralisis	paralysis
paralitic	paralytic
parallax	
parallel ¹ /ogram/ism	

paraly se ² /sis/tic	
parameter	
paramilitary	
paramilitrey	paramilitary
paramiter	parameter
paramoor	paramour
paramount	
paramour	
paramownt	paramount
paranoi a /c/d	
parapet	
paraphernalia	
paraphrase ²	
paraplegi a /c	
parapleja	paraplegia +
paraselene	
parashoot	parachute ²+
parashootist	parachutist
parasilene	paraselene
parasit e /ic/ical	
parasol	
paratifoid	paratyphoid
paratroop /er	
paratyphoid	
parboil ¹	
parcel ³	
parch ¹ /ment	
pardon ¹ /able/er	
pardonabul	pardonable
pare ²★ (trim)	
pare	pair ¹★
pare	pear ★+
parent /age/al/ally	
parenthes is /es (pl.)	
parenthesise ²	
parenthetic /ally	
parentige	parentage
pariah	
parie	parry ⁴
parish /es/ioner	
parishoner	parishioner
Parisi an /enne (fem.)	
pariside	parricide +
parisidul	parricidal
parit y /ies	

park ^{1} /er		part ^{1} /ly/-time	
parket	parquet	partak e /en/er/ing	
parking-meter		partial /ly	
parlament	parliament $^+$	partialit y /ies	
parlance		participant	
parlans	parlance	participat e ^{2} /ion/or	
parlay ^{1*} (bet)		particip le /ial	
parlay	parley ^{1*}	participul	participle $^+$
parlementarey	parliamentary	particle	
parlementarian	parliamentarian	particul	particle
parler	parlour $^+$	particular /ity/ly	
parlermade	parlour-maid	particularis e ^{2} /ation	
parley ^{1*} (discuss)		partie	party $^+$
parley	parlay ^{1*}	partisan /ship	
parliament /arian/ary		partishun	partition $^{1+}$
parlour /-maid		partisipant	participant
parlous		partisipashun	participation
parlus	parlous	partisipate	participate $^{2+}$
parm	palm $^{1+}$	partisipation	participation
Parmesan		partisipul	participle $^+$
parmist	palmist	partit ion ^{1} /ive	
parochial /ism/ly		partly	
parod y ^{4} /ies		partner ^{1} /ship	
parokial	parochial $^+$	partook	
paroksism	paroxysm	partridge	
parole ^{2}		partrige	partridge
parot	parrot $^{1+}$	part y /ies	
paroxysm		parvenew	parvenu
parquet		parvenu	
parricid e /al		pary	parry ^{4}
parrot ^{1} /-fish		pas	pass $^+$
parry ^{4}		pasable	passable $^+$
parse ^{2}		pasabul	passable $^+$
parsec		pascher	pasture $^+$
parsel	parcel ^{3}	pase	pace $^{2+}$
parshal	partial $^+$	pasemaker	pace-maker
parshialitey	partiality $^+$	pasenger	passenger
parsimon ious /y		paserbie	passer-by
parsimonius	parsimonious $^+$	paserby	passer-by
parsley		pasha	
parslie	parsley	pashence	patience $\star$
parsly	parsley	pashens	patience $\star$
parsnip		pashent	patient $^+$
parson /age/ic		pashonat	passionate
parsonige	parsonage	pashun	passion $^+$

pasidge	passage
pasific	pacific +
pasifier	pacifier
pasifism	pacifism +
pasifist	pacifist
pasify	pacify 4+
pasige	passage
pasiv	passive +
pasivitey	passivity
pasover	passover
paspartoo	passe-partout
pasport	passport
pass /book/es/ing/key	
passabl e /y	
passage	
passed ★ (did pass)	
passed	past ★
passenger	
passe-partout	
passer /-by	
passige	passage
passion /ate/ately	
passive /ly	
passivity	
passover	
passport	
password	
past ★ (just over)	
past	passed ★
pasta	
paste 2 /board	
pastel	
paster	pastor +
pasterise	pasteurise 2+
pastern	
pasteuris e 2 /ation	
pastie	pasty +
pastil	pastille
pastille	
pastime	
pastmaster	
pastor /al/ate	
pastrey	pastry +
pastr y /ies	
pastur e /age	

pasturn	pastern
past y /ies	
paswerd	password
pasword	password
pat 3 /ly/ness	
patay	pâté
patch 1 /es/work/y	
pâté	
patella	
paten	pattern 1
patency	
patensey	patency
patent 1 /able/ee/ly	
pater	patter 1+
patern	pattern 1
paternal /ism/ly	
paternalist /ic	
paternity	
path /way	
pathetic /ally	
pathological /ly	
patholog y /ist	
pathos	
patie	patty +
patience ★†	
†(forbearance)	
patient /s ★ (under	
doctor's care)	
patina	
patio /s	
patiserey	pâtisserie
pâtisserie	
patois	
patriarch /al/y	
patriark	patriarch +
patrician	
patricide	
patrimon y /ies	
patriot /ism	
patriotic /ally	
patrishun	patrician
patriside	patricide
patrol 3	
patron /ess (fem.)	
patron age /al	

P.D.P.S.—O

patronige	patronage +	payabul	payable
patronise 2 /r		paynt	paint 1+
patten		pe	pea+
patter 1 /er		pea /nut	
pattern 1		peace * (calm)	
patt y /ies		peace	piece 2*+
paturnal	paternal +	peaceabl e /y	
paturnitey	paternity	peaceabul	peaceable +
patwa	patois	peaceful /ly/ness	
paucity		peace-offering	
paunch /y		peach /es	
pauper /ism		pea cock /fowl/hen	
pauperis e 2 /ation		peak 1* (top)	
pause 2* (stop)		peak	peek 1*
pause	paws*	peak	pique *
pave 2 /ment		peal 1* (of bells)	
pavier	paviour	peal	peel 1*
pavilion		peap	peep 1
pavilyun	pavilion	pear * (fruit) /-shaped	
paviour		pear	pare 2*
paw 1* (foot, feet) /s *		pear	peer 1*+
paw	pore 2*	pear	pier *
pawcelain	porcelain	pearage	peerage +
pawch	porch +	pearce	pierce 2
pawferey	porphyry	pearl * (gem) /y	
pawk	pork +	pearl	purl 1*+
pawkupine	porcupine	peasant /ry	
pawl	pall 1+	peat	
pawlbarer	pall-bearer	pebbl e /y	
pawlfrey	palfrey	pebul	pebble +
pawltrey	paltry +	pecadillo	peccadillo
pawlzid	palsied	pecan	
pawlzy	palsy +	peccadillo	
pawn 1 /broker/shop		peck 1 /er/ish	
pawnch	paunch +	pecock	peacock +
pawnografey	pornography +	pectin	
pawnography	pornography +	pectoral	
pawper	pauper +	peculat e 2 /ion/or	
pawperise	pauperise 2+	peculiar /ly	
pawpus	porpoise	peculiarit y /ies	
paws	pause 2*	pecuniary	
pawselin	porcelain	pedagog	pedagogue +
pawshun	portion 1	pedagogic /al	
pawsitey	paucity	pedagog ue /y	
pay /able/ee/ing/ment		pedal 3* (of bicycle)	

pedant /ic/ry	
peddle ²★ (sell)	
pedestal	
pedestrian crossing	
pediatric s /ian	
pediatrishun	pediatrician
pedi cure /gree/ment	
pedlar	
pedler	pedlar
pedometer	
pedul	pedal ³★
pedul	peddle ²★
peech	peach +
peek ¹★ (peep)	
peek	peak ¹★
peek	pique ★
peel ¹★ (remove skin)	
peel	peal ¹★
peep ¹	
peer ¹★† /ess (fem.)	
†(look, noble)	
peer	pier ★
peer age /less/lessly	
peet	peat
peev ed /ish/ishness	
peg ³	
pehen	peahen
peice	piece ²★+
peiceofring	peace-offering
pejorative	
pekanese	pekinese
pekansey	piquancy +
pekant	piquant
pekinese	
pekish	peckish
pektin	pectin
pektoral	pectoral
pelican	
pelit	pellet
pellet	
pell-mell	
pellucid	
pelmel	pell-mell
pelmet	
pelota	

pelt ¹	
pelusid	pellucid
pelvi s /c	
pemmican	
pen ³ /-friend/-name	
penal	
penalis e ² /ation	
penalt y /ies	
penance ★ (repentance)	
penance	pennants ★
penans	penance ★
penant	pennant +
pence	
pencil ³	
pendant ★ (ornament)	
pendent ★ (hanging)	
pending	
pendulous	
pendulum /s	
pendulus	pendulous
penetrab le /ility	
penetrabul	penetrable +
penetrashun	penetration
penetrat e ² /ion/ive	
penguin	
pengwin	penguin
penicillin	
penie	penny +
peniless	penniless +
peninsula ★(n.) /r ★(adj.)	
penis	
penisilin	penicillin
peniten ce /t	
penitens	penitence +
penitensharey	penitentiary +
penitentiar y /ies	
penkni fe /ves (pl.)	
pennant /s ★ (flags)	
pennife	penknife +
penniless /ness	
pennives	penknives
pennon	
penn y /ies	
penon	pennon
pens	pence

211

penshun	pension [1+]	perchance	
penshunabul	pensionable	perchans	perchance
penshuner	pensioner	perchase	purchase [2+]
pensil	pencil [3]	percolat *e* [2] /ion/or	
pension [1] /able/er		percushun	percussion [+]
pensive /ly/ness		percuss *ion* /ive	
pentagon /al		perda	purdah
pentameter		perdishun	perdition
pentathlon		perdition	
Pentecost		peregrin *e* /ation	
penthouse		peremptor *y* /ily/iness	
penthows	penthouse	peremtrey	peremptory [+]
penticost	Pentecost	perenial	perennial [+]
penultimate /ly		perennial /ly	
penumbra		perfecshun	perfection [+]
penurey	penury [+]	perfect [1] /ible	
penurius	penurious	perfection /ist	
penur *y* /ious		perfidey	perfidy [+]
penut	peanut	perfidius	perfidious
peonie	peony [+]	perfid *y* /ious	
peon *y* /ies		perforashun	perforation
people [2]		perforat *e* [2] /ion/or	
peper	pepper [1+]	perforce	
pepercorn	peppercorn	perform [1] /ance/er	
peperey	peppery	performans	performance
pepper [1] /corn/mint/y		perfors	perforce
pepsin /ogen		perfume [2] /ry/ries	
pep-talk		perfunctor *y* /ily	
peptic		perfunctrey	perfunctory [+]
peptides		pergative	purgative [+]
pepul	people [2]	pergatrey	purgatory
per	purr [1]	perge	purge [2+]
per annum		perhaps	
per capita		pericarp	
peradvencher	peradventure	periferal	peripheral
peradventure		periferey	periphery [+]
perambulat *e* [2] /ion/or		periferic	peripheric
perblind	purblind	perifery	periphery [+]
perceiv *e* [2] /able		perigee	
percentage		peril /ous/ously	
percepshun	perception [+]	perilus	perilous
perceptibl *e* /y		perimeter	
perceptibul	perceptible [+]	period	
percept *ion* /ive		periodic /al/ally	
perch [1] /es		periosteum	

peripatetic	
peripher *y* /al/ic	
periscope	
perish [1] /able/ables	
peristalsis	
periton *eum* /itis	
periwinkle	
periwinkul	periwinkle
perjur *e* [2] /y	
perk [1] /iness/s/y	
perkushun	percussion +
perkusiv	percussive
perl	pearl ★+
perl	purl [1]★+
perloin	purloin [1]
perlu	purlieu
perm [1]	
permanenc *e* /y	
permanens	permanence +
permanent /ly	
permanganate	
permeab *le* /ility	
permeabul	permeable +
permeat *e* [2] /ion	
permishun	permission +
permisibul	permissible
permisiv	permissive +
permiss *ion* /ible	
permissive /ness	
permit [3]	
permutashun	permutation
permut *e* [2] /ation	
pernicious /ly/ness	
pernickety	
pernikitey	pernickety
pernishus	pernicious +
perokside	peroxide
peroxide	
perpechooal	perpetual +
perpechooate	perpetuate [2]+
perpechual	perpetual +
perpechuate	perpetuate [2]+
perpendicular /ity	
perpetrashun	perpetration
perpetrat *e* [2] /ion/or	

perpetrater	perpetrator
perpetual /ly	
perpetuat *e* [2] /ion	
perpetuity	
·perple .	purple
perpleks	perplex [1]+
perplex [1] /ity/ities	
perport	purport [1]
perpose	purpose +
perse	purse [2]+
persecut *e* [2] /ion/or	
persepshun	perception +
perseptible	perceptible +
perseption	perception +
perseptiv	perceptive
perseve	perceive [2]+
persever *e* [2] /ance	
pershun	Persian
Persian	
persist [1] /ent/ently	
persistenc *e* /y	
persistens	persistence +
person /able/age	
persona /(non) grata	
personal ★ (private) /ly	
personal	personnel ★
personalit *y* /ies	
personat *e* [2] /ion/or	
personel	personal ★+
personel	personnel ★
personifi	personify [4]+
personif *y* [4] /ication/ier	
personnel ★ (employees)	
personnel	personal ★+
perspective	
perspeks	perspex
perspektiv	perspective
perspex	
perspicaci *ous* /ty	
perspicashus	perspicacious +
perspicu *ous* /ity	
perspicuus	perspicuous +
perspirashun	perspiration
perspir *e* [2] /ation	
persuad *e* [2] /able/er	

persuashun	persuasion	pestle	
persuasion		pesul	pestle
persuasive /ly/ness		pet ³ /-name	
perswadable	persuadable	petal ³	
perswadabul	persuadable	peteat	petite
perswade	persuade ²⁺	peter ¹ /sham	
perswasion	persuasion	peticoat	petticoat
perswasiv	persuasive ⁺	petie	petty ⁺
pert /ly/ness		petiole	
pertain ¹		petish	pettish
pertane	pertain ¹	petishun	petition ¹⁺
pertinaci ous /ty		petite	
pertinashus	pertinacious ⁺	petition ¹ /er	
pertinen ce /t		petrel ★ (sea bird)	
pertinens	pertinence ⁺	petrel	petrol ★⁺
perturb ¹ /ation		petrifacshun	petrifaction
perva de ² /sive		petrifaction	
perverse /ly/ness		petrifi	petrify ⁴⁺
pervershun	perversion ⁺	petrif y ⁴ /ication	
pervers ion /ive		petrol ★ (gasoline) /eum	
pervert ¹ /er		petrol	petrel ★
pervious		petrolog y /ist	
pervius	pervious	petrul	petrel ★
pervurs	perverse ⁺	petrul	petrol ★⁺
pervurshun	perversion ⁺	petticoat	
pervursiv	perversive	pettish	
pervurt	pervert ¹⁺	pett y /ièr/iest/ily/iness	
pesable	peaceable ⁺	petul	petal ³
pesabul	peaceable ⁺	petulan ce /t	
pesant	peasant ⁺	petulans	petulance ⁺
pesarey	pessary ⁺	petunia	
pese	peace ★	peved	peeved ⁺
pese	piece ²★⁺	pevish	peevish
peseful	peaceful ⁺	pew	
peseofring	peace-offering	pewit	
peseta		pewter	
pesimism	pessimism ⁺	phaeton	
pesimist	pessimist	phalanks	phalanx ⁺
pesimistic	pessimistic	phalan x /ges/xes (pls.)	
pessar y /ies		phall ic /us	
pessimis m /t/tic		phantasm	
pest /icide		phantasmagori a /c	
pester ¹		phantom	
pestilen ce /t/tial		Pharaoh	
pestilens	pestilence ⁺	pharingeal	pharyngeal ⁺

pharinx	pharynx	phisicist	physicist
Pharis *ee* /aic		phisics	physics
pharmaceutic /al		phisik	physique *
pharmacist		phisiologey	physiology +
pharmacolog *y* /ist		phisionomey	physiognomy
pharmacopoeia		phisiotherapist	physiotherapist +
pharmac *y* /ies		phisiotherapy	physiotherapy
pharmasey	pharmacy +	phisique	physique *
pharmasist	pharmacist	phlebitis	
pharmasutical	pharmaceutical	phlegm /atic	
pharo	Pharaoh	phlem	phlegm +
pharyng *eal* /itis		phloem	
pharynx		phloks	phlox *
phase ²		phlox * (flower)	
phayton	phaeton	phobia	
pheasant		Phoebus	
phebus	Phoebus	phoenix	
pheniks	phoenix	phon * (unit of sound)	
phenix	phoenix	phone ²* (telephone)	
phenobarbitone		phonetic /ally	
phenol		phonograf	phonograph +
phenomenal /ly		phonograph /ic	
phenomen *on* /a (pl.)		phonolog *y* /ical	
phesant	pheasant	phony	
phial * (bottle)		phosfate	phosphate
philander ¹ /er		phosforesence	phosphorescence
philanthrop *y* /ic/ist		phosforesent	phosphorescent
philarmonic	philharmonic	phosforous	phosphorous *+
philatel *y* /ist		phosforus	phosphorus *
philharmonic		phosphate	
philip	fillip ¹	phosphoresce ² /nce/nt	
Philistine		phosphor *ous* * (adj.) /ic	
philolog *y* /ical/ist		phosphorus * (n.)	
philosofer	philosopher +	photo /-electric/stat	
philosofey	philosophy	photocopie	photocopy +
philosofical	philosophical +	photocop *y* /ies	
philosofise	philosophise ²	photo-finish	
philosoph *er* /y		photogenic	
philosophical /ly		photograf	photograph ¹+
philosophise ²		photograph ¹ /ic/y	
philter	philtre *	photomet *er* /ric/ry	
philtre * (love potion)		photon	
phisic	physic *	photosynthesis	
phisical	physical +	phototropism	
phisician	physician	phrase ²* (words) /ology	

phrenetic		piece ²★ (part) /meal	
phrenolog*y* /ist		piece	peace ★
phthisis		piece-work	
phylum		pier ★ (jetty)	
physic ★ (remedy)		pier	peer ¹★⁺
physic	physique ★	pierce ²	
physical /ly		piers	pierce ²
physician		piety	
physicist		pig ³ /-iron/let	
physics		pigeon ★ (bird)	
physiognomy		pigeon	pidgin ★
physiolog*y* /ical/ist		pigeon-hole ²	
physiotherap*ist* /y		pigerey	piggery ⁺
physique ★ (body)		pigger*y* /ies	
pi ★ (maths)		piggyback	
pi	pie ★⁺	pigheaded /ness	
pianist		pigheded	pigheaded ⁺
piano /forte		pigiback	piggyback
piatsa	piazza	pigin	pidgin ★
piazza		pigin	pigeon ★
pibald	piebald	pigment ¹ /ation	
picador		pig *skin* /tail	
picalilli	piccalilli	pigsti	pigsty ⁺
picancy	piquancy ⁺	pigst*y* /ies	
picaniny	piccaninny	pigtale	pigtail
picant	piquant	pijamas	pyjamas
piccalilli		pikaxe	pickaxe
piccaninny		pike ² /staff	
piccolo /s		piks	pyx ¹
pich	pitch ¹⁺	piksy	pixie ⁺
pichfork	pitchfork ¹	pil	pill ⁺
pick ¹ /axe/pocket		pilage	pillage ²⁺
pickcher	picture ²⁺	pilchard	
picket ¹		pile ²	
pickle ²		piler	pillar ⁺
picnic /ked/ker/king		pilerbox	pillar-box
Pict /ish		pilfer ¹ /age/er	
pictorial /ly		pilgrim /age	
picture ² /sque		pilgrimige	pilgrimage
picturesk	picturesque	pilige	pillage ²⁺
pidgin ★ (jargon)		pilion	pillion
pidgin	pigeon ★	pill /-box	
pie ★ (food) /crust		pillage ² /r	
pie	pi ★	pillar /-box	
piebald		pillion	

216

pillor *y* [4] /ies		pirat *e* [2] /ical	
pillow		pire	pyre
pilon	pylon	piric	Pyrrhic [+]
pilorey	pillory [4+]	pirite	pyrite
pilot [1] /age		pirooet	pirouette [2]
pilow	pillow	pirotecnic	pyrotechnic [+]
pilyun	pillion	pirouette [2]	
pimento		pirric	Pyrrhic [+]
pimpernel		pistachio /s	
pimpl *e* /y		pistil ★ (flower)	
pimpul	pimple [+]	pistol ★ (gun)	
pin [3] /-prick/-up		piston	
pinacle	pinnacle [2]	pit [3] /fall/man	
pinacul	pinnacle [2]	pitance	pittance
pinafore		pitans	pittance
pince-nez		pit-a-pat /ter	
pincers		pitch [1] /blende/er/es	
pinch [1] /er/es		pitchfork [1]	
pincushion		pitch-pine	
pincushun	pincushion	piteous /ly/ness	
pine [2] /-cone		pith /ily/iness/y	
pineapple		pithon	python
pineapul	pineapple	pitiabl *e* /y	
ping-pong		pitiabul	pitiable [+]
pinion [1]		pitie	pity [4+]
pink [1]		pitiful /ly	
pinnacle [2]		pitius	piteous [+]
pinpoint [1]		pitsicato	pizzicato
pinsers	pincers	pittance	
pint		pittans	pittance
pinyun	pinion [1]	pituitary	
pionear	pioneer [1]	pituitrey	pituitary
pioneer [1]		pit *y* [4] /iless	
pious /ly		pius	pious [+]
pip [3] /-squeak		pivot [1] /al	
pipe [2] /r		pix	pyx [1]
pipe -*clay* /line		pixie /s	
pipet	pipette	pixy	pixie [+]
pipette		pizzicato	
pippin		placab *le* /ility	
piquan *cy* /t		placabul	placable [+]
pique ★ (anger)		placard [1]	
piracy		placat *e* [2] /ion	
piramid	pyramid [+]	place [2]★ (position)	
pirasey	piracy	place	plaice ★

217

placenta /l		plate	plait [1]
placid /ity/ly		plateau /x (pl.)	
placket		platelet	
plagarise	plagiarise [2+]	plater	platter
plage	plague [2]	platform	
plagiaris e [2] /m/t		platichood	platitude [+]
plague [2]		platinum	
plaice * (fish)		platipus	platypus [+]
plaid		platitud e /inous	
plain * (flat land)		platitudinus	platitudinous
plain	plane [2*]	plato	plateau [+]
plain er /ness/song		platonic /ally	
plaintiff * (legal)		platoon	
plaintive * (sad) /ly		platter	
plait [1]		platypus /es	
plait	plate [2+]	plaudit	
plajarise	plagiarise [2+]	plausib le /ility/ly	
plak	plaque	plausibul	plausible [+]
plaket	placket	plawdit	plaudit
plan [3] /ner		plawsible	plausible [+]
plane [2*] (smooth, aircraft)		play [1] /er/ing/mate	
plane	plain *	playfellow	
planet /arium/ary		playful /ly/ness	
planetrey	planetary	playground	
plank		playgrownd	playground
plankton		playrite	playwright
plant [1] /ain/ation/er		playwright	
plantashun	plantation	ple	plea [+]
plantif	plaintiff *	plea /s * (appeal)	
plantin	plantain	plead [1] /er	
plantiv	plaintive *+	pleasant /ly/ry	
plaque		please [2*] (request)	
plase	place [2*]	pleasur e /able/ably	
plase	plaice *	pleat [1]	
plasenta	placenta [+]	plebean	plebeian
plasid	placid [+]	plebeian	
plasma		plebian	plebeian
plasmolysis		plebiscite	
plaster [1] /cast/er		plebisit	plebiscite
plastic /ally/ity		plectrum	
plasticine		pledge [2]	
plastiseen	plasticine	pleed	plead [1+]
plastisine	plasticine	pleet	pleat [1]
plate [2] /ful/glass		plege	pledge [2]
		plenary	

plenipotensharey	plenipotentiary
plenipotentiary	
plenitude	
plentie	plenty [+]
plentiful /ly/ness	
plentius	plenteous
plent*y* /eous	
plesant	pleasant [+]
plese	pleas ★
plese	please [2]★
plesurable	pleasurable
plesurabul	pleasurable
plesure	pleasure [+]
plethor *a* /ic	
pleural ★ (membrane)	
pleural	plural ★[+]
pleurisy	
pli	ply [4+]
pliab *le* /ility	
pliabul	pliable [+]
plian *cy* /t	
pliansey	pliancy [+]
pliers	
plight /ed	
Plimsoll /line/mark	
plimsolls	
plinth	
plite	plight [+]
pliwood	plywood
plod [3] /der	
ploi	ploy
plooto	Pluto
plootocracy	plutocracy [+]
plootocrat	plutocrat [+]
plootonium	plutonium
ploovial	pluvial
plot [3] /ter	
plough [1] /man/share	
plover	
plow	plough [1+]
ploy	
pluck [1] /ier/iest/ily/y	
plug [3] /ger	
plum ★ (fruit)	
plum	plumb [1]★[+]

plumage	
plumb [1]★ (weight) /line	
plumbago	
plumber	
plume [2]	
plumer	plumber
plumet	plummet [1]
plumige	plumage
plumline	plumbline
plummet [1]	
plump [1] /er/est/ness	
plunder [1] /er	
plunge [2] /r	
pluperfect	
plural ★ (a few) /ism/ity	
plural	pleural ★
plurisey	pleurisy
plus	
plush /y	
Pluto	
plutocrac *y* /ies	
plutocrasey	plutocracy [+]
plutocrat /ic	
plutonium	
pluvial	
ply [4] /wood	
pnemonic	mnemonic
pneumatic	
pneumonia	
poach [1] /er	
poch	poach [1+]
pock /-marked	
pocket [1] /-book/-knife	
pocket-money	
podgy	
podium	
poem	
poet /ess (fem.)	
poetic /al/ally	
poetry	
pogo-stick	
poignan *cy* /t/tly	
poim	poem
poinancy	poignancy [+]
poinansey	poignancy [+]

poinant	poignant
point [1] /edly/er/less	
point -*blank* /-duty	
poise [2]	
poisenous	poisonous
poisenus	poisonous
poison [1] /er/ous	
pok *e* [2] /er/y	
poker-face /d	
pokey	poky
pokmarked	pock-marked
poks	pox
pol	poll [1]★+
polar /ity	
polar bear	
polard	pollard +
Polaris	
polaris *e* [2] /ation/er	
pole ★ (tall staff) /cat	
pole	poll [1]★+
pole-jump [1]	
polemic /al	
polen	pollen
poler	polar +
polerbare	polar bear
polerbear	polar bear
polese	police [2]+
pole-star	
pole-vault [1]	
poliandrey	polyandry +
poliandrus	polyandrous
polianthus	polyanthus
police [2] /man/woman	
polic *y* /ies	
poligamey	polygamy +
poligamus	polygamous
poliglot	polyglot
poligon	polygon
polihedron	polyhedron +
polimer	polymer
polinashun	pollination
polinate	pollinate [2]+
polination	pollination
polinesian	Polynesian
polio /myelitis	

polip	polyp
polisey	policy +
polish [1]	
polisilable	polysyllable +
polite /ly/ness	
politecnic	polytechnic
politey	polity
politheism	polytheism +
polithene	polythene
politic /ian/s	
political /ly	
politishun	politician
polity	
polka /dot	
poll [1]★ (vote) /-tax	
poll	pole ★+
pollard /ed	
pollen	
pollinat *e* [2] /ion	
pollster	
pollut *e* [2] /ion	
polonaise	
polonase	polonaise
polo-neck	
polonium	
poltax	poll-tax
poltegist	poltergeist
polterer	poulterer
poltergeist	
poltice	poultice
poltis	poultice
poltrey	poultry
polushun	pollution
polute	pollute [2]+
polution	pollution
polyandrey	polyandry +
polyandr *y* /ous	
polyanthus	
polygam *y* /ous	
polyglot	
polygon	
polyhedr *on* /al	
polymer	
polymeris *e* [2] /ation	
polyneshun	Polynesian

Polynesian		poor *er* /est/ly	
polyp		pop³ /corn/gun	
polysyllab *le* /ic		pop *e* /ery/ish	
polytechnic		popet	poppet
polytheis *m* /t/tic		pop-eyed	
polythene		popicock	poppycock
pomace ★ (pulp)		popie	poppy⁺
pomade²		popinjay	
pomegranate		poplar ★ (tree)	
pomegranit	pomegranate	poplar	popular ★⁺
pomel	pommel³	poplin	
Pomeranian		poppet	
pomfret /cake		popp *y* /ies	
pomfrit	pomfret⁺	poppycock	
pomiculcher	pomiculture	populace	
pomiculture		popular ★† /ity/ly	
pommel³		†(well known)	
pomology		popularis *e*² /ation	
pomp /osity/ous		popularitey	popularity
pompus	pompous	populas	populace
ponder¹ /able		populashun	population
ponderous /ly		populat *e*² /ion	
ponderus	ponderous⁺	populer	popular ★⁺
pondrabul	ponderable	populous	
poney	pony⁺	populus	populous
poniard		popy	poppy⁺
ponie	pony⁺	por	paw¹★⁺
ponitale	pony-tail	por	pore²★
pontiff		porcelain	
pontificate²		porch /es	
pontoon		porcupine	
pon *y* /ies /y-tail		pore²★ (of skin)	
ponyard	poniard	pore	poor★
poo	pooh¹⁺	pore	pour¹★
poodle		porer	poorer⁺
poodul	poodle	porfrey	porphyry
poof	pouffe	poridge	porridge
pooh¹ /-pooh		porige	porridge
pool		poringer	porringer
pooley	pulley	pork /er/y	
poolit	pullet	porkupine	porcupine
poop¹		pornografey	pornography⁺
poor ★ (needy)		pornograph *y* /ic	
poor	pore²★	poro *us* /sity	
poor	pour¹★	porphyry	

porpoise		posse	
porpus	porpoise	possess [1] /ion/ive/or	
porridge		possi	posse
porringer		possib *le* /ility/ly	
porselin	porcelain	possibul	possible [+]
porshun	portion [1]	possum	
porslin	porcelain	post [1] /-card	
port /age/-hole		post office	
portab *le* /ility		postage /-stamp	
portabul	portable [+]	postal	
portal		post-date [2]	
portcullis		poster	
portend [1]		posterier	posterior
portent /ous		posterior	
portentus	portentous	posterity	
porter /house		postern	
portfolio		post-graduate	
portico		post-haste	
portion [1]		posthumous /ly	
portkulis	portcullis	posthumus	posthumous [+]
portl *y* /iness		postige	postage [+]
portmanteau		postilion	
portrait /ure		postilyon	postilion
portray [1] /al		post-impressionist	
portrit	portrait [+]	post *man* /mark	
portul	portal	post *master* /mistress	
porus	porous [+]	post-meridiem	
poscher	posture [2]	post-mortem	
pose [2]		postofiss	post office
poseshun	possession	postpone [2] /ment	
posess	possess [1+]	postulant	
posession	possession	postulate [2]	
posessiv	possessive	postumus	posthumous [+]
posey	posy [+]	posture [2]	
posh		post-war	
poshun	potion	posum	possum
posibilitey	possibility	pos *y* /ies	
posible	possible [+]	potash	
posibul	possible [+]	potasium	potassium
posie	posy [+]	potassium	
posishun	position [+]	potato /es	
position /al		pot-bell *y* /ied	
positive /ly/ness		poteen	
positivism		poten *cy* /t	
positron		potene	poteen

potensey	potency [+]	praer	prayer [+]
potenshul	potential [+]	pragmati*c* /sm	
potentate		prairey	prairie
potential /ity/ly		prairie	
poter	potter [1]	praise [2] /worthy	
poterey	pottery [+]	prance [2]	
pot-hol*e* /er/ing		prank	
pot-hook		prans	prance [2]
potie	potty	prarey	prairie
potion		prase	praise [2+]
pot-pourri		prasee	précis [1]
potter [1]		praseworthey	praiseworthy
potter*y* /ies		prate [2]	
potty		prattle [2]	
pouch [1] /es		pratul	prattle [2]
pouffe		prawn [1]	
poulterer		pray [1][*] (say prayers)	
poultice		pray	prey [1][*]
poultry		prayer /book/ful	
pounce [2]		preach [1] /er	
pound [1] /age		preamble [2]	
pour [1][*] (to flow)		preambul	preamble [2]
pour	poor [*]	prearrange [2]	
pour	pore [2][*]	precarious /ly/ness	
pout [1]		precarius	precarious [+]
poverty /-stricken		precaution /ary	
powch	pouch [1+]	precawshun	precaution [+]
powder [1] /y		precede [2][*] (go before)	
power [1] /less/-station		precede	proceed [1][*+]
powerful /ly/ness		precedence [*] (priority)	
pownce	pounce [2]	precedent [*][†] /s [*][†]	
pownd	pound [1+]	†(previous law[s])	
powns	pounce [2]	precedent	president [*+]
powt	pout [1]	precentor	
pow-wow [1]		precept /or	
pox		preceshun	procession
practicab*le* /ility		prech	preach [1+]
practicabul	practicable [+]	precinct	
practical /ity/ly		precious /ly	
practice [*] (n.)		precipice	
practician		precipis	precipice
practise [2][*] (v.)		precipitanc*e* /y	
practishun	practician	precipitans	precipitance [+]
practishuner	practitioner	precipitat*e* [2] /ion/or	
practitioner		precipitous /ly	

precipitus	precipitous +	preferens	preference
précis [1]		preferenshal	preferential +
precise /ly		preferential /ly	
preclu *de* [2] /sion/sive		preferment	
preclushun	preclusion	prefiks	prefix [1]
precocious /ness		prefis	preface [2+]
precocity		prefix [1]	
preconceive [2]		pregnanc *y* /ies	
preconception		pregnansey	pregnancy +
preconsepshun	preconception	pregnant	
preconseve	preconceive [2]	prehensile	
precoshus	precocious +	prehistor *ic* /y	
precositey	precocity	pre-ignition	
precursor /y		prejudge [2]	
predater	predator +	prejudice [2]	
predator /y		prejudicial /ly	
predecessor		prejudis	prejudice [2]
predesesor	predecessor	prejudishal	prejudicial +
predestinashun	predestination	prejuge	prejudge [2]
predestin *e* [2] /ation		prelate	
predetermine [2]		prelim	
predicament		preliminar *y* /ies	
predicate [2]		preliminrey	preliminary +
predicshun	prediction	prelude [2]	
predict [1] /able/ion		premature /ly	
predictabul	predictable	premeditat *e* [2] /ion	
predilecshun	predilection	premier *† /ship	
predilection		†(Prime Minister)	
predispos *e* [2] /ition		première *†	
prediturmine	predetermine [2]	†(first performance)	
predominance		premise [2]* (postulate)	
predominans	predominance	premises (house)	
predominant /ly		premiss * (logic)	
predominate [2]		premium /s	
preegsist	pre-exist [1+]	premonishun	premonition +
pre-eminen *ce* /t		premonit *ion* /ory	
pre-empt [1] /ion		prenatal	
preemshun	pre-emption	prene	preen [1]
preen [1]		preoccupi	preoccupy [4+]
pre-exist [1] /ence		preoccup *y* [4] /ation	
prefabricat *e* [2] /ion		preocupashun	preoccupation
prefa *ce* [2] /tory		preocupy	preoccupy [4+]
prefect /orial/ure		prepade	prepaid
prefer [3] /able/ably		prepaid	
preference		preparashun	preparation

preparatrey	preparatory
prepar *e* ² /ation/atory	
prepay /ing/ment	
preponderan *ce* /t	
preponderate ²	
preposess	prepossess ¹⁺
preposishun	preposition ⁺
preposition /al	
prepossess ¹ /ion	
preposterous /ly	
preposterus	preposterous ⁺
prerekwisit	prerequisite
prerequisite	
prerogative	
pres	press ¹⁺
presage ²	
presbiterian	Presbyterian
Presbyterian	
pre-school	
prescribe ²⋆†	
†(give directions)	
prescribe	proscribe ²⋆
prescripshun	prescription ⁺
prescript *ion* /ive	
presede	precede ²⋆
presedence	precedence ⋆
presedence	precedents ⋆
presedent	precedent ⋆⁺
presedent	president ⋆⁺
preseed	precede ²⋆
presence	
presens	presence
present ¹ /ation/ly	
presentabl *e* /y	
presentashun	presentation
presentiment	
presentor	precentor
presept	precept ⁺
preservashun	preservation
preservative	
preserv *e* ² /ation	
preseshun	procession
presession	procession
presher	pressure ²⁺
presherise	pressurise ²⁺

preshus	precious ⁺
presid *e* ² /ial	
presidency	
presidensey	presidency
presidenshal	presidential
president ⋆† /ial/s ⋆†	
†(elected head[s])	
president	precedent ⋆⁺
presige	presage ²
presinct	precinct
presipice	precipice
presipis	precipice
presipitance	precipitance ⁺
presipitans	precipitance ⁺
presipitate	precipitate ²⁺
presipitation	precipitation
presipitous	precipitous ⁺
presipitus	precipitous ⁺
presise	precise ⁺
press ¹ /er	
press-stud	
pressure ² /-cooker	
pressuris *e* ² /ation	
prest	priest ⁺
prestege	prestige ⁺
presthood	priesthood
prestig *e* /ious	
prestigus	prestigious
presto	
presum *e* ² /ably	
presumpt *ion* /ive/uous	
presumshun	presumption ⁺
presumshus	presumptuous
presumtuous	presumptuous
presuppos *e* ² /ition	
pretekst	pretext
pretence	
pretend ¹ /er	
pretens	pretence
pretenshun	pretension
pretenshus	pretentious ⁺
pretension	
pretentious /ly/ness	
preterite	
pretext	

pretie	pretty [+]	principal ★ (chief) /ly	
prett y /ily/iness		principal	principle ★
prety	pretty [+]	principalit y /ies	
prevail [1]		principle ★†	
prevalen ce /t		†(moral code)	
prevalens	prevalence [+]	principle	principal ★[+]
prevaricat e [2] /ion/or		prins	prince [+]
prevayl	prevail [1]	prinsess	princess
prevenshun	prevention	prinsipal	principal ★[+]
prevent [1] /able/ion/ive		prinsipality	principality [+]
preview [1]		print [1] /er	
previous /ly		prior /ess (fem.)/y	
previus	previous [+]	priorit y /ies	
prevue	preview [1]	prise [2]★ (lever)	
pre-war		prise	price [2+]
prey [1]★ (devour)		prise	prize [2]★
prey	pray [1]★	prisie	prissy
prezbiterian	Presbyterian	prism /atic	
pri	pry [4]	prison /er	
price [2] /less		prissy	
prick [1]		pristene	pristine
prickl e [2] /y		pristine	
pricul	prickle [2+]	prithee	
pride [2]		prity	pretty [+]
prier	prior [+]	privacy	
prierey	priory	privaricate	prevaricate [2+]
priest /hood/ly		privasey	privacy
prig /gish		privashun	privation
prim /ly/mer/mest/ness		private /ly	
prima donna		privateer	
prima facie		privation	
prima cy /te		privet	
primar y /ies/ily		privie	privy
primasey	primacy [+]	privilege [2]	
prime [2] /r		privilige	privilege [2]
Prime Minister		privit	private [+]
primeval		privy	
primitiv e /ism		prize [2]★ (award)	
primogenit al /or/ure		prize	prise [2]★
primordial		prizm	prism [+]
primrey	primary [+]	probab le /ility/ly	
primrose		probabul	probable [+]
primula		probashun	probation [+]
primus		probate	
prince /ly/ss (fem.)		probation /ary/er	

probe ²
problem
problematic /al/ally
proboscis
procedure
proceed ¹★ (go on) /s
proceed   precede ²★
proceshun   procession
process ¹ /ion/ional
proclaim ¹
proclamashun   proclamation
proclamation
proclaym   proclaim ¹
procrastinat e ² /ion
procreat e ² /ion
proctor /ial
procura ble /tion/tor
procurabul   procurable ⁺
procurater   procurator
procure ² /ment
prod ³
prodigal /ity
prodigey   prodigy ⁺
prodigious /ly/ness
prodigus   prodigious ⁺
prodig y /ies
produc e ² /er/ible
product /ion/ive
produse   produce ²⁺
produser   producer
profan e ² /ation
profanit y /ies
profecy   prophecy ★
profecy   prophesy ⁴★
profer   proffer ¹
profeser   professor ⁺
profesey   prophecy ★
profeshonal   professional ⁺
profeshun   profession ⁺
profesi   prophesy ⁴★
profesor   professor ⁺
profess ¹ /edly
profession /alism
professional /ly
professor /ial

profet   prophet ⁺
profetical   prophetical
proffer ¹
proficien cy /t
profilactic   prophylactic ⁺
profile
profishency   proficiency ⁺
profishensey   proficiency ⁺
profishent   proficient
profit ¹ /less
profitab le /ility/ly
profitabul   profitable ⁺
profiteer ¹
profliga cy /te
profound /ly
profownd   profound ⁺
profundity
profus e ² /ion
profushun   profusion
progenitor
progeny
prognos is /es (pl.)/tic
prognosticat e ² /ion
program ³★ (computer)
programme ★†
     †(list of events)
progreshun   progression
progress ¹ /ion/ional
progressive /ly
prohibishun   prohibition
prohibit ¹ /ion/ive/ory
proibit   prohibit ¹⁺
projecshun   projection
project ¹ /ile/ion/or
projeney   progeny
projeniter   progenitor
proksey   proxy ⁺
proksimate   proximate ⁺
proksimitey   proximity
prolapse ²
proletaria n /t
proliferashun   proliferation
proliferat e ² /ion
prolific /ally
prolog   prologue ²

prologue²		propitiat *e*² /ion/or	
prolong¹		propitious /ly	
prolongat *e*² /ion		propolis	
promenade² /r		proporshonal	proportional⁺
promethium		proporshonate	proportionate
prominen *ce* /t		proporshun	proportion¹⁺
prominens	prominence⁺	proportion¹ /ate	
promiscu *ous* /ity		proportional /ly	
promiscuus	promiscuous⁺	proposal	
promis *e*² /sory		propos *e*² /ition	
promoshun	promotion⁺	proposishun	proposition
promote² /r		propound¹	
promotion /al		propownd	propound¹
prompt¹ /er/ness		proprietary	
promulgat *e*² /ion		proprieter	proprietor
prone /ly/ness		proprietey	propriety⁺
prong¹		proprietor	
pronoun		proprietrey	proprietary
pronounce² /ment		propriet *y* /ies	
pronown	pronoun	propulshun	propulsion⁺
pronowns	pronounce²⁺	propuls *ion* /ive	
pronunciation		prorog	prorogue²⁺
pronunsiashun	pronunciation	prorog *ue*² /ation	
prood	prude⁺	prosaic /ally	
proof¹ /-reader		proscribe²★ (outlaw)	
proon	prune²	proscribe	prescribe²★
proov	prove²⁺	proscripshun	proscription⁺
prop³		proscript *ion* /ive	
propaganda		prose	
propagashun	propagation	prosecushun	prosecution
propagat *e*² /ion		prosecut *e*² /ion/or	
propane		prosedure	procedure
propel³ /ler		proseed	proceed¹★⁺
propell *ant* (n.) /ent (adj.)		proselight	proselyte²
propensit *y* /ies		proselyte²	
proper /ly		proselytise² /r	
propert *y* /ies		prosess	process¹⁺
prophecy★ (n.)		prosicushun	prosecution
prophesy⁴★ (v.)		prosilite	proselyte²
prophet /ess (fem.)/ical		prosilitise	proselytise²⁺
prophilactic	prophylactic⁺	prosody	
prophyl *actic* /axis		prospect¹ /ive/or	
propishiate	propitiate²⁺	prospectus /es	
propishous	propitious⁺	prosper¹ /ity/ous	
propishus	propitious⁺	prosperus	prosperous

prostate * (gland)		provision /al/ally	
prostitushun	prostitution	proviso /ry	
prostitut e ² /ion		provocat ion /ive	
prostrat e ²* (lay flat)		provoke ²	
protactinium		provost	
protagonist		prow	
protecshun	protection	prowd	proud +
protect ¹ /ion/ive/or		prowess	
protectorate		prowibishun	prohibition
proteen	protein	prowibition	prohibition
protégé /e (fem.)		prowl ¹ /er	
protein		proximate /ly	
protejay	protégé +	proximity	
protene	protein	prox y /ies	
protest ¹ /ation		prozaic	prosaic +
Protestant /ism		prud e /ery/ish	
protocol		pruden ce /t	
proton		prudens	prudence +
protoplasm		prudenshal	prudential +
prototipe	prototype +	prudential /ly	
prototyp e /al/ical		prune ²	
protract ¹ /ion/or		prurien ce /t	
protrood	protrude ²	pruriens	prurience +
protrooshun	protrusion +	prushan	Prussian
protrude ²		Prussian	
protrus ion /ive		pry ⁴	
protuberan ce /t		psalm /ist	
protuberans	protuberance +	psalter /y	
proud /ly/ness		pseudo /nym	
prov e ² /able		psycedelic	psychedelic
provenance		psyche	
provenans	provenance	psychedelic	
provender		psychiatr ist /y	
proverb /ial		psychic /al	
provide ² /r		psychoanalys e ² /is/t	
providence		psychological /ly	
providens	providence	psycholog y /ist	
providenshul	providential	psychopath /ic	
provident /ial/ially		psycho sis /tic	
provijun	provision +	psychosomatic	
provijunal	provisional	psychotherap ist /y	
provinc e /ial		psycoanalise	psychoanalyse ²+
provins	province +	psycologey	psychology +
provinshal	provincial	psycological	psychological +
provishun	provision +	psycopath	psychopath +

229

psycosis	psychosis +	pulie	pulley
psycosomatic	psychosomatic	pulkritude	pulchritude
psycotherapist	psychotherapist +	pull [1]	
psykey	psyche	pullet	
psykick	psychic +	pulley	
ptarmigan		Pullman	
pterodactyl		pullover	
Ptolemaic system		pulman	Pullman
ptomaine		pulmonary	
ptyalin		pulmonrey	pulmonary
pu	pew	pulover	pullover
pub		pulp [1] /y	
puberty		pulpit	
pubescen ce /t		pulsar	
pubesens	pubescence +	pulsashun	pulsation
pubesent	pubescent	pulsat e [2] /ion	
pubic		pulse [2] /less	
pubis		pulser	pulsar
public /an/ation/ly		pulveris e [2] /ation	
publicis e [2] /t		puma	
publicity		pumel	pummel [3]
publish [1] /er		pumice [2]* (lava) /-stone	
publisitey	publicity	pumice	pomace *
publisize	publicise [2]+	pumis	pomace *
puce		pumis	pumice [2]*+
puck		pumkin	pumpkin
pucker [1]		pummel [3]	
pudding		pump [1] /er	
puddle [2]		pumpernickel	
puding	pudding	pumpkin	
pudul	puddle [2]	pumy	pumice [2]*+
pueril e /ity		pun [3] /ner/nist	
puff [1] /iness/y		punch [1] /eon/es	
puffin		punchun	puncheon
pufin	puffin	punctilious /ly/ness	
pug		punctilius	punctilious +
pugilis m /t/tic		punctual /ity/ly	
pugnaci ous /ty		punctuat e [2] /ion	
pugnashus	pugnacious +	puncture [2]	
pugnasitey	pugnacity	pundit	
puka	pucker [1]	pungen cy /t	
puke [2]		pungensey	pungency +
puker	pucker [1]	punie	puny +
pulchritude		punish [1] /able/ment	
pulcritude	pulchritude	punitive /ly	

punjency	pungency [+]
punjensey	pungency [+]
punjent	pungent
punt [1] /er	
pun y /ier/iest/ily	
pupa /e (pl.)	
pupat e [2] /ion	
pupie	puppy [+]
pupil	
pupit	puppet [+]
puppet /eer/ry	
pupp y /ies	

> *If you cannot find your word under* **pur** *look under* **per**

pur anum	per annum
puray	purée
purblind	
purceive	perceive [2+]
purcentige	percentage
purchas e [2] /able	
purchis	purchase [2+]
purda	purdah
purdah	
pure /ly/r/st	
purée	
purgat ive /ory	
purgatrey	purgatory
purg e [2] /ation	
purifi	purify [4+]
purif y [4] /ication	
purile	puerile [+]
purist	
puritan /ical	
purity	
purje	purge [2+]
purjer	perjure [2+]
purjerey	perjury
purl [1★] (knitting) /y	
purl	pearl [★+]
purlieu	
purloin [1]	
purlu	purlieu
puroolence	purulence [+]

purple	
purport [1]	
purpose /ful/fully/ly	
purpul	purple
purr [1]	
purse [2] /r	
pursuan ce /t	
pursue [2] /r	
pursuit	
pursute	pursuit
purulen ce /t	
purvay	purvey [1+]
purvey [1] /ance/or	
puse	puce
push [1] /-chair/y	
pusillanim ity /ous	
puss /y	
pussy-willow	
put	
putative	
puter	pewter
putie	putty [4]
putrefi	putrefy [4+]
putref y [4] /action	
putrid	
putrifi	putrefy [4+]
putt [1] /er	
putty [4]	
puty	putty [4]
puzle	puzzle [2+]
puzzle [2] /ment	
pyatsa	piazza
pye	pie [★+]
pygmy	
pyjamas	
pylon	
pyramid /al	
pyre	
pyrenoid	
pyric	Pyrrhic [+]
pyrite	
pyrotechnic /als/s	
Pyrrhic victory	
python	
pyx [1]	

Q

quack [1]
quad
quadrang *le* /ular
quadrangul   quadrangle [+]
quadrant
quadratic
quadrennial
quadrenyal   quadrennial
quadril   quadrille
quadrilateral
quadrille
quadruped
quadruple [2] /t/x
quadruplicat *e* [2] /ion
quadrupul   quadruple [2+]
quaff [1]
quagmire
quail [1]
quaint /er/est/ly/ness
quake [2]
Quaker /ism
qualifactory
qualifi   qualify [4+]
qualif *y* [4] /ication
qualitative
qualit *y* /ies
qualm
quandar *y* /ies
quandrey   quandary [+]
quantifi   quantify [4+]
quantif *y* [4] /ication
quantitative
quantit *y* /ies
quant *um* /a (pl.)
quarantine [2]
quarel   quarrel [3+]
quarey   quarry [+]
quarrel [3] /some
quarr *y* /ies
quart
quarter [1] /ly/master
quartern
quartet

quarto /s
quarts [*] (fluid measure)
quartz [*] (mineral) /ite
quasar
quash [1]
quaternary
quatrain
quaver [1]
quay [*] (by sea)
que   cue [2*]
que   queue [2*]
queas *y* /iness
queen /ly
queer [1] /er/est/ly/ness
quell [1]
quench [1] /able/less
querey   query [4+]
quern
querulous /ly/ness
querulus   querulous [+]
quer *y* [4] /ies
queschun   question [1+]
quest [1]
question [1] /able/ably/naire
quetzal
queue [2*] (line)
quibble [2] /r
quibul   quibble [2+]
quich   quitch
quick /er/est/ly/ness
quicken [1]
quick *sand* /silver
quid
quid pro quo
quiescen *ce* /t
quiesense   quiescence [+]
quiet [1] /er/est/ly
quieten [1]
quietude
quiff
quill [1]
quilt [1]
quin
quince
quincentenary

quinine		quot *e* [2] /able/ation	
quins	quince	quotidian	
quinsy		quotient	
quintesence	quintessence [+]		
quintessen *ce* /tial			
quintet			
quintupl *e* /et/icate		**R**	
quintupul	quintuple [+]		
quip [3]		rabbi /s	
quire ★ (of paper)		rabbit [1]★ (animal)	
quire	choir ★	rabbit	rarebit ★
quirk		rabble	
quisling		rabes	rabies
quit [3] /ter		rabi	rabbi [+]
quitch		rabid /ly	
quite		rabies	
quits		rabit	rabbit [1]★
quiver [1]		rabit	rarebit ★
quixot *ic* /ry		rable	rabble
quiz [3]		rabul	rabble
quizzical /ly		race /-course/-horse	
quod	quad	rachit	ratchet
quodrangul	quadrangle [+]	racial /ism/ist/ly	
quodrant	quadrant	racis *m* /t	
quodratic	quadratic	rack [1]★ (shelf)	
quodrenial	quadrennial	rack	wrack ★
quodril	quadrille	racket [1] /eer	
quodrilateral	quadrilateral	racoon	
quodrooped	quadruped	rac *y* /ily	
quodruplicate	quadruplicate [2+]	radar	
quof	quaff [1]	raddle [2]	
quogmire	quagmire	rade	raid [1+]
quoit		radial /ly	
quolitativ	qualitative	radian *ce* /t	
quolitey	quality [+]	radians	radiance [+]
quontify	quantify [4+]	radiashun	radiation
quontitativ	quantitative	radiat *e* [2] /ion/or	
quontitey	quantity [+]	radiater	radiator
quontum	quantum [+]	radical ★ (political) /ly	
quorantine	quarantine [2]	radicle ★ (rootlet)	
quorrel	quarrel [3+]	radio [1] /wave	
quorrey	quarry [+]	radioactiv *e* /ity	
quorum		radio-astronomy	
quoshent	quotient	radiografer	radiographer [+]
quota		radiogram	
		radiograph *er* /y	

radioisotope		ramifi	ramify [4+]
radiolog *y* /ist		ramificashun	ramification
radiotherapy		ramif *y* [4] /ication	
radish /es		ramp [1]	
radium		rampage [2] /ous	
radi *us* /i (pl.)		rampagus	rampageous
radon		rampan *cy* /t	
radul	raddle [2]	rampart	
radyal	radial [+]	rampige	rampage [2+]
raffia		ramshackle	
raffish		ramshacul	ramshackle
raffle [2]		ranch [1] /er/es	
rafia	raffia	rancid /ity	
rafish	raffish	rancor	rancour [*+]
raft [1] /er		ranco *ur* [*] (hate) /rous	
raful	raffle [2]	random	
rag [3] /ger/time/wort		randum	random
ragamuffin		rane	rain [1*+]
ragamufin	ragamuffin	ranee	
rage [2]		ranefall	rainfall
raglan		range [2] /finder/r	
raid [1] /er		rangle	wrangle [2+]
rail [1] /road/way		rangul	wrangle [2+]
raillery		rank [1] /er [*] (soldier)	
raiment		ranker	rancour [*+]
rain [1*] (water) fall/y		rankle [2]	
rain	reign [1*]	rankul	rankle [2]
rain	rein [1*]	ransack [1]	
raindeer	reindeer	ransid	rancid [+]
raise [2*] (lift)		ransom [1] /er	
raise	rays [*]	ransum	ransom [1+]
raise	raze [2*]	rant [1] /er	
raisin		raon	rayon
raith	wraith	rap [3*] (knock) /per [*]	
raja		rap	wrap [*+]
rak *e* [2] /ish		rapaci *ous* /ty	
rakoon	racoon	rapashus	rapacious [+]
rale	rail [1+]	rapasitey	rapacity
ralerey	raillery	rapcher	rapture [+]
ralie	rally [4+]	rap *e* [2] /er/ine/ist	
rall *y* [4] /ies		rapid /ity/ly	
ram [3] /mer/rod		rapier	
ramble [2] /r		rapper	wrapper [*]
rambul	ramble [2+]	rapscallion	
rament	raiment	rapscalyon	rapscallion

rapsodey	rhapsody +	ratif y 4 /ication/ier	
rapsodise	rhapsodise 2	ratio /s	
rapt * (absorbed)		ration 1	
rapt	wrapped *	rational * (adj.) /ity/ly	
raptur e /ous		rationale * (n.)	
rapturus	rapturous	rationalis e 2 /ation/m	
rare /ly/r/st		rattle 2 /snake	
rarebit * (food)		ratul	rattle 2+
raref y 4 /ication		raucous /ly	
rarifi	rarefy 4+	raucus	raucous +
rarit y /ies		ravage 2 /r	
rasberie	raspberry +	rave 2	
rasbery	raspberry +	ravel 3	
rascal /ity/ly		raven	
rase	raise 2*	ravene	ravine
rase	raze 2*	ravenous /ly/ness	
rasecorse	race-course	ravenus	ravenous +
rasehorse	race-horse	ravige	ravage 2+
rash /er/est/ly/ness		ravine	
rashal	racial +	ravioli	
rashalism	racialism	ravish 1	
rashalist	racialist	raw /er/est/ness	
rashio	ratio +	rawcus	raucous +
rashul	racial +	rayon	
rashun	ration 1	rays * (light beams)	
rashunal	rational *+	raze 2* (demolish)	
rashunalise	rationalise 2+	raze	raise 2*
rashunalitey	rationality	razer	razor +
rashyo	ratio +	razor /-bill/-blade	
rasie	racy +	reach 1	
rasin	raisin	reacshun	reaction +
rasism	racism +	react 1 /ive/or	
rasist	racist	reaction /ary	
raskal	rascal +	read *† /able/er/ing	
rasp 1		†(book)	
raspberr y /ies		read	red *+
rat 3 /-race/ter		read	reed 1*
ratable	rateable	readdress 1	
ratabul	rateable	readi ly /ness	
ratafia		readmishun	readmission
ratchet		readmission	
rate 2 /able/payer		readmit 3 /tance	
rath	wrath +	readress	readdress 1
rather		ready /-made	
ratifi	ratify 4+	reaf	reef 1+

reagent		rebellious /ly/ness	
reak	reek [1]★	rebelyun	rebellion
reak	wreak [1]★	rebelyus	rebellious [+]
real ★ (actual) /ly		reberth	rebirth
real	reel [1]★	rebild	rebuild [+]
realey	really	rebilt	rebuilt
realisashun	realisation	rebirth	
realis e [2] /able/ation		rebound [1]	
realis m /t		rebownd	rebound [1]
realistic /ally		rebuff [1]	
realit y /ies		rebuild /ing	
realm		rebuilt	
realter	realtor	rebuk e [2] /ingly	
realtor		rebut [3] /tal	
ream		rebutal	rebuttal
reanimat e [2] /ion		recalcitran ce /t	
reap [1] /er		recall [1]	
reapear	reappear [1+]	recalsitrance	recalcitrance [+]
reapearance	reappearance	recant [1] /ation	
reappear [1] /ance		recap [3]	
rear [1] /guard		recapcher	recapture [2]
rear-admiral		recapitulat e [2] /ion	
rearange	rearrange [2+]	recapture [2]	
reargard	rearguard	recast	
rearm [1] /ament		recede [2]	
rearrange [2] /ment		receipt [1]★ (document)	
reasemble	reassemble [2]	receit	receipt [1]★
reasembul	reassemble [2]	receiv e [2] /able/er	
reasershun	reassertion	recent ★ (of late) /ly	
reasert	reassert [1+]	recepshun	reception [+]
reasertion	reassertion	recepshunist	receptionist
reasess	reassess [1+]	receptacle	
reashorance	reassurance	receptacul	receptacle
reashorans	reassurance	reception /ist/-room	
reashore	reassure [2+]	receptive /ly/ness	
reason [1] /able/ably		receptivity	
reassemble [2]		receptor	
reassembul	reassemble [2]	receshun	recession [+]
reassert [1] /ion		recess [1] /ive	
reassess [1] /ment		recession /al	
reassur e [2] /ance		rech	retch [1]★
reath	wreath ★	rech	wretch ★
reath	wreathe [2]★	recharge [2] /able	
rebate [2]		recicle	recycle [2]
rebel [3] /lion		recidivis m /t	

recieve	receive [2+]
recipe	
recipi	recipe
recipient	
reciproc *al* /ally/ity	
reciprocat *e* [2] /ion	
recita *l* /tion/tive	
recitashun	recitation
recite [2]	
reck	wreck [1+]
reckage	wreckage
reckidge	wreckage
reckless /ly/ness	
reckon [1]	
reclaim [1]	
reclamashun	reclamation
reclamation	
reclaym	reclaim [1]
recline [2]	
recluse	
recognis *e* [2] /able/ably	
recognishun	recognition
recognition	
recoil [1]	
recolect	recollect [1+]
recollect [1] /ion	
recomence	recommence [2+]
recomend	recommend [1+]
recomens	recommence [2+]
recommence [2] /ment	
recommend [1] /ation	
recommendabl *e* /y	
recompense [2]	
reconcil *e* [2] /able/iation	
reconcilement	
recondishun	recondition [1]
recondite	
recondition [1]	
reconker	reconquer [1]
reconnoitre [2]	
reconoiter	reconnoitre [2]
reconquer [1]	
reconsider [1] /ation	
reconsile	reconcile [2+]
reconstitut *e* [2] /ion	

reconstruct [1] /ion/ive	
recoop	recoup [1+]
record [1] /er/-player	
recorse	recourse
recount [1]★ (tell)	
re-count [1]★†	
†(count again)	
recoup [1] /ment	
recouperate	recuperate [2+]
recourse	
recover [1] /y	
recownt	recount [1]★
recownt	re-count [1]★
recreant /ly	
recreat *e* [2]★ (entertain) /ion ★	
re-creat *e* [2]★ (form anew) /ion ★	
recriminat *e* [2] /ion	
recriminat *ive* /ory	
recruit [1]	
rectang *le* /ular	
rectangul	rectangle [+]
recter	rector [+]
rectifi	rectify [4+]
rectif *able* /er	
rectifiabul	rectifiable [+]
rectif *y* [4] /ication	
rectilinea *r* /l	
rectilinier	rectilinear [+]
rectitude	
recto	
rector /y/ies	
rect *um* /al	
recumben *cy* /t	
recuperat *e* [2] /ion/ive	
recur [3] /rence/rent	
recurens	recurrence
recycle [2]	
recycul	recycle [2]
red ★† /-handed	
†(colour)	
red	read ★+
redbreast	
redbrest	redbreast
redbrick	
redden [1]	

redd *er* /est/ish
redeem [1] /able/er
redempt *ion* /ive
redemshun — redemption [+]
reden — redden [1]
redeploi — redeploy [1+]
redeploy [1] /ment
reder — redder [+]
redevelop [1] /ment
redie — ready [+]
rediffusion
redifushun — rediffusion
redifusion — rediffusion
rediley — readily [+]
redimade — ready-made
rediploi — redeploy [1+]
rediploy — redeploy [1+]
redirecshun — redirection
redirect [1] /ion
redistribut *e* /ion
redivelop — redevelop [1+]
redolen *ce* /t
redouble [2]
redoubt /able
redound [1]
redress [1] /ment
redskin
reduble — redouble [2]
reduc *e* [2] /ible/tion
reducshun — reduction
redundanc *y* /ies
redundansey — redundancy [+]
redundant
reduplicat *e* [2] /ion
redwood
re-echo [1]
reed [1]* (water-plant)
reed — read *[+]
reef [1] /er/-knot
reegsamin — re-examine [2+]
reek [1]* (smell)
reek — wreak [1]*
reeko — re-echo [1]
reeksport — re-export [1+]
reel [1]* (wind in)

reel
re-elect [1] /ion
reem — ream
re-enter [1]
re-entr *y* /ies
reep — reap [1+]
reer — rear [1+]
reer admiral — rear-admiral
reergard — rearguard
re-establish [1] /ment
reeve [2]
re-examin *e* [2] /ation
re-export [1] /ation
refashion [1]
refashun — refashion [1]
refector *y* /ies
refer [3] /able/ence
referee /d/ing
referend *um* /a/ums (pls.)
referens — reference
refewel — refuel [3]
refill [1] /able
refine [2] /ment
refiner *y* /ies
refit [3]
reflashun — reflation [+]
reflate [2]
reflation /ary
reflect [1] /ion/ive/or
refleks — reflex [+]
refleksiv — reflexive
reflex /ive
refloat [1]
reflote — refloat [1]
reform [1] /ation/er
reformashun — reformation
reformator *y* /ies
reformatrey — reformatory [+]
refracshun — refraction
refract [1] /able/ion/ive
refractor *y* /iness
refrain [1]
refresh [1] /er/ment
refrigerat *e* [2] /ion/or
refuel [3]

real *[+]

ream

refuge ★ (shelter) /e ★†
  †(fugitive)
refulgen ce /t
refulgens   refulgence +
refund [1]
refurbish [1]
refus e [2] /al
refutashun   refutation
refut e [2] /able/al/ation
regain [1]
regal ★† /ia/ly
  †(of a king)
regale [2]★ (to feast)
regane   regain [1]
regard [1] /less
regatta /s
regen cy /t
regenerat e [2] /ion/ive/or
regicid e /al
regime /n
regiment [1] /al/ation
region /al/alism/ally
regiside   regicide +
regist er [1] /ration
registrar
registrashun   registration
registr y /ies
regreshun   regression
regress [1] /ion/ive
regret [3] /ful/fully
regretabul   regrettable +
regrettabl e /y
regular /ity/ly
regularis e [2] /ation
regularitey   regularity
regulashun   regulation
regulat e [2] /ion/or
reguler   regular +
regurgitat e /ion
rehabilitat e [2] /ion
rehash [1]
rehears e [2] /al
rehersal   rehearsal
reherse   rehearse [2]+
Reich

reign [1]★ (rule)
reimburse [2] /ment
rein [1]★ (of horse)
rein   reign [1]★
reincarnashun   reincarnation
reincarnat e [2] /ion
reindeer
reinforce [2] /able/ment
reinfors   reinforce [2]+
reinshore   re-insure [2]+
reinstate [2] /ment
re-insur e [2] /ance
reinvest [1] /ment
reiterashun   reiteration
reiterat e [2] /ion
rejecshun   rejection
reject [1] /ion
rejeme   regime +
rejoic e [2] /ingly
rejoin [1] /der
rejoise   rejoice [2]+
rejoovenate   rejuvenate [2]+
rejuvenat e [2] /ion
rekindle [2]
rekindul   rekindle [2]
rekwest   request [1]
rekwiem   requiem
rekwisishun   requisition
rekwisit   requisite +
rekwisition   requisition
rekwite   requite [2]+
relaks   relax [1]+
relaksashun   relaxation
relaksation   relaxation
relapse [2]
relashun   relation
relat e [2] /ion
relative /ly
relativity
relax [1] /ation
relay [1]
releaf   relief
release [2]
relegashun   relegation
relegat e [2] /ion

releif	relief
relent [1] /less/lessly	
relese	release [2]
relevan ce /t	
relevans	relevance [+]
releve	relieve [2+]
reli	rely [4]
reliabilitey	reliability
reliab le /ility/ly	
reliabul	reliable [+]
relian ce /t	
relians	reliance [+]
relic	
relief	
reliev e [2] /able	
religion	
religious /ly/ness	
religun	religion
religus	religious [+]
relinkwish	relinquish [1+]
relinquish [1] /ment	
relish [1] /able	
relm	realm
reluctan ce /t/tly	
reluctans	reluctance [+]
rely [4]	
remain [1] /der/s	
remand [1]	
remaridge	remarriage
remarie	remarry [4+]
remarige	remarriage
remark [1] /able/ably	
remarr y [4] /iage	
remed y [4] /ies	
rememb er [1] /rance	
remembrans	remembrance
remind [1] /er	
reminisce [2] /nce/nt	
reminisence	reminiscence
reminisens	reminiscence
reminisent	reminiscent
reminiss	reminisce [2+]
remishun	remission
remiss /ion/ly	
remit [3] /tal/tance	

remitans	remittance
remnant	
remonstran ce /t	
remonstrans	remonstrance [+]
remonstrat e [2] /ion/ive	
remoov	remove [2+]
remooval	removal
remorse /ful/fully	
remorseless /ly/ness	
remote /ly/r/st	
remount [1]	
removal	
remov e [2] /able/ability	
remownt	remount [1]
remunerat e [2] /ion/ive	
ren	wren
Renaissance *†	
†(historic period)	
renal	
renascen ce *† /t	
†(rebirth)	
rench	wrench [1]
rend [1]	
render [1]	
rendezvous [1]	
renegade [2]	
renew [1] /able/al	
renit	rennet
renium	rhenium
rennet	
renounce [2] /ment	
renouns	renounce [2+]
renovashun	renovation
renovat e [2] /ion/or	
renown /ed	
renowns	renounce [2+]
rent [1] /al/er	
rentul	rental
renue	renew [1+]
renunciat e [2] /ion	
reorganis e [2] /ation	
re-orientat e [2] /ion	
repade	repaid
repaid	
repair [1] /er	

repara *ble* /tion	
reparashun	reparation
repartee /s	
repast	
repatriashun	repatriation
repatriat *e* ² /ion	
repay /able/ing/ment	
repeal ¹	
repeat ¹ /able/edly	
repel ³ /lent	
repent ¹ /ance/ant	
repentans	repentance
repercushun	repercussion
repercussion	
repertoire	
repertory	
repetishun	repetition ⁺
repetishus	repetitious
repetiti *on* /ous/ve	
repetitiv	repetitive
repetrey	repertory
repine ²	
replace ² /able/ment	
replase	replace ²⁺
replay ¹	
replenish ¹ /ment	
replet *e* /ion	
repli	reply ⁴⁺
replica	
repl *y* ⁴ /ies	
report ¹ /able/er	
repose ² /ful	
reposito*r y* /ies	
repositrey	repository ⁺
reprable	reparable ⁺
reprabul	reparable ⁺
reprehend	
reprehenshun	reprehension ⁺
reprehensibul	reprehensible
reprehensi *on* /ble	
represent ¹ /ation	
representashun	representation
representative	
represhun	repression
repress ¹ /ible/ion/ive	

reprieve ²	
reprimand ¹	
reprint ¹	
reprisal	
reproach ¹ /ful/fully	
reprobate ²	
reproduc *e* ² /ible	
reproducshun	reproduction
reproduction	
reproof /s	
reprov *e* ² /al/ingly	
reptil *e* /ian	
republic /an	
repudiat *e* ² /ion/or	
repugnan *ce* /t	
repugnans	repugnance ⁺
repuls *e* ² /ion	
repulshun	repulsion
repulsive /ly/ness	
reputashun	reputation
reput *e* ² /able/ation	
reputedly	
request ¹	
requiem	
require ² /ment	
requisishun	requisition
requisit *e* /ion	
requit *e* ² /al	
rerite	rewrite ⁺
reritten	rewritten
rerote	rewrote
rescind ¹	
rescue ² /r	
research ¹ /er	
reseat ★ (seat again)	
reseat	receipt ¹★
resede	recede ²
reseed	recede ²
reseipt	receipt ¹★
resembl *e* ² /ance	
resembul	resemble ²⁺
resent ¹★ (grudge) /ment	
resent	recent ★⁺
resentful /ly	
resepshonist	receptionist

resepshun	reception +	resistans	resistance +
reseptacul	receptacle	resit /ting	
reseption	reception +	resitashun	recitation
reseptionist	receptionist	resitation	recitation
reseptiv	receptive +	resite	recite ²
reseptor	receptor	resle	wrestle ²+
reserch	research ¹+	resler	wrestler
reservashun	reservation	resole ²	
reserv e ² /ation/ist		resoloot	resolute +
reservoir		resolushun	resolution
reseshun	recession +	resolute /ly/ness	
resess	recess ¹+	resolution	
resession	recession +	resolve ²	
resessiv	recessive	reson	reason ¹+
reset /ting		resonable	reasonable
reseve	receive ²+	resonabul	reasonable
reshuffle ²		resonan ce /t/tly	
reshuful	reshuffle ²	resonans	resonance +
resicle	recycle ²	resonat e ² /or	
reside ² /nce		resorce	resource +
residenc y /ies		resort ¹	
residens	residence	resound ¹	
residensey	residency +	resource /ful/fully	
residenshal	residential	respect ¹ /ful/fully	
resident /ial		respectab le /ility/ly	
residivism	recidivism +	respectabul	respectable +
residivist	recidivist	respective /ly	
residu e /al/ary/um		respirashun	respiration
resign ¹ /ation		respirater	respirator
resignashun	resignation	respir e ² /ation/ator	
resilien ce /t/tly		respite	
resiliens	resilience +	resplenden ce /t	
resin /ous		respond ¹ /ence/ent	
resind	rescind ¹	respons e /ive/iveness	
resinus	resinous	responsib le /ility/ly	
resipe	recipe	responsibul	responsible +
resipie	recipe	rest ¹★ (repose)	
resipient	recipient	rest	wrest ¹★
resiprocal	reciprocal +	restaurant	
resiprocate	reciprocate ²+	resterant	restaurant
resiprositey	reciprocity	restful /ly/ness	
resist ¹ /er/ive		restitushun	restitution
resistab le /ility/ly		restitution	
resistabul	resistable +	restive /ness	
resistan ce /t		restle	wrestle ²+

restler	wrestler	retract¹ /able/ile/ion	
restless		retrase	retrace²
restorashun	restoration	retread ★ (walk again)	
restor e² /ation/ative		re-tread¹★ (tyre)	
restrain¹ /t		retreat¹	
restrict¹ /ion/ive		retred	retread ★
restruccher	restructure²	retred	re-tread¹★
restructure²		retreive	retrieve²+
resul	wrestle²+	retrench¹ /ment	
result¹ /ant		retribushun	retribution
resumay	résumé ★	retribut e² /ion	
resume²★ (restart)		retriev e² /able/al/er	
résumé ★ (summary)		retroactive	
resumption		retrograde	
resurecshun	resurrection	retrogress¹ /ion/ive	
resurection	resurrection	retrospect¹ /ion/ive	
resurgen ce /t		return¹ /able	
resurgens	resurgence +	reunion	
resurrect¹ /ion		reunite²	
resus	rhesus	reunyun	reunion
resuscitat e² /ion		rev³	
resusitashun	resuscitation	revali	reveille
resusitate	resuscitate²+	revaluashun	revaluation
resusitation	resuscitation	revalu e² /ation	
retail¹ /er		reve	reeve²
retain¹ /er		reveal¹	
retale	retail¹+	reveille	
retaliat e² /ion/ory		revel³ /ler/ry	
retard¹ /ation/er		revelashun	revelation
retayn	retain¹+	revelation	
retch¹★ (vomit)		revelrey	revelry
retch	wretch ★	revenew	revenue
retenshun	retention +	revenge² /ful/fully	
retent ion /ive		revenue	
reticen ce /t		reverberat e² /ion/or	
retina		revere² /nce	
retinew	retinue	reverend ★ (priest)	
retinue		reverens	reverence
retire² /ment		reverent ★† /ly	
retisens	reticence +	†(respectful)	
retisent	reticent	reverey	reverie
retoric	rhetoric +	reverie	
retorical	rhetorical	revers e² /al/ible/ion	
retort¹		revershun	reversion
retrace²		revert¹ /ible	

review [1]★ (survey) /er
| review | revue ★ |
| revijun | revision |
revile [2]
revis *e* [2] /ion
| revishun | revision |
reviv *e* [2] /al
revocabl *e* /y
| revokashun | revocation |
revo *ke* [2] /cation
revolt [1]
revolushun	revolution
revolushunise	revolutionise [2]
revolushunrey	revolutionary +
revolution
revolutionar *y* /ies
revolutionise [2]
revolve [2] /r
revue ★ (entertainment)
revue	review [1]★+
revulshun	revulsion
revulsion
reward [1]
rewrit *e* /ten/ing
rewrote
rhapsodise [2]
rhapsod *y* /ies
rhenium
rhesus
rhetoric /al
rheumat *ic* /ism
rhinoceros /es
rhizome
rhizomorph
rhodium
rhododendron
rhomb *us* /i (pl.) /oid
rhubarb
rhyme [2]★ (poetry)
rhythm
rhythmic /al/ally
rib [3]
ribald /ry
ribbon
ricalsitrant	recalcitrant

rice ★ (food)
rich /er/es/est/ly/ness
| ricital | recital + |
| ricite | recite [2] |
rick [1] /ety
rickets
rickshaw
| ricline | recline [2] |
| ricluse | recluse |
ricochet [1]
ricooperate	recuperate [2]+
ricroot	recruit [1]
ricshore	rickshaw
ricumbent	recumbent
ricur	recur [3]+
ricuver	recover [1]+
rid /dance
ridance	riddance
ridans	riddance
riddle [2]
rid *e* /den/er/ing
rideem	redeem [1]+
rideemable	redeemable
rideemabul	redeemable
rideemer	redeemer
ridemshun	redemption+
ridge [2]
ridicule [2]
ridiculous /ly/ness
ridiculus	ridiculous +
ridownd	redound [1]
ridowt	redoubt +
ridress	redress [1]+
riduce	reduce [2]+
riducshun	reduction
ridul	riddle [2]
ridundansey	redundancy +
ridundant	redundant
riduse	reduce [2]+
ridusible	reducible
ridusibul	reducible
rie	rye ★
rie	wry ★+
rife
riff-raff

rifinerey	refinery +
rifle ² /-range	
riflecshun	reflection
riflect	reflect ¹⁺
riflecter	reflector
riflectiv	reflective
riform	reform ¹⁺
rifract	refract ¹⁺
rifrane	refrain ¹
rifresh	refresh ¹⁺
rifrigerate	refrigerate ²⁺
rifrigerater	refrigerator
rift /-valley	
rifulgens	refulgence +
rifulgent	refulgent
rifusal	refusal
rifuse	refuse ²⁺
rifutal	refutal
rifute	refute ²⁺
rig ³ /ger	
rigard	regard ¹⁺
rigardless	regardless
rigata	regatta +
rige	ridge ²
riger	rigor ★
riger	rigour ★
riggle	wriggle ²
right ¹★ (correct)	
right	rite ★
right	write ★⁺
righteous /ly/ness	
rightful /ly	
rigid /ity/ly	
rigmarole	
rigor ★ (stiffness)	
rigour ★ (severity)	
rigreshun	regression
rigresiv	regressive
rigress	regress ¹⁺
rigret	regret ³⁺
rigretable	regrettable +
rigretabul	regrettable +
rigretful	regretful
rigul	wriggle ²
rike	Reich

rikwest	request ¹
rikwire	require ²⁺
rikwite	requite ²⁺
rile ²	
riluctance	reluctance +
riluctans	reluctance +
riluctant	reluctant
rim ³	
rimainder	remainder
rimand	remand ¹
rimane	remain ¹⁺
rimark	remark ¹⁺
rimarkable	remarkable
rime ²★ (frost)	
rime	rhyme ²★
rimember	remember ¹⁺
rimembrance	remembrance
rimembrans	remembrance
rimind	remind ¹⁺
riminder	reminder
rimishun	remission
rimiss	remiss +
rimit	remit ³⁺
rimitance	remittance
rimitans	remittance
rimonstrativ	remonstrative
rimoov	remove ²⁺
rimorse	remorse +
rimorsless	remorseless +
rimote	remote +
rimunerate	remunerate ²⁺
rimuneration	remuneration
rinasance	Renaissance ★
rinasance	renascence ★⁺
rinasant	renascent
rind	
rinew	renew ¹⁺
rinewable	renewable
rinewabul	renewable
rinewal	renewal
ring ¹★ (circle, bell)	
ring	wring ★
ring er ★† /leader/let †(horse)	
ringer	wringer ★

245

rink	
rinkle	wrinkle [2]
rinkul	wrinkle [2]
rinoceros	rhinoceros [+]
rinoserus	rhinoceros [+]
rinounce	renounce [2+]
rinownse	renounce [2+]
rinse [2]	
rinuable	renewable
rinuabul	renewable
rinual	renewal
rinue	renew [1+]
rinunsiashun	renunciation
rinunsiate	renunciate [2+]
rinunsiation	renunciation
riot [1] /ous/ously	
riotus	riotous
rip [3] /per	
ripair	repair [1+]
ripare	repair [1+]
ripe /r/st/ly/ness	
ripeel	repeal [1]
ripeet	repeat [1+]
ripel	repel [3+]
ripen [1]	
ripent	repent [1+]
ripentance	repentance
ripentans	repentance
ripentant	repentant
ripine	repine [2]
riple	ripple [2]
riplete	replete [+]
ripli	reply [4+]
riport	report [1+]
ripose	repose [2+]
ripositrey	repository [+]
ripple [2]	
ripreshun	repression
ripress	repress [1+]
ripreve	reprieve [2]
riprisal	reprisal
riproch	reproach [1+]
riprochful	reproachful
riproof	reproof [+]
riproov	reprove [2+]

ripublic	republic [+]
ripublican	republican
ripudiate	repudiate [2+]
ripugnance	repugnance [+]
ripugnans	repugnance [+]
ripugnant	repugnant
ripul	ripple [2]
ripulse	repulse [2+]
ripulshun	repulsion
ripulsiv	repulsive [+]
ripute	repute [2+]
riquest	request [1]
riquire	require [2+]
riquite	requite [2+]
ris *e* *(get up)/en/er/ing*	
rise	rice *
risemblans	resemblance
risemble	resemble [2+]
risembul	resemble [2+]
risent	resent [1*+]
risentful	resentful [+]
riserch	research [1+]
riserve	reserve [2+]
riservist	reservist
riside	reside [2+]
risign	resign [1+]
risilience	resilience [+]
risilient	resilient
risilyant	resilient
risilyens	resilience [+]
risist	resist [1+]
risistable	resistable [+]
risistabul	resistable [+]
risistance	resistance [+]
risistans	resistance [+]
risistant	resistant
risital	recital [+]
risite	recite [2]
risk [1] /ier/iest/y	
riski *ly* /ness	
risolve	resolve [2]
risorce	resource [+]
risorceful	resourceful
risort	resort [1]
risotto	

risound	resound [1]	riter	writer
risource	resource +	rithe	writhe [2]
risourceful	resourceful	rithm	rhythm
risownd	resound [1]	rithmic	rhythmic +
rispect	respect [1+]	riting	writing
rispectable	respectable +	ritire	retire [2+]
rispectful	respectful	ritort	retort [1]
rispectiv	respective +	ritracshun	retraction
rispire	respire [2+]	ritract	retract [1+]
rispite	respite	ritraction	retraction
risplendence	resplendence +	ritreet	retreat [1]
risplendens	resplendence +	ritrevable	retrievable
risplendent	resplendent	ritreval	retrieval
rispond	respond [1+]	ritreve	retrieve [2+]
rispondence	respondence	ritten	written
rispondens	respondence	ritual /ism/ist	
risponsible	responsible +	riturn	return [1+]
risponsibul	responsible +	rityoual	ritual +
risponsiv	responsive	rival [3] /ry	
rissole		riveal	reveal [1]
rist	wrist +	rivenge	revenge [2+]
ristband	wristband	rivengeful	revengeful
ristlet	wristlet	river	
ristore	restore [2+]	rivere	revere [2+]
ristrain	restrain [1+]	rivet [1]	
ristraint	restraint	rivijun	revision
ristrict	restrict [1+]	rivile	revile [2]
ristwatch	wrist-watch	rivise	revise [2+]
risult	result [1+]	rivishun	revision
risultant	resultant	rivision	revision
risume	resume [2★]	rivival	revival
risurgence	resurgence +	rivive	revive [2+]
risurgens	resurgence +	rivocable	revocable +
risurgent	resurgent	rivocabul	revocable +
rit	writ	rivoke	revoke [2+]
ritaliate	retaliate [2+]	rivolt	revolt [1]
ritard	retard [1+]	rivolv	revolve [2+]
ritchus	righteous +	rivolver	revolver
rite ★ (ceremony)		rivue	review [1★+]
rite	right [1★]	rivue	revue ★
rite	write ★+	rivulet	
riteful	rightful +	rivulshun	revulsion
ritenshun	retention +	rivulsion	revulsion
ritention	retention +	rivursal	reversal
ritentiv	retentive	rivurse	reverse [2+]

247

rivurt	revert [1+]	roli poli	roly-poly
riward	reward [1]	rolick	rollick [1+]
ro	roe [*+]	roll [1*] (move) /-call/er	
ro	row [1*+]	roller-skate [2]	
roach [1] /es		rollick [1] /er	
road [*] (highway)		rolling-pin	
road	rode [*]	roly-poly	
roadworth y /iness		Roman Catholic	
roam [1]		romance [2]	
roan		romans	romance [2]
roar [1] /er		romantic /ally/ism	
roast [1]		Romany	
rob [3] /ber		romboid	rhomboid
robber y /ies		rombus	rhombus [+]
robe [2]		rome	roam [1]
roberey	robbery [+]	romp [1] /er	
robin redbreast		rondayvoo	rendezvous [1]
robot		rondo /s	
robust /ly/ness		rone	roan
roch	roach [1+]	rong	wrong [1+]
rock [1] /er/y		rongful	wrongful [+]
rock -cake /garden		roo	rue [2+]
rocker y /ies		roobarb	rhubarb
rocket [1] /eer/ry		rooble	rouble
rocking -chair /-horse		roobul	rouble
rococo		rood [*] (church)	
rode [*](did ride)		rood	rude [*+]
rode	road [*]	roodiment	rudiment [+]
rodedendron	rhododendron	roodimentrey	rudimentary
rodent		roof [1] /less	
rodeo /s		rooful	rueful
rodeworthey	roadworthy [+]	rooge	rouge [2]
rodio	rodeo [+]	rooin	ruin [1+]
rodium	rhodium	rooinashun	ruination
roe [*] (deer) /buck		rooination	ruination
roe	row [1*+]	rooinous	ruinous [+]
rog	rogue [+]	rooinus	ruinous [+]
rogish	roguish	rook [1] /ery/eries	
rogu e /ery/ish		rool	rule [2+]
roial	royal [+]	roolet	roulette
roialtey	royalty	room /ful/iness/y	
rol	role [*]	roomatic	rheumatic [+]
rol	roll [1*+]	roomatism	rheumatism
rolcall	roll-call	roomer	rumour [1]
role [*] (of an actor)		roomey	roomy

248

roon	rune
roopee	rupee
rooral	rural +
roose	ruse
roost [1] /er	
root [1]★ /-crop/less	
root	route ★
roothless	ruthless +
rootine	routine
rootstock	
rop e [2] /iness/y	
rope-ladder	
ropey	ropy
ror	roar [1]+
rort	wrought +
rosarey	rosary +
rosar y /ies	
rose ★ /-bud/-tree	
rose	rows ★
roset -	rosette
rosette	
rosewood	
rosie	rosy +
rost	roast [1]
roster	
rostrum /s	
ros y /ily/iness	
rot [3] /ter	
rota /s	
rotarey	rotary +
rotar y /ies	
rotashun	rotation
rotat e [2] /able/ion	
rote ★ (repetition)	
rote	wrote ★
roten	rotten +
roter	rotor
roth	wrath +
rotor	
rotten /ly/ness	
rotund /a/ity	
rouble	
rouge [2]	
rough ★ (coarse) /age	
rough-and-ready	

rough-and-tumble	
roughen [1]	
rough er /est/ly/ness	
rough-shod	
rought	wrought +
roulette	
round [1] /er/est/ly/ness	
roundabout	
Roundhead	
round -table /-up	
rous e [2] /ingly	
rout [1]★ (defeat)	
route ★ (way)	
routeen	routine
routine	
rove [2] /r	
row [1]★ (boat) /er	
rowdie	rowdy +
rowd y /ies/ily/iness	
rownd	round [1]+
rowndabout	roundabout
rowndhed	Roundhead
rowndup	round-up
rows ★ (lines)	
rowse	rouse [2]+
rowt	rout [1]★
rowze	rouse [2]+
royal /ly/ty	
royaltey	royalty
rub [3] /ber	
rubarb	rhubarb
rubbish /y	
rubble	
rubicund	
rubie	ruby +
rubish	rubbish +
rubric	
rubul	rubble
rub y /ies	
rucksack	
rudder	
rudd y /iness	
rude ★(offensive)/ly/r/st	
rude	rood ★
ruder	rudder

249

rudie	ruddy +
rudiment /ary	
rue ² /ful/fully	
ruf	rough *+
ruf	ruff *
ruf and redy	rough-and-ready
ruf and tumbul	rough-and-tumble
ruff * (collar, bird)	
ruff	rough *+
ruffage	roughage
ruffen	roughen ¹
ruffian /ism/ly	
ruffle ²	
ruffley	roughly
rufidge	roughage
rufige	roughage
rufle	ruffle ²
rufshod	rough-shod
ruful	rueful
rufyan	ruffian +
rugbe	Rugby
Rugby	
rugged /ly/ness	
rugid	rugged +
ruin ¹ /ation	
ruinashun	ruination
ruinous /ly	
ruinus	ruinous +
ruksac	rucksack
rule ² /r	
rum /ba/my	
rumatic	rheumatic +
rumatism	rheumatism
rumble ²	
rumbul	rumble ²
rumer	rumour ¹
rumidge	rummage ²
rumige	rummage ²
ruminat e ² /ion/ive	
rummage ²	
rumour ¹	
rump /steak	
rumple ²	
rumpul	rumple ²
rumpus /es	

run /ner/ning/way	
runaway	
rune	
runerup	runner-up
rung *†	
†(step, did ring)	
rung	wrung *
runner-up	
runt	
rupcher	rupture ²
rupea	rupee
rupee	
rupture ²	
rural /ly	
ruse	
rush ¹	
rushun	Russian
rusit	russet
rusk	
rusler	rustler
russet	
Russian	
rust ¹ /less/y	
rustic /ity	
rusticat e ² /ion	
rusti er /est/ly/ness	
rustle ² /r	
rust-proof	
rusul	rustle ²+
rut ³	
ruthenium	
ruthless /ly/ness	
rye * (grain)	
rye	wry *+
ryly	wryly
rythm	rhythm
rythmic	rhythmic +

S

saans	seance
sabath	sabbath +
sabatical	sabbatical
sabbat h /ical	

saber	sabre +	sail	sale *+
sable		sailsman	salesman
sabotage ²		saint /hood/ly	
sabre /-toothed		sake	
sabul	sable	sakshorn	saxhorn
sacarin	saccharin	saksofone	saxophone +
saccharin		sakson	Saxon +
sacerdotal		saksophone	saxophone +
sachel	satchel	salar y ⁴ /ies	
sachet		sale *† /ability/able	
sack ¹ /ful		†(of goods)	
sackarin	saccharin	sale	sail ¹*+
sacrament		salesman	
sacred /ly/ness		salie	sally ⁴+
sacrement	sacrament	salien ce /t	
sacrific e ² /ial		saliens	salience +
sacrifise	sacrifice ²+	salin e /ity	
sacrifishal	sacrificial	saliva /ry/tion	
sacrileg e /ious		sallow /ness	
sacrilige	sacrilege +	sall y ⁴ /ies	
sacriligus	sacrilegious	salm	psalm +
sacrosanct		salmon	
sacsophone	saxophone +	salon	
sad /der/dest/ly/ness		saloon	
sadden ¹		saloot	salute ²+
saddle ² /r/ry		salow	sallow +
saden	sadden ¹	salsify	
sadis m /t		salt ¹ /iness/y	
sadul	saddle ²+	salt -cellar /-lick	
safari /s		salter	psalter +
safe /ly/r/st/ty		saltpeter	saltpetre
safegard	safeguard ¹	saltpetre	
safeguard ¹		salubri ous /ty	
saffron		salubrius	salubrious +
safire	sapphire	salutar y /iness	
saftie	safety	salutashun	salutation
sag ³		salut e ² /ation	
saga /s		salvage ²	
sagaci ous /ty		salvashun	salvation
sagashus	sagacious +	salvation	
sagasitey	sagacity	salv e ² /able	
sage /ly/ness		salver	
sago		salvidge	salvage ²
said		salvige	salvage ²
sail ¹* (of boat) /or		salvo /s	

samaritan		sap [3]	
samarium		saper	sapper
same /ness		sapien *ce* /t	
samon	salmon	sapiens	sapience [+]
samovar		sapling	
sample [2] /r		sapper	
sampul	sample [2+]	sapphire	
sanatorium /s		sarcasm	
sancshun	sanction [1]	sarcastic /ally	
sanctifi	sanctify [4+]	sarcofagus	sarcophagus [+]
sanctif *y* [4] /ication		sarcophag *us* /i (pl.)	
sanctimonious /ly		sardine	
sanctimonius	sanctimonious [+]	sardonic /ally	
sanction [1]		sargant	sergeant [+]
sanctity		sari	
sanctuar *y* /ies		sarjent	sergeant [+]
sanctum /s		sarm	psalm [+]
sand [1] /y		sartorial	
sandal /-wood		sary	sari
sandle	sandal [+]	saserdotle	sacerdotal
sandpaper [1]		sash /es	
sandwhich	sandwich [1+]	sashable	satiable
sandwich [1] /es		sashabul	satiable
sane ★ (not mad) /ly/ness		sashay	sachet
sane	seine [2★]	sashiate	satiate [2]
sang-froid		Satan /ic	
sanguin *e* /ary		satchel	
sangwin	sanguine [+]	sate [2]	
sanitary		sateen	
sanitashun	sanitation	satelight	satellite
sanitation		satellite	
sanitey	sanity	saten	sateen
sanitrey	sanitary	saterday	Saturday
sanity		satiable	
sankshun	sanction [1]	satiabul	satiable
sanktify	sanctify [4+]	satiate [2]	
sanktimonius	sanctimonious [+]	satin	
sanktitey	sanctity	satir *e* /ist	
sanktuarey	sanctuary [+]	satirical /ly	
sanktum	sanctum [+]	satirise [2]	
Sanskrit		satisfacshun	satisfaction
sant	saint [+]	satisfactor *y* /ily	
Santa Claus		satisfactrey	satisfactory [+]
Santa klaws	Santa Claus	satisfiabul	satisfiable
santeem	centime	satisf *y* [4] /iable/action	

saturashun	saturation	say /ing	
saturat *e*² /ion		sayance	seance
Saturday		scab³ /by	
Saturn		scabbard	
sauce ★ (liquid) /boat/pan		scabees	scabies
sauce	source ★	scabies	
saucer		scaffold	
saucerer	sorcerer +	scald¹	
saucerey	sorcery	scal *e*² /y	
sauci *er* /est/ly/ness		scaliwag	scallywag
saucy		scallop	
sauna		scallywag	
saunter¹		scalp¹ /er	
sausage		scalpel	
sausie	saucy	scamp¹	
savage² /ly/ry		scamper¹	
savana	savannah	scampi	
savannah		scan³ /ner	
save²★ (hoard)		scandal /ous/ously	
saver	savour¹★+	scandalise²	
savier	saviour	scandium	
savige	savage²+	scanshun	scansion
savigrey	savagery	scansion	
saviour		scant /ily/iness/y	
savorey	savoury	scapegoat	
savour¹★ (flavour) /y		scapula /r	
savyer	saviour	scar³	
saw ★ (cut) /n		scarab	
saw	soar¹★	scarce /ly/ness/r	
saw	sore ★+	scarcit *y* /ies	
sawcer	saucer	scare² /crow/monger/y	
sawcy	saucy	scaretso	scherzo
sawdid	sordid +	scar *f* /fs/ves (pls.)	
sawdust		scarf-pin	
sawna	sauna	scarif *y*⁴ /ication	
sawnter	saunter¹	scarlatina	
saws	sauce ★+	scarlet	
saws	source ★	scarsitey	scarcity +
sawser	saucer	scate	skate²+
sawsey	saucy	scathe² /less	
sawsier	saucier +	scatter¹ /-brain	
saxhorn		scavenge² /r	
saxofone	saxophone +	sceme	scheme²+
Saxon /y		scenario /s	
saxophon *e* /ist		scene ★ (of a play) /ry	

scenic /ally
scent [1]* (smell)
scepter   sceptre
sceptic /al/ally/ism
sceptre
scerge   scourge [2]
scermish   skirmish [1]+
schedule [2]
schematic /ally
scheme [2] /r
scherzo /s
schism /atic
schist
schizofrenia   schizophrenia +
schizoid
schizophreni *a* /c
schnaps
scholar /ly/ship
scholastic /ism
school [1] /boy/girl
schooner
sciatic /a
scien *ce* /tist
scientific /ally
scintillat *e* [2] /ion
scion
scission
scissors
scitsofrenia   schizophrenia +
sclerosis
sclerotic
scoff [1] /er
scolar   scholar +
scolarship   scholarship
scolastic   scholastic +
scold [1] /er
scone
scool   school [1]+
scoop [1]
scoot [1] /er
scorch [1] /er/ingly
score [2] /r
scorn [1] /ful/fully
scorpion
scorpyun   scorpion

Scot /ch/tish
scot-free
Scots *man* /woman
scoundrel /ism/ly
scour [1] /er
scourge [2]
scout [1]
scower   scour [1]+
scowl [1]
scowndrel   scoundrel +
scowt   scout [1]
scrabble [2]
scrabul   scrabble [2]
scrag [3] /gy
scram [3]
scramble [2]
scrambul   scramble [2]
scrap [3] /-book/-heap
scrape [2] /r
scrapp *y* /ily/iness
scrapy   scrappy +
scratch [1] /es
scrawl [1]
scrawny
scream [1] /er
scree
screech [1] /es/-owl
screed [1]
screen [1]
screw [1] /driver/y
screwtinise scrutinise [2]
scribble [2] /r
scribe [2]
scribul   scribble [2]+
scrimige   scrimmage
scrimmage
scrimp [1] /y
scripcher   scripture +
script /-writer
scriptur *e* /al
scroful *a* /ous
scroll
scroo   screw [1]+
scrotum
scrounge [2] /r

scrownge	scrounge [2+]	seam	seem [1★]
scrub [3] /ber/by		seaman /ship	
scruff /ier/iest/y		seamstress	
scrum half		seam *y* /ier/iest	
scrummage		sean	scene [★+]
scrumptious /ly/ness		sean	seen [★]
scrumshus	scrumptious [+]	seance	
scrunch [1] /es		seans	seance
scruple [2]		sear [1★] (scorch)	
scrupul	scruple [2]	sear	seer [★]
scrupulous /ly/ness		search [1] /es/er	
scrutinise [2]		sea *shore* /side/weed	
scrutin *y* /ies/eer		seasick /ness	
scud [3]		season [1] /able/ably	
scuffle [2]		seasonal /ly	
scuful	scuffle [2]	seasor	seesaw [1]
scul	scull [1★+]	seat [1]	
scul	skull [★+]	seaworth *y* /iness	
sculerey	scullery [+]	sebaceous	
scull [1★] (boat) /er		sebashus	sebaceous
sculler *y* /ies		secaters	secateurs
sculpcher	sculpture [2]	secateurs	
sculpt *or* /ress (fem.)		secede [2]	
sculpture [2]		seceshun	secession
scum [3] /my		secession	
scupper [1]		seclu *de* [2] /sion	
scurf /iness/y		second [1] /ly/-rate	
scurge	scourge [2]	secondar *y* /ily	
scurie	scurry [4]	secondrey	secondary [+]
scurilus	scurrilous [+]	secrecy	
scurrilous /ly		secresey	secrecy
scurry [4]		secret /ive/ly	
scurv *y* /ily		secretaria *l* /t	
scury	scurry [4]	secretar *y* /ies	
scuttle [2]		secret *e* [2] /ion	
scutul	scuttle [2]	sect /arian	
scythe [2]		section /al/ally	
sea ★ (water) /-gull		sector	
sea	see [★+]	secular /ism	
seafar *er* /ing		seculatis *e* [2] /ation	
seal /ed/er/ing ★ (fasten)		secur *e* [2] /able/ely	
sea *-level* /-lion		securitey	security [+]
sealing	ceiling ★	securit *y* /ies	
sealskin		sed	said
seam ★ (join in cloth)		sedashun	sedation [+]

sedate /ly/ness		seesfire	cease-fire
sedat *ion* /ive		seesher	seizure
sedentary		seeshore	seashore +
sedentrey	sedentary	seesick	seasick +
seder	cedar	seeside	seaside
sedge		seet	seat [1]
sedila	cedilla	seeth	seethe [2]
sediment /ation		seethe [2]	
sedishun	sedition +	seeworthey	seaworthy +
sedishus	seditious	seeze	seize [2]
sedit *ion* /ious		sefalic	cephalic +
seduce [2] /r		sefalitis	cephalitis
seducshun	seduction	sege	sedge
seduction		segment /ation	
seductive /ly		segregashun	segregation
sedulous /ly		segregat *e* [2] /ion/ive	
sedulus	sedulous +	seige	siege
seduse	seduce [2+]	seine [2]★ (fishing net)	
see ★† /ing/n ★†		seism *ic* /ometer	
†(with eyes)		seismograph /ic	
see	sea ★+	seismolog *y* /ist	
seed [1]★ (of plants)		seize [2]	
seed	cede [2]★	seizure	
seed *iness* /ling/y		sekaters	secateurs
seefarer	seafarer +	sekstant	sextant
seege	siege	sekstet	sextet
seek /er/ing		sekston	sexton
seel	seal +	seksual	sexual +
seeling	ceiling ★	sekt	sect +
seeling	sealing ★	sekwel	sequel
seem [1]★ (appear)		sekwence	sequence +
seem	seam ★	sekwens	sequence +
seeman	seaman +	sekwester	sequester [1]
seemey	seamy +	sekwestrate	sequestrate [2+]
seeml *y* /ier/iest/iness		sekwin	sequin
seemstress	seamstress	selandine	celandine
seen	scene ★+	selcius	Celsius
seenerey	scenery	seldom /ly	
seenic	scenic +	selebritey	celebrity +
seep [1] /age		select [1] /ion/or	
seepige	seepage	selective /ly	
seer ★ (prophet)		selenium	
seer	sear [1]★	seler	cellar ★
seesaw [1]		seler	seller ★
seese	cease [2+]	selerey	celery

seleritey	celerity
self /ish/ishness	
self-assured	
self-centred	
self-confiden *ce* /t	
selfconfidens	self-confidence [+]
self-conscious /ly/ness	
selfconshus	self-conscious [+]
self-contained	
self-control	
self-respect /ing	
self-righteous /ly/ness	
self-service	
selibacy	celibacy [+]
selibasey	celibacy [+]
selibat	celibate
selibrant	celebrant
selibrate	celebrate [2+]
sell ★ (goods) /er ★	
sell	cell ★
seller	cellar ★
Sellotape	
selofane	cellophane
selsius	Celsius
selt	Celt [+]
seltic	Celtic
selular	cellular
selule	cellule
seluloid	celluloid
selulose	cellulose
selvage	
selvige	selvage
semafor	semaphore
semantic /s	
semaphore	
semblance	
semblans	semblance
semen	
semester	
semibreve	
semicercul	semicircle [+]
semicirc *le* /ular	
semicolon	
semi-conductor	
semi-detached	

semi-final	
semikwaver	semiquaver
semilunar	
seminal	
seminar /y	
semi-precious	
semipreshus	semi-precious
semiquaver	
Semit *e* /ic	
semitone	
semitrey	cemetery [+]
semolena	semolina
semolina	
sena	senna
senario	scenario [+]
senat	senate [+]
senat *e* /or	
senater	senator
send /er	
senil *e* /ity	
senilitey	senility
senior /ity	
senna	
senotaf	cenotaph
sensashun	sensation
sensashunal	sensational [+]
sensation	
sensational /ism/ly	
sense [2] /less	
senser	censer ★
senser	censor [1★+]
sensher	censure [2+]
senshience	sentience [+]
senshooal	sensual [+]
sensib *le* /ility/ly	
sensibul	sensible [+]
sensitise [2]	
sensitiv *e* /ely/ity	
sensitivitey	sensitivity
sensorey	sensory
sensorious	censorious
sensorius	censorious
sensory	
sensual /ist/ity/ly	
sensus	census [+]

sent * (did send)	
sent	cent *
sent	scent ¹*
sentenarey	centenary +
sentenarian	centenarian
sentence ²	
sentenial	centennial +
sentens	sentence ²
sentenshus	sententious +
sententious /ly	
sentenyal	centennial +
senter	centre ²+
senter forwud	centre-forward
sentien ce /t	
sentigrade	centigrade
sentigram	centigram
sentileter	centilitre
sentiment	
sentimental /ist/ity/ly	
sentimentalise ²	
sentimeter	centimetre
sentinel	
sentipede	centipede
sentor	centaur
sentral	central +
sentralise	centralise ²+
sentralitey	centrality
sentrey	sentry +
sentrifugal	centrifugal +
sentrifuge	centrifuge
sentripetal	centripetal
sentr y /ies	
sentuple	centuple
senturey	century +
senturion	centurion
senyor	senior +
senyoritey	seniority
separat e ² /ion/ist/or	
seperate	separate ²+
sephalic	cephalic +
sephalitis	cephalitis
sepia	
sepoi	sepoy
sepoy	
September	

septer	sceptre
septic	
septicaemia	
septisemia	septicaemia
sepulchr e /al	
sepulker	sepulchre +
sequel	
sequen ce /tial	
sequester ¹	
sequestrat e ² /ion/or	
sequin	
ser	sir
seraf	seraph +
serafic	seraphic
seramic	ceramic +
seraph /s/ic	
serch	search ¹+
serebral	cerebral +
serees	series
serenade ²	
serendipity	
seren e /ely/ity	
serenitey	serenity
seres	series
sereze	cerise
serf * (slave) /dom	
serf	surf ¹*+
sergeant /-major	
serial *† /ly	
†(part of a story)	
serial	cereal *
serialis e ² /ation	
seribelum	cerebellum
seribrum	cerebrum
serid	serried
series	
serimonial	ceremonial +
serimonius	ceremonious +
serimuney	ceremony +
serious /ly/ness	
serius	serious +
serlier	surlier +
serloin	sirloin
serly	surly *
sermise	surmise ²

sermon	
sermonise [2]	
sermownt	surmount [1]
sername	surname
serpass	surpass [1]
serpent /ine	
serplis	surplice ★
serplus	surplus ★
serprise	surprise [2]
serrated	
serried	
sertaks	surtax [+]
sertax	surtax [+]
sertifi	certify [4+]
sertifiable	certifiable [+]
sertificat	certificate [2+]
sertify	certify [4+]
sertintey	certainty [+]
sertitude	certitude
serum	
servant	
servay	survey [1+]
servaylans	surveillance
serve [2] /r	
servical	cervical
service [2] /ability/able	
serviet	serviette
serviette	
serviks	cervix [+]
servil e /ity	
servitude	
servival	survival
servive	survive [2+]
serviver	survivor
servix	cervix [+]
sesashun	cessation
sese	cease [2+]
seseed	secede [2]
seseshun	secession
seshun	cession ★
seshun	session ★
sesion	cession ★
sesion	session ★
sesium	caesium
sesless	ceaseless

sesmic	seismic [+]
seson	season [1+]
sesonable	seasonable
sesonabul	seasonable
sesonal	seasonal [+]
sespit	cesspit
sespool	cesspool
sessashun	cessation
sessesion	secession
session ★ (period)	
session	cession ★
set /ting/-square	
setea	settee
seter	setter
setle	settle [2+]
settee	
setter	
settle [2] /ment/r	
setul	settle [2+]
setulment	settlement
seudo	pseudo [+]
seudonim	pseudonym
sevear	severe [+]
seven /teen/teenth/th	
sevent y /ies/ieth	
sever [1] /ance	
several /ly	
severans	severance
sever e /ely/ity	
severitey	severity
sew [1★†] /er ★† /ing/n ★†	
†(with a needle)	
sew er [1★†] /age/erage	
†(public drain)	
sewn	sown ★
sex /ed/iness/less	
sextant	
sextet	
sexton	
sexual /ity/ly	
sezarian	Caesarean
Sezer	Caesar
sfere	sphere [2+]
sferical	spherical
sferoid	spheroid

sfincter	sphincter
sfinks	sphinx +
sfinx	sphinx +
sha	shah
shabbi *ly* /ness	
shabb *y* /ier/iest	
shaby	shabby +
shack	
shackle ²	
shad *e* ² /y	
shadervre	chef-d'oeuvre
shadow ¹ /y	
shaft	
shagay da fare	chargé-d'affaires
shagg *y* /iness	
shagie	shaggy +
shagrin	chagrin +
shah	
shak	shack
shake *† /down/n/r	
†(agitate)	
shake	sheik *
shakey	shaky +
shak *y* /ily/iness/ing	
shal	shall
shalaton	charlatan
shalay	chalet
shale	
shalet	chalet
shall	
shallot	
shallow /er/est/ness	
sham ³ /mer	
shamble ²	
shambul	shamble ²
shame ² /-faced/less	
shameful /ly	
shampane	champagne
shampoo ¹	
shamrock	
shamwa	chamois
shandeleer	chandelier
shandie	shandy +
shand *y* /ies	
shank	

shan't (shall not)	
shant	shan't
shant *y* /ies	
shape ² /liness/ly	
shaperon	chaperon ¹+
sharad	charade
share ² /holder/r	
shark	
sharlot	charlotte
sharp /er/est/ly/ness	
sharpen ¹ /er	
sharpshooter	
shasee	chassis
shater	shatter ¹
shatow	chateau +
shatter ¹	
shave ² /n/r	
shawl	
shea *f* ¹ /ves (pl.)	
shear * (clip) /s	
shear	sheer ¹*
sheath * (n.)	
sheathe ²* (v.)	
shed /ding	
shedule	schedule ²
sheef	sheaf ¹+
sheek	chic *
sheek	sheik *
sheen	
sheep /-dog/skin	
sheepish /ly/ness	
sheer ¹* (thin, steep)	
sheer	shear *+
sheet ¹	
shef	chef
sheik * (Arab chief)	
sheik	chic *
sheild	shield ¹
shel	shell ¹+
shelac	shellac +
sheld	shield ¹
shel *f* /ves (pl.)	
shelfish	shellfish
shell ¹ /fish	
shellac /ked/king	

shelter [1] /er	
shelve [2]	
shemeez	chemise
sheperd	shepherd [1+]
sheperds pie	shepherd's pie
shepherd [1] /ess (fem.)	
shepherd's pie	
sherbet	
sherie	sherry [+]
sherif	sheriff [+]
sheriff /s	
sheroot	cheroot
sheropodey	chiropody [+]
sherr *y* /ies	
shery	sherry [+]
sheth	sheath ★
sheth	sheathe [2] ★
shevaler	chevalier
sheves	sheaves
shevron	chevron
shi	shy [4+]
shic	chic ★
shic	sheik ★
shicanerey	chicanery
shield [1]	
shifon	chiffon
shift [1] /ily/iness/less/y	
shiling	shilling
shilling	
shilly-shall *y* [4] /ier	
shily shaly	shilly-shally [4+]
shimeric	chimeric [+]
shimmer [1] /y	
shin [3]	
shin *e* [2] /er/y	
shingle [2]	
shingles	
shingul	shingle [2]
shinguls	shingles
ship [3] /ment/per	
shipreck	shipwreck [1]
ship *shape* /wright	
shipwreck [1]	
shire	
shirk [1] /er	

shirt /ing/y	
shivalrey	chivalry [+]
shivalrous	chivalrous
shivalrus	chivalrous
shiver [1] /y	
shnaps	schnaps
shoal [1]	
shock [1] /-absorber/er	
shoddi *ly* /ness	
shodd *y* /ier/iest	
shodie	shoddy [+]
shody	shoddy [+]
shoe /lace/string	
shofer	chauffeur
sholder	shoulder [1]
shole	shoal [1]
shoo	shoe [+]
shood	should [+]
shook	
shoolace	shoelace
shoostring	shoestring
shoot ★ (gun) /er	
shoot	chute ★
shooting /-brake	
shop [3] /keeper/per	
shoplift [1] /er	
shop-soiled	
shop-steward	
shore [2] ★ (prop up)	
shore	sure ★[+]
shoretey	surety [+]
shorley	surely ★
shorn	
short /age/ly	
short *bread* /cake	
short-circuit [1]	
shorten [1]	
shorthand	
short-sighted /ness	
short sited	short-sighted [+]
shot	
should /n't	
shoulder [1]	
shout [1] /er	
shove [2]	

shovel³ /ler	
shovinism	chauvinism⁺
shovinist	chauvinist
show /down/ily/ing/n/y	
shower¹ /-bath/y	
showt	shout¹⁺
shrank	
shrapnel	
shred³ /der	
shreek	shriek¹
shrew /ish/ishly	
shrewd /er/est/ly/ness	
shriek¹	
shrift	
shrike	
shrill¹ /er/est/ness/y	
shrimp	
shrine²	
shrink /age/ing	
shrivel³	
shroo	shrew⁺
shrood	shrewd⁺
shroud¹	
Shrovetide	
shrowd	shroud¹
shrub /bery	
shrug³	
shrunk /en	
shudder¹	
shuffle² /r	
shuful	shuffle²⁺
shugar	sugar¹⁺
shun³	
shunt¹	
shurbet	sherbet
shurk	shirk¹⁺
shurt	shirt⁺
shut /ter/ting	
shuttle² /cock	
shutul	shuttle²⁺
shuv	shove²
shuvel	shovel³⁺
shy⁴ /er/est/ly/ness	
si	sigh¹
sianide	cyanide

siatic	sciatic⁺
sibernetics	cybernetics
sibilant	
sibling	
sicamore	sycamore
sicedelic	psychedelic
siciatrey	psychiatry
sicick	psychic⁺
sick /ly/ness	
sicken¹	
sickle	
siclamate	cyclamate
siclamen	cyclamen
siclic	cyclic⁺
siclist	cyclist⁺
siclometer	cyclometer
siclone	cyclone⁺
siclops	Cyclops
siclostile	cyclostyle
siclotron	cyclotron
sicoanalise	psychoanalyse²⁺
sicofant	sycophant⁺
sicologey	psychology⁺
sicological	psychological⁺
sicopath	psychopath⁺
sicosis	psychosis⁺
sicosomatic	psychosomatic
sicotherapey	psychotherapy
sicotherapist	psychotherapist⁺
sicotic	psychotic
sicul	cycle²
side² /board/line/ways	
sider	cider
sidle²	
sie	sigh¹
siege	
sienna	
siense	science⁺
sientific	scientific⁺
sientist	scientist
siesta	
sieve²	
sieze	seize²
sifer	cipher¹
sifilis	syphilis⁺

sifon	siphon [1+]	silidge	silage
sift [1]		silie	silly [+]
sigar	cigar [+]	silige	silage
sigaret	cigarette	silinder	cylinder
sigh [1]		silindrical	cylindrical [+]
sight [1]* (see) /less		silk /ily/iness/y	
sight	cite [2*+]	sill	
sight	site [2*]	sillable	syllable [+]
sightsee r /ing		sillabub	
sign [1]* /er/-writer		sill y /ier/iest/ily/iness	
sign	sine *	silo	
signacher	signature	silogise	syllogise [2+]
signal [3] /ler		silogism	syllogism
signalise [2]		silooet	silhouette [2]
signator y /ies		siluet	silhouette [2]
signature		silvan	
signet * (ring)		silver [1] /y	
signet	cygnet *	sily	silly [+]
signifi	signify [4]	simbiosis	symbiosis [+]
significan ce /t/tly		simbiotic	symbiotic
significans	significance [+]	simbol	cymbal [*+]
signify [4]		simbol	symbol [*+]
signpost [1]		simbolical	symbolical [+]
signul	signal [3+]	simbolise	symbolise [2+]
sikedelic	psychedelic	simbolism	symbolism
sikey	psyche	siment	cement [1+]
sikiatrist	psychiatrist [+]	simer	simmer [1]
sikiatry	psychiatry	simfoney	symphony [+]
sikick	psychic [+]	simian	
siks	six [+]	similar /ly	
sikstey	sixty [+]	similarit y /ies	
silable	syllable [+]	similer	similar [+]
silabus	syllabus [+]	similitude	
silage		simmer [1]	
silence [2] /r		simmetrey	symmetry [+]
silens	silence [2+]	simpathetic	sympathetic [+]
silent /ly		simpathise	sympathise [2+]
silestial	celestial [+]	simpathy	sympathy [+]
silf	sylph [+]	simper [1]	
silhouette [2]		simple /r/st/ton	
siliam	cilium	simplifi	simplify [4+]
silic a /osis		simplif y [4] /ication	
silicon * (hard mineral)		simplisitey	simplicity
silicone * (compound in polish)		simpl y /icity	
		simposium	symposium [+]

simptom	symptom [+]	sinopsis	synopsis [+]
simptomatic	symptomatic	sinoptic	synoptic
simpul	simple [+]	sinoshoor	cynosure
simpulton	simpleton	sinovial	synovial
simulashun	simulation	sinse	since
simulat *e* [2] /ion/or		sinsere	sincere [+]
simultaneous /ly		sinseritey	sincerity
simultanius	simultaneous [+]	sintactic	syntactic
sin [1] /ner		sintaks	syntax [+]
sinagog	synagogue	sintax	syntax [+]
sinamon	cinnamon	sinthesis	synthesis [+]
since		sinthesise	synthesise [2+]
sincer *e* /ity		sinthetic	synthetic
sinch	cinch [+]	sinue	sinew [+]
sincopate	syncopate [2+]	sinuous	
sindicalism	syndicalism [+]	sinus /es/itis	
sindicate	syndicate [2+]	sinuus	sinuous
sindrome	syndrome	sion	scion
sine ★ (maths)		sip [3]	
sine	sign [1★+]	sipher	cipher [1]
sinecamera	cine camera	siphon [1] /age	
sinecure		sipress	cypress
sinepost	signpost [1]	sir	
sinew /y		sirca	circa
sinful /ly/ness		sircharge	surcharge [2]
sing /er/ing		siren	
singe [2]		siringe	syringe [2]
single [2] /-minded		sirloin	
singul	single [2+]	siro stratus	cirro-stratus
singular /ity		sirocco	
singuler	singular [+]	sirocumulus	cirro-cumulus
sinic	cynic [+]	sirosis	cirrhosis
sinical	cynical [+]	sirup	syrup [+]
sinima	cinema [+]	sise	size [+]
sinimatograf	cinematograph [+]	sishun	scission
sinimatograph	cinematograph [+]	sismic	seismic [+]
sinisism	cynicism	sismograf	seismograph [+]
sinister		sismologey	seismology [+]
sink /er/ing		sissers	scissors
sinkromesh	syncromesh	sist	cyst [+]
sinkronise	synchronise [2+]	sistem	system [+]
sinod	synod [+]	sistematic	systematic
sinonim	synonym [+]	sistematise	systematise [2+]
sinonimus	synonymous	sister(s)/-in-law	
sinonym	synonym [+]	sistern	cistern

sistitis	cystitis	skeptic	sceptic +
sistole	systole	skepticul	sceptical
sit /-in/ter/ting		skeptisism	scepticism
sitadel	citadel	skermish	skirmish ¹+
sitashun	citation	skert	skirt ¹+
site ²★ (place)		skerting bord	skirting-board
site	cite ²★+	skertso	scherzo +
site	sight ¹★+	sketch ¹ /ier/ily/iness/y	
siteseeing	sightseeing	skew ¹ /-whiff	
siteseer	sightseer +	skewer ¹	
sitey	city +	ski ¹★ (sport) /er	
sithe	scythe ²	ski	sky ⁴★+
sitie	city +	skid ³	
sitizen	citizen +	skiff ¹	
sitologey	cytology	skil	skill +
sitric acid	citric acid	skilful /ly/ness	
sitron	citron +	skilite	skylight
sitrus	citrus	skill /ed	
situashun	situation	skim ³ /-milk	
situat e ³ /ion		skimp ¹ /ily/iness/y	
siv	sieve ²	skin ³ /ner/ny	
sivere	severe +	skin-deep	
sivic	civic +	skin-div er /ing	
sivil	civil +	skiney	skinny.
sivilian	civilian	skinflint	
sivilisashun	civilisation	skintilate	scintillate ²+
sivilise	civilise ²+	skip ³	
sivilitey	civility +	skipper	
sivit	civet	skirl ¹	
six /th/thly		skirmish ¹ /es	
sixteen /th		skirt ¹ /ing-board	
sixt y /ies/ieth		skiscraper	skyscraper
siythe	scythe ²	skism	schism +
size /able/ably		skist	schist
sizemic	seismic +	skit /tish	
sizers	scissors	skitsofrenia	schizophrenia +
sizul	sizzle ²	skittle ²	
sizzle ²		skitul	skittle ²
skate ² /board/r		skitzoid	schizoid
skedule	schedule ²	sku	skew ¹+
skee	ski ¹★+	skulk ¹	
skein		skull ★ (head) /-cap	
skelet on /al		skull	scull ¹★+
skematic	schematic +	skunk	
skeme	scheme ²+	skurl	skirl ¹

> *If you cannot find your word under* **skw** *look under* **squ**

skwable	squabble [2]
skwod	squad
skwodron	squadron
skwolid	squalid [+]
sky [4][★][†] /-blue/-high †(atmosphere)	
sky	ski [1][★][+]
skyatic	sciatic [+]
skylark	
skylight	
skylite	skylight
skyscraper	
slack [1] /er/est/ly/ness	
slacken [1]	
slain	
slake [2]	
slaken	slacken [1]
slam [3]	
slander [1] /er/ous	
slane	slain
slang /y	
slant [1]	
slap [3] /dash/stick	
slash [1] /er	
slat e [2] /y	
slattern /ly	
slaughter [1] /-house	
Slav /onic	
slav e [2] /ish/ishness/ery	
slawter	slaughter [1][+]
slay ★ (kill) /ing	
slay	sleigh ★
sleazy	
sled	
sledge /-hammer	
sleek /ness	
sleep /ing/y	
sleepi er /est/ly/ness	
sleepless /ness	
sleet [1] /y	
sleeve /d/less	
slege	sledge [+]
sleigh ★ (for snow)	
slender /ness	
sleuth	
slew	
sli	sly [+]
slice [2]	
slick [1]	
slid e /ing	
slight [1] /er/est/ly/ness	
slim [3] /mer/mest/ness	
slim e /ier/iest/y	
sling /er	
slip [3] /way	
slipper /iness/y	
slipshod	
slise	slice [2]
slit /ting	
slite	slight [1][+]
slither [1]	
sliver	
slo	sloe ★
slo	slow [1][★][+]
slobber [1] /er	
sloe ★ (plum)	
sloe	slow [1][★][+]
slog [3] /ger	
slogan	
sloop	
sloose	sluice [2]
slooth	sleuth
slop [3] /py	
slope [2]	
sloppi er /est/ly/ness	
slosh [1]	
slot [3] /machine	
sloth /ful	
slouch [1]	
slough [1][★] (dead skin)	
slough ★ (swamp)	
sloven /liness/ly	
slow [1][★][†] /er/ly/-worm †(not quick)	
slow	slough ★
slowch	slouch [1]

slowerm	slow-worm
sludg *e* /y	
slue	slew
sluff	slough [1]★
slug /gard/gish	
sluge	sludge +
sluice [2]	
slum [3] /mer/my	
slumber [1] /ous	
slump [1]	
slung	
slunk	
slur [3]	
slush /y	
slut /tish	
sly /er/est/ly/ness	
smack [1]	
small /er/est/pox	
smarmy	
smart [1] /er/est/ly/ness	
smarten [1]	
smash [1] /er	
smatter [1]	
smear [1] /y	
smeer	smear [1]+
smell [1] /ier/iest/ing/y	
smelling-salts	
smelt [1] /er	
smirch [1] /es	
smirk [1]	
smit *e* /ing	
smith /y/ies	
smithereens	
smithey	smithy
smitten	
smock [1]	
smog	
smoke [2] /r/-stack	
smok *ier* /iest/y	
smolder	smoulder [1]
smooth [1] /er/est/ly/ness	
smote	
smother [1]	
smoulder [1]	
smudg *e* [2] /y	

smug /ger/gest/ly/ness	
smuge	smudge [2]+
smuggle [2] /r	
smugul	smuggle [2]+
smurch	smirch [1]+
smurk	smirk [1]
smut /tiness/ty	
snack	
snag [3]	
snail [1]	
snake [2] /-bite	
snale	snail [1]
snap [3] /dragon/shot	
snapp *er* /ily/ish/y	
snare [2]	
snarl [1] /er	
snatch [1] /es	
sneak [1] /ingly/ily	
sneek	sneak [1]+
sneer [1]	
sneeze [2]	
snicker [1]	
snide	
sniff [1] /er/y	
sniffle [2]	
sniful	sniffle [2]
snigger [1]	
snip [3] /pet	
snipe [2] /r	
snivel [3] /ler	
sno	snow [1]+
snobb *ery* /ish/ishness	
snoberie	snobbery +
snobish	snobbish
snooker [1]	
snoop [1] /er	
snooze [2]	
snore [2] /r	
snorkel	
snorkle	snorkel
snort [1] /er	
snot /ty	
snout	
snow [1] /drift/drop/fall	
snowball [1]	

snow-plough		soften [1]	
snowt	snout	software	
snub [3]		softwear	software
snuff [1]		sogg y /iness	
snuffle [2]		sogie	soggy [+]
snuful	snuffle [2]	Soho	
snuggle [2]		soia	soya
snugul	snuggle [2]	soil [1]	
so * (in this way)		soiray	soirée
so	sew *[+]	soirée	
so	sow [1]*	soiya	soya
soak [1]		sojern	sojourn [1+]
soap [1] /y		sojourn [1] /er	
soar [1]* (to fly)		soke	soak [1]
soar	sore *[+]	solace [2]	
sob [3]		solar /ium	
sober [1]		solar plexus	
sobriety		solar system	
sobrikay	sobriquet [+]	solas	solace [2]
sobriquet /s		solder [1]	
soccer		soldering iron	
sociab le /ility/ly		soldier [1] /ly/y	
sociabul	sociable [+]	sole * (shoe) /ly	
social /ite/ly		sole	soul *[+]
socialis e [2] /ation		solecism	
socialis m /t/tic		soleful	soulful [+]
societ y /ies		solem	solemn [+]
sociolog y /ical/ist		solemn /ity/ly	
sock [1]		solemnis e [2] /ation	
socker	soccer	solemnitey	solemnity
socket		solenoid	
soda /-water		solesism	solecism
sodden		sol-fa	
soden	sodden	solger	soldier [1+]
sodium		solicit [1] /ation/ude	
sodom y /ite		solicit or /ous	
sofen	soften [1]	solid /er/est/ity/ly	
sofism	sophism [+]	solidarity	
sofist	sophist	solidifi	solidify [4+]
sofisticashun	sophistication	solidif y [4] /ication	
sofisticate	sophisticate [2+]	solilokwise	soliloquise [2]
sofistication	sophistication	solilokwy	soliloquy [+]
sofistrey	sophistry	soliloquise [2]	
sofmore	sophomore	soliloqu y /ies	
soft /er/est/ly/ness		solisit	solicit [1+]

solisiter	solicitor +
solisitous	solicitous
solisitus	solicitous
solitar *y* /ily/iness	
solitrey	solitary +
solitude	
soljer	soldier ¹+
solo /ist	
solstice	
solstis	solstice
solub *le* /ility	
solubul	soluble +
solushun	solution
solution	
solv *e* ² /able	
solven *cy* /t	
solvensey	solvency +
somber	sombre +
sombraro	sombrero +
sombre /ly/ness	
sombrero /s	
some *★† /body/how	
†(a few)	
some	sum ³★
some *one* /what/where	
somersalt	somersault ¹
somersault ¹	
somnolen *ce* /t	
somnolens	somnolence +
son ★(male child)	
sonar	
sonata	
sonde	
soner	sonar
song /-bird/ster	
sonic	
son(s)-in-law	
sonnet	
sonor *ous* /ity	
sonorus	sonorous +
soo	sue ²
soocher	suture
sooflay	soufflé
sooit	suet
soon /er	

soop	soup
soot ★ (black powder) /y	
soot	suit ¹★+
sooth /sayer	
soothe ²	
soovenir	souvenir
sop ³ /py	
sope	soap ¹+
sophis *m* /t/try	
sophisticat *e* ² /ion	
sophomore	
soporific	
soprano /s	
sorcer *er* /ess (fem.)/y	
sord	sword
sordid /ly/ness	
sordust	sawdust
sore ★ (hurt) /ly/r/st	
sore	saw ★+
sore	soar ¹★
sorey	sorry +
sorie	sorry +
sorna	sauna
sornter	saunter ¹
sorow	sorrow ¹+
sorrel	
sorrow ¹ /ful/fully	
sorr *y* /ier/iest	
sors	sauce ★+
sors	source ★
sort ¹★ (kind) /er	
sort	sought ★
sortee	sortie
sortie	
sorul	sorrel
soshable	sociable +
soshabul	sociable +
soshal	social +
soshalise	socialise ²+
soshalism	socialism +
soshalist	socialist
soshalistic	socialistic
soshiologey	sociology +
soshiologist	sociologist
sosidge	sausage

sosietey	society +
sosige	sausage
sot /tish	
sotto voce	
soufflé	
sought * (did seek)	
soul * (spirit) /less	
soul	sole *+
soulful /ly	
sound [1] /er/est/less/ness	
soundproof [1]	
soup	
sour [1] /er/est/ish/ness	
source * (origin)	
source	sauce *+
souse [2]	
south /erly/ern	
souvenir	
sou'-wester	
sovereign /ty	
soverin	sovereign +
soviet	
sovrentey	sovereignty
sow [1]* (cast seed, pig)	
sow	sew [1]*+
sown * (seed)	
sown	sewn *
sownd	sound [1]+
sowndproof	soundproof [1]
sowr	sour [1]+
sowse	souse [2]
sowth	south +
sow-wester	sou'-wester
soya	
spac e [2] /ious	
spade /-work	
spagetti	spaghetti
spaghetti	
span [3]	
spaner	spanner
spangle [2]	
spangul	spangle [2]
Spaniard	
spaniel	
spank [1]	

spanner	
Spanyard	Spaniard
spanyel	spaniel
spar [3]	
spare [2]	
spark [1] /ing-plug	
sparkle [2] /r	
sparkul	sparkle [2]+
sparo	sparrow +
sparrow /-hawk	
spars	sparse +
sparse /ly/ness	
sparsity	
Spartan	
spase	space [2]+
spashal	spatial
spashus	spacious
spasm	
spasmodic /ally	
spastic /ism	
spate	
spatial	
spatter [1]	
spatula /te	
spawn [1]	
speak /er/ing	
spear [1] /head	
special /ist/ly	
specialis e [2] /ation	
specialt y /ies	
species	
specifi	specify [4]+
specific /ally	
specif y [4] /ication	
specimen	
specious /ness	
speck [1]	
speckle [2]	
spectacle	
spectacular /ly	
spectator	
specter	spectre +
spectr e /al	
spectrograf	spectrograph
spectrograph	

spectroscop *e* /ic
spectr *um* /a (pl.)
speculashun   speculation
speculat *e* ² /ion/or
speculative /ly
speech /less
speed ¹ /y
speedi *er* /est/ly/ness
speedometer

speek   speak ⁺
speeker   speaker
speeking   speaking
speer   spear ¹⁺
speerhed   spearhead
spekul   speckle ²
spel   spell ⁺
spelbownd   spellbound
spel *l* /ling/t
spellbound
spend /er/thrift
sperm /-whale
spermatozo *on* /a (pl.)

spern   spurn ¹
spert   spurt ¹
speshal   special ⁺
speshalise   specialise ²⁺
speshalist   specialist
speshaltey   specialty ⁺
speshes   species
speshialtey   specialty ⁺
speshus   specious ⁺
spesifi   specify ⁴⁺
spesific   specific ⁺
spesificashun   specification
spesify   specify ⁴⁺
spesimen   specimen
spew ¹
spher *e* ² /ical/ically
spheroid
sphincter
sphinx /es
spi   spy ⁴⁺
spic *e* ² /y
spici *er* /est/ly/ness
spick and span

spider /y
spik *e* ² /y
spil *l* /ling/t
spin ³ /ner/neret
spinach
spinaker   spinnaker
spindl *e* /y
spindul   spindle ⁺
spin *e* /al/eless
spiney   spinney ⁺
spinidge   spinach
spinige   spinach
spinnaker
spinney /s
spinster /hood
spiracle
spiral ³ /ly
spire
spirichooal   spiritual ⁺
spirichooalise   spiritualise ²⁺
spirichooalist   spiritualist ⁺
spirit ¹ /less
spiritual /ly
spiritualis *e* ² /ation
spiritualist /ic
spise   spice ²⁺
spisey   spicy
spisier   spicier ⁺
spit /ting/toon
spite ² /ful/fulness
spitfire
spittle
spitul   spittle
splash ¹ /-down
splay ¹
spleen
splender   splendour
splendid
splendour
splice ²
splint ¹
splinter ¹
splise   splice ²
split /ting
splutter ¹

spoil[1] /sport/t	
spoke /n	
spokes *man* /woman	
spoliashun	spoliation +
spoliat *ion* /or	
spong *e*[2] /er/y	
sponser	sponsor[1]
sponsor[1]	
spontaneity	
spontaneous /ly/ness	
spontanius	spontaneous +
spontenaitey	spontaneity
spoof[1] /er	
spool	
spoon[1] /-fed/ful	
spoonerism	
spoor[1]★ (track)	
spoor	spore ★
sporadic /ally	
sporan	sporran
spore ★ (seed, germ)	
spore	spoor[1]★
sporn	spawn[1]
sporran	
sport[1] /ive/ively	
sportsman	
spot[3] /-check/ty	
spotlight[1]	
spotlite	spotlight[1]
spouse	
spout[1]	
spowse	spouse
spowt	spout[1]
sprain[1]	
sprane	sprain[1]
sprang	
sprawl[1]	
spray[1] /er	
spread /ing	
spread-eagle[2]	
spred	spread +
spree	
spri	spry +
sprightl*y* /ier/iest	
spring /-board/bok	

springtime	
spring*y* /iness/ing	
sprinkle[2] /r	
sprinkul	sprinkle[2]+
sprint[1]	
sprite /ly	
sprocket	
sproose	spruce +
sprout[1]	
sprowt	sprout[1]
spruce /ly	
sprung	
spry /er/est	
spu	spew[1]
spume[2]	
spunge	sponge[2]+
spunk	
spur[3]	
spurious /ly/ness	
spurius	spurious +
spurm	sperm +
spurn[1]	
spurt[1]	
sputter[1]	
sputum	
sp*y*[4] /ies	
squabble[2]	
squabul	squabble[2]
squad	
squadron	
squalid /ly	
squall[1]	
squalor	
squander[1]	
square[2] /ly	
squash[1]	
squat[3] /ter	
squaw	
squawk[1] /er	
squeak[1] /er/y	
squeal[1] /er	
squeamish /ly/ness	
squeeze[2]	
squelch[1]	
squerm	squirm[1]

squert	squirt [1]	stale /ness	
squib		stalemate [2]	
squid		stalion	stallion
squiggle [2]		stalk [1] /er	
squigul	squiggle [2]	stall [1]	
squint [1]		stallion	
squir e [2] /archy		stalwart	
squirm [1]		stalwert	stalwart
squirrel		stalyun	stallion
squirt [1]		stamen	
squod	squad	stamer	stammer [1+]
squodron	squadron	stamina	
squoler	squalor	stammer [1] /er	
squolid	squalid [+]	stamp [1] /er	
squonder	squander [1]	stampede [2]	
squosh	squash [1]	stance	
squot	squat [3+]	stanch [1]★ (stop flow)	
stab [3]		stanch	staunch ★
stabilis e [2] /ation/er		stand /-by/point/still	
stability		standard	
stable [2]		standardis e [2] /ation	
stabul	stable [2]	standerd	standard
staccato		standerdise	standardise [2+]
stacher	stature	stane	stain [1+]
stachooery	statuary	stank	
stack [1]		stans	stance
stadi um /a/ums (pls.)		stanza	
staf	staff [1+]	stapes	
staff [1] /s		staple [2] /r	
stag		stapul	staple [2+]
stage [2] /-coach		star [3] /less/light/ry	
stager	stagger [1]	starboard	
stagger [1]		starbord	starboard
stagnant		starch [1]	
stagnashun	stagnation	stare [2]★ (gaze)	
stagnat e [2] /ion		stare	stair ★+
staid ★ (steady)		starecase	staircase
staid	stayed ★	starie	starry
stain [1] /less		stark	
stair ★ (step) /case		starling	
stair	stare [2]★	start [1] /er	
stake [2]★ (post)		startle [2]	
stake	steak ★	startul	startle [2]
stalactite ★ (down)		starvashun	starvation
stalagmite ★ (up)		starv e [2] /ation/eling	

stashun	station [1+]
stashunrey	stationary ★
stashunrey	stationery ★
state [2] /less/ment	
statel y /ier/iest/iness	
static /ally/s	
station [1] /ary ★ (at rest)	
stationer /y ★ (paper)	
statistic /ian/s	
statistical /ly	
statistishun	statistician
statuary	
statue /sque/tte	
statuesk	statuesque
statuet	statuette
stature	
status	
statut e /ory	
staunch ★ (true)	
staunch	stanch [1]★
stave [2]	
stawk	stalk [1+]
stay /ed ★† /ing	
†(remained)	
stayed	staid ★
steadfast /ly/ness	
steadie	steady [4+]
stead y [4] /ier/iest/ily	
steak ★ (beef)	
steak	stake [2]★
steal ★ (take) /ing	
steal	steel [1]★+
stealth /ily/iness/y	
steam [1] /er	
stedfast	steadfast +
stedy	steady [4+]
steed	
steel [1]★ (metal) /y	
steel	steal ★+
steem	steam [1+]
steep [1] /er/est/ly/ness	
steeple /chase/jack	
steepul	steeple +
steer [1] /able/age	
stelar	stellar

stellar	
stelth	stealth +
stem [3]	
stench /es	
stencil [3] /ler	
stenografey	stenography +
stenograph y /er/ic	
stenotipe	stenotype [2]
stenotype [2]	
stensil	stencil [3+]
step [3]★ (pace) /-ladder	
step	steppe ★
step brother /sister	
step daughter /son	
step father /mother	
steppe ★ (plain)	
ster	stir [3]
sterdey	sturdy +
stereo /phonic	
stereoscop e /ic	
stereotype [2]	
steril e /ity	
sterilis e [2] /ation	
sterilitey	sterility
sterio	stereo +
steriofonic	stereophonic
sterioscope	stereoscope +
steriotipe	stereotype [2]
sterjun	sturgeon
sterling	
stern /er/est/ly/ness	
sternum	
stethoscope	
stevedore	
stew [1]	
steward /ess (fem.)	
sti	sty [4+]
stich	stitch [1+]
stick /er/ing/s ★ (wood)	
sticking-plaster	
stickleback	
stickler	
Sticks	Styx ★
stick y /ily/iness	
stif	stiff +

stifen	stiffen [1+]
stiff /er/est/ly	
stiffen [1] /er	
stifle [2]	
stiful	stifle [2]
stigma /s/ta (pls.)	
stigmatise [2]	
stil	still [1+]
stilberth	still-birth [+]
stile ★ (steps)	
stile	style [2★+]
stiletto /s	
stilise	stylise [2+]
stilish	stylish
stilist	stylist
still [1] /ness	
still -*birth* /-born	
stilt [1]	
stilus	stylus [+]
stimie	stymie [+]
stimulashun	stimulation
stimulat e [2] /ion/ive/or	
stimul us /i (pl.)/ant	
sting /er/ing	
sting y /ier/iest/ily/iness	
stink /er/ing	
stint [1]	
stipel	stipple [2]
stipend	
stipendiar y /ies	
stipple [2]	
stiptic	styptic
stipul	stipple [2]
stipulashun	stipulation
stipulat e [2] /ion/or	
stir [3]	
stirrup	
stirup	stirrup
stitch [1] /es	
stoat	
stock [1] /broker/taking	
stockade	
stockie	stocky [+]
stocking	
stockman	

stockpile [2]	
stock-still	
stock y /ier/iest/iness	
stodg e [2] /y	
stoge	stodge [2+]
stoic /al/ally	
stoicism	
stoisism	stoicism
stoke [2] /r	
stole /n	
stolid /ity	
stoma /s/ta (pls.)	
stomach [1] /-ache	
stone [2] /mason	
stonewall [1] /er	
ston y /ier/iest/ily	
stood	
stooge [2]	
stook [1]	
stool [1]	
stoop [1]	
stop [3] /cock/page/per	
stoper	stopper
storage	
store [2] /house	
storekeeper	
storey ★ (floor level) /s	
storey	story [★+]
storidge	storage
storie	storey [★+]
storie	story [★+]
storige	storage
stork	
storm [1] /ier/iest/y	
stormi ly /ness	
stor y ★ (narrative) /ies	
story	storey [★+]
stote	stoat
stout /er/est/ly/ness	
stove [2]	
stow [1] /age/away	
stowige	stowage
stowt	stout [+]
straddle [2]	
stradul	straddle [2]

275

straf	strafe [2]
strafe [2]	
straggle [2] /r	
stragul	straggle [2]+
straight * (line),	
straight	strait *
straightaway	
straighten [1]	
straightforward	
strain [1] /er	
strait * (sea passage)	
strait	straight *
straitaway	straightaway
straiten	straighten [1]
straitforwerd	straightforward
strait-jacket	
strait-laced	
strand [1]	
strane	strain [1]+
strange /ly/ness/r/st	
strangle [2]	
strangul	strangle [2]
strangulat e [2] /ion	
strap [3] /hanger	
stratagem	
strate	straight *
strate	strait *
strategey	strategy +
strategic /ally	
strateg y /ies/ist	
stratifi	stratify [4]+
stratif y [4] /ication	
stratoscope	
stratosfere	stratosphere +
stratospher e /ic	
strat um /a (pl.)	
straw	
strawberie	strawberry +
strawberr y /ies	
stray [1]	
streak [1] /y	
stream [1]	
streamline [2]	
streek	streak [1]+
streem	stream [1]

streemline	streamline [2]
street	
strength	
strengthen [1]	
strenth	strength
strenthen	strengthen [1]
strenuous /ly/ness	
strenuus	strenuous +
streptococc us /i (pl.)/al	
stress [1]	
stretch [1] /er	
strew /ing	
strewn	
striccher	stricture
stricken	
stricneen	strychnine
strict /er/est/ly/ness	
stricture	
strid e /ing	
striden cy /t	
stridensey	stridency +
strife	
strik e /er/ing	
strike-break er /ing	
string /ing/y	
stringen cy /t	
stringensey	stringency +
strip [3] /per	
stripe [2]	
stripling	
striv e /en/ing	
stroboscop e /ic	
strode	
stroke [2]	
stroll [1] /er	
strong /er/est/ly/ness	
strontium	
stroo	strew +
strooen	strewn
strove	
struck	
struckcher	structure +
structur e /al/ally	
struggle [2]	
strugul	struggle [2]

276

strum³ /mer		sturgon ·	sturgeon
strung		sturgun	sturgeon
strut³		sturling	sterling
strychnine		sturn	stern⁺
stu	stew¹	sturnum	sternum
stuard	steward⁺	stuter	stutter¹⁺
stub³		stutter¹ /er	
stubbl e /y		stuward	steward⁺
stubborn /ly/ness		st y⁴ /ies	
stubern	stubborn⁺	styl e ²★† /ish/ist	
stubul	stubble⁺	†(manner)	
stucco¹		style	stile ★
stuck		stylis e² /ation	
stud³		stylus /es	
student		stymie /d	
studey	study⁴⁺	styptic	
studio /s		Styx ★ (river)	
studious /ly/ness		suage	sewage
studius	studious⁺	suav e /ely/ity	
stud y⁴ /ies		subaltern	
stuf	stuff¹⁺	subcomitee	subcommittee
stuff¹ /y		subcommittee	
stuffi er /est/ly/ness		subconscious /ly	
stuko	stucco¹	subconshus	subconscious⁺
stultifi	stultify⁴⁺	subcontinent	
stultif y⁴ /ication		subcontract¹ /or	
stumac	stomach¹⁺	subdivide²	
stumble²		subdivishun	subdivision⁺
stumbul	stumble²	subdivisi on /ble	
stump¹		subdue²	
stun³		subedit¹ /or	
stung		suberb	suburb⁺
stunk		suberban	suburban
stunt¹		sub-human	
stupefi	stupefy⁴⁺	subjecshun	subjection
stupef y⁴ /action		subject¹ /ion/ive/ivity	
stupendous /ly/ness		subjoogate	subjugate²⁺
stupendus	stupendous⁺	subjugat e² /ion	
stuper	stupor	subjunctive	
stupid /er/est/ity/ly		sublet /ting	
stupify	stupefy⁴⁺	sublimat e² /ion	
stupor		sublim e /inal	
sturdie	sturdy⁺	submachine-gun	
sturd y /ier/iest/ily/iness		submarine	
sturgeon		submerg e² /ence/ible	

submershun	submersion +	subtenant	
submersi *on* /ble		subtend [1]	
submishun	submission +	subterfuge	
submisiv	submissive	subterranean	
submiss *ion* /ive		sub-title [2]	
submit [3]		subtitul	sub-title [2]
submurge	submerge [2]+	subtle /ness/r/st	
subnormal		subtlet *y* /ies	
subordinat *e* [2] /ion		subtly	
suborn [1] /ation/er		subtracshun	subtraction
subpena	subpoena [1]	subtract [1] /ion	
sub-plot		subtropical	
subpoena [1]		suburb /an/ia	
subscribe [2] /r		subvershun	subversion +
subscription		subvers *ion* /ive	
subsekwent	subsequent +	subversiv	subversive
subsequent /ly		subvert [1] /er	
subservien *ce* /t		subvurt	subvert [1]+
subserviens	subservience +	subway	
subsidarey	subsidiary +	succeed [1]	
subside [2] /nce		success /ful/fully	
subsidens	subsidence	success *ion* /ive/or	
subsidey	subsidy +	succinct	
subsidiar *y* /ies		succour [1]★ (help)	
subsidis *e* [2] /ation		succulen *ce* /t	
subsid *y* /ies		succumb [1]	
subsist [1] /ence		such	
subsistens	subsistence	sucher	suture
subsoil		suck [1]	
subsonic		sucker ★ (victim, one who sucks)	
subsoyl	subsoil		
substance		sucker	succour [1]★
substandard		suckle [2]	
substans	substance	suckshun	suction
substanshal	substantial +	suckulens	succulence +
substanshiate	substantiate [2]+	suckulent	succulent
substantial /ly/ity		suckumb	succumb [1]
substantiat *e* [2] /ion		sucrose	
substantive		sucseed	succeed [1]
substashun	substation	sucseshun	succession +
substation		sucsess	success +
substitushun	substitution	sucsesser	successor
substitut *e* [2] /ion		sucsessful	successful
substrat *um* /a (pl.)		sucsessiv	successive
subtefuge	subterfuge	sucsint	succinct

278

suction	
sudden /ly/ness	
sudo	pseudo [+]
sudonim	pseudonym
suds	
sue [2]	
suède	
suer	sewer [1][*][+]
suet	
sufer	suffer [1][+]
suffer [1] /ance/er	
suffice [2]	
sufficien cy /t	
suffiks	suffix [1][+]
suffise	suffice [2]
suffishency	sufficiency [+]
suffishent	sufficient
suffix [1] /es	
suffocat e [2] /ion	
suffrage /tte	
suffus e [2] /ion	
sufocashun	suffocation
sufocate	suffocate [2][+]
sufocation	suffocation
sufrajet	suffragette
sufrance	sufferance
sufrige	suffrage [+]
sufuse	suffuse [2][+]
sugar [1] /y	
sugeschun	suggestion
sugest	suggest [1][+]
sugestion	suggestion
sugestiv	suggestive
suggest [1] /ion/ive	
suicid e /al	
suige	sewage
suiside	suicide [+]
suit [1][*][†] /ability	
†(clothes)	
suit	suet
suitab le /ility/ly	
suite [*] (rooms)	
suitor	
sulfate	sulphate
sulfer	sulphur [+]

sulferus	sulphurous
sulfide	sulphide
sulfuric asid	sulphuric acid
sulie	sully [4]
sulk [1] /ily/iness/y	
sullen	
sully [4]	
sulphate	
sulphide	
sulphur /ous	
sulphuric acid	
sultan /a (fem.)/ate	
sultrey	sultry [+]
sultr y /ily/iness	
suly	sully [4]
sum [3][*] (total)	
sum	some [*][+]
sumbody	somebody
sumhow	somehow
summari ly /ness	
summarise [2]	
summar y [*] (account)/ies	
summer /time/y [*][†]	
†(of summer)	
summerise	summarise [2]
summit	
summon [1][*] (call forth)	
summons [1][*] (before court)	
sump	
sumptuous /ly/ness	
sumshus	sumptuous [+]
sumun	summon [1][*]
sumuns	summons [1][*]
sumwere	somewhere
sumwun	someone [+]
sun [3][*][†] /beam/dial/ny	
†(planet)	
sun	son [*]
sun inlaw	son(s)-in-law
sunbathe [2]	
sunbern	sunburn [+]
sunburn /t	
sundae [*] (ice cream)	
Sunday [*] (day of week)	
sundrey	sundry [+]

279

sundr *y* /ies
sung
sunk /en
sunlight
sunlite   sunlight
sunni *er* /est/ly/ness
sun *rise* /stroke
sun-tan [3]
sup [3] /per ★ (meal)
super ★ (fantastic)
super   supper ★
superabundan *ce* /t
superannuat *e* [2] /ion
superb /ly
supercargo /es
supercharge [2]
supercilious /ly/ness
superconductor
superficial /ity/ly
superfine·
superfishal   superficial +
superfloous   superfluous +
superflu *ous* /ity
superhuman
superier   superior +
superimpos *e* [2] /ition
superintend [1] /ent
superior /ity
superlative
super *man* /men (pl.)
supermarket
supernacheral supernatural +
supernatural /ly
supernova
supernumerar *y* /ies
superpos *e* [2] /ition
supersede [2]
supersilious supercilious +
supersilius   supercilious +
supersonic
superstishun superstition +
superstishus superstitious
superstitio *n* /us
superstructure
superven *e* [2] /tion

supervis *e* [2] /ion/or/ory
supervishun supervision
supine
suplant   supplant [1]+
suple   supple +
suplement   supplement [1]+
suplicate   supplicate [2]+
suport   support [1]+
suposishun   supposition
suposition   supposition
supositrey   suppository +
supplant [1] /er
supple /ness
supplement [1] /ation
supplementary
suppli   supply [4]+
suppliant
supplicat *e* [2] /ion/ory
suppl *y* [4] /ier/ies
support [1] /er
suppos *e* [2] /ition
supposito *r y* /ies
suppress [1] /ible/ion/or
suppurat *e* [2] /ion
supremasey   supremacy
suprem *e* /acy/ely
supreshun   suppression
supress   suppress [1]+
supression   suppression
suprintend   superintend [1]+
supul   supple +
sur   sir
surayalism   surrealism +
surayalist   surrealist
surca   circa
surcharge [2]
surcit   circuit [1]+
surcitrey   circuitry
surcitus   circuitous
surcul   circle [2]
surcularise   circularise [2]+
surculashun   circulation
surculate   circulate [2]+
surculer   circular
surcumfleks   circumflex

surcumflex	circumflex	surogat	surrogate
surcumfrance	circumference	suround	surround [1]
surcumfrans	circumference	surownd	surround [1]
surcumnavigate	circumnavigate [2+]	surpass [1]	
surcumscribe	circumscribe [2]	surplice ★ (robe)	
surcumscripshun	circumscription	surplis	surplice ★
surcumscription	circumscription	surplus ★ (excess)	
surcumsise	circumcise [2+]	surprise [2]	
surcumsision	circumcision	surrealis *m* /t	
surcumspecshun	circumspection	surrender [1]	
surcumspect	circumspect [+]	surreptitious /ly/ness	
surcumstans	circumstance	surrogate	
surcumstanshul	circumstantial [+]	surround [1]	
surcumstantial	circumstantial [+]	surt	cert
surcumvent	circumvent [1+]	surtaks	surtax [+]
surcus	circus [+]	surtax /es	
sure ★† /ly ★†/r/st		surtin	certain [+]
†(certain[ly])		surtn	certain [+]
sure	shore [2]★	survant	servant
sureptishus	surreptitious [+]	survay	survey [1+]
sureptitious	surreptitious [+]	survaylans	surveillance
suret *y* /ies		surve	serve [2+]
surf [1]★ (sea) /er		surveillance	
surf	serf ★[+]	survey [1] /or	
surface [2]		survice	service [2+]
surfdom	serfdom	surviet	serviette
surfeet	surfeit [1]	survile	servile [+]
surfeit [1]		survilitey	servility
surfis	surface [2]	survis	service [2+]
surfit	surfeit [1]	surviv *e* [2] /al/or	
surge [2]		susceptib *le* /ility	
surgeon		suseptible	susceptible [+]
surger *y* /ies		suseptibul	susceptible [+]
surgun	surgeon	suspect [1]	
surley	surely ★	suspend [1] /er	
surli *er* /est/ly/ness		suspense	
surloin	sirloin	suspenshun	suspension [+]
surly ★ (uncivil)		suspens *ion* /ory	
surly	surely ★	suspicion	
surmise [2]		suspicious /ly/ness	
surmon	sermon	suspishun	suspicion
surmonise	sermonise [2]	suspishus	suspicious [+]
surmount [1]		sustain [1]	
surmownt	surmount [1]	sustayn	sustain [1]
surname		sustenance	

sustenans	sustenance	swerve ²	
sut	soot ★+	swet	sweat ¹+
sutable	suitable +	sweter	sweater
sutabul	suitable +	swich	switch ¹+
suter	suitor	swift /er/est/ly/ness	
suthen	southern	swig ³	
sutherley	southerly	swill ¹ /er	
sutle	subtle +	swim /mer/-suit	
sutletey	subtlety +	swimming /-pool	
sutul	subtle +	swindle ² /r	
suture		swindul	swindle ²+
swab ³		swin e /ish	
swaddle ²		swing ★ (move) /ing	
swade	suède	swinge ★ (beat) /ing	
swadul	swaddle ²	swipe ²	
swagger ¹ /er		swirl ¹	
swain		swish ¹	
swallow ¹ /er		Swiss /roll	
swam		switch ¹ /back	
swamp ¹ /y		swivel ³	
swan ³ /sdown		swizul	swizzle ²
swane	swain	swizzle ²	
swank ¹ /y		swob	swab ³
sware	swear +	swollen	
swarm ¹		swollow	swallow ¹+
swarthy		swomp	swamp ¹+
swash ¹		swon	swan ³+
swastika		swoon ¹	
swat ³ /ter		swoop ¹	
swath ★ (line of cut grass)		swop ³	
swathe ²★ (bandage)		sword	
sway ¹		swor e /n	
swear /-word		swostika	swastika
sweat ¹ /er/y		swot ³ /ter	
Swed e /ish		swum	
sweep /er/ing/stake		swung	
sweet ★ (sugary)		swurl	swirl ¹
sweet	suite ★	swurv	swerve ²
sweetchestnut		sybarit e /ic	
sweeten ¹		sycamore	
sweet heart /ly/meat		sycedelic	psychedelic
sweetpea		syciatrey	psychiatry
swell ¹		syciatrist	psychiatrist +
swelter ¹		sycick	psychic +
swept		sycoanalise	psychoanalyse ²+

sycoanalisis	psychoanalysis
sycofant	sycophant +
sycologey	psychology +
sycological	psychological +
sycologist	psychologist
sycopath	psychopath +
sycophant /ic	
sycosis	psychosis +
sycosomatic	psychosomatic
sycotherapey	psychotherapy
sycotherapist	psychotherapist +
sycotic	psychotic
syfilis	syphilis +
sygnet	cygnet ★
sylf	sylph +
syllab *le* /ic	
syllabus /es	
syllogis *e* ² /m	
sylph /like	
symbio *sis* /tic	
symbol ★ (sign) /ic	
symbol	cymbal ★+
symbolical /ly	
symbolis *e* ² /m	
symmetr *y* /ical/ically	
sympathetic /ally	
sympathey	sympathy +
sympathise ² /r	
sympath *y* /ies	
symphon *y* /ies/ic	
symplify	simplify ⁴+
symposi *um* /a (pl.)	
symptom /atic	
synagog	synagogue
synagogue	
synchronis *e* ² /ation/m	
syncopat *e* ² /ion	
syncope	
syncromesh	
syndicalis *m* /t	
syndicat *e* ² /ion	
syndrome	
synic	cynic +
synod /al/ical	
synonym /ous/ously	

synops *is* /es (pl.)	
synoptic	
synovial	
syntaks	syntax +
synta *x* /ctic	
synthes *is* /es (pl.)	
synthe *sise* ² /tic/tically	
sypher	cipher ¹
syphili *s* /tic	
syphon	siphon ¹+
syringe ²	
syrup /y	
system /atic/atically	
systematis *e* ² /ation	
systole	

T

tab ³	
tabard	
tabb *y* /ies	
tabernacle	
tabernacul	tabernacle
tabie	tabby +
table ²	
tableau /x (pl.)	
tablespoon /ful	
tabl *et* /oid	
tablit	tablet +
tablo	tableau +
tabloyd	tabloid
taboo ¹ /s	
tabor	
tabul	table ²
tabular	
tabulashun	tabulation
tabulat *e* ² /ion/or	
tabuler	tabular
tabulspoon	tablespoon +
taby	tabby +
tacit /ly	
taciturn /ity	
tack ¹	
tackey	tacky +

283

tackle ² /r	
tackul	tackle ²⁺
tack y /iness	
tact /less/lessly	
tactful /ly/ness	
tactic /al/ian/s	
tactile	
tactishun	tactician
tacul	tackle ²⁺
tadpole	
taffeta	
tafita	taffeta
tag ³	
tail ¹★† /less	
†(follow, of animals)	
tail	tale ★
tailor ¹ /-made	
taint ¹	
tak e /en/ing	
takey	tacky ⁺
taks	tax ¹⁺
taksashun	taxation
taksi	taxi ⁺
taksidermey	taxidermy ⁺
talc /um	
tale ★ (story)	
tale	tail ¹★⁺
talent /ed	
talie	tally ⁴⁺
talie ho	tally-ho
talisman /s	
talk ¹ /ative/er	
talk	talc ⁺
talkum	talcum
tall /est/ness	
tallow	
tall y ⁴ /ies	
tally-ho	
talon	
talor	tailor ¹⁺
talow	tallow
tamarisk	
tamber	tambour ⁺
tamboreen	tambourine
tambour /ine	

tam e ² /able	
tam-o'-shanter	
tamper ¹	
tampon	
tan ³ /ner/nery/neries	
tandem	
taner	tanner
tang	
tangent /ial	
tangerine	
tangib le /ility/ly	
tangibul	tangible ⁺
tangle ²	
tango ¹ /s	
tangul	tangle ²
tanic	tannic ⁺
tanjent	tangent ⁺
tanjerene	tangerine
tank /age/ard/er/ful	
tanni c /n	
tant	taint ¹
tantalis e ² /ingly	
tantalum	
tantamount	
tantamownt	tantamount
tantrum	
tap ³ /-dancing/-root	
tape ² /worm	
tape measure	
tape recorder	
taper ¹★ (candle, narrow)	
taper	tapir ★
tapestr y /ies	
tapioca	
tapir ★ (animal)	
tapistrey	tapestry ⁺
tar ³	
taragon	tarragon
tarantella ★ (dance)	
tarantula ★ (spider)	
tardie	tardy ⁺
tard y /ily/iness	
tare ★ (weed)	
tare	tear ★⁺
target	

targit	target
tarie	tarry [4]
tarif	tariff
tariff	
tarmac	
tarmigan	ptarmigan
tarn	
tarnish [1]	
tarpaulin	
tarporlin	tarpaulin
tarragon	
tarry [4]	
tarsals	
tarsus	
tart /let	
tartan	
tartar	
tarter	tartar
tartrate	
tasit	tacit [+]
tasiturn	taciturn [+]
task /master	
tassel [3]	
tassul	tassel [3]
taste [2] /less/r	
tasteful /ly/ness	
tast ier /iest/y	
tatle	tattle [2]
tatoo	tattoo [1+]
tatter [1]	
tattle [2]	
tattoo [1] /er	
tatul	tattle [2]
taught * (did teach)	
taught	tort *
taunt [1] /er	
Taurus	
taut * (tight) /ly/ness	
taut	taught *
taut	tort *
tauten [1]	
tautolog y /ical	
taven	tavern
tavern	
tawdr y /ily/iness	

tawny	
tax [1] /able/ation	
taxashun	taxation
taxi /cab/meter/s	
taxiderm y /ist	
Te Deum	
tea * (drink) /cup/pot	
tea	tee *[+]
teach /able/er/ing	
teajuncshun	T-junction
teak	
teal	
team [1] * (group) /ster	
team	teem [1]*
team-work	
tear * (crying) /ful	
tear * (rip) /ing	
tear	tier *
tease [2] /r	
teaspoon /ful	
teat	
teath	teeth *
teathe	teethe [2]*
teatime	
teatotler	teetotaller
teatotul	teetotal [+]
tech	teach [+]
techer	teacher
technical /ly	
technicalit y /ies	
techni cian /que	
technocrac y /ies	
technocrat /ic	
technolog y /ical/ically	
tecneek	technique
tecnical	technical [+]
tecnicalitey	technicality [+]
tecnician	technician [+]
tecnishun	technician [+]
tecnocracy	technocracy [+]
tecnologey	technology [+]
teddy-bear	
tedibare	teddy-bear
tedi um /ous/ously	
tedius	tedious

tee * (golf) /d/ing

tee	tea *+
teech	teach +
teek	teak
teel	teal

teem [1]* (swarm)

teem	team [1]*+

teenage /r

teese	tease [2]+
teet	teat

teeter [1]

teeth * (pl. of tooth)

teethe [2]* (develop teeth)

teetotal /ism/ler

tegument

tekneek	technique
teknical	technical +
teknicalitey	technicality +
teknician	technician +
teknishun	technician +
teknocracy	technocracy +
teknocrasey	technocracy +
teknologey	technology +
teknological	technological
tekscher	texture
tekst	text +
tekstile	textile

telecommunications

telefone	telephone [2]+
telefonist	telephonist
telegraf	telegraph [1]+

telegram

telegraph [1] /ic/ist/y

teleks	telex [1]

telemeter

telepath y /ic

telephon e [2] /ic/ist

telephoto /graph

teleprinter

telescop e [2] /ic/y

teletipe	teletype

teletype

televise [2]

televishun	television

television

---

telex [1]

telicomunications	telecommunications
telie	telly
telifone	telephone [2]+
telifoto	telephoto +
teligraf	telegraph [1]+
teligram	telegram
telimeter	telemeter
teliprinter	teleprinter
teliscope	telescope [2]+
teliscopic	telescopic
telitipe	teletype
telivise	televise [2]
telivishun	television
telivision	television

tell /er/ing/-tale

tellurium

telly

telurium	tellurium

temerity

temper [1]

temperacher	temperature

temperament /al

temperance

temperans	temperance

temperat e /ure

temperit	temperate +

tempest /uous

tempestuus	tempestuous

temple

tempo /s

temporal /ly

temporar y /ily

temporis e [2] /r

temprament	temperament +
temprecher	temperature
tempremental	temperamental

tempt [1] /ation/er

temptashun	temptation
tempul	temple
temtashun	temptation

ten /fold/th/thly

tenab le /ility

tenabul	tenable +

tenacious /ly

tenacity	
tenanc y /ies	
tenansey	tenancy +
tenant /ry	
tenashus	tenacious +
tenasitey	tenacity
tend 1	
tendenc y /ies	
tendensey	tendency +
tendenshus	tendentious
tendentious	
tender 1 /er/est/ly/ness	
tenderhooks	tenterhooks
tendon	
tendril	
tenement /-house	
tener	tenor ★
tenet	
teniment	tenement +
tenis	tennis
tennis	
tenon /-saw	
tenor ★ (voice)	
tenor	tenure ★
tense /ly/ness/r/st	
tenshun	tension
tensile	
tension	
tent	
tentacle	
tentacul	tentacle
tentative /ly	
tenterhooks	
tenuous /ly/ness	
tenure ★ (possession)	
tenuus	tenuous +
tenyer	tenure ★
tepid /ity/ly	
teracota	terracotta
terafurma	terra firma
terain	terrain
terapin	terrapin
terass	terrace 2
terban	turban +
terbid	turbid +

terbine	turbine
terbium	
terbo	turbo +
terbot	turbot
terbulence	turbulence +
terbulens	turbulence +
terbulent	turbulent
tergid	turgid +
terible	terrible +
teribul	terrible +
terific	terrific +
terify	terrify 4
teritorey	territory +
teritorial	territorial +
terjid	turgid +
terkey	turkey +
terkish	Turkish
terkwoise	turquoise
term 1	
termagant	
terminable	
terminabul	terminable
terminal /ly	
terminat e 2 /ion	
terminological /ly	
terminolog y /ies	
termin us /i (pl.)	
termite	
termoil	turmoil
tern ★ (bird)	
tern	turn 1★+
ternip	turnip
terodactil	pterodactyl
teror	terror +
terorism	terrorism
terorist	terrorist
terpentine	turpentine
terpitude	turpitude
terra firma	
terrace 2	
terracotta	
terrain	
terrapin	
terrestrial	
terribl e /y	

terribul	terrible +	thach	thatch [1+]
terrier		thalidomide	
terrifi	terrify [4]	thallium	
terrific /ally		than	
terrify [4]		thank [1] /less	
territorial /ly		thankful /ly	
territor y /ies		thanksgiving	
terror /ism/ist		that /'s (that is)	
terroris e [2] /ation		thatch [1] /er	
terse /ly/ness		thaw [1]	
tershan	tertian +	thay	they +
tertia n /ry		the	
tertle	turtle	theater	theatre
teselashun	tessellation	theatre	
teselate	tessellate [2+]	theatrical /ly	
teselation	tessellation	theft	
tespoon	teaspoon +	theif	thief +
tessellat e [2] /ion		their * (possession) /s *	
test [1] /-tube		their	there *
testament		theirs	there's *
testat e /or/rix (fem.)		theis m /t/tical	
testes	testis +	theives	thieves
testicle		theivish	thievish
testicul	testicle	them /selves	
testie	testy +	them e /atic	
testifi	testify [4+]	thence /forth/forward	
testif y [4] /ier		thens	thence +
testimon y /ial		theocra cy /tic	
testimonyal	testimonial	theocrasey	theocracy +
test is /es (pl.)		theodolite	
test y /ily/iness		theolog y /ian/ical/ist	
tetanic	titanic	theolojun	theologian
tetanus		theorem	
tetatet	tête-à-tête	theoretic /al/ally	
tête-à-tête		theorey	theory +
tether [1]		theorise [2]	
tetragon /al		theor y /ies/ist	
tetrahedr on /al		theosofey	theosophy +
tetrarch /y		theosoph y /ical/ist	
tetrark	tetrarch +	therapeuti c /st	
Teutonic		therapey	therapy +
texcher	texture	theraputic	therapeutic +
text /ual/ually		therap y /ist	
textile		therd	third +
texture		there * (that place)	

there	their *+	thiroyd	thyroid
there	they're *	thirst [1] /ily/y	
therefore		thirteen /th	
therem	theorem	thirtie	thirty +
there's * (there is)		thirt y /ies/ieth	
theres	theirs *	thisis	phthisis
theretic	theoretic +	thisle	thistle +
theretical	theoretical	thisorus	thesaurus +
therey	theory +	thistl e /y	
therise	theorise [2]	thisul	thistle +
therist	theorist	thither	
therm /al/ally		tho	though
thermion /ic		thole	
thermite		thong	
thermocouple		thor	thaw [1]
thermocuple	thermocouple	thoraks	thorax +
thermodynamic /s		thora x /cic	
thermo-electric /ity		thorium	
thermomet er /ric/ry		thorn /y	
thermonuclear		thorough /ly	
thermos		thorough bred /fare	
thermostat /ic/ically		thort	thought
thersday	Thursday	thortful	thoughtful +
therst	thirst [1]+	thortless	thoughtless +
therstey	thirsty	those	
therteen	thirteen +	though	
therty	thirty +	thought	
thesaur us /i (pl.)		thoughtful /ly/ness	
these		thoughtless /ly/ness	
thes is /es (pl.)		thousand /th	
they /'re * (they are)		thowsand	thousand +
thi	thigh	thrall [1]	
thick /er/est/ly/ness/set		thrash [1]	
thicken [1] /er		thread [1] /bare	
thie f /ves (pl.)/vish		threat	
thigh		threaten [1]	
thimble /ful		thred	thread [1]+
thimbul	thimble +	thredbare	threadbare
thime	thyme *	three-dimensional	
thin [3] /ly/ner/nest		three fold /pence	
thine		three-quarters	
thing		thresh [1] /er	
think /er/ing		threshold	
third /ly		thret	threat
thirm	therm +	threten	threaten [1]

threw ★ (did throw)	
threw	through ★
threwout	throughout
thrice	
thrift /less/y	
thrifti er /est/ly/ness	
thrill ¹ /er	
thrise	thrice
thriv e /en/ing	
throat /y	
throb ³	
throe ★ (pain) /s ★	
throe	throw ★+
thrombosis	
throne ★ (chair of state)	
throne	thrown ★
throng ¹	
throo	threw ★
throo	through ★
throt	throat +
throttle ²	
throtul	throttle ²
through ★ (penetrated)	
through	threw ★
throughout	
throve	
throw ★† /ing/n ★†/s ★†	
†(hurl[ed, s])	
throw	throe ★+
thrum ³	
thrush /es	
thrust /er/ing	
thud ³	
thug /gery	
thulium	
thum	thumb ¹
thumb ¹	
thump ¹	
thunder ¹ /bolt/ous	
thunderstorm	
thunderstruck	
thunderus	thunderous
thurer	thorough +
thurerbred	thoroughbred +
thurerfare	thoroughfare

thurm	therm +
thurmal	thermal
thurmion	thermion +
thurmite	thermite
thurmocuple	thermocouple
thurmodinamic	thermodynamic +
thurmoelectric	thermo-electric +
thurmometer	thermometer +
thurmonucliar	thermonuclear
thurmos	thermos
thurmostat	thermostat +
thurmyon	thermion +
Thursday	
thurst	thirst ¹+
thurteen	thirteen +
thurty	thirty +
thus	
thwack ¹	
thwart ¹	
thwort	thwart ¹
thyme ★ (herb)	
thyroid	
tialin	ptyalin
tiara /s	
tibia	
tic ★ (twitch)	
tick ¹★ (sound) /er	
ticket	
tickl e ² /er/ish	
tickul	tickle ²+
ticoon	tycoon
tidal	
tiddler	
tiddlywinks	
tide /less	
tidie	tidy ⁴+
tidi ly /ness	
tidings	
tidliwinks	tiddlywinks
tidul	tidal
tid y ⁴ /ier/iest/ily/iness	
tie /d	
tier ★ (layer)	
tier	tire ²★+
tier	tyre ★

tiff [1]		tipist	typist
tiffin		tipit	tippet
tifoid	typhoid	tiple	tipple [2+]
tifoon	typhoon [+]	tipografey	typography [+]
tifus	typhus [+]	tippet	
tig *er* /ress (fem.)		tipple [2] /r	
tight /-laced/rope		tipsey	tipsy [+]
tighten [1]		tips *y* /ily/iness	
tight *er* /est/ly/ness		tiptoe [2]	
tights		tipul	tipple [2+]
tike	tyke	tirade	
tile [2]		tiraney	tyranny [+]
tilige	tillage	tiranical	tyrannical [+]
till [1] /able/age/er		tiranise	tyrannise [2+]
tilt [1]		tirannical	tyrannical [+]
timber [1]		tirant	tyrant
time [2]★† /keeper/less		tiranus	tyrannous
†(duration)		tire [2]★† /less/lessly	
time	thyme ★	†(grow weary)	
timepeace	timepiece	tire	tyre ★
timepiece		tiresome /ly/ness	
timid /er/est/ity		tiresum	tiresome [+]
timorous /ly/ness		tiro	
timorus	timorous [+]	tishoo	tissue [+]
timpan *o* /i (pl.)/ist		tishue	tissue [+]
timpanum	tympanum [+]	tissue /-paper	
tin [3] /foil/ny		Titan	
tincture		titanic	
tinder /y		titanium	
tinge [2]		titbit	
tingle [2]		tite	tight [+]
tingul	tingle [2]	titen	tighten [1]
tinie	tiny [+]	titer	tighter [+]
tinkcher	tincture	titerope	tightrope
tinker [1]		tites	tights
tinkle [2]		tithe /-barn	
tinkul	tinkle [2]	titillat *e* [2] /ion	
tinsel [3] /ly		titivat *e* [2] /ion	
tint [1]		title /d	
tin *y* /ier/iest/ily/iness		titm *ouse* /ice (pl.)	
tip [3] /ster		titmowse	titmouse [+]
tipe	type [2+]	titrat *e* [2] /ion	
tiperiter	typewriter [+]	titter [1]	
tipical	typical [+]	tittle-tattle	
tipify	typify [4]	titul	title [+]

titul tatul	tittle-tattle	toll¹ /-bar/-gate	
titular		tolrable	tolerable +
tituler	titular	tolrabul	tolerable +
T-junction		tomahawk	
to ★ (towards) /day		tomahork	tomahawk
to	too ★	tomane	ptomaine
to	two ★+	tomato /es	
to and fro		tomb /stone	
toad /stool/y		tomboi	tomboy
toast¹ /er		tomboy	
tobacco /nist		tome	
tobaco	tobacco +	tomfoolery	
toboggan¹ /er		tomorrow	
tocsic	toxic +	tomtit	
tocsicologey	toxicology +	ton ★ (weight) /nage	
tocsin ★ (bell)		ton	tun ★
tocsin	toxin ★	tonal /ity	
toddle² /r		tone /less	
toddy		tongs	
tode	toad +	tongue² /-tied/-twister	
todle	toddle ²+	tonic	
todstool	toadstool	tonight	
todul	toddle ²+	tonite	tonight
tody	toddy	tonsher	tonsure +
toe ★ (on foot)		tonsil /litis	
toe	tow¹★+	tons *ure* /orial	
tofee	toffee	too ★ (also)	
toffee		too	to ★+
together		too	two ★+
toggle		took	
togul	toggle	tool¹	
toi	toy¹+	toom	tomb +
toil¹ /er		toomstone	tombstone
toilet /ry		toor	tour¹+
token		toot¹	
toksic	toxic +	tooth /ache/less	
toksicologey	toxicology +	toothake	toothache
tole	toll¹+	tootle²	
tolemaic sistem	Ptolemaic system	tootul	tootle²
tolerabl*e* /y		top³ /-heavy/sail	
tolerabul	tolerable +	topas	topaz
toleran*ce* /t		topath	towpath
tolerans	tolerance +	topaz	
tolerashun	toleration	topic /al/ally	
tolerat*e*² /ion		tople	topple²

topografer	topographer	tortuus	tortuous [+]
topografey	topography [+]	torus	Taurus
topografic	topographic	Tor y /ies	
topograph y /er/ic/ical		toss [1] /-up	
topple [2]		tost	toast [1+]
topsy-turvy		total [3] /ity/ly	
topul	topple [2]	totalis e [2] /ator	
torch /light		totalitey	totality
torcher	torture [2+]	totem pole	
torchlite	torchlight	totter [1]	
tordrey	tawdry [+]	totul	total [3+]
toreador		touch [1] /ier/iness/y	
torenshal	torrential	touchstone	
torent	torrent [+]	touchwood	
torential	torrential	tough /er/est/ly/ness	
torero		toughen [1]	
torey	Tory [+]	tour [1] /ism/ist	
torid	torrid	tournament	
torie	Tory [+]	tourniket	tourniquet
torism	tourism	tourniquet	
torist	tourist	tousle [2]	
torment [1] /or		tout [1]	
tornado /es		tow [1★] (pull) /age	
tornament	tournament	tow	toe ★
torney	tawny	toward /s	
tornt	taunt [1+]	towel [3]	
torpedo [1] /-boat/es		tower [1]	
torper	torpor	town /hall	
torpid /ity		towpath	
torpor		towsl	tousle [2]
torrenshal	torrential	towt	tout [1]
torrent /ial		toxic /ity	
torrid		toxicolog y /ist	
torshun	torsion [+]	toxin ★ (poison)	
torsion /al		toxin	tocsin ★
torso /s		toy [1] /s/shop	
tort ★ (law)		toylet	toilet [+]
tort	taught ★	toyul	toil [1+]
tort	taut ★[+]	trace [2] /able/r/ry	
torten	tauten [1]	trache a /otomy	
tortoise /-shell		tracing-paper	
tortologey	tautology [+]	track [1] /er	
tortuous /ly/ness		tracshun	traction
torture [2] /r		tract	
tortus	tortoise [+]	tract able /ion/or	

tracter	tractor	transendental	transcendental
trade² /r/sman		transept	
tradishun	tradition⁺	transfer³ /able/ence	
tradishunal	traditional	transferens	transference
tradition /al/ally		transfiger	transfigure²⁺
traduce²		transfigur e² /ation	
traduse	traduce²	transfiks	transfix¹
traffic /ked/king		transfix¹	
trafic	traffic⁺	transform¹ /ation/er	
traged y /ies		transformashun	transformation
tragic /al/ally		transfus e² /ion	
trail¹ /er		transfushun	transfusion
train¹ /ee/er		transgreshun	transgression
traipse²		transgress¹ /ion/or	
trait		transien ce /t/tly	
traitor /ous		transiens	transience⁺
trajector y /ies		transishun	transition⁺
trajectrey	trajectory⁺	transister	transistor
trajedey	tragedy⁺	transistor	
trakia	trachea⁺	transistoris e²	
trakiotomey	tracheotomy	transit /ive/ory	
trakshun	traction	transition /al	
tram /car/-line		translashun	translation
trammel³		translat e² /able/ion/or	
tramp¹		translater	translator
trample²		translucen ce /t	
trampoline		translusens	translucence⁺
trampul	trample²	translusent	translucent
tramul	trammel³	transmigrat e² /ion	
trance		transmishun	transmission
trane	train¹⁺	transmission	
trankwil	tranquil⁺	transmit³ /ter	
trankwilise	tranquillise²⁺	transmut e /ation	
trankwilitey	tranquillity	transparen ce /cy/t	
tranquil /lity/ly		transparens	transparence⁺
tranquillis e² /er		transparensey	transparency
trans	trance	transpir e² /ation	
transact¹ /ion		transplant¹ /ation	
transatlantic		transport¹ /ation/er	
transceiver		transportashun	transportation
transcend¹ /ence/ental		transpos e² /ition	
transcribe²		transsever	transceiver
transcript /ion		trans-ship³ /ment	
transend	transcend¹⁺	transverse /ly	
transendence	transcendence	transvershun	transversion

transversion		treetment	treatment
transvesti *sm* /te		trefoil	
trap [3] /per		trefoyul	trefoil
trapez *e* /ium/oid		trek [3] /ker	
trapse	traipse [2]	trellis-work	
trase	trace [2+]	tremble [2]	
trash /y		trembul	tremble [2]
trasing paper	tracing-paper	tremendous /ly	
trate	trait	tremendus	tremendous [+]
trater	traitor [+]	tremer	tremor
traterous	traitorous	tremor	
traterus	traitorous	tremulous	
trauma /tic		tremulus	tremulous
travail [1]		trench [1] /es	
travale	travail [1]	trenchan *cy* /t	
travel [3] /ler/ogue		trenchansey	trenchancy [+]
travelog	travelogue	trend [1] /y	
traverse [2]		treo	trio [+]
travest *y* /ies		trepidashun	trepidation
trawl [1] /er		trepidation	
trawma	trauma [+]	treshur	treasure [2+]
tray /s		treshurey	treasury [+]
treacherey	treachery [+]	treson	treason [+]
treacher *y* /ous		trespass [1] /er/es	
treacl *e* /y		tressul	trestle
treacul	treacle [+]	trestle	
tread /ing/le		tri	try [4+]
treason /able/ous		trial	
treasonus	treasonous	triang *le* /ular	
treasure [2] /r		triangul	triangle [+]
treasur *y* /ies		triangulat *e* [2] /ion	
treat [1] /able/ment		trianguler	triangular
treatise		trib *e* /al/alism	
treatiss	treatise	tribul	tribal
treat *y* /ies		tribulashun	tribulation
trebl *e* [2] /y		tribulation	
trebul	treble [2+]	tribun *e* /al	
trecherey	treachery [+]	tributar *y* /ies	
trecherus	treacherous	tribute	
tred	tread [+]	tributrey	tributary [+]
tree		trice	
treecul	treacle [+]	triceps	
treet	treat [1+]	tricicul	tricycle
treetie	treaty [+]	trick [1] /ery/ster/y	
treetis	treatise	tricki *er* /est/ly/ness	

trickle ²		trooant	truant
tricuspid		troobadoor	troubadour
tricycle		trooism	truism
trident		trooley	truly
trifle ² /r		troop ¹★ (military)	
triful	trifle ²⁺	troop	troupe ★
trigger ¹		troos	truce
trigonometr y /ic		trooth	truth
trill ¹		troothful	truthful ⁺
trilogy		troph y /ies	
trim ³ /mer		tropic /al/ally	
trimaran		tropism	
trinity		troposfere	troposphere
trinket		troposphere	
trio /s		trorma	trauma ⁺
triode		trormatic	traumatic
trip ³★ (fall)		trot ³ /ter	
tripartite		troubadour	
tripe ★ (food)		trouble ² /-maker	
triple ² /t		troubleshooter	
triplicat e ² /ion		troublesome	
tripod		trough	
tripos		trounce ²	
triptick	triptych	trouns	trounce ²
triptych		troup	troop ¹★
tripul	triple ²⁺	troupe ★ (actors)	
trise	trice	trousers	
trisicul	tricycle	trousseau /x (pl.)	
trite /ly		trout	
triumf	triumph ¹⁺	trowel	
triumph ¹ /al/ant		trownce	trounce ²
trivia /l/ly		trowns	trounce ²
trivialise ²		trowsers	trousers
trivialit y /ies		trowt	trout
trod /den		truan cy /t	
trofey	trophy ⁺	truansey	truancy ⁺
troley	trolley ⁺	truble	trouble ²⁺
trolie	trolley ⁺	trubul	trouble ²⁺
troll ¹		truce	
trolley /s		truck	
trollop		truculen ce /t	
trolop	trollop	trudge ²	
trombon e /ist		tru e /er/est/ism/ly/th	
troo	true ⁺	truf	trough
trooancy	truancy ⁺	truffle	

truful	truffle	tumultuus	tumultuous
truge	trudge ²	tumulus	
trulie	truly	tun ★ (large cask)	
trump ¹		tun	ton ★⁺
trumpet ¹ /er		tuna	
truncat e ² /ion		tundra	
truncheon		tun e ² /able/er	
trunchon	truncheon	tuneful /ly/ness	
trundle ²		tuney	tunny ⁺
trundul	trundle ²	tung	tongue ²⁺
trunk /-line		tungsten	
trusow	trousseau ⁺	tungtied	tongue-tied
truss ¹ /es		tunic	
trust ¹ /ee/ful/fully		tunie	tunny ⁺
trustwerthey	trustworthy ⁺	tunige	tonnage
trustworth y /iness		tunnel ³ /ler	
truthful /ly/ness		tunn y /ies	
tr y ⁴ /ier/ies		tunul	tunnel ³⁺
trycicle	tricycle	turban /ed	
tsar		turbid /ity	
tub ³ /biness/by		turbine	
tuba /s		turbo /-alternator	
tub e ² /ular		turbo-generator	
tuber /cle/cular		turbo-jet	
tubercul osis /ous		turbo-prop	
tuch	touch ¹⁺	turbot	
tuchstone	touchstone	turbulen ce /t	
tuchwood	touchwood	turbulens	turbulence ⁺
tuchy	touchy	tureen	
tuck ¹ /er		turet	turret ⁺
Tuesday		turf ¹ /s/ves (pls.)	
tuf	tough ⁺	turgid /ity	
tuffen	toughen ¹	turjid	turgid ⁺
tuft ¹		turkey /s	
tug ³ /-of-war		Turkish	
tuishun	tuition	turkwoise	turquoise
tuition		turm	term ¹
tuk	tuck ¹⁺	turminable	terminable
tuksedo	tuxedo	turminabul	terminable
tulip		turminal	terminal ⁺
tumble ² /r		turminate	terminate ²⁺
tumbul	tumble ²⁺	turmination	termination
tumer	tumour	turminologey	terminology ⁺
tumour		turminological	terminological ⁺
tumult /uous		turminus	terminus ⁺

turmite	termite	twilight	
turmoil		twilite	twilight
turn [1]* (rotate) /er		twill [1]	
turn	tern *	twin [3]	
turn *coat* /key/pike		twine [2]	
turnikay	tourniquet	twinge [2]	
turniket	tourniquet	twinkle [2]	
turnip		twinkul	twinkle [2]
turn *stile* /table		twirl [1]	
turpentine		twise	twice
turpitude		twist [1] /er	
turquoise		twit [3]	
turret /ed		twitch [1] /es	
turse	terse [+]	twitter [1]	
turshan	tertian [+]	two * (number) /-way	
tursharey	tertiary	two	to *[+]
turtian	tertian [+]	two	too *
turtle		twodle	twaddle [2]
turtul	turtle	two *fold* /pence	
tusday	Tuesday	twurl	twirl [1]
tusk [1] /er		tyalin	ptyalin
tussle [2]		tycoon	
tusul	tussle [2]	tyfoid	typhoid
tutel *age* /ary		tyfoon	typhoon [+]
tutelige	tutelage [+]	tyfus	typhus [+]
tuter	tutor [1+]	tyke	
tutonic	Teutonic	tympano	timpano [+]
tutor [1] /ial		tympan *um* /a (pl.)	
tuxedo		type [2] /script	
twaddle [2]		typeriter	typewriter [+]
twain		typewrit *er* /ing/ten	
twang [1]		typho *on* /nic	
twayn	twain	typh *us* /oid	
tweak [1]		typical /ly	
tweed		typifi	typify [4]
tweek	tweak [1]	typify [4]	
tweezers		typist	
twel *fth* /ve		typografey	typography [+]
twelth	twelfth [+]	typograph *y* /er/ic	
twent *y* /ies/ieth		tyranical	tyrannical [+]
twice		tyrannical /ly	
twich	twitch [1+]	tyrann *ise* [2] /ous	
twiddle [2]		tyran *ny* /t	
twidul	twiddle [2]	tyre * (of a car)	
twig [1]		tyre	tire [2*+]

U

u	ewe *
ubikwitey	ubiquity +
ubikwitus	ubiquitous
ubiquit y /ous	
U-boat	
ucalyptus	eucalyptus +
Ucarist	Eucharist
uclid	Euclid
udder	
ufemism	euphemism
ufemistic	euphemistic +
ufoney	euphony +
uforia	euphoria +
uforic	euphoric
ug	ugh
ugenic	eugenic +
ugh	
uglie	ugly +
ugl y /ier/iest/iness	
ukaliptus	eucalyptus +
ukarist	Eucharist
ukelalee	ukulele
uksorius	uxorious
ukulele	
ulcer /ous	
ulcerat e² /ion	
ulna	
ulogey	eulogy +
ulogise	eulogise 2+
ulogism	eulogism
ulser	ulcer +
ulserate	ulcerate 2+
ulserous	ulcerous
ulserus	ulcerous
ulterier	ulterior
ulterior	
ultimate /ly	
ultimatum /s (pl.)	
ultramarine	
ultramicroscopic	
ultrasonic	
ultra-violet	
umbilical	

umbrage	
umbrella	
umbridge	umbrage
umpire ²* (referee)	
umpire	empire *
umpteen	
unable	
unabridged	
unabriged	unabridged
unabul	unable
unacceptable	
unaccompanied	
unaccompnid	unaccompanied
unaccountable	
unaccustomed	
unacowntable	unaccountable
unacquainted	
unacseptable	unacceptable
unacseptabul	unacceptable
unacumpanid	unaccompanied
unacustomd	unaccustomed
unaded	unaided
unadulterated	
unaffected	
unafrade	unafraid
unafraid	
unaided	
unalloyed	
unaloid	unalloyed
unanimity	
unanimous /ly	
unanimus	unanimous +
unanserable	unanswerable +
unanswer able /ed	
unapproachable	
unaprochable	unapproachable
unaprochabul	unapproachable
unarmed	
unashamed	
unasked	
unaskt	unasked
unassisted	
unassuming	
unatacht	unattached
unatainable	unattainable

unattached		uncann *y* /ily/iness	
unattainable		uncared-for	
unattended		unceremonious /ly	
unauthorised		unceremonius	unceremonious +
unavail *able* /ing		uncertain /ty/ties	
unavalabul	unavailable +	unchangable	unchangeable
unavaling	unavailing	unchangeable	
unavoidabl *e* /y		uncharitable	
unavoydable	unavoidable +	uncharitabul	uncharitable
unaware /s		uncharted	
unawthorised	unauthorised	unchristian	
unbalanced		uncivil /ised	
unbalanst	unbalanced	unclaimed	
unbarable	unbearable +	unclamed	unclaimed
unbarabul	unbearable +	uncle	
unbearabl *e* /y		unclean	
unbeat *able* /en		uncomfortabl *e* /y	
unbecoming		uncomfortabul	uncomfortable +
unbeknown		uncomftable	uncomfortable +
unbeleif	unbelief	uncomited	uncommitted
unbelevable	unbelievable +	uncommitted	
unbelevabul	unbelievable +	uncommon	
unbelief		uncommunicative	
unbeliev *able* /ing		uncompromising	
unbelievabul	unbelievable +	unconcern /ed	
unbend /ing		uncondishnal	unconditional +
unbenown	unbeknown	unconditional /ly	
unberden	unburden [1]	unconected	unconnected
unbeten	unbeaten	unconfirmed	
unbiased		unconfurmd	unconfirmed
unbiast	unbiased	uncongenial	
unbidden		unconnected	
unblemished		unconquerable	
unblemisht	unblemished	unconscionable	
unborn		unconscious /ly/ness	
unbounded		unconshonable	unconscionable
unbowed		unconshonabul	unconscionable
unbownded	unbounded	unconshus	unconscious +
unbridled		unconstitutional	
unbriduld	unbridled	uncontrolabul	uncontrollable
unbroken		uncontrollable	
unburden [1]		unconvenshunal	unconventional
unbutton [1]		unconventional	
uncalled-for		unco-operative	
uncanie	uncanny +	unco-ordinated	

uncooth	uncouth
uncorroborated	
uncouple [2]	
uncoupul	uncouple [2]
uncouth	
uncover [1]	
uncristian	unchristian
uncritical	
uncshun	unction [+]
unct *ion* /uous	
uncul	uncle
uncultivated	
uncumftable	uncomfortable [+]
uncuple	uncouple [2]
uncuver	uncover [1]
undated	
undaunted	
undawnted	undaunted
undeceive [2]	
undecided	
undecieve	undeceive [2]
undefended	
undeniable	
undeniabul	undeniable
under /arm/bid	
undercarige	undercarriage
undercarriage	
undercloth *es* /ing	
undercover	
undercurrent	
undercut /ting	
undercuver	undercover
underdog	
underdone	
underdun	underdone
underfed	
undergo /ing/ne	
undergraduate	
undergroth	undergrowth
underground	
undergrownd	underground
undergrowth	
underhand	
underl *ie* /ying	
underline [2]	

underling	
undermand	undermanned
undermanned	
undermine [2]	
underneath	
undernourish [1] /ment	
undernurish	undernourish [1+]
underpass [1]	
underprivileged	
underrate [2]	
underrite	underwrite [+]
underrote	underwrote
undersell /ing	
undersigned	
undersined	undersigned
undersised	undersized
undersized	
understand /able	
understatement	
understood	
understud *y* [4] /ies	
undertak *e* /er/ing	
underto	undertow
undertone	
undertook	
undertow	
underwait	underweight
underware	underwear
underwater	
underwear	
underweight	
underwerld	underworld
underworld	
underwrit *e* /ing/ten	
underwrote	
undeservd	undeserved
undeserved	
undeseve	undeceive [2]
undesirable	
undesirabul	undesirable
undeterd	undeterred
undetermind	undetermined
undetermined	
undeterred	
undieing	undying

301

undifended	undefended	unfaned	unfeigned
undignifide	undignified	unfare	unfair [+]
undignified		unfasen	unfasten [1]
undisciplined		unfashionable	
undisided	undecided	unfashnable	unfashionable
undisiplind	undisciplined	unfasten [1]	
undo /ing/ne		unfathful	unfaithful [+]
undornted	undaunted	unfavourabl e /y	
undoubted /ly		unfavrable	unfavourable [+]
undowted	undoubted [+]	unfeigned	
undress [1]		unfit [3] /ness	
undu e /ly		unfold [1]	
undulat e [2] /ion/ory		unforeseen	
undying		unforgetabul	unforgettable
unearned		unforgettable	
unearth [1] /ly		unfortunate /ly	
uneas y /ily		unfounded	
uneatable		unfownded	unfounded
uneatabul	uneatable	unfriendl y /iness	
unecessary	unnecessary [+]	unfurl [1]	
uneconomic /al/ally		unfurnished	
uneducated		unfurnisht	unfurnished
uneek	unique [+]	ungainly	
unekspected	unexpected	unganley	ungainly
unekwal	unequal [+]	ungarded	unguarded
unemploiabul	unemployable [+]	ungodly	
unemploy able /ed/ment		ungovernable	
unenterprising		ungracious /ly	
unequal /led/ly		ungrammatical /ly	
unequivocal		ungrashus	ungracious [+]
unering	unerring	ungrateful	
unerned	unearned	ungreatful	ungrateful
unerring		unguarded	
unerth	unearth [1+]	unguent	
unesessary	unnecessary [+]	unguvernabul	ungovernable
unesey	uneasy [+]	unguvnable	ungovernable
unetable	uneatable	unguvnabul	ungovernable
uneven /ness		unhallowed	
uneventful		unhalowd	unhallowed
unexpected		unhapie	unhappy [+]
unfailing /ly		unhappi ly /ness	
unfaind	unfeigned	unhapp y /ier/iest	
unfair /ly/ness		unhealthy	
unfaithful /ly/ness		unheard-of	
unfaling	unfailing [+]	unhelthy	unhealthy

unherdov	unheard-of	unkshus	unctuous
unhinge [2]		unkwalified	unqualified
unholesum	unwholesome	unkweschunable	unquestionable +
unholy		unlawful /ly	
unhurdov	unheard-of	unleash [1]	
unicellular		unleavened	
unicicle	unicycle	unlesh	unleash [1]
unicorn		unless	
unicycle		unlevend	unleavened
unidentified		unlicensed	
unifi	unify [4+]	unlike /ly	
uniform /ity		unlimited	
unif y [4] /ication		unlisensd	unlicensed
unikwivocal	unequivocal	unload [1]	
unilateral /ly		unlock [1]	
unimpeachable		unlode	unload [1]
uninhabit able /ed		unluck y /ier/iest/ily	
uninteligibul	unintelligible +	unlukey	unlucky +
unintelligib le /ility		unmanageable	
union /ism/ist		unmanigable	unmanageable
unique /ly/ness		unmannerly	
uniquivocal	unequivocal	unmarid	unmarried
uniselular	unicellular	unmarried	
unisicul	unicycle	unmask [1]	
unison		unmenshunable	unmentionable
unit /ary		unmentionable	
unitarian /ism		unmistakabl e /y	
unite [2]		unmistakabul	unmistakable +
unit y /ies		unmitigated	
uniun	onion	unmoovd	unmoved
universal /ity/ly		unmoved	
universe		unnacheral	unnatural +
universit y /ies		unnamd	unnamed
univursal	universal +	unnamed	
univurse	universe	unnatural /ly	
univursitey	university +	unnecessar y /ily	
unjust		unnerv ed /ing	
unjustifi able /ed		unnesessarey	unnecessary +
unjustifiabul	unjustifiable +	unnowing	unknowing +
unkempt		unnown	unknown
unkemt	unkempt	unnumberd	unnumbered
unkind /ness		unnumbered	
unknow ing /n		unnurvd	unnerved +
unkristian	unchristian	unobserv ant /ed	
unkshun	unction +	unobtrusive	

303

unoccupied		unread *y* /iness	
unocupied	unoccupied	unreal /istic	
unoffending		unreasnable	unreasonable +
unofficial /ly		unreasonabl *e* /y	
unoficial	unofficial +	unrecognis *able* /ed	
unofishul	unofficial +	unrecognisabul	unrecognisable +
unopend	unopened	unredabul	unreadable
unopened		unredey	unready +
unorthorised	unauthorised	unreel	unreal +
unpack [1]		unrekwited	unrequited
unpaid		unreleved	unrelieved
unparaleld	unparalleled	unreliab *le* /ility	
unparalleled		unreliabul	unreliable +
unparlamentrey	unparliamentary	unrelieved	
unparliamentary		unremitting	
unpayd	unpaid	unrequited	
unpick [1]		unreservedly	
unpleasant /ness		unresnable	unreasonable +
unplesant	unpleasant +	unresponsive	
unpopular /ity		unrest	
unpopuler	unpopular +	unrestraind	unrestrained
unpractical		unrestrained	
unprecedented		unrighteous	
unprejudiced		unrimitting	unremitting
unprejudist	unprejudiced	unripe	
unpremeditated		unritchus	unrighteous
unprepard	unprepared	unritten	unwritten
unprepared		unrivald	unrivalled
unprepossessing		unrivalled	
unpresedented	unprecedented	unroll [1]	
unpretenshus	unpretentious	unruffled	
unpretentious		unrufld	unruffled
unprincipled		unrufuld	unruffled
unprinsipld	unprincipled	unruly	
unprintable		unsafe	
unprintabul	unprintable	unsaid	
unprofeshnal	unprofessional +	unsatisfactor *y* /ily	
unprofessional /ly		unsatisfactrey	unsatisfactory +
unqualified		unsatisfied	
unquestionabl *e* /y		unsavorey	unsavoury +
unquestionabul	unquestionable +	unsavour *y* /iness	
unrap	unwrap [3]	unscathed	
unravel [3]		unscientific	
unreadable		unscrupulous /ly	
unreadabul	unreadable	unscrupulus	unscrupulous +

unseasnabul	unseasonable	unsucsesful	unsuccessful [+]
unseasonable		unsuitable	
unseat [1]		unsuitabul	unsuitable
unsed	unsaid	unsullied	
unseeing		unsupported	
unseeml y /iness		unsurmountable	insurmountable
unseen		unsurtan	uncertain [+]
unseet	unseat [1]	unsuspected	
unselfish /ly/ness		unsutable	unsuitable
unseremonius	unceremonious [+]	unsutabul	unsuitable
unsermowntable	insurmountable	untactful /ly	
unsertan	uncertain [+]	untenable	
unsettle [2]		untenabul	untenable
unsetul	unsettle [2]	unthinkable	
unsientific	unscientific	unthinkabul	unthinkable
unsightl y /iness		unti	untie [+]
unsitely	unsightly [+]	untide	untied
unsivil	uncivil [+]	untid y /ier/iest/ily/iness	
unsivilised	uncivilised	unt ie /ied/ying	
unskathd	unscathed	untieing	untying
unskild	unskilled	until	
unskilful		untimely	
unskilled		untimley	untimely
unsociabl e /y		unto	
unsofisticated	unsophisticated	untold	
unsolicited		untouchable	
unsolisited	unsolicited	untouchabul	untouchable
unsootable	unsuitable	untoward	
unsootabul	unsuitable	untraceable	
unsophisticated		untrasable	untraceable
unsoshable	unsociable [+]	untrasabul	untraceable
unsoshabul	unsociable [+]	untroo	untrue
unsound		untrooth	untruth
unsownd	unsound	untroothful	untruthful [+]
unspeakabl e /y		untrue	
unspekabul	unspeakable [+]	untruth	
unspoiled		untruthful /ly/ness	
unspoyld	unspoiled	untuchable	untouchable
unstable		untuchabul	untouchable
unstabul	unstable	untuterd	untutored
unstead y /ily/iness		untutored	
unstedey	unsteady [+]	unuch	eunuch
unsubstanshiated	unsubstantiated	unuk	eunuch
unsubstantiated		unushual	unusual [+]
unsuccessful /ly		unusual /ly	

unvail	unveil [1]	upon	
unvareying	unvarying	upper /most	
unvarnished		uppish /ness	
unvarnisht	unvarnished	upright	
unvarying		upris e /ing	
unveil [1]		uprite	upright
unwanted		uproar /ious/iously	
unwarey	unwary +	uprore	uproar +
unwarrant able /ed		uprorius	uproarious
unwarrantabul	unwarrantable +	upset /ting	
unwar y /ily		upshot	
unweldey	unwieldy	upside-down	
unwell		upstairs	
unwerkable	unworkable	upstares	upstairs
unwerkabul	unworkable	upstart	
unwerthey	unworthy +	upstream	
unwholesome		upstreem	upstream
unwieldy		upward	
unwilling		upwerd	upward
unwind /ing		ur	err [1]
unwise /ly		uranium	
unwitting /ly		Uranus	
unworantable	unwarrantable +	Urazian	Eurasian
unworantabul	unwarrantable +	urban	
unworkable		urban e /ely/ity	
unworkabul	unworkable	urbanis e [2] /ation	
unworldl y /iness		urbun	urban
unworth y /iness		urchin	
unwound		urea	
unwownd	unwound	ureter	
unwrap [3]		urethra	
unwritten		urge [2] /ncy/nt	
unyun	onion	urinate [2]	
upbrade	upbraid [1]	urin e /al/ary	
upbraid [1]		urithmics	eurhythmics
upbringing		urjensey	urgency
update [2]		urjent	urgent
upheaval		url	earl +
upheld		urley	early +
upheval	upheaval	urlier	earlier +
uphill		urmin	ermine
uphold /ing		urn ★ (vase)	
upholster [1] /er/y		urn	earn [1]★+
uphoney	euphony +	urnest	earnest +
upkeep		urolog y /ist	

Uropian	European	vacseen	vaccine
urstwile	erstwhile	vacsinashun	vaccination
urth	earth [1+]	vacsination	vaccination
urthen	earthen [+]	vacsine	vaccine
urthkwake	earthquake	vacu *ous* /ity	
urthquake	earthquake	vacuum	
us *e²* /able/age/er		vacuus	vacuous [+]
useful /ly/ness		vagabond /age	
useless		vagar *y* /ies	
userp	usurp [1+]	vage	vague [+]
usher [1] /ette (fem.)		vagina	
usheret	usherette	vagran *cy* /t	
usless	useless	vagransey	vagrancy [+]
usorius	usurious	vague /ly/r/st	
usual /ly		vail	vale ★
usurp [1] /ation/er		vail	veil [1★]
usur *y* /ious		vain ★(proud)/er/est/ly	
utensil		vain	vane ★
uter	utter [1+]	vain	vein [1★]
uter *us* /ine		vainglor *ious* /y	
uthanasia	euthanasia	vainglorius	vainglorious [+]
uther	other [+]	vajina	vagina
utherwise	otherwise	valance	
utilis *e²* /able/ation		valans	valance
utilitarian /ism		valay	valet [1]
utilit *y* /ies		vale ★ (valley)	
utmost		vale	veil [1★]
Utopia /n		valedicshun	valediction [+]
utríc *le* /ular/ulus		valedict *ion* /ory	
utter [1] /ance/ly		valentine	
uvula /r		valer	valour [+]
uxorious		valerus	valorous
uxorius	uxorious	valese	valise
		valet [1]	
		valiant	
V		valid /ity	
		validashun	validation
		validat *e²* /ion	
vacanc *y* /ies		valise	
vacansey	vacancy [+]	valley /s	
vacant /ly		valor	valour [+]
vacashun	vacation	valo *ur* /rous	
vacat *e²* /ion		valt	vault [1]
vaccinat *e²* /ion/or		valuashun	valuation
vaccine		valu *e²* /able/ation/er	
vacillat *e²* /ion			

valueless		varnish¹ /er	
valv e /ular		var y⁴ /iation/ious	
valy	valley⁺	vascular	
valyu	value²⁺	vase	
valyuble	valuable	Vaseline	
valyubul	valuable	vasillate	vacillate²⁺
valyuer	valuer	vasleen	Vaseline
valyuless	valueless	vast /er/est/ly/ness	
vamp¹		Vatican	
vampire		vault¹	
Van de Graaff generator		vaunt¹	
vanadium		veal	
vandal /ism		vech	vetch⁺
vane ★ (weather)		vector	
vane	vain★⁺	veel	veal
vane	vein¹★	veemence	vehemence⁺
vangard	vanguard	veemens	vehemence⁺
vanglorey	vainglory	veement	vehement
vanglorious	vainglorious⁺	veer¹	
vanglorius	vainglorious⁺	vegetable	
vanguard		vegetarian /ism	
vanilla		vegetashun	vegetation
vanish¹		vegetat e² /ion/ive	
vanity /-bag		vegtable	vegetable
vankwish	vanquish¹	vegtabul	vegetable
vanquish¹		vehemen ce /t	
vantage		vehic le /ular	
vantidge	vantage	veiculer	vehicular
vantige	vantage	veil¹★ (disguise)	
vaper	vapour⁺	veil	vale★
vapid		vein¹★ (blood)	
vaporis e² /ation/er		vein	vain★⁺
vaporus	vaporous	vein	vane★
vapo ur /rous		veks	vex¹⁺
varia ble /bility/tion		veksashun	vexation
variabul	variable⁺	veksashus	vexatious
varian ce /t		veksation	vexation
varians	variance⁺	veksatious	vexatious
variashun	variation	vekter	vector
varicose		veld	
varie	vary⁴⁺	vellum	
variegated		velocit y /ies	
variet y /ies		veloors	velours
varikose	varicose	velositey	velocity⁺
varius	various	velours	

velt	veld
velum	vellum
velvet /een	
vena cava	
venal /ity/ly	
vencher	venture [2+]
vend [1] /or	
vendetta	
veneer [1]	
venerab le /ility	
venerabul	venerable [+]
venerashun	veneration
venerat e [2] /ion	
venereal	
venerial	venereal
veneshun	Venetian
Venetian	
venge ance /ful	
vengence	vengeance [+]
vengens	vengeance [+]
venial	
venison	
venom /ous	
venomus	venomous
venous ★ (of veins)	
venous	Venus ★
vent [1]	
ventilashun	ventilation
ventilat e [2] /ion/or	
ventral /ly	
ventrical	ventricle
ventricle	
ventrilokwism	ventriloquism [+]
ventriloquis m /t	
venture [2] /some	
venturous	
venturus	venturous
Venus ★ (planet)	
venus	venous ★
venyet	vignette
veraci ous /ty	
veranda	
verashus	veracious [+]
verasitey	veracity
verb /al/ally/atim	

verbiage	
verbos e /ity	
verdant	
verdict	
verdur e /ous	
verge [2]	
verger	
verie	very
verifi	verify [4+]
verif y [4] /iable/ication	
verily	
verisimilitude	
verit y /ies/able/ably	
vermicelli	
vermilion	
vermin /ous	
vermouth	
vernacular	
vernal	
versatil e /ity	
verse /s ★ (poetry)	
verses	versus ★
versif y [4] /ication	
version	
versus ★ (against)	
vertebra /e (pl.)/l/te	
verteks	vertex [+]
vert ex /ices (pl.)	
vertical /ly	
vertig o /inous	
verve	
very	
vesa	visa
vescher	vesture [2]
vespers	
vessel	
vest [1] /ment	
vestal	
vestibule	
vestig e /ial	
vestrie	vestry [+]
vestr y /ies	
vestul	vestal
vesture [2]	
vesul	vessel

vet³	
vetch /es	
vetenarey	veterinary+
vetenrey	veterinary+
veteran	
veterinar y /ies	
veto¹ /es	
vex¹ /ation/atious	
vexashun	vexation
vexashus	vexatious
veza	visa
vezave	vis-à-vis
vi	vie+
via	
viab le /ility	
viabul	viable+
viaduct	
vial * (glass)	
vial	vile *+
vial	viol *+
viands (pl.)	
vibrant	
vibrashun	vibration
vibrat e² /ion/or	
vicar /age	
vicarious /ly	
vicarius	vicarious+
vice	
vice versa	
vice-chancellor	
vice-president	
vicer	vicar+
viceregal	
viceroi	viceroy+
viceroy /alty/alties	
vicinity	
vicious /ly/ness	
vicissitude	
vicount	viscount+
vicownt	viscount+
victim	
victimis e² /ation	
victor /ious/iously	
victorey	victory+
victorius	victorious

victor y /ies	
victual³ /ler	
video /-frequency	
vidio	video+
vie /d	
vieing	vying
view¹ /er	
view-point	
viger	vigour+
vigil /ance/ant/ante	
vigilans	vigilance
vignette	
vigorus	vigorous
vigo ur /rous/rously	
vijun	vision+
Viking	
viksen	vixen
vilan	villain+
vile *† /ly/ness/r/st	
†(loathsome)	
vile	vial *
vile	viol *+
vilidge	village+
vilifi	vilify 4+
vilif y⁴ /ication/ier	
vilige	village+
villa	
village /r	
villain /ous/y	
villaney	villainy
villanus	villainous
vill us /i (pl.)	
vindicashun	vindication
vindicat e² /ion/or	
vindictive	
vine /ry	
vinegar /y	
viniger	vinegar+
vintage	
vintidge	vintage
vintige	vintage
vinul	vinyl
vinyet	vignette
vinyl	
viol * (music) /a/in/inist	

viol	vial ★
viol	vile ★+
violashun	violation
violat e ² /ion/or	
violen ce /t	
violens	violence +
violet	
violoncello /s	
violonchelo	violoncello +
viper /ish/ous	
virgin /al/ity	
Virgo	
viril e /ity	
virilitey	virility
virolog y /ist	
virtual /ly	
virtu e /osity/ous	
virtuoso	
virulen ce /t	
virulens	virulence +
virus	
visa	
visage	
vis-à-vis	
viscera /l	
viscid /ity	
viscos e /ity	
viscositey	viscosity
viscount /ess (fem.)	
viscous	
viscuus	viscous
vise	vice
vise chanseler	vice-chancellor
vise president	vice-president
visera	viscera +
viseregal	viceregal
viseroi	viceroy +
visevursa	vice versa
vishiate	vitiate ²+
vishun	vision +
vishunrey	visionary
vishus	vicious +
visib le /ility/ly	
visibul	visible +
visid	viscid +

visiditey	viscidity
visinitey	vicinity
vision /ary	
visionrey	visionary
visissitude	vicissitude
visit ¹ /ant/ation/or	
visitashun	visitation
visiter	visitor
viskositey	viscosity
vista	
visual /ly	
visualis e ² /ation	
visul	visual +
visulise	visualise ²+
vital /ity/ly/s	
vital	victual ³+
vitalis e ² /ation	
vitalitey	vitality
vitamin	
vitaminis e ² /ation	
vitiat e ² /ion	
vitreous	
vitrifi	vitrify ⁴+
vitrif y ⁴ /ication	
vitriol /ic	
vitrius	vitreous
vitul	vital +
vituperat e ² /ion/ive/or	
viul	vial ★
viul	vile ★+
viva voce	
vivac ious /ity	
vivashus	vivacious +
vivasitee	vivacity
vivavosi	viva voce
vivid /ly/ness	
vivifi	vivify ⁴+
vivif y ⁴ /ication	
viviparous	
viviparus	viviparous
vivisecshun	vivisection
vivisect ¹ /ion/or	
vixen	
vocabular y /ies	
vocal /ist/ly	

vocalis *e*² /ation	
vocashun	vocation +
vocation /al	
vocative	
vocifer *ate*² /ous	
vociferus	vociferous
vodka	
voge	vogue
vogue	
voice²	
void¹	
voiige	voyage²⁺
voiiger	voyager
voile	
vois	voice²
volatil *e* /ity	
volatilis *e*² /ation	
volcanic	
volcano /es	
voley	volley¹⁺
volishun	volition +
volition /al	
volkano	volcano +
volley¹ /s	
volt /age/meter	
volub *le* /ility/ly	
volubul	voluble +
volum *e* /etric/inous	
voluminus	voluminous
voluntar *y* /ily	
volunteer¹	
voluntrey	voluntary +
voluptu *ous* /ary	
voluptuus	voluptuous +
vomit¹	
voraci *ous* /ty	
vorashus	voracious +
vorasitey	voracity
vornt	vaunt¹
vorteks	vortex +
vort *ex* /exes/ices (pls.)	
vorticella	
vosiferate	vociferate²⁺
vosiferus	vociferous
votar *y* /ies	

vote² /r	
votive	
vouch¹ /er	
vouchsafe²	
vow¹	
vowch	vouch¹⁺
vowchsafe	vouchsafe²
vowel	
vowul	vowel
voyage² /r	
voyd	void¹
voys	voice²
vue	view¹⁺
vulcanis *e*² /ation	
vulcher	vulture
vulgar /ity	
vulgaris *e*² /ation/m	
vulnerab *le* /ility	
vulnerabul	vulnerable +
vulnrable	vulnerable +
vulture	
vulva	
vurb	verb +
vurchoo	virtue +
vurchual	virtual +
vurchuous	virtuous
vurchuus	virtuous
vurgin	virgin +
vurginitey	virginity
vurgo	Virgo
vurtue	virtue +
vurtuoso	virtuoso
vurtuous	virtuous
vwal	voile
vye	vie +
vying	

W

wack	whack¹
wad /ding	
waddle²	
wade² /r	
wadle	waddle²

wadul	waddle ²	walow	wallow ¹
wafe	waif	walrus /es	
wafer		walts	waltz ¹⁺
waffle ² /-iron		waltz ¹ /er	
wafle	waffle ²⁺	wan ★ (pale) /ness	
waft ¹		wan	won ★
waful	waffle ²⁺	wander ¹★ (roam) /er/lust	
wag ³ /gish/tail		wander	wonder ¹★⁺
wage ²		wane ²	
wager ¹		wangle ² /r	
waggle ²		wangul	wangle ²⁺
wagon /er/ette		wanskot	wainscot ¹⁺
wagul	waggle ²	want ¹	
waif		wanton /ness	
wail ¹★ (cry)		war ³ /-paint/-path	
wail	whale ★⁺	warant	warrant ¹⁺
wainscot ¹ /ing		warantee	warranty ⁺
waist ★ (body) /coat		warble ² /r	
waist	waste ²★⁺	warbul	warble ²⁺
wait ¹★† /er/ress (fem.)		ward ¹ /er/room	
†(stay for)		warden	
wait	weight ★⁺	wardrobe	
waitey	weighty	ware ★ (avoid) /s ★†	
waive ²★ (give up)		†(goods for sale)	
waive	wave ²★⁺	ware	wear ★⁺
waiver ¹★ (law)		ware	where ★
waiver	waver ¹★⁺	warehouse	
wake ² /ful/fulness		warehowse	warehouse
waken ¹		waren	warren
waks	wax ¹⁺	wares	wears ★
wakswork	waxwork	warey	wary ⁺
walabey	wallaby ⁺	warf	wharf ⁺
wale	wail ¹★	war *fare* /like	
wale	whale ★⁺	warior	warrior
walk ¹ /-over		warm ¹ /er/est/ly/ness/th	
walkie-talkie		warmonger ¹	
walking-stick		warn ¹	
wall ¹ /flower/paper		warp ¹	
wallab *y* /ies		warrant ¹ /able	
wallah		warrant *y* /ies	
wallet		warren	
wallop ¹		warrior	
wallow ¹		wart /y	
walnut		warves	wharves
walop	wallop ¹	war *y* /ily/iness	

was	
wash [1] /able/er	
washed-up	
wasl	wassail [1]
wasn't (was not)	
wasnt	wasn't
wasp /ish	
wassail [1]	
wast *e* [2]*† /age/er/rel	
†(squander)	
waste	waist *+
wasteful /ly/ness	
wat	watt *+
wat	what *+
watch [1] /ful/fulness	
wate	wait [1]*+
wate	weight *+
water [1] /cress/fall	
waterlogged	
water *mark* /tight	
waterproof [1]	
watt * (power) /age	
wave [2]*† /form/length	
†(water, gesture)	
wave	waive [2]*
waver [1]* (falter) /er	
waver	waiver [1]*
wawlts	waltz [1]+
wax [1] /en/work	
way * (direction) /side	
way	weigh [1]*+
way	whey *
waybridge	weighbridge
wayfare [2] /r	
way *lay* /laid/laying	
wayward	
waywerd	wayward
we * (us)	
we	wee *
weak *† /ling/ness	
†(feeble)	
weak	week *+
weaken [1]	
weak *er* /est/ly *† /ness	
†(sickly)	

weakly	weekly *+
weal * (state)	
weal	wheel [1]*+
weald * (district)	
weald	wield [1]*
wealth /ier/iest/iness/y	
wean [1]	
weapon	
wear *† /able/er/ing/s *†	
†(have on the body)	
wear	ware *+
wear	where *
wearey	weary [4]+
wearisome	
wears	wares *
wear *y* [4] /ier/iest/ily/iness	
weasel	
weat	wheat +
weather [1]*† /cock	
†(atmosphere)	
weather	whether *
weathervane	
weatmeal	wheatmeal
weave [2]* (make fabric) /r	
weave	we've *
web [3] /-footed/-toed	
wed [3] /ding/lock	
Wedensday	Wednesday
wedge [2]	
Wednesday	
wee * (small)	
weed [1] /s/y	
weedul	wheedle [2]
week *† /day/end	
†(seven days)	
week	weak *+
weeken	weaken [1]
weekling	weakling
weekl *y* * (every week) /ies	
weel	weal *
weel	wheel [1]*+
weelbarrow	wheelbarrow
weeld	weald *
weeld	wield [1]*
weelrite	wheelwright

ween	wean [1]	were * (to be)	
weep /er/ing/y		were	where *
weevil		were	whirr [1]*
weeze	wheeze [2]+	we're * (we are)	
wege	wedge [2]	wereabouts	whereabouts
weigh [1]*† /bridge		wereas	whereas +
†(how heavy)		wereby	whereby
weight *† /less/lessness/y		werefor	wherefore
†(heaviness)		weren't (were not)	
weild	weald *	werever	wherever
weild	wield [1]*	werewol f /ves (pl.)	
weir * (dam)		werey	weary [4]+
weird /er/est		werisum	wearisome
weja	ouija	werk	work [1]+
welch [1]* (cheat)		werkbox	workbox +
welch	Welsh *	werker	worker
welcome [2]		werkshop	workshop
weld [1] /er		werl	whirl [1]*+
welfare		werl	whorl [1]*
welk	whelk	werld	world +
welkin		werldwide	worldwide
we'll * (we will)		werligig	whirligig
well [1]* (spring) /-advised		werm	worm [1]+
well-appointed		werse	worse +
well-balanced		wersen	worsen [1]
well-behaved		wership	worship [3]+
well-*being* /-bred		werst	worst
wellingtons		wersted	worsted
well-meaning		werth	worth +
well-*nigh* /-to-do		werthey	worthy +
welp	whelp [1]	werthwiul	worthwhile
Welsh * (from Wales)		werwoolf	werewolf +
welter [1]		wesel	weasel
welth	wealth +	Wesleyan	
wen	when +	weslian	Wesleyan
wence	whence	west /erly/ern/ward	
wench [1] /es		westernis *e* [2] /ation	
wend [1]		westwerd	westward
wenever	whenever	wet [3]*† /ness/ter/test	
went		†(soaked)	
wepon	weapon	wet	whet [3]*
wept		wether	weather [1]*+
wer	weir *	wether	whether *
werd	weird +	wethercock	weathercock
werd	word +	wethervane	weathervane

315

we've * (we have)	
weve	weave 2*+
wevil	weevil
whack 1	
whal e *† /er/ing †(mammal)	
whar f /ves (pl.)	
what *† /ever/soever †(question)	
what	watt *+
wheat /en/meal	
whedul	wheedle 2
wheedle 2	
wheel 1* /barrow	
wheelwright	
wheez e 2 /ily/y	
whelk	
whelp 1	
when /ever/soever	
whence	
whens	whence
where * (which place)	
where	ware *+
where	wear *+
where	were *
whereabouts	
where as /by/ever	
wherefore	
where upon /withal	
wherl	whirl 1*+
wherl	whorl 1*
whet 3* (sharpen)	
whether * (if)	
whether	weather 1*+
whey * (milk)	
which * (which one)	
which	witch *+
whiff 1	
Whig * (political)	
whil e * (during) /st	
while	wile 2*+
whim /sical	
whimper 1	
whimsie	whimsy +
whims y /ies	

whine 2* (complain)	
whinn y 4 /ies	
whip 3 /cord	
whipper-snapper	
whippet	
whirl 1*† /igig †(swing round)	
whirl	whorl 1*
whirr 1* (whirl)	
whisk 1	
whisker /ed	
whiskey *† †(alcohol—Irish)	
whisky *† †(alcohol—Scotch)	
whisper 1 /er	
whist	
whistle 2 /r	
whisul	whistle 2+
whit * (particle, jot)	
white /bait/r/st	
whiten 1	
whitewash 1	
whither * (where)	
whiting	
Whitsun	
whittle 2	
whitul	whittle 2
whiz 3	
who /ever	
whoa * (stop)	
whole * (complete)	
whole	hole 2*+
whole-hearted	
wholesale /r	
wholesome /ly	
wholly * (fully)	
wholly	holey *
wholly	holy *
whom	
whoop 1* (shout)	
whoop	hoop 1*
whooping cough	
whop 3	
whore 2 /monger	

whorl [1]*†	
†(ring of leaves)	
whorl	whirl [1]*+
who's * (who is or has)	
whose * (possessive)	
whur	whirr [1]*
whurl	whirl [1]*+
whurl	whorl [1]*
why	
wick /er	
wicked /er/est/ly	
wide /ly/r/st	
wide *awake* /spread	
widen [1]	
widow [1] /er	
width	
wield [1]* (hold and use)	
wield	weald *
wi*fe* /ves (pl.)	
wiff	whiff [1]
wig [3]* (hair)	
wig	Whig *
wiggl *e* [2] /y	
wigul	wiggle [2]+
wigwam	
wild /er/est/ly/ness	
wilderness	
wil *e* [2]* (trick) /iness/y	
wile	while *+
wilful /ly/ness	
will [1] /power/-o'-the-wisp	
willow /y	
willy-nilly	
wilst	whilst
wilt [1]	
wim	whim +
wimin	women +
wimper	whimper [1]
wimsey	whimsy +
wimsical	whimsical
win /ner/ning	
wince [2]	
winch [1] /es	
wind [1]*† /bag/ward	
†(make short of breath)	

wind * (turn)/er/ing	
window /-pane/-sill	
wind *y* /ier/iest/iness	
wine * (drink) /-cellar	
wine	whine [2]*
wineglass /es	
wing [1]	
wink [1]	
winkle [2]	
winkul	winkle [2]
winnow [1]	
winsome /ness	
winter [1]	
wintrie	wintry
wintry	
wip	whip [3]+
wipcord	whipcord
wipe [2] /r	
wipper snapper	whipper-snapper
wippet	whippet
wire [2] /less	
wir *iness* /y	
wirl	whirl [1]*+
wirl	whorl [1]*
wirr	whirr [1]*
wisdom	
wise /acre/ly/r/st	
wish [1] /ful	
wishy-washy	
wisk	whisk [1]
wisker	whisker +
wiskey	whiskey *
wiskey	whisky *
wisp	
wisper	whisper [1]+
wist	whist
wistful /ly/ness	
wistle	whistle [2]+
wisul	whistle [2]+
wit * (flair, humour)	
wit	whit *
witch * (hag) /es	
witch	which *
witcher *y* /ies	
wite	white +

317

witen	whiten [1]	wolop	wallop [1]
witer	whiter	wolow	wallow [1]
witewash	whitewash [1]	woman /kind/ly	
with /al		womb	
withdraw /al/ing/n		women (pl.) /folk	
withdrew		won ★ (did win)	
withdroo	withdrew	won	wan ★+
wither [1]★ (decay)		wonder [1]★† /ful/fully	
wither	whither ★	†(remarkable thing)	
withers		wonder	wander [1]★+
withheld		wondrous	
withhold /ing		wondrus	wondrous
within		wont ★ (accustomed)	
without		wont	want [1]
withstand /ing		wont	won't ★
witing	whiting	won't ★ (will not)	
witness [1] /es		wonton	wanton +
witsun	Whitsun	woo [1] /er	
witti *cism* /ness		wood ★ (lumber) /cut	
wittle	whittle [2]	wood	would ★
witt *y* /ier/iest/ily		wooden /ly/ness	
witul	whittle [2]	woof	
wiz	whiz [3]	wool /len/liness	
wizard		woolf	wolf [1]+
wizened		wooll *y* /ies	
wo	whoa ★	wooman	woman +
wo	woe ★+	woomb	womb
wobbl *e* [2] /y		woond	wound [1]★
woble	wobble [2]+	wop	whop [3]
wobul	wobble [2]+	wor	war [3]+
woch	watch [1]+	worant	warrant [1]+
wod	wad +	worantie	warranty +
wodle	waddle [2]	worble	warble [2]+
wodul	waddle [2]	worbul	warble [2]+
woe ★ (grief) /begone		word /ily/ing/y	
woe	whoa ★	word	ward [1]+
woeful /ly		worden	warden
wofle	waffle [2]+	wordrobe	wardrobe
woft	waft [1]	wore	
woful	waffle [2]+	woren	warren
woful	woeful +	worf	wharf +
wolabey	wallaby +	worfare	warfare +
wolet	wallet	work [1] /able/aday/er	
wol *f* [1] /ves (pl.)		work *box* /shop	
wolla	wallah	worl	whirl [1]★+

worl	whorl [1]★
world /liness/ly/wide	
worm [1] /wood	
worm	warm [1]+
wormunger	warmonger [1]
worn /-out	
worn	warn [1]
worp	warp [1]
worrier	warrior
worr*y* [4] /ies/ier	
wors*e* /t	
worsen [1]	
worship [3] /per	
worsted	
wort	wart +
worth /less/while	
worth*y* /ier/iest/ily	
wos	was
wosh	wash [1]+
wosht up	washed-up
wosl	wassail [1]
wosnt	wasn't
wosp	wasp +
wot	watt ★+
wot	what ★+
wotch	watch [1]+
wotchful	watchful
wotever	whatever
wotsoever	whatsoever
would ★ (conditional)	
would	wood ★+
wound [1]★ (injure)	
wound ★ (did turn)	
wove /n	
wrack ★ (seaweed)	
wraith	
wrangle [2] /r	
wrangul	wrangle [2]+
wrap ★ (pack) /per ★ /ping	
wrapped ★ (packed)	
wrath /ful	
wreak [1]★ (inflict)	
wreath ★ (flowers)	
wreathe [2]★ (twist)	
wreck [1] /age	

wren	
wrench [1]	
wrest [1]★ (pull away)	
wrestle [2] /r	
wresul	wrestle [2]+
wretch ★†	
†(unhappy person)	
wri	wry ★+
wriggle [2]	
wrigul	wriggle [2]
wring ★ (squeeze)	
wringer ★ (machine)	
wrinkle [2]	
wrinkul	wrinkle [2]
wrist /band/let/-watch	
writ	
writ*e* ★† /er/ing/ten	
†(put words on paper)	
writhe [2]	
wrong [1] /doer	
wrongful /ly	
wrort	wrought +
wrote ★ (did write)	
wrought /-up	
wrung ★ (squeezed)	
wry ★ (distorted) /ly	
wun	one ★+
wun	won ★
wunce	once
wunder	wonder [1]★+
wundrus	wondrous
wuns	once
wunself	oneself
wur	whirr [1]★
wurey	worry [4]+
wurl	whirl [1]★+
wurl	whorl [1]★
wurligig	whirligig

X

xenofobia	xenophobia +
xenophob*ia* /e/ic	
xeroks	Xerox [1]

Xerox [1]	
X-ray [1]	
xylofone	xylophone
xylophone	

Y

y	why
yacht [1] /sman	
yak	
yam	
yank [1]	
Yankee	
yap [3]	
yard /age	
yarn [1]	
yashmak	
yaw [1]★ (of ship)	
yaw	yore ★
yaw	your ★+
yawl [1]	
yawn [1]	
yay	yea
yea	
yeald	yield [1]
year /ling	
yearn [1]	
yeast	
yeer	year +
yeest	yeast
yeld	yield [1]
yell [1]	
yellow /ish	
yelow	yellow +
yelp [1]	
yeoman /ry	
yerling	yearling
yern	yearn [1]
yes	
yest	yeast
yesterday	
yet	
yeti	
yety	yeti

yew ★ (tree)	
yew	ewe ★
yew	you ★
yewse	use [2]+
yewsery	usury +
yewshual	usual +
yewsual	usual +
yiddish	
yield [1]	
yodel [3] /ler	
yodle	yodel [3]+
yoga	
yogert	yogurt
yogurt	
yoke ★ (round neck)	
yoke	yolk ★
yokel	
yokle	yokel
yolk ★ (of egg)	
yolk	yoke ★
yoman	yeoman +
yonder	
yore ★ (years ago)	
yore	yaw [1]★
yore	your ★+
yorself	yourself +
yorselves	yourselves
yot	yacht [1]+
yotsman	yachtsman
you ★ (person)	
you	ewe ★
you	yew ★
youboat	U-boat
you'll ★ (you will)	
young /er/est/ster	
your ★† /s	
†(belonging to you)	
your	yaw [1]★
your	yore ★
your	you're ★
you're ★ (you are)	
yourself /ves (pl.)	
youth /ful	
ytterbium	
yttrium	

yule *† /tide	
†(Christmas)	
yule	
yung	you'll *
yungster	young +
yurn	youngster
yuse	yearn 1
yuseful	use 2+
yuserey	useful +
yusual	usury +
yutensil	usual +
yuterine	utensil
yuterus	uterine
yuth	uterus +
yutilise	youth +
yutilitarian	utilise 2+
yutilitee	utilitarian +
yutopia	utility +
	Utopia +

Z

zan y /ies	
zar	tsar
zeal /ous	
zealot	
zebra	
zeel	zeal +
zefer	zephyr
zelot	zealot
zelus	zealous
zenith	

zenofobia	xenophobia +
zenophobia	xenophobia +
zepher	zephyr
zephyr	
zeplin	Zeppelin
Zeppelin	
zerconium	zirconium
zero /s	
zeroks	Xerox 1
zerox	Xerox 1
zest /ful	
Zeus	
zigospore	zygospore
zigote	zygote
zigzag 3	
zilofone	xylophone
zilophone	xylophone
zinc	
zink	zinc
Zion /ism/ist	
zip 3 /per/-fastener	
zirconium	
zither	
zodiac	
zon e 2 /al	
zoo /logical/logy	
zoologey	zoology
zoom 1	
Zulu	
zus	Zeus
zygospore	
zygote	

APPENDIX I
Some Spelling Rules

A. y always stays when adding -ing but changes to **i** before adding -ed, e.g.:

      carry, carrying, carried   terrify, terrifying, terrified

B. i before e except after c, e.g.:

      field, mischievous, relief   deceive, perceive, receipt

   Note that there are exceptions to the above rules.

C. q is always followed by u, e.g.: conquer, frequent, queen

D. all at the beginning of a word loses one l, e.g.: already, altogether, always
The double l is retained in hyphenated words such as all-fours and all-round, but the words all right should always be written as two separate words.

E. A word accented on its last syllable and ending with a single consonant preceded by a vowel doubles that consonant on adding **-ed** and **-ing** e.g.:

          prefer   preferred   preferring

Words of this type, not accented on the last syllable, do **not** double the last consonant, e.g.:

          benefit   benefited   benefiting

With words ending in -l, the final consonant is generally doubled whether the last syllable is accented or not, e.g.:

          travel   travelled   travelling

THE FORMATION OF PLURALS

1. Most words, including those ending in silent -e, add **-s**, e.g.:
   airport, airports
   sausage, sausages

2. Words ending in -ay, -ey, -oy, or -uy add **-s**, e.g.:
   day, days   toy, toys
   abbey, abbeys   guy, guys

3. Words ending in -fe change f to **v** and add **-s**, e.g.:
   knife, knives

4. Some words ending in -f change f to **v** and add **-es**, e.g.:
   half, halves   loaf, loaves

5. Some words ending in -f add **-s**, e.g.:
   chief, chiefs
   handkerchief, handkerchiefs
   But note that some words ending in -f can either add **-s** or change f to **v** and add **-es**, e.g.:
   hoof, hoofs *or* hooves
   scarf, scarfs *or* scarves

6. Words ending in -ff usually add **-s**, e.g.:
   cliff, cliffs
   sheriff, sheriffs

7. Words ending in -o add **-s** or **-es**, e.g.:
   concerto, concertos
   dynamo, dynamos
   buffalo, buffaloes
   domino, dominoes

8. Words ending in -ch, -s, -sh, -x, or -z add **-es**, e.g.:
   church, churches   thrush, thrushes
   gas, gases   box, boxes
   dress, dresses   buzz, buzzes

9. Words ending in -y (but not -ay, -ey, -oy, or -uy: see Note 2) change the y to an **i** and add **-es**, e.g.:
   baby, babies
   family, families

10. Some words form their plurals mainly by changing their vowels (or some of their vowels), e.g.:

foot, feet   mouse, mice
goose, geese tooth, teeth
man, men   woman, women

11. One word adds -en:
ox, oxen
One word adds -ren:
child, children

12. Words ending in -us change us to i, e.g.:
bacillus, bacilli
fungus, fungi
radius, radii
rhombus, rhombi
terminus, termini

13. Words ending in -is change is to -es, e.g.:
analysis, analyses
basis, bases
metamorphosis, metamorphoses

14. Words ending in -ex add -es or change ex to -ices, e.g.:
apex, apexes or apices
index, indexes or indices
vortex, vortexes or vortices

15. Words ending in -ix add -es or change ix to -ices, e.g.:
appendix, appendixes or appendices
helix, helices
matrix, matrixes or matrices

16. Some words ending in -a simply add -s, e.g.:
aroma, aromas
drama, dramas
idea, ideas
but note:
alga, algae
antenna, antennae
formula, formulas or formulae
stoma, stomas or stomata

17. Some words ending in -um simply add -s, e.g.:
museum, museums
premium, premiums
but note:
aquarium, aquariums or aquaria

bacterium, bacteria
curriculum, curricula
memorandum, memorandums
               or memoranda
stadium, stadiums or stadia

18. Words ending in -on usually add -s, e.g.:
electron, electrons
neutron, neutrons
but note:
phenomenon, phenomena

19. Words ending in -eau add -x, e.g.:
bureau, bureaux
chateau, chateaux
plateau, plateaux
Note that some dictionaries allow a plural in -s for some of these words.

20. Some words have the same spelling for both the singular and the plural forms, e.g.:

bison	grouse	sheep
deer	salmon	trout

21. Compound words.
Logically, the most important word should be changed into the plural, as, for example:
brother-in-law, brothers-in-law
man-of-war, men-of-war
but note:
court-martial, court-martials
lord justice, lords justices

22. Some words are used only in the singular form, e.g.:

arithmetic	goodness	magic
courage	logic	music

23. Some words are used only in the plural form, e.g.:
mathematics
Among words frequently used in their plural form are:

acoustics	physics	tactics
athletics	politics	

24. Pairs.
The following nouns do not have a singular form:

entrails	pliers	trousers
pincers	scissors	tweezers

APPENDIX II
Abbreviations in General Use

A. Advanced (level of G.C.E.)
A.A. Automobile Association
A.B.M. anti-ballistic missile
acc., a/c account
A.D. in the year of our Lord
A.D.C. aide-de-camp
A.F.C. Air Force Cross
A.F.M. Air Force Medal
a.m. before noon
Ave. avenue
A.W.O.L. absent without leave

B.A. Bachelor of Arts
Bart. Baronet
B.B.C. British Broadcasting Corporation
B.C. before Christ
B.D. Bachelor of Divinity
B.Ed. Bachelor of Education
B.E.M. British Empire Medal
Benelux Belgium–Netherlands–Luxembourg Union
B.M. Bachelor of Medicine
B.M.A. British Medical Association
B.Mus. Bachelor of Music
B.R. British Rail
B.R.C.S. British Red Cross Society
B.Sc. Bachelor of Science
B.S.T. British standard time, British summer time

C. Centigrade
c., ca. about
C.A.B. Citizens' Advice Bureau
C.A.C.M. Central American Common Market
CARICOM Caribbean Community
C.B.E. Commander of the British Empire
C.B.I. Confederation of British Industry
C.C. County Council
C.E.N.T.O. Central Treaty Organisation
C.G.M. Conspicuous Gallantry Medal
C.G.S. Chief of General Staff
C.H. Companion of Honour
Ch.B. Bachelor of Surgery

C.I.D. Criminal Investigation Department
C.-in-C. Commander-in-Chief
C.M.E.A. (COMECON) Council for Mutual Economic Assistance
C.N.D. Campaign for Nuclear Disarmament
C.O. Commanding Officer
c/o care of
C.O.D. cash on delivery
Con. Conservative
C.S.E. Certificate of Secondary Education

D.B.E. Dame Commander of the British Empire
D.C.L. Doctor of Civil Law
D.C.M. Distinguished Conduct Medal
D.D. Doctor of Divinity
D.D.T. dichlor-diphenyl-trichlorethane (insecticide)
D.F.C. Distinguished Flying Cross
D.F.M. Distinguished Flying Medal
D.M. Doctor of Medicine
D.Mus. Doctor of Music
DNA deoxyribonucleic acid
D.O.E. Department of the Environment
D.Phil. Doctor of Philosophy
Dr. Doctor
D.Sc. Doctor of Science
D.S.C. Distinguished Service Cross
D.S.M. Distinguished Service Medal
D.S.O. Distinguished Service Order

E.E.C. European Economic Community
E.F.T.A. European Free Trade Association
e.g. for example
E.S.N. educationally subnormal
E.S.P. extrasensory perception
Esq. Esquire

F. Fahrenheit
F.A. Football Association

F.A.O. Food and Agriculture Organisation

F.B.A. Fellow of the British Academy

f.o.c. free of charge

F.R.S. Fellow of the Royal Society

G.A.T.T. General Agreement on Tariffs and Trade

G.B. Great Britain

G.B.E. Dame or Knight Grand Cross of the British Empire

G.C. George Cross

G.C.E. General Certificate of Education

G.D.P. gross domestic product

G.D.R. German Democratic Republic

G.H.Q. General Headquarters

G.L.C. Greater London Council

G.M. George Medal

G.M.T. Greenwich mean time

G.N.P. gross national product

G.P. general practitioner

G.P.O. General Post Office

H.E. His Excellency; His Eminence

H.M. Her Majesty

H.M.I. Her Majesty's Inspector

H.M.S. Her Majesty's Ship

H.M.S.O. Her Majesty's Stationery Office

H.N.C. Higher National Certificate

H.N.D. Higher National Diploma

Hon. honorary; Honourable

h.p. hire purchase; horsepower

H.Q. Headquarters

H.R.H. Her (His) Royal Highness

I.B.R.D. International Bank for Reconstruction and Development (World Bank)

I.C.C. International Chamber of Commerce

I.C.F.T.U. International Confederation of Free Trade Unions

I.C.I. Imperial Chemical Industries

i.e. that is

I.L.O. International Labour Organisation

I.M.F. International Monetary Fund

I.O.U. I owe you

I.Q. intelligence quotient

I.R.A. Irish Republican Army

I.T.V. Independent Television

J.E.T. Joint European Torus

J.P. Justice of the Peace

K.B.E. Knight Commander of the British Empire

K.C.B. Knight Commander of the Bath

Kt. Knight

Lab. Labour

L.A.F.T.A. Latin American Free Trade Association

lat. latitude

lbw leg before wicket

L.E.A. Local Education Authority

Lib. Liberal

LL.B., LL.D. Bachelor, Doctor of Laws

long. longitude

L.P. long-playing (of gramophone records, etc.)

L.S.D. lysergic acid diethylamide (hallucinogenic drug)

L.T.A. Lawn Tennis Association

Ltd. Limited

L.V. luncheon voucher

M.A. Master of Arts

M.B. Bachelor of Medicine

M.B.E. Member of the British Empire

M.C. Military Cross; Master of Ceremonies

M.C.C. Marylebone Cricket Club

M.D. Doctor of Medicine

M.F.H. Master of Foxhounds

M.O.H. Medical Officer of Health

M.P. Member of Parliament

m.p.g. miles per gallon

m.p.h. miles per hour

MS., MSS. manuscript(s)

M.Sc. Master of Science

N.A.S.A. National Aeronautics and Space Administration

N.A.T.O. North Atlantic Treaty Organisation

N.B. note well

N.C.O. non-commissioned officer

N.H.S. National Health Service

N.I. National Insurance

No. number

nr. near

N.S.P.C.C. National Society for the Prevention of Cruelty to Children

O. Ordinary (level of G.C.E.)
O.A.P. old aged pensioner
O.A.S. Organisation of American States
O.A.U. Organisation of African Unity
O.B.E. Officer of the British Empire
O.D.E.C.A. Organisation of Central American States
O.E.C.D. Organisation for Economic Co-operation and Development
O.H.M.S. On Her Majesty's Service
O.M. Order of Merit
O.N.C. Ordinary National Certificate
O.N.D. Ordinary National Diploma
op. cit. in the work named
O.P.E.C. Organisation of the Petroleum Exporting Countries

P.A.Y.E. pay as you earn
P.E. physical education
Ph.D. Doctor of Philosophy
P.M. Prime Minister
P.O. post office; postal order
P.O.W. prisoner of war
P.S. postscript
P.T.O. please turn over

Q.C. Queen's Counsel

R. Regina; Rex
R.A. Royal Academy; Royal Artillery
R.A.C. Royal Automobile Club
R.A.D.A. Royal Academy of Dramatic Art
R.A.F. Royal Air Force
R.A.M. Royal Academy of Music
R.C. Roman Catholic
R.C.A. Royal College of Arts
R.C.M. Royal College of Music
Rev., Revd. Reverend
R.G.S. Royal Geographical Society
R.H.S. Royal Horticultural Society
R.I.P. may he (she, they) rest in peace
R.M. Royal Marines; Royal Mail
R.N. Royal Navy
r.p.m. revolutions per minute
R.S.P.C.A. Royal Society for the Prevention of Cruelty to Animals
R.S.V.P. please reply
Rt. Hon. Right Honourable

s.a.e. self-addressed envelope
S.A.L.T. Strategic Arms Limitation Treaty

S.A.Y.E. save as you earn
S.C.M. State Certified Midwife
S.E.A.T.O. South-East Asia Treaty Organisation
S.O.S. distress signal
S.R.N. State Registered Nurse
St. Saint; street
S.T.D. subscriber trunk dialling

T.A.S.S. Soviet Telegraph Agency
T.B. tuberculosis
T.N.T. trinitrotoluene (high explosive)
T.U.C. Trades Union Congress

U.A.R. United Arab Republic
U.D.C. Urban District Council
U.D.I. Unilateral Declaration of Independence
U.F.O. unidentified flying object
U.N. United Nations
U.N.D.P. United Nations Development Programme
U.N.E.S.C.O. United Nations Educational, Scientific and Cultural Organisation
U.N.I.C.E.F. United Nations International Children's Emergency Fund
U.S. United States
U.S.A. United States of America
U.S.S.R. Union of Soviet Socialist Republics

V.A.T. value added tax
V.C. Victoria Cross
V.D. venereal disease
V.H.F. very high frequency
V.I.P. very important person

W.C.C. World Council of Churches
W.H.O. World Health Organisation
W.I. West Indies; Women's Institute
W.R.A.C. Women's Royal Army Corps
W.R.A.F. Women's Royal Air Force
W.R.N.S. Women's Royal Naval Service
W.R.V.S. Women's Royal Volunteer Service

Y.H.A. Youth Hostels Association
Y.M.C.A. Young Men's Christian Association
Y.W.C.A. Young Women's Christian Association

APPENDIX III
Common Forenames

MEN
Adrian
Alan, Allan
Andrew
Anthony, Antony
Barry
Brian, Bryan
Bruce
Charles
Christopher
Claude
Clive
Cyril
Derek
Desmond
Douglas
Edmund
Edward, Ted
Eugene
Ewen, Ewin
Francis
Frederick, Fred
Gareth
Gary
Geoffrey
George
Gerald, Gerry
Giles
Gordon
Graham
Guy
Harold, Harry
Howard, Howerd
Hugh
Humphrey
Ian
Jack
James, Jim
Jeremy, Jerry
John
Jonathan
Julian
Keith
Kenneth
Leonard

Lewis
Malcolm
Mathew, Matt
Michael, Mike
Neil
Nicholas, Nick
Nigel
Oliver
Patrick, Paddy
Peter
Philip
Richard, Dick
Robert, Bob
Roger
Ronald
Roy
Sean
Sidney
Simon
Stephen, Steven
Terence, Terry
Thomas
Timothy
Tony
Trevor
Wayne
William

WOMEN
Alice
Alison
Angela, Angie
Ann, Anne
Anthea
Barbara
Belinda
Bridget
Carol, Carole
Caroline
Carolyn
Catherine, Cathy
Charlotte
Christine
Clare
Daphne

Dawn
Deborah, Debby
Denise
Diana
Doreen
Eileen
Elaine
Elizabeth, Betty
Ellen
Emily
Emma
Evelyn
Felicity
Fiona
Frances
Gillian, Jill
Hazel
Heather
Helen
Hilary
Irene
Isabel, Isobel
Jacqueline
Jane
Janet
Janice
Jean
Jennifer, Jenny
Jill
Joan
Joanna
Joy
Joyce
Judith, Judy
Julia
Julie
Karen
Laura
Lesley
Lilian
Linda, Lynda
Lisa, Liza
Lorna
Louise
Lynn

Margaret, Maggie
Marian
Marie
Marilyn
Marion
Marjorie
Mary
Miranda
Miriam
Monica
Natalie
Olivia
Pamela
Patricia
Paula
Pauline
Penelope, Penny
Phillipa
Phillis, Phyllis
Rachel
Rebecca
Rosemary
Ruth
Sally
Sandra, Sandy
Sarah
Sharon
Sheila
Shirley
Sonia
Stephanie
Susan, Sue
Suzanne
Sylvia
Theresa, Tessa
Tina
Tracy
Vera
Veronica
Victoria, Vicky
Virginia
Vivian
Wendy
Yvonne
Zoe

The British Isles

APPENDIX V

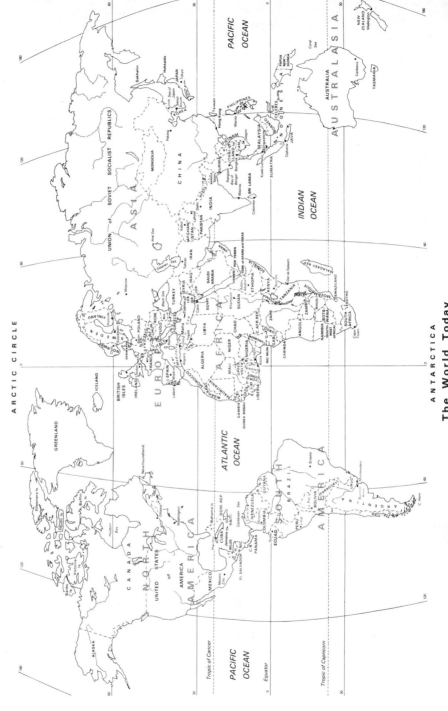

The World Today

APPENDIX VI

Metric Measures

Imperial Measures

Length

Metric				Imperial	
1 millimetre (mm)		= 0.039 in	1 inch (in)		= 2.540 cm
1 centimetre (cm)	= 10 mm	= 0.394 in	1 foot (ft)	= 12 in	= 30.48 cm
1 metre (m)	= 100 cm	= 1.094 yd	1 yard (yd)	= 3 ft	= 0.914 m
1 kilometre (km)	= 1000 m	= 0.621 mile	1 mile	= 1760 yd	= 1.609 km
			1 nautical mile	= 6080 ft	= 1.852 km

Surface or Area

Metric			Imperial		
1 sq cm (cm²)		= 0.155 in²	1 sq in (in²)		= 6.452 cm²
1 sq m (m²)	= 100 mm²	= 1.196 yd²	1 sq ft (ft²)	= 144 in²	= 9.290 dm²
1 sq km (km²)	= 10000 cm²	= 0.386 mile²	1 sq yd (yd²)	= 9 ft²	= 0.836 m²
1 hectare (ha)	= 100 ha	= 11960 yd²	1 rood	= 1210 yd²	= 1012 m²
	= 10000 m²		1 acre	= 4840 yd²	= 0.405 ha
			1 sq mile	= 640 acres	= 259.0 ha

Volume and Capacity

Metric			Imperial		
1 cu cm (cm³)		= 0.061 in³	1 cu in (in³)		= 16.39 cm³
1 cu dm (dm³)	= 1000 cm³	= 61.02 in³	1 cu ft (ft³)	= 1728 in³	= 0.028 m³
1 cu m (m³)	= 1000 dm³	= 1.308 yd³	1 cu yd (yd³)	= 27 ft³	= 0.765 m³
1 litre (l)	= 1 dm³	= 1.760 pints	1 pint	= 4 gills	= 0.568 l
1 hectolitre (hl)	= 100 l	= 2.750 bushels	1 gallon (gal)	= 8 pints	= 4.546 l
			1 bushel	= 8 gal	= 36.37 l
			1 fluid ounce	= 8 fl drachms	= 28.41 cm³
			1 pint	= 20 fl oz	= 568.2 cm³

Weight

Metric			Imperial		
1 milligram (mg)		= 0.015 grain	1 ounce (oz)		= 28.35 g
1 gram (gm)	= 1000 mg	= 0.035 oz	1 pound (lb)	= 16 oz	= 0.454 kg
1 kilogram (kg)	= 1000 g	= 2.205 lb	1 stone	= 14 lb	= 6.350 kg
1 tonne (t)	= 1000 kg	= 0.984 ton	1 cwt	= 8 st	= 50.80 kg
			1 ton	= 20 cwt	= 1.016 tonnes

Temperature Conversion

$C = \frac{5}{9} (F - 32)$ $F = (\frac{9}{5} C) + 32$

98.4° Fahrenheit	= 36.9° Centigrade
32° Fahrenheit	= 0° Centigrade
50° Fahrenheit	= 10° Centigrade
68° Fahrenheit	= 20° Centigrade
212° Fahrenheit	= 100° Centigrade

Time

1 min	= 60 sec	
1 hr	= 60 min	= 3600 sec
1 day	= 24 hr	
1 year	= 365 days (366 in leap year)	

APPENDIX VII
Common Chemical Compounds

Common name	Chemical name	Formula
Alcohol, grain	Ethanol	CH_3CH_2OH
Alcohol, wood	Methanol	CH_3OH
Baking soda	Sodium hydrogen carbonate	$NaHCO_3$
Borax	Disodium tetraborate	$Na_2B_4O_7$
Brimstone	Sulphur	S
Calomel	Mercury(I) chloride	Hg_2Cl_2
Carbolic acid	Phenol	C_6H_5OH
Carbon tetrachloride	Tetrachloromethane	CCl_4
Carborundum	Silicon carbide	SiC
Chalk	Calcium carbonate	$CaCO_3$
Chloroform	Trichloromethane	$CHCl_3$
Cooking salt	Sodium chloride	NaCl
Corn syrup	Glucose, dextrose	$C_6H_{12}O_6$
Diamond	Carbon	C
Dry ice	Carbon dioxide (solid)	CO_2
Ethyl	Lead tetraethyl	$Pb(C_2H_5)_4$
Fire damp	Methane	CH_4
Glycerine	Glycerol	$C_3H_5(OH)_3$
Graphite	Carbon	C
Iron pyrites	Iron disulphide	FeS_2
Laughing gas	Dinitrogen oxide	N_2O
Lime water	Calcium hydroxide solution	$Ca(OH)_2$
Lye (or caustic soda)	Sodium hydroxide	NaOH
Magnesia	Magnesium oxide	MgO
Marble	Calcium carbonate	$CaCO_3$
Marsh gas	Methane	CH_4
Milk of magnesia	Magnesium hydroxide (with water)	$Mg(OH)_2$
Moth balls	Naphthalene	$C_{10}H_8$
Muriatic acid	Hydrochloric acid	HCl
Oil of vitriol	Sulphuric acid	H_2SO_4
Peroxide	Hydrogen peroxide	H_2O_2
Potash	Potassium carbonate	K_2CO_3
Quartz	Silicon dioxide	SiO_2
Quicklime	Calcium oxide	CaO
Quicksilver	Mercury	Hg
Sal ammoniac	Ammonium chloride	NH_4Cl
Saltpetre	Potassium nitrate	KNO_3
Sand	Silicon dioxide (impure)	SiO_2
Soap	Sodium stearate	$C_{17}H_{35}COONa$
Sugar (cane or beet)	Sucrose	$C_{12}H_{22}O_{11}$
Vinegar	Ethanoic acid (with water)	CH_3COOH
Water glass	Sodium silicate	Na_2SiO_3
Zinc white	Zinc oxide	ZnO

APPENDIX VIII

Physical Constants, Conversion Factors and Units

	Quantity	Name of unit	Symbol
There are nine basic units in the SI system (Système international d'unités)	length	metre	m
	mass	kilogram	kg
	time	second	s
	electric current	ampere ★	A
	thermodynamic temperature	kelvin ★	K
	amount of substance	mole	mol
	luminous intensity	candela	cd
	plane angle	radian	rad
	solid angle	steradian	sr
In addition there are a number of derived units	force	newton ★	N
	energy	joule ★	J
	power	watt ★	W
	electric charge	coulomb ★	C
	potential difference	volt ★	V
	electric resistance	ohm ★	Ω
	frequency	hertz ★	Hz
	customary temperature	degree Celsius	°C

The asterisk (★) indicates that the names of the relevant units begin with a small letter when they are written out in full, but are symbolised by a capital letter.

	Multiple	Prefix	Symbol
Special prefixes and symbols are used to indicate multiples and sub-multiples of the basic units in powers of ten	10^{18}	exa	E
	10^{15}	peta	P
	10^{12}	tera	T
	10^{9}	giga	G
	10^{6}	mega	M
	10^{3}	kilo	k
	10^{-1}	deci	d
	10^{-2}	centi	c
	10^{-3}	milli	m
	10^{-6}	micro	μ
	10^{-9}	nano	n
	10^{-12}	pico	p
	10^{-15}	femto	f
	10^{-18}	atto	a

PERIODIC TABLE OF THE ELEMENTS

H 1 Hydrogen																	He 2 Helium
Li 3 Lithium	Be 4 Beryllium											B 5 Boron	C 6 Carbon	N 7 Nitrogen	O 8 Oxygen	F 9 Fluorine	Ne 10 Neon
Na 11 Sodium	Mg 12 Magnesium											Al 13 Aluminium	Si 14 Silicon	P 15 Phosphorus	S 16 Sulphur	Cl 17 Chlorine	Ar 18 Argon
K 19 Potassium	Ca 20 Calcium	Sc 21 Scandium	Ti 22 Titanium	V 23 Vanadium	Cr 24 Chromium	Mn 25 Manganese	Fe 26 Iron	Co 27 Cobalt	Ni 28 Nickel	Cu 29 Copper	Zn 30 Zinc	Ga 31 Gallium	Ge 32 Germanium	As 33 Arsenic	Se 34 Selenium	Br 35 Bromine	Kr 36 Krypton
Rb 37 Rubidium	Sr 38 Strontium	Y 39 Yttrium	Zr 40 Zirconium	Nb 41 Niobium	Mo 42 Molybdenum	Tc 43 Technetium	Ru 44 Ruthenium	Rh 45 Rhodium	Pd 46 Palladium	Ag 47 Silver	Cd 48 Cadmium	In 49 Indium	Sn 50 Tin	Sb 51 Antimony	Te 52 Tellurium	I 53 Iodine	Xe 54 Xenon
Cs 55 Caesium	Ba 56 Barium	La 57 Lanthanum	Hf 72 Hafnium	Ta 73 Tantalum	W 74 Tungsten	Re 75 Rhenium	Os 76 Osmium	Ir 77 Iridium	Pt 78 Platinum	Au 79 Gold	Hg 80 Mercury	Tl 81 Thallium	Pb 82 Lead	Bi 83 Bismuth	Po 84 Polonium	At 85 Astatine	Rn 86 Radon
Fr 87 Francium	Ra 88 Radium	Ac 89 Actinium	104	105													

Ce 58 Cerium	Pr 59 Praseodymium	Nd 60 Neodymium	Pm 61 Promethium	Sm 62 Samarium	Eu 63 Europium	Gd 64 Gadolinium	Tb 65 Terbium	Dy 66 Dysprosium	Ho 67 Holmium	Er 68 Erbium	Tm 69 Thulium	Yb 70 Ytterbium	Lu 71 Lutetium
Th 90 Thorium	Pa 91 Protactinium	U 92 Uranium	Np 93 Neptunium	Pu 94 Plutonium	Am 95 Americium	Cm 96 Curium	Bk 97 Berkelium	Cf 98 Californium	Es 99 Einsteinium	Fm 100 Fermium	Md 101 Mendelevium	No 102 Nobelium	Lr 103 Lawrencium

Acknowledgements

In preparing this dictionary the following books have been particularly useful to me as resource material:

Cassell's New Spelling Dictionary
L. B. and D. Firnberg, Cassell, 1976

Authors' and Printers' Dictionary
F. Howard Collins, Oxford University Press, 11th rev. ed., 1973

The Concise Oxford Dictionary
Ed. J. B. Sykes, Oxford University Press, 6th ed., 1976

Maxwell's Illustrated Colour Dictionary
Ed. J. P. Brasier-Creach, M.A. and
B. A. Workman, M.A. ILSC, London, 1969

The Oxford School Dictionary
Joan Pusey, Oxford University Press, 3rd rev. ed., 1974

The Perfect Speller
Harriet Wittels and Joan Griesman, Grosset & Dunlap, New York, 1973

I have benefited greatly from the help and advice of many people and schools. I would like to acknowledge the help of: Miss Judy Black, Miss Georgina Cox, Mr Gordon Files, Mrs Edna Goldman, Mr Oliver Gregory, Mrs Gretchen Ingram, Mr C. R. Jacobs, Mrs Jean Price, Mrs Olive Robinson, Miss Avital Talmor and the teachers of Shepherds' Hill Middle School, Oxford. However, any mistakes contained in the dictionary are entirely my responsibility.

Special thanks are also due to Mr Vince Edmonds, Mr Ben Bolt, and in particular to Mr John Hine of the Editorial Production Department at Pergamon Press, Oxford.

The final acknowledgement goes to my family who helped me out in so many ways and particularly to my father, without whose invaluable advice, constant encouragement and support this project would never have got off the ground.